Prostitutes and Courtesans
in the Ancient World

Publication of this volume has been made possible through the generous support and enduring vision of WARREN G. MOON.

Prostitutes and Courtesans in the Ancient World

Edited by
CHRISTOPHER A. FARAONE
and
LAURA K. MCCLURE

THE UNIVERSITY OF WISCONSIN PRESS

The University of Wisconsin Press
1930 Monroe Street
Madison, Wisconsin 53711

www.wisc.edu/wisconsinpress/

3 Henrietta Street
London WC2E 8LU, England

5   4   3   2   1

Printed in the United States of America

Library of Congress Cataloging-in-Publication Data
  Prostitutes and courtesans in the ancient world / edited by
Christopher A. Faraone and Laura K. McClure.
     p.   cm.—(Wisconsin studies in classics)
  Papers from the conference, "Prostitution in the Ancient World,"
held in Madison, April 12–14, 2002, hosted by the Classics and
Hebrew and Semitic Studies department at the University.
  Includes bibliographical references and index.
  ISBN 0-299-21310-2 (cloth: alk. paper)
  ISBN 0-299-21314-5 (pbk.: alk. paper)
   1. Prostitution—Greece—History—Congresses.   2. Prostitution—
Rome—History—Congresses.   3. Courtesans—Greece—History—
Congresses.   4. Courtesans—Rome—History—Congresses.   5. Sex
role—Greece—History—To 1500—Congresses.   6. Sex role—
Rome—History—To 1500—Congresses.   I. Faraone, Christopher A.
II. McClure, Laura, 1959-   III. Series.
  HQ113P76   2005
  306.74´0938—dc22   2005005455

Contents

Prostitution, Comedy, and Public Performance

Acknowledgments

The editors would like to acknowledge the Anonymous Fund of the College of Letters and Science at the University of Wisconsin for their generous funding of the conference at which these papers were first delivered, "Prostitution in the Ancient World," held in Madison, April 12–14, 2002. We are also grateful to colleagues in the Classics and Hebrew and Semitic Studies Department at Wisconsin for their hospitality during the conference. The series editor for UW Press, Patricia Rosenmeyer, deserves special thanks for her support of the manuscript at an early stage. The volume benefited from the remarks of the readers for the press, Judith Hallett and Ellen Greene, especially on the Roman materials. Thanks also to our editor, Sheila Moermond, for her help in the preparation of the manuscript and to Alex Pappas in Madison and Martin Devecka in Chicago for their help with the bibliography and indices. Lastly, we would like to thank all of our contributors for their patience with what has been a rather protracted editing process, especially given the postponement of the original conference date due to the events of September 11, 2001. We hope that their thoughtful reflections on a complex yet integral aspect of the ancient world will engender further dialogue in the fields of ancient gender studies and cultural criticism.

Abbreviations and Transliteration

Abbreviations for frequently cited books, journals, and reference works appear in the list below. All other references to modern works consist of the author's name and the date of publication; full citations can be found in the bibliography at the end of this volume. In transliterating Greek, it has seemed reasonable, if not entirely consistent, to use the familiar Latinized spelling of those names for which this has become "normal" English usage and in other cases to use a direct transliteration from the Greek.

ARV²	J. D. Beazley. *Attic Red-Figure Vase-Painters*. 2nd ed. Oxford, 1963.
BDB	*Brown-Driver-Briggs Hebrew and English Lexicon*.
BM	British Museum.
CCSL	*Corpus christianorum: Series latina*.
CEG	P. A. Hansen, ed. *Carmina epigraphica graeca, saeculorum VIII–V a. Chr. n.*Berlin, 1983.
CEG 2	P. A. Hansen, ed. *Carmina epigraphica graeca, saeculi IV a. Chr. n.*Berlin, 1989.
Etym. Magn.	*Etymologicum magnum*. Venice, 1499.
FGrH.	F. Jacoby, ed. *Die Fragmente der griechischen Historiker*. Berlin, 1923–.
HAL	L. Koehler, W. Baumgartner, and J. J. Stamm, eds. *Hebräisches und aramäisches Lexikon zum Alten Testament*. Leiden, 1967–1995.
IG 1³	D. Lewis, ed. *Inscriptiones graecae*. 3rd ed. of vol. 1. Berlin, 1981.
IG 2²	J. Kirchner, ed. *Inscriptiones graecae*. 2nd ed. of vol. 2. Berlin, 1913–40.

ILLRP	A. Degrassi, ed. *Inscriptiones latinae liberae rei publicae*. 2 vols. Florence, 1957–63.
KJV	King James Version.
LIMC	Hans Christoph Ackermann and Jean-Robert Gisler, eds. *Lexicon iconographicum mythologiae classicae*. Zurich, 1981–1999.
LSAG²	L. H. Jeffery. *Local Scripts of Archaic Greece*. Rev. ed. Ed. A. W. Johnston. Oxford, 1990.
LSCG suppl.	F. Sokolowski, ed. *Lois Sacrées des cités grecques: Supplément*. Paris, 1962.
LSJ H.	G. Liddell and R. Scott, eds. *A Greek-English Lexicon*. Rev. and aug. throughout by H. S. Jones. 9th ed. Oxford, 1968.
NJPS	*Tanakh: The Traditional Hebrew Text and the New JPS Translation*. Philadelphia, 1999.
NRSV	New Revised Standard Version.
OED	*Oxford English Dictionary*. Oxford, 2002.
PG	J.-P. Migne, ed. *Patrologia graeca*. 161 vols. Paris, 1857–66.
RA	*Révue d'assyriologie et d'archéologie*.
RSV	Revised Standard Version.
SEG	*Supplementum epigraphicum graecum*. Amsterdam, 1923–.
SBH	G. Reisner. *Sumerisch-babylonische Hymnen nach Thontafeln griechischerf Zeit*. Berlin, 1896.
UET	Ur Excavations: Texts. London, 1928–1976.

Prostitutes and Courtesans
in the Ancient World

Introduction

LAURA K. MCCLURE

The study of prostitution in the classical world has been until recently but a footnote to scholarship on ancient sexuality and gender. And yet, as David Halperin noted in his introduction to the landmark volume, *Before Sexuality*, a comprehensive view of ancient sexualities must include "the varieties of prostitution and prostitutes, from the cultured and powerful Athenian courtesans of the fourth century, to the professional dancer performing at men's symposia, to the poor streetwalker" (Halperin, Winkler, and Zeitlin 1990, 18). The neglect of this subject cannot be explained by a dearth of primary sources, as the German scholar Friedrich Karl Forberg long ago demonstrated: his *Apophoreta*, published in 1824, catalogued and classified hundreds of references to Greek and Latin sexual practices from ancient authors of all periods. Much later, Paul Brandt observed in his *Sexual Life in Ancient Greece (Sittengeschichte Griechenlands)*, published under the pseudonym Hans Licht (Licht 1932, 329): "If in the course of the previous discussion of Greek morals and culture I have had to remark that it was a question of working upon entirely new ground, or that, in the case of a particular chapter, preliminary works of reference were non-existent, no such complaint can be made with regard to the depiction of Greek prostitution. Rather the contrary would be true, and an author might almost apologize for the abundance of [ancient] works treating of his subject, the number of which in this case can scarcely be estimated." Translated into

English in 1932 by J. H. Freese, Brandt's work quickly became for classical scholars the standard text on ancient sexuality and prostitution—a subject to which he devotes over eighty pages. Around the same time, two German monographs substantially devoted to the representation of the courtesan in the Greek comic tradition appeared, *Die Gestalt der Hetäre in der griechischen Komödie* (Hauschild 1933), and *Motivstudien zur griechischen Komödie* (Wehrli 1936). But while German scholars like Forberg, Brandt, and Hauschild pondered the shocking directness and profusion of Greco-Roman accounts of sexuality and prostitution, Anglophone scholarship largely remained silent on the question until well into the second half of the twentieth century.

By the early 1970s, the proliferation of feminist scholarship in multiple disciplines kindled an interest in issues of gender and sexuality among Anglo-American classical scholars. The pioneering work of J. P. Sullivan, Jeffrey Henderson, and Sir Kenneth Dover led to advances in our understanding of sexual terminology and the social construction of gender and sexuality in the ancient world. The subject of prostitution figured in broad surveys of women in ancient Greece, such as that of Pomeroy (1975), and in analyses of erotic vocabulary and behavior in Athenian comedy and oratory, e.g., Henderson's *Maculate Muse* (1975) and Dover's *Greek Homosexuality* (1978). The publication of *Menander's Courtesans and the Greek Comic Tradition* by Madeleine Henry in 1985 furnished a feminist perspective on the question of the portrayal of the courtesan in Greek New Comedy initiated by Hauschild and Wehrli. Around the same time, the large number of images of prostitutes found in classical art, particularly in Attic vase painting, engendered Otto Brendel's lengthy essay, "The Scope and Temperament of Erotic Art in the Graeco-Roman World" (Brendel 1970) and the subsequent studies of Keuls (1985), Peschel (1987), and Reinsberg (1989). On the Roman side, feminist scholars such as Amy Richlin, Judith Hallett, and Marilyn Skinner published important studies of ancient Roman constructions of gender and sexuality during the 1980s, most notably Richlin's *The Garden of Priapus* (1983), a study of Latin sexual vocabulary and its social meanings.

The profound influence of Michel Foucault, palpable in almost every study of ancient Greek sexuality from 1990 onward, occasioned a shift of focus in scholarly discourse and privileged a Hellenic perspective. Instead of emphasizing historical realities, these studies have taken up the role of prostitution as one of many cultural discourses produced by Athenians during the archaic and classical periods. The fact that the topic has figured prominently in many larger projects of cultural criticism attests to its pivotal importance for understanding ancient constructions of gender, sexuality, and even political ideology. Halperin, following on Dover and Keuls, elucidates the political repercussions of male prostitution in classical Athens in a chapter of *One Hundred Years of Homosexuality* (1990). More recently, James Davidson's *Courtesans and Fishcakes* (1997) has examined prostitution as a major aspect of the consuming passions enjoyed and regulated by Athenian men of the classical period. Finally, Leslie Kurke devotes two chapters to the subject in *Coins, Bodies, Games and Gold* (1999), in which she explores how concepts of prostitution reflected conflicting aristocratic and democratic political ideologies in the drinking parties of Athenian men.

Although debate about prostitution in the Greek world has proliferated in the last two decades, much less discussion has occurred on the Roman side until very recently. Most influential has been Thomas McGinn's massive study of Roman prostitution, *Prostitution, Sexuality and the Law in Ancient Rome* (1998). The book maps out the social position of prostitutes in Roman society, their legal status as it bore on marriage and taxation, and the ways in which they were protected under private law. Similarly, the imprint of Catherine Edwards' seminal essay, "Unspeakable Professions: Public Performance and Prostitution in Ancient Rome," which appeared in the 1997 volume *Roman Sexualities* edited by Hallett and Skinner, can be felt in many recent discussions of Roman prostitution and its construction in literary and legal discourses, including Anne Duncan's and Sharon James's essays on Roman Comedy in this volume.

The essays collected here originated as papers delivered at a conference on prostitution in the ancient world held at the University of Wisconsin–Madison on April 12–14, 2002. They cover a vast historical span, from ancient Mesopotamia to the early Christian period. They range over a wide variety of genres and sources, from legal and religious tracts to the high poetic genres of lyric poetry, love elegy, and comic drama, and even to graffiti scrawled on the walls of ancient Pompeii. While these essays do not pretend to provide a comprehensive, unified survey of ancient prostitution, they do reflect the variety and vitality of the debates engendered by the last three decades of research on the subject. In particular, they confront the ambiguities of terms for prostitutes in ancient languages, the difficulty of distinguishing the prostitute from the woman who is merely promiscuous or adulterous, the question of whether sacred or temple prostitution actually existed

in the ancient Near East and Greece, and the political and social implications of literary representations of prostitutes and courtesans. The organization of this volume into three sections reflects, to a certain extent,
some of these debates. The first section, "Prostitution and the Sacred,"
examines the relation of prostitution to religious worship and sacred
space in the Mesopotamian, biblical, and Greek traditions. The second
section, "Legal and Moral Discourses on Prostitution," explores the use
of prostitutes in Greek and Roman oratory to vilify opponents and enforce moral agendas as well as considers their economic function. The
third part, "Prostitution, Comedy, and Public Performance," analyzes
the development of prostitution as a comic trope on both the Greek and
Roman stages, and finally, in the comic dialogues of Lucian of the Second Sophistic period. Although sometimes divergent in methodology
and theme, all of these essays demonstrate that while prostitutes in the
ancient world may have been socially marginal, they were symbolically
and even socially central, intersecting with almost every aspect of daily
life.

Defining Prostitutes

As the sociologist Iwan Bloch observed in 1912, any study of prostitution must contend with the difficulty of defining the practice; clear
boundaries between nonmarital sexual relations, such as concubinage and adultery and sex for pay, are often elusive. The promiscuous
woman often has the same social meaning whether an adulteress or
prostitute: in ancient Rome, for example, both the prostitute and the
woman disgraced by adultery donned the male toga (McGinn 1998c,
340; see also Olson in this volume). As observed by several contributors
to this volume, terms for prostitutes are much contested in nearly every
ancient language, not only in Greek, where the exact relation of *hetaira*
(courtesan) and *pornê* (brothel worker) has long been debated, but also
in the languages of ancient Mesopotamia and in biblical Hebrew. In the
Greco-Roman tradition, the preponderance of euphemisms and metaphorical terms that refer to sexual activities and practitioners generates
further confusion. The problem of terminology reflects in part our inadequate access to the social practices depicted by the literary accounts,
even as it reveals the ambiguous status of such socially outcast and
marginal figures in the ancient world.

    Among Hellenists, there has been a long and vigorous debate about
ancient Greek terminology for prostitution, particularly the words

"*pornê*" and "*hetaira.*" Both James Davidson (1997) and Leslie Kurke (1999) have argued that these terms express a binary opposition between two types of prostitutes that in turn reflect competing social and political ideologies. The term "*hetaira*," the feminine form of "*hetairos*" (male friend), denoted a woman, usually celebrated, who was maintained by one man in exchange for his exclusive sexual access to her; typically she did not reside in his home. She participated in and embodied an economy of gift exchange that maintained, rather than severed, the connection between individuals. Alternately seductive and persuasive, providing her services in exchange for gifts, the *hetaira* perpetually left often the possibility that she might refuse her favors; indeed, "the very name *hetaira*—'companion,' 'friend'—is ambiguous, a euphemism" (Davidson 1997, 135). The *pornê*, in contrast, belonged to the streets: she was the *hetaira's* nameless, faceless brothel counterpart and participated in a type of commodity exchange that continually depersonalized and reified, exemplified by crass transactional names such as "Didrachmon" and "Obole," both terms for Attic currency (Davidson 1997, 118–19). And yet, as reasonable as these distinctions might sound, the two terms are frequently applied to the same woman in all periods of the Greek literary tradition (McClure 2003, 9–24; see also Cohen in this volume). Indeed, as Edward Cohen argues, both types of prostitute may have originated in the brothel, with the name "*hetaira*" serving to advertise a woman's manumission from sexual slavery and her acquisition of free status.

In contrast, considerably less attention has been given to Latin vocabulary for prostitution both in this volume and elsewhere, even though Adams in his 1983 essay enumerated over fifty such terms. The most common Latin terms are "*scortum*" and "*meretrix.*" The word "*scortum*" ("leather," "hide") may refer to the female genitalia and, synechdocally, to the woman who sells her sexual services; as such, it has a more pejorative meaning. In Plautus, it refers to figures who tend not to be named but rather might participate in temporary liaisons at dinner parties (Adams 1983, 325). In contrast, "*meretrix*" denotes named prostitutes in New Comedy who serve as the objects of romantic intrigue and individual ardor. However, like the Greek terms "*hetaira*" and "*pornê*," a clear status distinction between the words "*meretrix*" and "*scortum*" is not always evident: Horace in *Satires* 1.2 seems to lump together the actress *(mima)*, the brothel worker *(in fornice)*, and the *meretrix,* at least in their opposition to the respectable wife or *matrona*. Most other Latin terms for prostitutes suggest various aspects of transacting their business, such as sitting or standing before the brothel *("proseda," "prostabulum"),* street walking *("circulatrix"),* aggressive soliciting *("petulca"),* or the time at which their liaisons occur *("nonaria").* By the late Republic, even the term *"puella"* ("girl"), an established euphemism of erotic language, could mean "whore" (Adams 1983, 346; see also James in this volume). Most of the essays concerned with the Roman literary tradition in this volume do not specifically address the question of prostitutional vocabulary, but rather focus on the *meretrix,* especially her intersection with the adulteress.

Prostitution and the Sacred

The specter of sacred or cultic prostitution raised by Herodotus in his account of the temple of Ishtar at Babylon has generated controversy and debate for well over a century. In the last decade, however, both Near Eastern and classical scholars have questioned the existence of this practice both in ancient Mesopotamia and in ancient Greece, concluding that female cultic personnel in the service of fertility goddesses such as Inana and Aphrodite did not engage in any type of sexual activity specific to their religious roles. As Martha Roth, Stephanie Budin, and Phyllis Bird suggest in their essays, the traditional view affirming cultic prostitution rests on flawed interpretations of terminology and unreliable ancient testimonia.

In Mesopotamian documents and in the tradition of the Hebrew Bible, however, the female prostitute is often difficult to distinguish from a sexually available or promiscuous woman. Some women have been interpreted as prostitutes who clearly were not, but whose behaviors "pushed the limits of social norms," as Martha Roth demonstrates in her discussion of the intersection of regulated and unregulated sexual activity in ancient Mesopotamian cultures. Such women threatened the stability of the household by potentially seducing married men away from their families; at the same time, they served to define both legal and social norms. Focusing on the Sumerian term *"kar.kid"* and the Babylono-Assyrian *"harīmtu,"* words typically translated as "prostitute," she shows the elusive status of women engaged in nonmarital sexual activities delineated in Mesopotamian documents. For example, the Laws of Lipit-Ishtar describe a *kar.kid* "of the street" as luring a husband away from his wife, but they do not allude to an actual commercial transaction. The reference to the street identifies the act or the person as originating outside of a legitimate household, as when Enkidu in the Gilgamesh story condemns the *kar.kid* who has seduced him to stand by the city wall. These promiscuous women—whether prostitutes, adulteresses, or merely sexually active females operating outside male control—occasioned fear because they did not submit to men and could disrupt legitimate marriages. They were of interest in the construction of Mesopotamian legal documents because of their impact on private and economic issues, such as inheritance devolution, rather than out of desire to regulate morality.

Stephanie Budin considers the question of sacred prostitution in the Near East from a Greek perspective. She observes that as no known direct testimonia of sacred prostitution survive from ancient Greece, scholars must rely on very late sources that often mistranslate key terms or distort the discussions of earlier classical authors. In many cases, late classical references to sacred prostitution are intended to denigrate the practices and beliefs of other ancient cultures. Budin defines sacred prostitution as the sale of the body, with a portion of the profits going to a deity, usually a fertility goddess like Inana or Aphrodite. The practice also includes the premarital sale of virginity, prostitution by temple personnel, as well as temporary prostitution on ritual occasions. Here, as well, terminology plays a critical role. In Budin's view, the ancient Near Eastern and Greek terms previously believed to refer to prostitutes actually designate temple personnel with no sexual function. Even words previously thought to refer to prostitutes, such as Babylono-Assyrian *"harīmtu,"* as discussed by Roth, do not necessarily designate a woman who sells her body for sex, but rather a promiscuous woman not under the immediate supervision of men. Budin's reading of two late sources previously believed to refer to sacred prostitution—a passage from Athenaeus concerning courtesans at Corinth (13.573e–f), and an inscription from Roman Tralles in Caria, Turkey—militates against their use as evidence for this practice in ancient Greece. In the latter case, the term *"pallakê"* ("concubine"), interpreted as a temple prostitute or concubine employed for ritual purposes, reveals a confusion with the word *"pallas"* ("maiden-priestess") among ancient commentators.

Phyllis Bird in her analysis of the Hebrew Bible shows how the process of translation and scholarly interpretation has distorted our understanding of biblical accounts of prostitution. Just as in the other traditions, terms for prostitutes in the Hebrew Bible admit of considerable ambiguity and often conflate promiscuous or adulterous female behavior with commercial sex. The most common term for prostitute is the feminine participle *"zonah,"* from the verb *"zanah"* ("to engage in extra-marital relations"), a word that normally applies only to female subjects. The original sense of *"zonah"* as habitual fornication outside of marriage eventually came to be applied to women offering sex for pay. Such women belonged to the streets and thus became identified with urban life in a number of proverbs, similes, and narratives; conversely, the city is often personified as a whore. The *zonah* represents the primary female example of the social outcast, defined by sexual activity normally prohibited. Tolerated but stigmatized, the biblical prostitute is frequently deployed as a symbol of generalized sexual immorality.

Catherine Keesling turns to the intersection of prostitution and the sacred in her discussion of dedicatory offerings made by or in honor of courtesans in ancient Greece. She discusses how many of these dedications transgress religious conventions by means of their enormous size, prohibitive expense, or high visibility. The most famous examples include the funerary monument of Pythionice located on the Sacred Way between Athens and Eleusis, the portrait statue of Phryne placed in the sanctuary of Apollo at Delphi, and the famous spits of Rhodopis, also dedicated to Apollo at Delphi. In her analysis of the material evidence, Keesling argues that Rhodopis' spits depart from dedicatory conventions in at least one significant way, but that, conversely, Phryne's statue reflects some contemporary conventions of portraiture. A base inscribed with the words "[*anethe*]*ke Rhod*[*opis*]" supports Herodotus's account of the courtesan's dedication of spits at Delphi. However, its substantial size, indicated by the letter height, suggests that the spits may have been on permanent display for the glorification of the dedicator rather than for use in sacrificial ritual. In other cases, the monuments associated with courtesans may represent an attempt on the part of later writers to bridge a gap left by the inscription. So we hear of Leaena's lion statue on the Athenian acropolis erected to commemorate her heroic silence and its role in the democratic revolution. The positioning of a portrait statue of a courtesan in a religious sanctuary, as in the case of Phryne, is unconventional and yet parallels the fourth-century practice of erecting honorific portraits of living subjects in public places.

Legal and Moral Discourses on Prostitution

Although prostitution did not carry—apart from the world of the Hebrew Bible—the same moral inflections for ancient societies as it does today, it did enter into moral discourses, particularly through the law courts, where it negotiated issues of inheritance, citizenship, and political ideology. While prostitution was a legal and highly visible practice on the streets of ancient cities, and patronizing prostitutes was not necessarily stigmatized—as long as it did not involve squandering one's patrimony—to be a prostitute incurred disgrace for both women and men. In Greek and Roman moral discourses, allegations of prostitution could serve to discredit an opponent, as in Aeschines' *Against Timarchus*, while consorting openly with courtesans could be used to undermine an individual's political authority by exposing a licentious and prodigal lifestyle, as in the case of Cicero's *Pro Caelio.* Indeed, Roman law branded prostitutes, along with actors and gladiators, as *"infames"* ("lacking in reputation"; Edwards 1997, 66-67). Moreover, the social status of prostitutes and courtesans as social outsiders or foreigners, coupled with the ambiguity of the terms relating to them, made their representations easily adaptable to a variety of rhetorical and political agendas.

Taking up Kurke's and Davidson's discussions of the political significance of the *hetaira/porn*ê dichotomy, Cohen in this volume explores contemporary fourth-century attitudes toward trade and commerce that underpinned prostitution in classical Athens. He argues that the two words denote a "complementary antithesis" that reflects the business context in which prostitution occurred. Inconsistencies in usage reveal the Athenian preoccupation with gauging the extent of a worker's freedom from another person's control, that is, where they belonged on the spectrum of freedom and slavery. Athenians disapproved of working for pay under the control of others; even supervisors in the world of Athenian commerce were normally slaves. A similar lack of distinction between commercial businesses and private households, found also in Roman towns as McGinn points out, explains the preponderance of literary and material evidence linking wool working to prostitution, particularly as found in the *phialai exeleutherikai* tablets that document the manumission of Athenian slaves. Servility or disgrace in Athens therefore did not devolve on the kind of task performed or even its locale— a slave and a free man could both serve as rowers on a trireme, for example—but on the presence or absence of supervision. A similar demarcation obtained in regard to female prostitutes in classical Athens. The term *"porn*ê*"* denoted a slave woman forced to have sex with whoever desired her and placed under the supervision of the *pornoboskos* (brothel keeper), while the *hetaira* more closely resembled a free-citizen wife in her ability to control her male partners' access to her body. In Cohen's words, the term *"hetaira"* "scrupulously trumpeted the calling of a free person, an honorific perhaps overly ostentatious for a formerly enslaved worker."

Although references to prostitutes abound in classical oratory, scholars have largely neglected the topic. Focusing on the pseudo-Demosthenic speech, *Against Neaira,* Alison Glazebrook explores the representation of courtesans in Athenian judicial oratory and shows how speakers constructed and manipulated images of prostitutes in service of hidden social and political agendas. In contrast to other literary discourses, oratory does not represent courtesans as witty and cultured but rather often depicts them as depraved and extravagant. Timarchus, for instance, squanders the wages of his own prostitution on exquisite meals, gambling, and prostitutes. The *hetaira* Neaira finances with her body an expensive lifestyle, including numerous servants and costly clothing. The unnamed companion of Olympiodorus also demands the same level of material prosperity, spending her time at parties and engaging in licentious behavior. These prostitutes and their consorts embody a prodigal lifestyle considered morally reprehensible by Athenians of the fourth century BCE. Judicial oratory further plays up the subversive aspects of such women by underscoring their ability to bring their partners under their sexual and economic control. At the same time, the speaker may attempt to vilify a citizen woman by attributing to her characteristics normally associated with prostitutes, such as prodigality, promiscuity, and manipulativeness. In all these contexts, the figure of the prostitute defines the boundaries of normative female behavior by serving as the antithesis of the chaste and secluded wives and daughters of the Athenian jurors.

Susan Lape revisits Aeschines' oration, *Against Timarchus,* to demonstrate the ways in which judicial oratory begins to deploy a moral discourse borrowed from contemporary philosophical thought about prostitution in fourth-century Athens, a time of political crisis that necessitated communal self-definition. Current scholarly consensus holds that Athenian law did not regulate the sexual behavior of citizens for moral reasons unless it interfered with the aims of the political community. But Lape argues that around 350 BCE, litigants increasingly appealed to the idea that irregular sexual practices could have a moral impact on the polis. Aeschines problematizes prostitution in moral terms, along with hedonism, using rhetoric culled from elite discourses critical of democratic culture. In Lape's view, he uses the rhetoric of shame and disgust to portray his opponent as "a pollutant that must be expelled from the citizen body." In so doing, the orator focuses on the state of Timarchus's soul, rather than on his body, to show how his very character has become deformed by excess. The concern for the souls of citizens is unparalleled in earlier judicial sources and shows a new political significance being attached to the moral domain developed more fully among philosophers such as Plato. Aeschines offers a new agenda for politics in which the interest in war and foreign affairs of the previous generation yields to prescription for civic education in the democratic state.

Thomas McGinn takes us out of the law courts and into the streets with his examination of the topography of Roman prostitution. The lack of moral stigma attached to prostitution in most ancient literary discourses is reflected in the topographical layout of Roman cities, where brothels mixed with residential houses and other commercial businesses. McGinn observes that the plan of the ancient city of Pompeii, with its preponderance of brothels, shows no evidence of a segregated red-light district, nor of any "moral zoning." Whereas in the Unites States, brothels tend to be isolated (as in the ranch brothels of the Nevada desert), illustrating our modern assumption that sex work should be segregated and unmentioned, Roman brothels were broadly dispersed throughout the city, clustering around combined residential and commercial districts with nearby lower-class housing. Only with the rise of Christianity does prostitution begin to appear to be linked to a concept of moral impurity. For example, the Bishop of Carthage first identifies the brothel with the sewer and the act of prostitution with befouling the body. The Roman emperor Constantine purportedly established the first dedicated red-light district in the ancient city of Zeugma in Asia Minor. Augustine in De ordine also concedes a place to prostitution as a safety valve for male lust and offers a Christian rationale for zoning their activities, as McGinn observes: "just as the human body segregates certain elements, so a well-ordered society isolates and renders as inconspicuous as possible the sale of sex."

Like Attic oratory, the moral discourse of the Roman law courts during the first century BCE marshals representations of prostitutes to defame opponents and to reinforce political ideology. In her discussion of Cicero's Pro Caelio, Marsha McCoy explores the implications of the unprecedented application of the term "meretrix" to an elite Roman woman. By affiliating Clodia, the wife of Metellus and lover of Catullus, with prostitution, Cicero attempted to turn the law courts into an arena for critiquing and shaping moral behavior. Apart from the genres of comedy, Cicero uses the word *"meretrix"* more frequently than any other Roman author; in each instance, the word is intended to disparage the subject he is attacking. In *Verres*, Cicero's flamboyant language and imagery convey his view that the courts provided the appropriate venue for an elite jury to pass judgment on the social behavior of its own members. Verres, by consorting with prostitutes, has turned his public behavior into private misbehavior and abused his civic duties. He pins the blame on a single *meretrix*, Chelidon, alleging that petitioners wishing access to Verres first had to resort to her and pay in cash for the privilege. The conflation of sexual and legal supplication, as well as the gender role inversions entailed by this reference to prostitution, all conspire to cast Verres in the worst light possible. The *Pro Caelio* dramatically expands on the argument laid out in the earlier prosecution: by confusing social boundaries, Clodia actually becomes a *meretrix* and in the process inverts the social order of her household. Cicero effectively marshals the figure of the prostitute to further his political agenda, the restoration of republican civil society.

   Although Latin terminology for prostitutes has not engendered the same degree of debate as the Greek terms discussed above, ambiguities of social status were manifested in other arenas of public life, particularly through clothing, as Kelly Olson observes in her essay. It has long been recognized that clothing in preindustrial societies served as a major means of reinforcing social hierarchies and yet, as she argues, actual practice probably did not rigidly adhere to ideological prescriptions. Indeed, in ancient Rome, the deliberate omission of distinctive garments that marked one's rank might be more common than previously suspected. Olson examines the types of garments and ornaments worn by Roman women and shows how the boundaries between the *matrona* and *meretrix* were frequently blurred. Among Roman men, clothing, although intended to designate rank, often did not accurately reflect the social status of the wearer. The difficulty of reinforcing sartorial policies led to the usurpation of equestrian symbols in the imperial period and the abandonment of the toga, the preeminent mark of the citizen, among elite Roman men. Clothing could also reinforce moral codes: so the *matrona* indicated her status as a legitimate wife by donning the *stola* (long upper garment) and the *palla* (mantle) and by wearing fillets in her hair. In contrast, prostitutes and adulterous women were obliged to wear the toga, a garment normally associated with citizen men. The lack of sartorial distinction between the promiscuous woman and the prostitute evident in the Roman custom of forcing such women to don the toga recalls similar ambiguities of terminology and social status found throughout the ancient world.

Prostitution, Comedy and Public Performance

Comic genres, whether Attic Old, Middle or New Comedy and its Roman successors, as well as the hybrid genres of the Second Sophistic period, prove our richest source of representations of courtesans and prostitutes from Greco-Roman antiquity. Although the *hetaira* is not a well-developed character in Attic Old Comedy, metaphors and images of prostitution pervade the genre. By the late fourth century BCE, the Greek *hetaira* had become a recognizable comic type, indispensable to plots of mistaken identity and romantic intrigue, and one that traveled well to non-Athenian theaters scattered throughout the ancient Mediterranean world. Plautus and Terrence transplanted this drama, with its stock characters and plots, to a Roman context, further reinforcing the role of the courtesan as a familiar staple of comic drama. Her feigned emotions and equivocal language invite comparisons with the dramatic actor and render her a ready metaphor for theatrical illusion in Plautine comedy as well as serve as reminders of the continuity of the ancient comic tradition.

In his discussion of Aristophanes' *Lysistrata*, Faraone argues against the prevailing view of the protagonist as a positive representation of female authority derived from women's religious roles in the Athenian polis. He argues instead that the comic poet in his portrayal of the character Lysistrata alternates between two very different images of female leadership, that of the historical priestess of Athena, Lysimache, and that of a madame placed in charge of a group of unruly *hetairas*. This juxtaposition also underlies the contrast between the oversexed, foolish young wives and the chorus of pious older women, wise in their years. For example, Myrrhine seduces her husband, Cinesias, using the *hetaira's* accoutrements and arts, but ultimately requires the intervention of Lysistrata to honor her oath. In contrast, the chorus of older women exemplifies female heroism in their performance of cultic and civic rituals and in their careful management of household economy. The figure of Lysistrata alternates surprisingly between *hetaira* and priestess, each persona in full control of her place of business (a brothel or sanctuary) and a group of young assistants (prostitutes or temple staff). The final scene plays up Lysistrata's identification with the brothel keeper: it represents her as using the *iynx*, a type of erotic spell normally associated with prostitutes, as she panders the personification of Hellenic peace, Reconciliation, to the assembled men of Greece. Throughout, Aristophanes brilliantly plays on the similarities between religious sanctuary and brothel and the authority and autonomy attributed to priestesses and courtesans.

The Roman obsession with the behavior of courtesans at table serves as the focus of Sharon James's discussion of Plautus's *Asinaria* and Ovid's *Amores* 1.4 and 2.5. These works demonstrate the anxieties produced in elite Roman males in the face of female freedom, subjectivity, and sexuality, as well afford insight into the lives of courtesans at Rome. By the time of Plautus, the Greek courtesan had become a familiar figure in elite Roman society. She could act as an agent on her own behalf and enter into contracts with her male lovers, just as in classical Athens. In turn, the lover paid an annual fee that guaranteed him exclusive access to an individual courtesan. James argues that the *puella* of Latin love elegy was modeled on the courtesan, by definition an unmarriageable woman not under the control of a father, husband or pimp, who made a living by sexually attracting propertied men. Because of her social and economic independence, her affections had to be won by a prospective lover and could not be permanently controlled. The *Asinaria* dramatizes this dilemma in its portrayal of a contract between a young lover, the *amator* Diabolus, and the courtesan Philaenis. His concern with every aspect of her behavior, from her facial expressions to her language, betrays the lover's comic obsession with controlling the behavior of an independent woman, the woman whom the Roman citizen actually wants but cannot marry. *Amores* 1.4 nicely dovetails with the contract scene of the *Asinaria* in its representation of the development of masculine anxieties over the inability to control a courtesan's thoughts and feelings as well as her behavior at a dinner party. Here the Ovidian *amator* advises a courtesan how to avoid her contracted lover while securing his attentions; she must use all of the ruses denied by the contract in *Asinaria*, such as secret communication and remaining sober while encouraging the contracted lover to get drunk. Both passages demonstrate the impossibility of controlling independent women such as courtesans while at the same time dramatizing the temporary identity crisis they provoked in elite Roman men.

Anne Duncan explores the relationship among actors, prostitutes, and theatricality in Roman Comedy from the perspective of Bakhtin's theory of carnival. In Rome, prostitutes and actors shared many similarities: both feigned emotions for a living, both cross-dressed, and both were branded as *infames* after Augustus's moral legislation. The Roman legal system repeatedly attempted to draw the line between such low-status individuals and the Roman elite by prohibiting upper-class individuals from marrying actors and women of senatorial rank from appearing onstage or registering as prostitutes in order to avoid charges of adultery. And while such figures invited moral suspicion as "low-Others," they also functioned as objects of desire for elite Roman males in the popular theater. Because of her capacity for deception, the *meretrix* in Roman Comedy is often closely identified with metatheatricality, that is, she calls attention to the play as a theatrical event and to its characters as actors. So in Plautus's *Miles Gloriosus,* the *meretrix* performs the part of the wife, dressed in the fillets that, as Olson's notes in her essay, signify female respectability. Elsewhere the verb *"simulare"* likens the performance of the *meretrix* to theatrical deception and invites us to view her as an actor playing a role. In *Truculentus,* Phronesium breaks the dramatic illusion and directly addresses the audience but remains fully in character. As a figure of substitution interchangeable with the actor, the *meretrix* comes to exemplify a kind of dishonesty and insincerity antithetical to Roman notions of elite subjectivity, thereby symbolically reinforcing normative boundaries of status and ideology.

In the final chapter, Kate Gilhuly transports us from the comedy of Plautus and Terrence to a much later period and comic genre. Her essay examines a fictional scene of sexual encounter between two courtesans and its relation to the earlier classical tradition in Lucian's *Dialogue of the Courtesans.* By referring to the central character, Megilla, as a *"hetairistria,"* Lucian parodically evokes the only other passage in extant Greek literature that uses the term in reference to female homosexuality, Plato's *Symposium* 189c-d. Although the names of most of Lucian's courtesans come from Attic comedy, that of Megilla recalls another Platonic passage, his account of Spartan pederasty enumerated by one Megillos in the *Laws.* Through the interplay of texts and names borrowed from the Greek literary past, Lucian displaces the phallic preoccupations of classical Athens onto a lesbian woman and in the process inverts Plato's erotic hierarchy of love between men. The fact that the original term *"hetairistria"* occurs in the character Aristophanes' account of the origins of sexual difference in Plato's *Symposium* also draws attention to Lucian's own method of splicing together comic and philosophical discourses. These Platonic allusions inherently problematize the authority and prestige of the Athenian past while identifying the author as a *barbaros,* an ethnic outsider to this Attic heritage.

Lucian's depiction of the phallic lesbian becomes emblematic of the discordant union of self in other in the shifting cultural and political matrix of the Second Sophistic period.

This volume is not intended to be the last word on the subject of prostitution in antiquity; rather, it attempts to reflect the diversity of contemporary directions and approaches to the questions and issues engendered by the subject. And yet all of the contributions in this volume demonstrate the centrality and ubiquity of prostitution in the ancient world. Prostitutes sat in brothels and walked the public streets, tempting fathers and husbands away from their families; they paid taxes and set up dedications in religious sanctuaries; they appeared as characters—sometimes admirable, sometimes despicable—on the comic stage and in the law courts; they lived lavishly, consorting with famous poets and politicians, or lived as slaves in poverty; they participated in the banquets and drinking parties of men, where they aroused jealousy among their anxious lovers. As the following essays show, these figures intersected with just about every aspect of ancient life. Much more work remains to be done about them.

Prostitution and the Sacred

Marriage, Divorce, and the Prostitute in Ancient Mesopotamia

MARTHA T. ROTH

Introduction

"The most shameful custom," Herodotus called it. He was writing, in his account of the events leading up to the war between Greece and Persia, about the goings-on at the temple of Ishtar in Babylon, in which, he claimed, once in her life every woman had to accept the sexual advances of a stranger in exchange for a silver coin in order to fulfill a duty to the goddess.

The most shameful custom the Babylonians have is this: every native woman must go sit in the temple of Aphrodite, once in her life, and have sex with an adult male stranger. Many of them disdain to mix with the rest, on the high horse of wealth, and so drive to the temple on covered carriages, taking their stand with a large retinue following behind them. But many more do as follows: they sit in the sanctuary of Aphrodite, these many women, their heads crowned with a band of bowstring. Some arrive while others depart. Roped-off thoroughfares give all manner of routes through the women and the strangers pass along them as they make their choice. Once a woman sits down there, she does not go home until a stranger drops money in her lap and has sex with her outside the temple. When he drops it he has to say "I call on the goddess My-litta." Assyrians call Aphrodite Mylitta. The money can be any value at all—it is not to be refused, for that is forbidden, for this money becomes sacred. She follows the first one who drops money and rejects none. When she has had sex, she has performed her religious dues to the goddess and goes home; and from that time on you will never make her a big enough gift to have her. All those who have looks and presence quickly get it over with, all those of them who have no looks wait for a long time unable to fulfill the law—some of them wait for a three- or four-year spell.[1]

This is the fifth and last of the Babylonian customs Herodotus found especially worthy of mention. The first and second, which Herodotus deemed the wisest and second wisest customs, involved a bride market with two auctions (one a straightforward bidding for the most beautiful, the other a Dutch auction for the ugliest [1.196]) and a method of medical diagnosis and treatment by which the Babylonians (whom he claimed had no physicians) laid out their sick in the public square to solicit and take the advice of all passersby who had ever suffered from similar ailments (1.197). The third custom noted by Herodotus is that the Babylonians bury their dead in honey (1.198). And the fourth custom of the five described is a postcoital ritual purification involving incense and washing (1.198).

It is certainly no accident that two of the five "customs" involve illness and death and the other three sex and marriage. These are the hot topics, those that attract and hold the attention of an audience. But, as is now generally accepted among scholars, Herodotus was not talking about a historical Babylon at all, but about the non-Greek "other," about the "anti-type of the Greek polis" by which the Greek population could define itself (Beard and Henderson 1998, 56–79; Kurke 1999, especially chapter 6). Nonetheless, his fantasies or musings found a receptive audience in antiquity, were echoed in Strabo (16.1.20) and in the apocryphal Letter of Jeremiah (= Baruch) 6:43, and retain their prurient appeal even to a modern audience. Although there is not a single modern piece of scholarship that gives any credence at all to any of Herodotus's other "Babylonian customs"—whether wise or shameful—his story about the ritual defloration and sexual accessibility of common women in the sacred realm ("Babylonian sacred prostitution") remains stubbornly embedded as an accepted fact in the literature.[2]

The goals of this essay are modest.[3] I do not intend to review all the individual pieces of ancient evidence from cuneiform sources, spanning two and a half millennia, relating to "prostitution" or more broadly to nonmarital sexual relations. I will, rather, try to focus on the intersection of and conflict between regulated and unregulated sexual reproduction; that is, the social and legal tensions between marriage that is about "fidelity and fecundity"[4] and nonmarital relations that can have other, competing, ends. First, however, the specter of the "sacred prostitute" raised by Herodotus must be confronted, if only to be eliminated from the discussion.

The "Sacred Prostitute"

Westenholz concluded in a 1989 article that "there was no such institution as sacred prostitution in Mesopotamia" (1989, 260 and bibliography, 246 n.1). The chapter in Frymer-Kensky's book on women and the biblical transformation of pagan myth that deals with Israel's putative "sexual orgiasticism" bears the subtitle "The Myth of Orgy," and concludes that in Mesopotamia, "there is no evidence that any [temple-associated women] performed sexual acts as part of their sacred duties" (1992, 201–2). We know of many categories of female cultic personnel— most of these are attested primarily during the Old Babylonian period only (about nineteenth to seventeenth centuries BCE)—and we do know a certain amount about these cultic women's private sexual, reproductive, and domestic lives. We know whether they were or were not permitted to marry, to bear children, to raise their children; which ones lived segregated in "cloisters"; which inherited property from their fathers; which had power to dispose of their inheritances to fellow devotees or to derive income from renting their houses, fields, and orchards. Interestingly, we know less about their cultic duties, which ceremonies they participated in and in what capacities. We do know, however, that not one engaged in any type of sexual activity specific to her role in the cult, other than the *ēntu*, who, in the late third millennium Ur III-Isin periods only, played a role in the sacred marriage ritual between the king and the goddess Inanna that served as "one way for the king to secure legitimacy and divine blessings, and to reaffirm his and his people's obligations to the gods" (Cooper 1993, 91).[5]

It is clear that, other than this highly restricted and structured "sacred marriage," there was no ritualized or institutionalized sexual intercourse associated with Mesopotamian religions or temples. Neither the female nor male cultic personnel, whether linked ritually or only lexically (the *ēntu* or the *ēnu*, *kezertu* or *kezru*, *qadištu* or *qadišu*, *šugītu* or *šugû*, etc.), can be identified as female or male prostitutes or catamites. Our discussion of the possible impact of prostitution on society and particularly on marriage must proceed without reference to religious practices.[6]

The Private Prostitute

The Mesopotamia world had a definite and appropriate place for women who exchanged sexual favors for pecuniary consideration, that is, "prostitutes." This simple statement is not uncontested. Although Lambert stated in 1992 that "there is one word for 'prostitute' which is not in doubt, the Babylono-Assyrian *harīmtu,* which corresponds to the Sumerian *kar-kid*" (1992, 127) in her 1998 work Assante argues that the *kar.kid/harīmtu* is not (or not only) a prostitute, and that she is "more than" Westenholz's a "wom[a]n whose sexuality is not regulated": she is, to Assante, the not-the-daughter, the not-the-wife, "in modern parlance 'the single woman'" (1998, 10). Assante does not insist that no *harīmtu* is a prostitute; rather, she argues that not every *harīmtu* is a prostitute. Her thesis is that the *harīmtu* "stand[s] outside of or separate from societal norms, that is, [from] the patriarchally controlled household. . . . [W]ithin this legal description, the *kar.kid/harīmtu* could be anything from a virgin to a prostitute" (1998, 13).

In the vast corpus of millions of legal, administrative, economic, and literary cuneiform texts from Mesopotamia, prostitution—that is, sex in exchange for wealth—is clearly documentable in only one passage: a song (or songs) addressed to the goddess Inanna (as Nanaja) known from a number of near-duplicates, all dating to the Old Babylonian period (Sjöberg 1977, 17–18, Alster 1993, 15–27, and ETCSL, "A Balbale to Inana as Nanaya").[7] The goddess's come-on to the male speaker is (lines 21–24):

Do not dig a canal, let me be your canal,
Do not plow a field, let me be your field,
Farmer, do not search for a damp place,
Let me be your damp place.

When he sweet-talks her with (lines 15–18):

When you speak with a man it is womanly,
When you look at a man it is womanly,
When you stand against the wall your nakedness is sweet,
When you bend over, your hips are sweet

her client is hooked and she gets down to business (lines 19–20):

When I stand against the wall it is one shekel,
When I bend over, it is one and a half shekels.

Other Sumerian and Old Babylonian Akkadian hymns and love poems
speak erotically about the delights of sex with the goddess, but this is
the only one that puts a price tag on it—and we are, remember, still
talking about the price for the goddess Inanna here, not about that for a
mortal whore.

The Threat of the Unmarried Woman:
Marriage, Divorce, and the Prostitute

There are many references in the cuneiform sources that refer to sexual
activities involving nonwives, but literary texts, omens, proverbs, and
so on, need to be read and understood within the limitations of their
genres; further, allusions to sexual behavior in such texts serve functions that are far too multifaceted and complex to yield simple conclu-
sions about moral or legal attitudes. Such documents rarely inform us
about that intersection of prostitution—whose practitioners were, in
some sense, free agents in the sexual and reproductive market—and
recognized marriage—the locus of controlled, regulated, and legitimate
sexual activities resulting in recognized inheritance devolution, to
which this essay now turns.

A married man who consorted with a prostitute was not committing
"adultery." In Mesopotamia as in many other places and times, as has
been well established, adultery resulted only if the female partner was
married to a third party; a married woman who had sexual relations
with a man other than her husband was denying the husband his exclusive sexual and reproductive access. For his part, her lover, whether unmarried or married, was "stealing" that which was the domain of another. There was no offense committed against the male lover's wife
comparable to that committed against the woman's husband. In other
words, there was but one wronged party—the married woman's husband (Roth 1988a, 186–206; Westbrook 1990, 542–76).

But what of consensual sexual relations of a man (whether married
or unmarried) with an unmarried and unbetrothed woman? While the
representation in the law collections is that anyone who had sexual
intercourse with a married or betrothed woman—by rape, mutual consent, or seduction—faced severe pecuniary and corporal punishment,
as did those who raped an unmarried woman, whether free or slave,[8]
the formal voice of the collections is less clear about noncoercive sex

with an unmarried woman. The situation seems to be considered in two cases, in the nineteenth-/eighteenth-century Sumerian Laws Exercise Tablet (hereafter SLEx) and in the fourteenth-century Middle Assyrian Laws (hereafter MAL).[9]

SLEx § 7′: If he deflowers in the street the daughter of a man, her father and her mother do not identify(?) him (but) he declares, "I will marry you"—her father and her mother shall give her to him in marriage. (Roth 1995, 44)

MAL A § 56: If a maiden should willingly give herself to a man, the man shall so swear; they shall have no claim to his wife; the fornicator shall pay "triple" the silver as the value of the maiden; the father shall treat his daughter in whatever manner he chooses. (Roth 1995, 175)

Thus, in the Sumerian law, the male actor (rapist?) may choose to marry the maiden if her parents consent. (This is also the solution in ancient Israel, proposed in Deuteronomy 22:28–29.) In the Assyrian law a half millennium later, the lover of a willing maiden need not pay for his act with his or his wife's life or honor but only with monetary compensation for her virginity, and the fate of the maiden is left to the discretion or whim of her father. The two situations differ widely but hold two assumptions in common: (1) the maiden's parents' unquestioned authority over (or ownership of) her virginity, and (2) the male lover's relatively minimal penalty (if any at all, it is considerably less than in the cases in which the woman is married or betrothed).

Are these women prostitutes? The woman in the Sumerian law is called "daughter of a man" (dumu.munus lu₂); the one in the Middle Assyrian provision is a "maiden" (batultu)—marriageable girl, virginity assumed (Roth 1987, 715–47). Given the presence of parental authority, it is highly unlikely that she was formally a prostitute. But there is another provision in the law collections that should be brought into this discussion: Laws of Lipit-Ishtar (hereafter LL) § 30. The woman involved here is not specified to be either slave or free, married or unmarried, daughter or maiden but is rather in another category—she is a kar.kid, the word Lambert identifies as the unambiguous term for "prostitute," a claim now disputed by Assante. The Sumerian law provision is one of three pieces of evidence in Raymond Westbrook's 1984 essay "The Enforcement of Morals in Mesopotamian Law" a title laden with gendered assumptions. The provision in the LL § 30 reads: "If a young married man has sexual relations with a prostitute of (or from) the street, and the judges order him not to go back to the prostitute (and if) afterwards he divorces his first-ranking wife and gives the silver of her divorce settlement to her (still) he shall not marry the prostitute" (Roth 1995, 32). In his discussion, Westbrook understands the "married status of the man [to be] . . . the crucial factor in the attitude of the law towards his actions" and concludes that the "purpose of the law is . . . not to protect the rights of individuals . . . but to uphold certain standards of morality" (753, 754). It is my argument, to the contrary, that these two issues—the married status of the male lover and any presumed "standards of morality"—are both irrelevant and imported from modern cultural assumptions. In fact, approaching this law provision from another angle and allowing for the gendered nuances of Mesopotamian legal constructs, it is at least equally valid to argue that this provision has the most direct and active impact on the person of the *woman* involved, the *kar.kid*. Thus LL § 30 denies the *kar.kid* (prostitute) the avenue of marriage with the man of her choice and lays the consequences of a continued relationship between them exclusively at her feet.

A brief digression: the SLEx and LL provisions both describe either the woman or the sexual act with reference to "the street" (*e.sir$_2$* in SLEx, *tilla$_2$* in LL). It has been argued convincingly that the "street" is a way of identifying the act or the person as originating from outside of a legitimate household (Assante 1998, 45–53).[10] Thus in the SLEx, the deflowering of the maiden takes place somewhere other than the sanctioned marriage bed; in the LL provision, the sex act and/or the *kar.kid* herself are located outside of the regulated social milieu.

The prostitute as outsider recalls the blessing (or countercurse) in the Epic of Gilgamesh. In the story, recall that the wild man Enkidu had been "civilized" by the ministrations of the prostitute Shamhat (a name that means literally "luscious one"), which included not only a weeklong sexual initiation, but also eating and drinking prepared foods and bathing and donning human-made garments. When Enkidu later lies dying, he blames Shamhat for luring him out of his natural, wild state and curses her vividly: "May the ground defile your finest garment! May the drunkard stain your festive gown with dirt! May you never acquire a well-equipped household! . . . May the shadow of the city wall be where you stand! . . . May drunk and sober strike your cheek!"[11] When he repents his harsh words, Enkidu blesses her: "May governors and noblemen love! He who is one league off shall slap his thighs, he who is two leagues off shall shake out his hair!, . . . Ishtar, the ablest of gods, shall gain you access to the man whose household is established and whose wealth is heaped high! For you his beloved first wife, the mother of seven, shall be divorced."[12] Enkidu, in other words, is blessing Shamhat in precisely the way the provision of LL anticipates: her charms will lure the most devoted of husbands away from his wife.

The fear that sexually available women could disrupt a marriage is, of course, not an uncommon one. Several pieces of "advice" from wisdom literature address this. An early second millennium composition, "Instructions of Shuruppak," warns about the dangers of bringing a prostitute into one's home: "Do not buy a prostitute: she is a mouth that bites. Do not buy a house-born slave: he is an herb that causes stomachache. Do not buy a free-born man: he will always loiter against the wall. Do not buy a palace slave-girl: the house will be on a bad track" (154–64).[13]

Another piece of advice a millennium later from the "Counsels of Wisdom" warns about the dangers of actually *marrying* such a woman, who will not remain sexually faithful:

Do not marry a *harīmtu* who has countless husbands,
An *ištarītu* who is dedicated to a god,
A *kulmašītu* whose favors (?) are many.
In your difficulties she will not support you,
In your disputes she will mock you.
There is no reverence or submissiveness with her,
Should she dominate your house, get her out!
Her attentions are directly elsewhere! (72–80)[14]

Of the three women singled out in this exhortation, the *harīmtu* is said to have many "husbands," the *ištarītu* to be more concerned with her duties to the temple than to her husband, the *kulmašītu* to distribute her favors(?) indiscriminately. At least the *harīmtu* and probably also the *kulmašītu* are what we would call promiscuous women, if not outright prostitutes. And marriage to them is dangerous. The Erra epic possibly makes a similar allusion when the city Uruk is described as "abode of Anu and Ishtar, city of *kezertu*-s, *šamhatu*-s, and *harīmtu*-s, whom Ishtar has deprived of husbands."[15] This seems to indicate that the city had been filled with sexually available women and when the married men abandoned their wives for these sexually available women, they abandoned family, home, farmstead, and so forth and, defending nothing, left the city open to the ravages of disease and destruction.

Did prostitutes ever find their way off the "streets" and into marriage? The scholastic legal composition *Ana ittišu*, a late second-millennium legal compendium used in the training of scribes, considers the possibility that a man might marry a prostitute, and even that the prostitute might supplant a first wife; in the latter, the "prostitute" is a temple dedicatee, the *qadištu*, and the suggestion that she is a prostitute comes from her association with "the street." *Ana ittišu* includes the following individual clauses among possible clauses in formal marriage contracts:

As a prostitute, he took her in from the street.
As a prostitute, he married her.
He gave her back her tavern.
He brought her into his house. (VII ii 23–26)[16]

Later, after clauses dealing with the bringing of the bride wealth to the house of the bride's father, the consummation of the marriage, the development of an aversion to the bride, and the payment of divorce monies to her, we find the following: "Afterward, he took in a *qadištu* from the street. Because of his love (for her), he married her in her status as *qadištu*" (VII iii 7–10).[17] At least some of the clauses in *Ana ittišu* follow a temporal sequence, and the inference that his taking in and marrying a *qadištu* "afterward" occurs subsequent to divorcing a first wife is plausible. A further inference that he divorced the first wife *because of* the *qadištu* "from the street" is not warranted, however.

But Mesopotamian men no doubt were tempted to wander off to sexually available women, and the civil authorities actually did have ways of enforcing restrictions on the behavior and movements of the populace, beyond the proverb or literary exhortation. An Old Babylonian record of the witnessed oaths sworn by a woman and man demonstrates this (RA 69 No. 8).[18] The oath of the woman, Shat–Marduk, is sworn to by the name of King Samsu-iluna and outlines a number of activities that she agrees to refrain from or to undertake. After first averring that she is "not beholden to him, not sworn to him," she agrees that she will refuse her admirer's offers of sexual intercourse, that she will not allow him to kiss her lips, that she will not herself initiate sexual intercourse with him, and that she will inform the authorities if he makes such overtures to her. Finally, should she not adhere to these conditions she will accept the appropriate punishment for one who violates the royal oath. Her lover's oath, also sworn to by King Samsu-iluna, is far simpler: "I shall not approach [her] with a proposal of sexual intercourse."

Commentators of this text interpret it as a divorce or a separation agreement between a married couple; Westbrook's interpretation of the oaths as a concession that the two will refrain from continuing their non-marital sexual liaison is undoubtedly correct, as is his conclusion that "*she* is being called upon to police the enforcement of the prohibition"

(1984, 755, emphasis added). But he then infers that Shat–Marduk must have been a public prostitute and that "the background to the prohibition was the unseemly association of a married man with a prostitute" (755). In fact, as Westbrook had already noted, there is no indication in the text that either party had any spousal status, and while it might be tempting to draw a parallel between the oath and LL § 30, there is no indication that the woman was a *kar.kid*. What is clear is that it is she who bears responsibility for any continuation of an officially prohibited relationship.

The next and final document Westbrook adduces in his discussion of "morals" is a Middle Babylonian record of a judge's order prohibiting contact between a woman named Ilatu and her lover, a man who divorced his wife for a (not fully clear) reason connected to Ilatu's behavior toward or intentions with respect to his wife (UET 7 8).[19] The matter was brought to the attention of the judge by the husband's own brother. After questioning by the judge, Ilatu seems to say that she was married earlier to the man, but now, after the judicial intervention, she formally agrees that (in Westbrook's elegant translation) "he shall not cross my bed-post." Again, we find that the woman is the party who assumes responsibility for terminating the relationship.[20] Once again, however, Westbrook prefers to understand the woman in this story, Ilatu, to be a prostitute, although there is nothing in the text to support the suggestion; rather, as we have just seen, she could have been his ex-wife (Gurney 1983, 44).[21] She is identified by a patronymic, often an indication of high social status, and without clarification of what she did to or about the wife to cause the husband to divorce,[22] we can say no more about her profession or person. It is clear only that it is *she* who publicly and officially has agreed to cease her relationship with him.

Two more cases (Cyr. 307 and 312),[23] dating to the Neo-Babylonian period during the reign of Cyrus the Great, are relevant. Cyr. 312 is a document that was written in Babylon in 531 BC (11–V–8 Cyrus) invalidating the marriage of a woman named Tablutu to one Nabu-ahhe-bullit; the marriage was arranged for the woman by her brother, but the groom acted alone and without the required approval of his father (Roth 1987, 723–27 and Roth 1989, 5–6) Again, the onus rests with the woman Tablutu to keep the couple apart; it is she who is threatened with enslavement should she see him again. The key portion of the text reads: "The agreement of marriage for Tablutu which Nabu-uballit sealed and gave to Nabu-ahhe-bullit without the consent of his father Nargija is invalid wherever it is found. From now on, should Tablutu [associate(?)] with Nabu-ahhe-bullit, she shall be subjected to the shackles and markings[24] of slavery" (Cyr. 312 [BM 33065, collated July 1993]).[25] The woman Tablutu acted with what appears to be due caution in establishing a marriage with Nabu-ahhe-bullit: the union had been arranged by her brother, a junior member of the palace bureaucracy, with the active approval of her brother's superior officer (perhaps patron). But the intended groom Nabu-ahhe-bullit acted on his own, without his father's consent. And we know from at least one other document (Cyr. 311 [Babylon 8-V-8 Cyrus]) dated three days earlier that almost simultaneously a match with yet another woman was being negotiated for Nabu-ahhe-bullit for which his father's approval was pending. These factors led to the official intervention to void the document recording the agreement to marry Tablutu, and the threat that she would be debased and enslaved if she continued to associate with him. If a similar threat was leveled at Nabu-ahhe-bullit, we have no record of it. All we can conclude is that the restraining order applies to the female half of this couple, and that it is she who is made responsible for terminating the relationship.

A similar scenario is described in another document (Cyr. 307) written a few weeks earlier in Sippar (3-IV-8 Cyrus). Again, the female member of the couple is threatened with slavery for the relationship (Cyr. 307 [BM 74923, collated July 1993]).[26]

(1–4) Should Tabat-Ishar, daughter of Jashe'ijama, ever be found with Kulu, son of Kalba—(4–5) even should he lead her away by subterfuge and an investigation confirms it (6–8) and/or she does not say to the head of the house (in which she is kept): "Send a message to Kalba, the father of Kulu!"—(8–9) she shall be subjected to the markings of slavery.

(10–15) Witnesses [names of three witnesses and a scribe]. (16–17) Sippar. Month IV, day 3, year 8. Cyrus, King of Babylon, King of the Lands.

(17–18) In the presence of Zitta, mother of Tabat-Ishar.

Again, we find a young woman and man whose relationship is prohibited. Under no circumstances may Tabat-Ishar agree to meet with her young man: she must not fall for any of his lies or tricks; if she is forcibly abducted she must appeal for help and try to get a message out to his father. Failure to take these or similar preventive measures may result in her subjugation to slavery (Cyr. 312:28; Cyr. 307:9).[27]

Although the woman in LL § 30 was called a kar.kid, and her sexual relationship to the married man is clearly linked to his divorce and subsequent desire to marry the kar.kid, these other women discussed were most probably not "prostitutes." They may have been women, married or unmarried, whose behaviors pushed the limits of social norms, but there is no indication that they had multiple sexual partners, or that they traded their bodies or their sexual favors for monetary compensation.

Note that both Kulu's father and Tabat-Ishar's mother are recognized in Cyr. 307 as interested parties who at least tacitly agree to the terms. Kulu's father will, if informed of his son's actions, intervene and rescue the girl, and Tabat-Ishar's mother agrees,[28] if her daughter allows herself to be duped, to the consequent enslavement.

Thus far the discussion about prostitution has related mostly to the woman's sexual activities. But it would be naïve to assume that the Babylonian judges, parents, and others involved in these cases were concerned about regulating sexual behavior or safeguarding anything like the western notion of the "sanctity of marriage." A major concern must have been to avoid the complications of property devolution that arise when the "women of the street" became pregnant and bore children. This must have been a relatively common event; although birth-control measures are not well documented in Mesopotamian sources,[29] such measures would have been generally relegated, cross-culturally, to the domain of women's folk medicine and thus do not occupy a place in formal medical treatises that survive. Note, however, that self-induced abortions are mentioned in MAL A § 53. Moreover, the cultural presumption appears to be that prostitutes would remain childless (or at least without natural heirs). A testamentary document disposing of the estate of a man from Emar, for example, leaves everything to his daughter the prostitute *(kar.kid)*, with his other two daughters, both married, serving as residual heirs (Arnaud 1986, no. 31). The implication here is that the prostitute daughter would not produce offspring. But should a prostitute indeed become pregnant and bear a child, and should that child make a claim to his father's estate, there will be a need to sort out competing claims. Several of the law collections include provisions clarifying such competing inheritance rights of offspring born to wives, second-ranked wives, concubines, and slaves; one provision addresses the inheritance rights of children of a prostitute.

The first possible situation is that in which a primary wife and a secondary wife both bear children; in LL § 24, Laws of Hammurabi (hereafter LH) § 167, and the Neo-Babylonian Laws (hereafter LNB) § 15, the sons of both the first and the second wives inherit (equally). The second possible situation is that in which both a wife and a female slave bear children to the husband/master; in LL § 25 and LH § 171, the slave's children are not deemed heirs (although they are manumitted). If, however, the husband/master has married the slave woman (LL § 26) or concubine (MAL A § 41), or if he has publicly acknowledged the slave's children (LH § 170), her children are (secondary) heirs; similar protection is accorded inheritance to a foster child/apprentice (LH § 191). All these permutations deal with children whose paternities are not in question. But what happens when a prostitute, potentially with many sexual partners, bears a child? One provision in the LL approaches this question, although curiously the husband's paternity is assumed: "If a man's wife does not bear him a child but a prostitute *(kar.kid)* from the street does bear him a child, he shall provide grain, oil, and clothing rations for the prostitute, and the child whom the prostitute bore to him shall be his heir; as long as his wife is alive, the prostitute will not reside in the house with his first-ranking wife" (LL § 27). Thus, according to LL § 27, a prostitute who bears a child whose paternity is not in question might see her child raised to the status of heir of his father, a free man. She herself can aspire to a steady income from the father of her child and will probably be set up in a separate residence, kept away from the man's wife. This is more reminiscent of the situation of a "mistress" than of a "prostitute from the street."

Not all prostitutes who bore children would have been as fortunate in securing either their own or their children's security. The children born to prostitutes might have been abandoned, ending up as the infant foundlings "taken from the street" in the literature.[30] Moreover, although the persons identified in our legal and economic documents only by matronymics (rather than only by patronymics) or without any reference to genealogy are generally assumed to be the children of slaves, there is no reason to exclude the possibility that they are the children of prostitutes or other women, slave or free, who were unable (or unwilling) to identify the father.[31] Dandamaev's observation that "a comparative study of the [Neo-Babylonian] documents reveals that a person who is called simply by name, without patronymic and title, is, as a rule, a slave" is qualified in his footnote by his recognition that "a number of these texts [in his study] concerns the sale of such persons" (1984, 404 and n.421). Certainly, elsewhere—for example, in witness lists or administrative texts—the absence of a patronymic could imply simply a fatherless child born to an unmarried woman.

Some of these children might be raised by family members. A Neo-Babylonian adoption from the thirty-second year of the rule of King Nebuchadnezzar (573 BC) (Pohl 1933, pl. 15*–16* No. 14) records that a prostitute's infant was taken in by her brother and made his secondary heir. The brother promised to raise the child along with his own son, to bear the costs of raising the infant until and unless the prostitute left her profession, and not to hand the child over to the prostitute's other siblings (Roth 1988b, 131–33). The key clauses read:

Innin-shum-ibni, son of Nabu-ahhe-ushallim, came to Balta, daughter of Nabu-ahhe-ushallim, his sister, and spoke as follows: "Please give to me Dannu-ahhe-ibni, your seventeen-day-old son. I will raise him. He will be my son." Balta agreed, and gave him Dannu-ahhe-ibni, her seventeen-day-old son, in adoption.

He (Innin-shum-ibni) recorded him (Dannu-ahhe-ibni) as an heir entitled to a secondary portion after Labashi, his (Innin-shum-ibni's) son.

As long as Balta continues as a prostitute, he (Innin-shum-ibni) will raise Dannu-ahhe-ibni. Should Balta go to the house of a *mār banî*, he (the *mār banî*) will pay one-third mina of silver (to Innin-shum-ibni) in consideration of the sustenance and upbringing costs of Dannu-ahhe-ibni and the food, beer, salt, cress, oil, and garments of Balta.

This document reveals that the prostitute Balta was supported by her brother, perhaps only for a time while she nursed her own son. The son would assume a recognized place in his uncle's household, but Balta would resume her professional activities. If and when Balta found a home with a *mār banî*, the expenses her brother incurred on her and her child's behalf would be reimbursed, but there is no indication that she could—then or at any other time—reclaim her child.

Conclusion

It is not simple to delineate the boundaries in ancient Mesopotamia between what we might term legal justice and moral justice, but it must be stressed that the documents and the evidence do not imply any valuation of the "morality" of the women or men involved in these cases. I would argue rather that the overriding motives in all these cases were not public moral or ethical ones, but private and economic. It is more likely that the sexual unions were proscribed with the individual families' aim of avoiding inheritance disputes and of clarifying the lines of property devolution rather than to conform to some community consensus about a duty to keep gullible and impressionable young men out of the clutches of unsuitable women.

In all these documents, spanning fifteen hundred years, we find demonstrated a pattern by which the woman is given responsibility for abstaining from a publicly prohibited relationship risking the imposition of a severe penalty if she fails to do so. The Mesopotamian gendered cultural assumptions about sexuality and procreation lead to the orders (at least those we have surviving) being directed to the women in these couples rather than to the men. Consensual sexual intercourse of a man and an unmarried woman is not in itself morally reprehensible; it can, however, lead to disruption in the normal lines of inheritance. Thus the "sexual free agent," although an erotic and even playful regular in literary texts, is an undesirable complication in daily life. Whether she is a "whore" or a "career girl," she is a disruptive threat to the economic integrity of marriage and inheritance and to the stability of the social fabric.

Notes

1. Text citations follow the abbreviations of the *The Assyrian Dictionary of the Oriental Institute of the University of Chicago (CAD)* and Roth (1995).
Herodotus 1.199. The somewhat earthy translation given here is after Beard and Henderson (1998, 58–59).

2. Curiously, the commendable point Herodotus makes about Babylonian wives' firm fidelity and resistance to temptation after their ritual defloration ("and from that time on you will never make her a big enough gift to have her") is largely ignored.

3. This essay is a revised version of a lecture originally prepared for the conference out of which this volume grew, "Prostitution in the Ancient World" at the University of Wisconsin at Madison. Originally scheduled for September 2001, it was postponed on account of the events of September 11th until April 2002. The lecture was later presented at the University of Chicago's Gender Studies Center (February 2003) and at Yale University's Department of Near Eastern Languages and Literatures (May 2003). Much of what follows was included in "Sexual Liaisons with Unmarried Women," part 3 of a paper circulated to participants of the Society of Biblical Literature panel on Gender and Law (November 1995); part 2 of that paper was published as Roth (1998). This final essay owes much to the comments and questions of the several audiences.

4. I owe the phrase to Glassner (2001).

5. See also Sweet (1994, 85–104) and Steinkeller (1999, 103–38).

6. Lerner (1986) is unreliable; she confuses and garbles the cuneiform evidence, miscites secondary sources, and perpetuates the notion of "cultic sexual service." One example: Oppenheim (1964 [and rev. ed. 1977]) neither stated nor implied that "the caring for the gods included, in some cases, offering them sexual services" (Lerner 1986, 239). Lerner is misunderstanding perhaps the

statement in Oppenheim (1977, 193) that "[t]here took place within the temple compound . . . nocturnal ceremonies and marriage festivals in which the deity met his spouse," a reference to ceremonies involving *statues,* such as the Seleucid ritual from Babylon (*SBH,* 145.VIII); see Cohen (1993, 311): "Nabû . . . as bridegroom . . . proceeds directly to the Ehursaba, parades radiantly, and enters before the goddess; everyone is there for the wedding. Inside the Ehursaba . . . [t]hey lie night after night on the nuptial bed in sweet sleep."

7. Reading at line 19 follows Bruschweiler (1989, 129); see also Attinger (1998) (reference kindly pointed out to me by J. Cooper).

8. Most of the cases are collected and analyzed in Finkelstein (1966, 355–72), where he groups the laws according to the marital status of the woman and the coercive nature of the sex act.

9. Finkelstein (1966, 366, fig. 1) agrees; however, he understands SLEx §§ 7´ and 8´ (his YBT I 28 Par. "a" and "b") to involve, respectively, coercive and consentive sex; in my understanding of the text, both might be noncoercive and the case variation involves identification of the fornicator, but SLEx § 8´ remains unsatisfactorily understood.

10. During the discussion at the conference in Madison, the observation was made by Anise Strong that the thematic tension of house versus street seems to run through the discussion of prostitution in this paper. Indeed, elsewhere I have commented on the theme of the domiciliation of widows (Roth, 1991–93), and Strong's point with respect prostitutes is insightful.

11. Translation after Lambert (1992, 129–31) and George (2003, 1:299).

12. See George (2003, 1:301).

13. Instructions of Shuruppak 154–64, in Alster (1974), Alster (1997) 569–70, and ETCSL http://www-etcsl.orient.ox.ac.uk/section5/c561.htm.

14. Translation after Lambert (1960) 102–3.

15. Cagni (1969, 128–29). Translation after Lambert (1992, 136) and Assante (1998, 39).

16. In Landsberger (1937, 96–97; corrections on 258).

17. In Landsberger (1937, 99–100).

18. Anbar (1975, 120–25, no. 8); see also Westbrook (1984, 753–56) and Charpin in Joannès (2000, 95–96, no. 51). The entire text reads:

> (1–4) Shat-Marduk, concerning Ahuni, son of Ilshu-ibbi, swore an oath by King Samsu-iluna, as follows: (5–15) "(I swear that) I am not beholden to/by Ahuni, son of Ilshu-ibbi; I am not besworn to/by him; he shall never again propose male-female relations to me; he shall never kiss my lips; I shall never agree to male-female relations with him; should he ever invite me to lie with him, I shall inform the Elders of the City and the Mayor! Should anyone discover me doing otherwise, may they treat me as one who scorned the oath by the king."
>
> (16–18) And Ahuni, son of Ilshu-ibbi, swore an oath by King Samsu-iluna, as follows: (19–21) "(I swear that) I shall never go to Shat-Marduk to propose male-female relations with her."

(22–29) Before (names of eight witnesses). (30–33) Month VI, day 25, Year 3 of Samsu-iluna [= 1747 BCE]; (sealings of the witnesses).

19. After Gurney (1982, 91–94); Wilcke (1980, 138–40); Gurney (1983, 41–45); Westbrook (1984, 755–56). The text reads:

(1–6) Sin-remanni, son of Sin-remanni [sic!], married [īhuzma] the daughter of Gula-erish, the herdsman of the district governor, and (later) Ilatu, daughter of Arkaya, detained her for napṭarūtu, and thus s/he caused him to divorce his wife. (7–9) Then Sin-bel-tabini, his brother, hauled Ilatu off to Sin-shapik-zeri the judge: (9–11) "She caused Sin-remanni, my brother, to divorce," he declared.

(11–12) The judge interrogated Ilatu: "Why have you caused Sin-remanni, the herdsman [sic!], to divorce?" he declared.

(14–20) Ilatu heard the words of the judge and "Sin-remanni, my lord/master's servant, up until now had married me [ītahzanni]. Ever since my lord/master interrogated me, he shall not cross my bed-post," she declared.

(20–26) Should Sin-remanni ever again enter the house of Ilatu, either passing the day or staying overnight, s/he will be arrested, investigated, and interrogated in accordance with the binding order of Sin-shapik-zeri (the judge).

(27–29) The sealed document was secured in the presence of Muranu, the mayor, Ninurta-andul, the divination priest, and Atu'u, son of Beliyatu. (30–33) Month IV, day 22, year 12 of Adad-shuma-usur, the King. Fingernail impression of Bana-sha-Sherish instead of his seal.

20. Although the woman clearly is the one to agree to cessation of relations, in the final clause of the document it is not certain who (Ilatu or her lover) would be subject to arrest, investigation, and interrogation as per the judge's order should the man enter her house either by day or night; see Gurney (1983, 45 and notes to rev. 8–9 and rev. 16).

21. Gurney, attempting an explanation of why the daughter of Gula-erish was "kept" or "detained" (ikla), suggests that Ilatu was the keeper of a brothel.

22. UET 7 8:4–6: "Ilatu detained her (the wife) for . . . -hood [ana napṭarūti] and caused him to divorce his wife." Westbrook (1994, 41–46) argues that in the OB period the napṭarūtum identified a "guest" or perhaps "resident alien"; the implications of the term or status in the later Middle Babylonian period are still unclear.

23. These Neo-Babylonian data were not adduced by Westbrook. See Roth (1987, 725 n.22).

24. Uncertain; both "šá-kin še?-pi" (in line 27) and "ši-in-da-tu GEME₂-ú-tu" (in line 28) are unusual; "šindātu" is a dissimilated plural of "šimtu" (see CAD

Š/3, s.v. *"šimtu* mng. 2" and compare *"ši-in-du šá* GEME₂-*ú-tu"* in Cyr. 307:9 [see below]).

25. Strassmaier (1890, 181–82, no. 312); Joannès (2000, 207, no. 149).

(1–5) Nargija, a royal official, son of Hanunu, the [. . .] official, brought Amurru-shar-usur (also) a royal official, the officer in charge of the inner quarters, before the senior officers and the judges of Cyrus, King of Babylon, King of the Lands, and spoke thus: (5–9) "Without my consent, Amurru-shar-usur, the officer in charge of the inner quarters, and Nabu-uballit, son of Nabu-shama', of the bureau of the officer in charge of the inner quarters, sealed an agreement of marriage of Tablutu, sister of Nabu-uballit, and gave it to Nabu-ahhe-bullit, my son."

(10) The senior officers and the judges interrogated the officer in charge of the inner quarters. (11–13) He swore an oath and spoke thus: (11–13) "He (i.e., Nargija) did not seal that document and before [. . .] he/I did not . . . as witness." This he confirmed.

(13–14) [The judges(?)] interrogated Tablutu . . . they confirmed.

(15–17) Nabu-uballit spoke thus: "I did seal an agreement of marriage for Tablutu, my sister; I gave it to Nabu-ahhe-bullit, the son of Nargia."

(18–19) [. . .] they investigated. Tablutu spoke thus: (19–20) "Nabu-uballit, my brother, . . ." (20–22) [. . .] his brother [. . .] the paternal estate [. . .]

(22–25) The agreement of marriage for Tablutu which Nabu-uballit sealed and gave to Nabu-ahhe-bullit without the consent of his father Nargija is invalid wherever it is found.

(26–28) From now on, should Tablutu [associate(?)] with Nabu-ahhe-bullit, she shall be subjected to the shackles and markings of slavery.

(29–35) Before (names of three high officers, six judges, and a scribe).

(35–37) Babylon. Month V, day 11, year 8. Cyrus, King of Babylon, King of the Lands.

26. Strassmaier (1890, 177–78, no. 307) and Dandamaev (1984, 105). Joannès (1994) differs.

27. It is specifically the markings of "slave-woman status" *(amūtu)* that are to be inflicted; whether such marks differed for male and female slaves is not known.

28. With regard to the *"ina ašābi"* clause, see Roth (1989, 21–22 with n.74).

29. On contraception and abortion, see Stol (2000, 37–42).

30. The motif of children abandoned in the streets, snatched from the mouths of dogs or rescued from wells, entered the legal and omen literature, as

well as found its way into personal names such as "Sha-pi-kalbi" "(Snatched)-from-the-mouth-of-a-dog"; see references quoted in *CAD* S, s.v. *sūqu* s. mng. 1a-2′, *CAD* K, s.v. *kalbu*, lex. section, and mng. 1a (Stamm 1939, 320). Certainly, such children would have been born not only to prostitutes, but might have been abandoned in times of distress by their (married or widowed) parents if, for example, they could not be sold; on the latter, see Oppenheim (1955, 69–89); Zaccagnini (1994, 1–4); Zaccagnini (1995, 92–109). See also the Neo-Babylonian documents VAS 6 116 and Nbk. 439 for the adoptions of such foundlings.

31. Note such personal names as "Abi-ul-idi" ("I-know-not-my-father," i.e., posthumous child or bastard); see Stamm (1939) 321. Systematic work on personal names remains to be done (Stol 1991, 191–212).

Prostitution in the Social World and Religious Rhetoric of Ancient Israel

PHYLLIS A. BIRD

Sources and History of Interpretation

Any attempt to speak of prostitution in ancient Israel must reckon first
with the literary sources that provide our sole means of access to the institution. All information about practices, incidence, and attitudes toward the practitioners must be drawn from a literature that contains a
particular, theological employment of the language of prostitution and
a history of interpretation that identified it with pagan religious practice. The legacy of this peculiar literary tradition reaches far beyond the
field of biblical studies owing to the Bible's role in western culture as a
common text and primary source for the religion and culture of the ancient Mediterranean world. While the rediscovery of classical sources
and the recovery of still more ancient documents from Mesopotamia,
Syria, Anatolia, and Egypt brought new data for the study of ancient
Near Eastern and Israelite society, old presuppositions persisted, influencing new interpretive constructs. This may be seen, for example, in
the concept of "sacred" or "cultic" prostitution, which has become a
given in interpretations of "Canaanite" and ancient "oriental" religions.

The Hebrew Bible (hereafter HB), or Christian Old Testament, is a collection of texts of different types, purposes, and perspectives, whose composition may span as much as a thousand years (older consensus) or as little as two to three centuries. Current debate concerning the period and nature of the writings makes historical reconstruction difficult, but certain general characteristics hold for any period. I shall assume that while the final shaping of all of the texts, and the composition of many, must be placed in the postexilic period (fifth to fourth centuries BCE) and understood as a response to the crisis of identity created by the destruction of the temple, state, and monarchy, much of the content of the books describing preexilic conditions stems from traditions and documents formed during the monarchy. Nevertheless, the form of the text that we have received is far removed from the time of the narrated events or actions, and all of the records are secondhand. Moreover, despite their diversity, all of the texts must be understood as male-authored and addressed primarily to males. Thus in all matters of sexual relations it is a male point of view that is expressed in the texts. In addition, the collection, and most of the individual compositions, must also be understood as the work of religious elites and created, selected, and preserved through a process that came to accord divine authority, and even authorship, to the texts. Religious purpose and particular theological interests exercised a significant role in the shaping and reception of the texts, as well as in later interpretation. Despite these limiting and distorting factors, however, it is still possible to recognize the prostitute as an identifiable "type" already in the earliest sources, a type that appears to have much in common with what we know about prostitutes in surrounding cultures and with the way they are represented in comparative literature.

Terminology

The terminology used to designate the prostitute in the HB provides important clues to Israel's understanding of the practice/profession. Extensive metaphorical or figurative use, however, has generated confusion in the secondary literature. This confusion has been further complicated by three passages in which the term for "prostitute" appears in parallelism or interchange with a term for a religious devotee ("*qede-šah,*" "consecrated woman"). This essay concentrates on the primary usage, which is clear and separable from the special uses. The metaphorical uses and the juxtaposition with the cultic term involve complex textual and socio-religious considerations, which cannot be treated adequately here.[1] Nevertheless, I offer an introduction to this secondary usage in order to illustrate some of the interpretive issues it raises.

The common term for a prostitute, and the only term generally recognized, is a feminine participle *"zonah"* of the verb *"zanah,"* whose basic meaning is "to engage in extramarital sexual relations." Standard Hebrew lexicons give the following definitions for the verb in its simple (Qal) stem: "commit fornication" *(BDB)*; "sich mit einem anderen Mann einlassen, buhlen" *(HAL)*.[2] As a general term for nonmarital sexual intercourse, the verb *"zanah"* is normally used only with female subjects, since it is only for women that marriage is the primary determinant of legal status and obligation. While male sexual activity is judged by the status of the female partner and prohibited only when it violates the recognized marital rights of another male, female sexual activity is judged according to the woman's marital status.

In Israel's moral code, a woman's sexuality belonged to her husband alone, for whom it was reserved both before marriage as well as after. Violation of a husband's sexual rights, the most serious sexual offense, is signified by the verb *"na'af,"* "to commit adultery;" all other instances of sexual intercourse outside marriage are designated by *"zanah."* These include premarital sex by a daughter, understood as an offense against her father and/or male kin, whose honor requires her chastity (Deuteronomy 22:13–21; Leviticus 21:9; cf. Genesis 34:31), or sex by a levirate-obligated widow (a woman promised or "betrothed" to her deceased husband's brother [Genesis 38:6–11, 24–26]). It also includes the activity of the prostitute, the professional "fornicator," who has no husband or sexual obligation to another male. Because her activity violates no man's rights or honor, it is free from the sanctions imposed on casual fornication. Strictly speaking, her activity is not illicit— and neither is her role. Despite frequent assumptions to the contrary, there is no evidence that prostitution was ever outlawed in ancient Israel or that the prostitute was ever punished simply for her activity as a prostitute. The denunciations and punishments recorded in the HB all pertain to metaphorical uses of ZNH[3] for crimes of apostasy and/or breach of covenant. Nevertheless, although prostitution found a place within Israelite society as a marginal institution, the language used to describe the prostitute is not neutral, but carries a sense of opprobrium, since in all other uses the same language describes activity that is prohibited and subject to heavy sanctions. Thus the prostitute appears as a kind of "legal outlaw" (Bird 1997, 205–6).

If Hebrew links the fornicator and the prostitute, it also distinguishes them, by syntactic and contextual means. A dramatic illustration of the linkage and the distinction is provided by the story of Judah and Tamar in Genesis 38. In one episode, Judah embraces a woman he identifies as a *zonah* (RSV has "he thought her to be a *harlot*" [v. 15]); in another, he condemns to death a woman whose crime is identified by the verb *"zanah"* (RSV reads "your daughter-in-law has *played the harlot* [*zanetah*] and moreover . . . is with child by *harlotry* [*harah liznunim*]" [v. 24]). The irony of the situation, on which the story turns, is that the two women are one, and so is the act they commit. But the act is construed differently according to the perceived circumstances, more specifically, the socio-legal status, of the woman involved. In the first instance, *ZNH*, in the form of a participle, describes the woman's (assumed) profession, as an ostracized but tolerated purveyor of sexual favors for men. In the second, *ZNH* in verbal form describes the activity of a woman whose socio-legal status (as daughter-in-law [*kallah*[4]]) makes such activity a crime.

In this passage we see one of the problems created by common English renderings of words from the root *ZNH*. The RSV introduces an unintended pun by its conventional translation of the verb as a denominative, "play the harlot." In this case, the statement is literally true (Tamar induced Judah to impregnate her by presenting herself as a harlot), but Judah does not intend to make this accusation with this remark. Judah intends only to say that his daughter-in-law has engaged in nonmarital sexual activity, the evidence of which is her pregnancy. The problem that besets all English translations is that there is no single English root word that can be used in both nominal and verbal forms to cover the range of usage exhibited by forms of Hebrew *ZNH*. Thus a number of different English terms, each with its own history and connotations, are used to translate the Hebrew participle in its specialized use for the professional prostitute.[5] English translations offer "whore," "harlot," and "prostitute," in various combinations depending on version and context. The variety of English terms may suggest different classes of prostitutes or differing attitudes toward them exhibited in different texts, but these distinctions have no linguistic base in the Hebrew.

The more serious problem concerns the English rendering of the Hebrew verbal forms, which typically suggest that the activity described constitutes or imitates the activity of the professional prostitute. Thus the KJV translated the simple verb (Qal) as "play the whore," "be a harlot" (Amos 7:17), while the NRSV substituted the more modern "prostitute oneself," "become prostituted."[6] In this usage the prostitute becomes the defining figure, reversing the Hebrew sense of the prostitute as a professional or habitual "fornicator," a promiscuous or unchaste woman, whose profession is defined by her sexual activity with men to whom she is not married.[7] The problem of translating— and interpreting—the verbal forms is further complicated by the fact that the great majority of the occurrences are in figurative uses in which the images of the prostitute, the "loose woman," and the adulteress combine to portray a lovesick woman unfaithful to her spouse. In addition, in some uses, the image is so attenuated that the verb becomes little more than a term for denouncing apostasy and political alliances (as illicit "affairs" with other gods and nations).

Despite the multitude of extended uses, however, it is still possible to obtain a relatively clear and coherent picture of the prostitute in ancient Israel. The evidence is found in sources representing a wide variety of periods, perspectives, and literary types, including narratives, cultic proscriptions, priestly regulations, wisdom counsel, and prophetic pronouncements. A brief survey must suffice.[8]

Priestly Legislation and Prostitution as Defiling

Priestly legislation specifies in Leviticus 21:7 that a priest may not marry a prostitute (literally, "a woman [who is a] zonah and defiled" ["ishshah zonah wachalalah"], i.e., "a woman defiled by prostitution/fornication") or "a woman divorced from her husband" ("ishshah gerushah me'ishah").[9] This text makes it clear by the association with the divorcée and by the interpretive addition of "defiled" that the prostitute is excluded as a marriage partner primarily on the basis of having had sexual relations with other men, but secondarily because her promiscuous relations are seen as "defiling" and thus a threat to the priest's sanctity. The same idea is found in two other texts relating to female members of a priest's family, both of which use verbal forms to describe the defiling activity. In Amos 7:17, the prophet proclaims the fate of the priest of the royal sanctuary at Bethel by decreeing loss of land and offspring, but also loss of sanctity: "Your wife shall fornicate/be a prostitute [tizneh] in the city . . . and you yourself shall die in an unclean land." Here the simple verb, "to fornicate/engage in promiscuous sex" is used, but the specification of the city as the place of the activity suggests that it is the prostitute's trade that is more narrowly intended. Nevertheless, the emphasis is not on the profession or the figure of the prostitute, but just on the idea of engaging in promiscuous and defiling sexual activity. In Leviticus 21:9 it is the priest's daughter that presents the threat of defilement. The connection with the father is explicit: "when the daughter of a priest defiles herself by *fornicating* [*techel liznot*], *it is her father that she defiles"* ("*et abiha hi me-challelet"*). The punishment: "she shall be burned with fire."[10]

The use of common language to describe both casual and professional sexual activity outside marriage is illustrated dramatically by the response of Simeon and Levi to the rape of their sister Dinah in Genesis 34. In answer to their father's reprimand for their violent revenge against the city of the offender who had "defiled" ["*tame*"] their sister (vv. 13, 27), they reply: "Should he treat [literally, "make"] our sister as a *zonah?"* ("*hakezonah ya`seh et achotenu"* [v. 31]). Even though she was raped, the unmarried daughter is put into the category of the prostitute, the woman who offers sex to other men. Consent plays no role; the only relevant point is that an unmarried woman is involved in a sexual act.[11]

The Prostitute in Proverbs: Counsel to Men

The prostitute is a recognizable figure of urban life in a number of proverbs, similes, and narratives. Proverbs 6–7 counsels a man to avoid the allures of a married woman. In 6:26 the cost of adultery is compared with that of a prostitute: "a *fornicator*-woman's fee is only a loaf of bread, but the wife of man stalks [a man's] very life."[12] In 7:5–27 the dangerous woman is described at length, where she is introduced as a "strange" woman ("*ishshah zarah*," RSV "loose woman" and NJPS "forbidden woman") and an "alien" or "outsider" ("*nokriyyah*," RSV "adventuress"), characterized as a woman of "smooth words" (v. 5). She is a married woman, who lures the senseless young man into her home by accosting him on the street at dusk "dressed as a *fornicator*" ("*shit zonah*"). It is not clear from this passage how much of the description of the woman's behavior is drawn from the figure of the prostitute, whom she impersonates in order to draw the unwary youth into her lair, but the description of her stalking the streets and market and "lurking at every corner" (v. 12) appears to reflect the general stereotypical behavior of the prostitute. Proverbs 23:27 parallels prostitute and "alien" woman in its warning: "A *fornicator* is a deep pit; an "alien woman' is a narrow well. She too lies in wait for prey." Proverbs 29:3 contrasts two loves: "A man who loves wisdom makes his father glad / But he who keeps company with *fornicators* will lose his wealth."

Personification of the City as a Prostitute

Another picture of the prostitute as a woman of the city streets is seen in the "Song of the Harlot" (Isaiah 23:15–16). Apparently a popular song about an aging prostitute, it gives us a picture not only of the prostitute's need to seek out customers, but also of her role as a musician and entertainer—well documented from cross-cultural studies, but otherwise unattested in the HB. The song is quoted in a prophetic oracle announcing the restoration of Tyre (vv. 15–18) after its destruction at the hands of the Assyrians (vv. 1–14). Here the great Phoenician maritime city is likened to a prostitute plying her trade with all the kingdoms of the world (v. 17). For seventy years the city will be forgotten, declares the prophet (v. 15), after which "it will happen to Tyre as in the song of the *fornicator* [*shirat hazzonah*]": "Take a harp, go about the city, O forgotten *fornicator!* / Make sweet melody, sing many songs, that you may be remembered" (16). The oracle continues under the figure of the prostitute, who will resume her trade, but now the profits will be devoted to the LORD (17–18): "She shall return to her hire [*etnan*] and *fornicate* [*wezanetah*] with all the kingdoms of the world. . . . But her merchandise [*sachrah*, "profits" in NJPS] and her hire [*we'etnannah*] shall be consecrated to the LORD." Here commercial aspects define the prostitute; more of the primary attributes of the profession attach to this picture of the prostitute than in other examples in the HB of the city personified as "whore."

The personification of the city as a prostitute is the counterimage to the more common personification of the city as a virgin daughter or bride.[13] Thus Isaiah 1:21 charges Israel/Zion with having become a prostitute: "How the faithful [*ne'emanah*] city has become a *fornicator!* She that was full of justice, righteousness lodged in her—but now murderers!" Here the prostitute is simply the antitype of the "good woman," and specifically sexual attributes play no role in the characterization— nor do other aspects of her profession. The association is with murderers, and the specific accusations target the rulers (v. 23) as "rogues and cronies of thieves," "greedy for gifts," who ignore the cause of the orphan and widow.

Prostitutes in Narrative Texts

Other passing references to prostitutes simply serve to corroborate the picture drawn from the more expansive texts. The Samson cycle depicts the hero's exploits, and fall, in association with women. The language of two contrasting episodes is instructive. Judges 16:1 reports that Samson "went to Gaza, and there he *saw* a *fornicator*-woman and 'went in to her.'" In 16:4, he "*loved* a woman in the Vale of Sorek"—Delilah by name. With the prostitute he is in complete control;[14] it is love that undoes him. The outsider status of the prostitute is suggested by a unique reference in the story of Jephthah that describes this tragic hero as a social outcast (Judges 11:1): he was "a mighty warrior, but the son of a *fornicator-woman.*" The sons of his father's wife drive him out, refusing to let him share in their father's inheritance because he is "the son of another woman" (v. 2). The low value of the prostitute—and association with cheap pleasure—is illustrated in Joel 4:2–3, which accuses the nations of dividing the LORD's land among themselves and casting lots for his people. The accusation (v. 3) concludes: "They have traded a boy for a *fornicator* and sold a girl for wine."

Prostitutes as a symbol of dishonor also appear in a notice on the ignominious demise of King Ahab of Israel. In an expanded report of the fulfillment of Elijah's prophecy (1 Kings 21:19) that dogs would lick up Ahab's blood in the place where they had licked the blood of his victim Naboth, 1 Kings 22:38 adds a reference to prostitutes: "They washed out the [blood-drenched] chariot by the pool of Samaria; thus the dogs licked up his blood, and the *fornicators* bathed [in it]." Despite the difficulties of this verse, it provides a picture of prostitutes as a fixture of urban life, in provocative association with dogs.

None of the examples cited thus far suggest that prostitution was prohibited in Israel—or had any cultic associations. All presuppose the existence of prostitutes as part of the urban scene, and all presuppose their low, or marginal, social status. Prostitution, like fornication (whose vocabulary it shares), presents a female profile, despite the fact that both activities require active male participation. This asymmetry of conception and nomenclature is a characteristic feature of patriarchal societies, reflecting a general pattern of asymmetry in gender-related roles, values, and obligations. The anomaly of the prostitute as a tolerated specialist in an activity prohibited to every other woman represents a patriarchal accommodation to the dual desires of men for exclusive control of their wives' sexuality (and hence offspring) and, at the same time, for sexual access to other women. The greater the inaccessibility of women as a result of restrictions on the wife and unmarried nubile woman, the greater the need for an institutionally legitimized "other woman." The prostitute is the "other woman," tolerated but stigmatized, desired but ostracized. Prostitution appears to be characterized by some degree of ambivalence in every society, and the biblical evidence does not support the common notion of a sharp distinction between Israelite and "Canaanite" society with respect to the prostitute's legal or social status.[15]

The tolerated but stigmatized status of the prostitute is illustrated in three narratives in which a prostitute, or presumed prostitute, plays a major role (Bird 1997, 197–218). In each case, the narrative plot depends on assumptions about the character and activities of the prostitute. One example must suffice, the famous account of the test of Solomon's wisdom by the conflicting claims of two prostitutes (1 Kings 3:16–28). I do not think we can conclude anything from this account about the rights of prostitutes—or other citizens—to bring legal disputes to the king for adjudication. The narrative is a story designed to make a point and the characters are chosen for that purpose (Solomon is not named in the story itself, where the chief actor is simply identified as "the king"). The test is to determine which of the two women who claim the child is telling the truth. The characterization of the two plaintiffs as prostitutes makes this the most difficult of cases. As prostitutes, they have no husbands to defend their claims or act on their behalf. As prostitutes who share a house without permanent male residents, there are no witnesses. Thus it is simply a case of one woman's word against another—but more specifically, one prostitute's word against the word of another prostitute, that is, the words of women whose words cannot be trusted. For in the ruling stereotype (as seen, for example, in Proverbs), the prostitute is a woman of smooth speech, self-serving and predatory. One does not expect truth from such as these. So it is a case to test the wisest judge. Solomon demonstrates his wisdom by not attempting to discern the truth through interrogation—a hopeless approach with habitual liars. His wisdom lies in recognizing a condition that will compel the truth. He—or the storyteller—appeals to another female stereotype, that of the mother, who is bound by the deepest emotional bonds to the fruit of her womb. That bond will not lie. And so the king orders a sword to be brought and the child to be divided between the two claimants. At this, the true mother reveals herself by relinquishing her claim in order to spare her child. The story is built on stereotypes attached to the prostitute and the mother. The audience is meant to see only two prostitutes, but Solomon in his wisdom sees what is hidden by that stereotype, namely a mother.

It is often assumed by modern readers that a more positive view of prostitutes obtained at the time stories such as this, or of Rahab the prostitute who saves the Israelite spies at Jericho (Joshua 2), were composed. But that is to mistake narrative interest for social status and role in the story for role in life. The stories are built on reversal of expectations—which requires the low status of the prostitute. And the valor or nobilty exhibited by the prostitute does not change her status. The harlot heroine remains a harlot. She is lifted up for a moment into the spotlight by the storyteller, but her place remains in the shadows of Israelite society.

Prostitution and the Cult

I have emphasized the female profile of prostitution in Israel. Male prostitution is homosexual and designated by distinct nomenclature. It appears to have been a minor phenomenon in ancient Israel, in keeping with a general abhorrence of male-male intercourse exhibited in a variety of texts (Bird 2000, 146–62; Nissinen 1998). The sole reference (if correctly interpreted) is found in a prohibition in Deuteronomy 23:18 [Heb. 23:19]: "You [m. singular] shall not bring the hire of a prostitute [etnan zonah] or the wages of a dog [mechir keleb] into the house of the LORD [in payment] for any vow." It is generally accepted that "dog" in this passage refers to a male prostitute. If this is in fact the case, the order in this gender-paired reference further emphasizes the secondary character of the male class; in contrast to the normal male-female order, the term for the female practitioner is the leading and defining term.

Of further note in this prohibition is the fact that it does not prohibit prostitution, but rather the dedication of income from prostitution as payment for religious vows. It has been suggested that women, who generally had no independent income, might engage in prostitution in order to obtain the money needed to pay their vows (Van der Toorn 1989)—perhaps with the active encouragement of temple personnel (the prohibition is formulated in the masculine, which, though conventional in the legal formulations of the HB, may suggest here that the law is targeting male instigators). The prohibition has more commonly been associated with some form of "sacred prostitution." Both interpretations have serious problems.[16]

An association of prostitutes with the sanctuary is also found in Hosea 4:13–14, where worshippers (and/or priests[17]) at the hilltop sanctuaries of the Northern Kingdom are accused of conducting their "worship" with prostitutes and "consecrated women." In this prophetic judgment oracle, men's cultic activity is aligned with women's sexual misconduct—and in a striking reversal of the usual norms, judgment is not passed on the promiscuous females but rather the males. The oracle focuses on the men's activity at the local shrines, sketched with heavy sexual innuendo (vv. 12–13a), and the female players are revealed only in the concluding verse. But while prostitutes/fornicators appear only in the final lines, the language of fornication pervades the passage.

(12) My people ['ammi, m. collective noun] consults his "stick" ['etso],
   And his "rod" [maqlo] gives him oracles!
For a "spirit of fornication" [ruach zenunim] has led [him/them] astray,
   And they have "fornicated from under" [wayyiznu mittachat] their God.
(13) They [m. plural] "sacrifice" on the tops of mountains,
   and "make offerings"[18] upon the hills,
under oak and poplar and terebinth
   —because their shade is good.
That is why your daughters fornicate [tiznenah]
   and your daughters-in-law (kallotekem)[19] commit adultery.
(14) I will not punish your daughters when they fornicate (tiznenah)
   or your daughters-in-law when they commit adultery [tena'apnah],
for they [the men] themselves "divide"[20] with the fornicators [hazzonot]
   and "sacrifice" with the "consecrated women" [haqqedeshot].

Here, for the first time in the HB, the language of prostitution/fornication is used in a metaphorical sense—in combination (only here) with a literal use (the reference to prostitutes, v. 14b, if not also the daughters' activity, v. 14a) (Bird 1997, 219–36).[21] The specialized usage that is inaugurated here and the question concerning the nature of the activity denounced by the prophet have generated much speculation and require a separate study. Nevertheless, some of the features of Hosea's innovative usage demand at least limited attention here. The message of the summary complaint in verse 12b is clear: the people have rejected submission to the LORD and sought religious "knowledge" in sexual "rites." The subjects are male, and the male phallus is the first sexual symbol alluded to. But the only language that Israel had for sexual misconduct, apart from the more specific terminology for adultery, was the language of fornication (ZNH). Thus language imprinted with a female image is used to admonish a nation whose primary actors are seen as male.

The tension between female image and male actor, which is underscored in this passage, is lacking or obscured in most other metaphorical uses of the language of prostitution/fornication in which Israel is personified as female, a promiscuous daughter or bride who has run after other lovers. Thus discussion concerning the activity alluded to by the metaphorical accusations has typically focused on the activity of women and the question of "sacred" or, as it is also known, "cultic prostitution." The opening chapters of Hosea have probably contributed more to this fixation on the female figure than any other source. Yet a careful reading of the text demonstrates that the usual identification is unwarranted.

The book begins with a word to the prophet, introducing the fornication language—and explaining its meaning. It sets the terms for the extended allegory in chapter 2 and for the use of this language in the rest of the book. It also contains a number of unique or innovative features:

(1:2) When the LORD first spoke through Hosea, the LORD said to Hosea: "Go, take for yourself [i.e., marry] a woman of *fornication(s)* [*eshet zenunim*] and [have] children of *fornication(s)* [*yalde zenunim*], for the land *fornicates greatly* [*zanoh tizneh*] "from after" [*me'achere*][22] the LORD.

The root *ZNH* is used four times in this verse, in the same forms found in the introductory words of the oracle in 4:12–14. Contrary to popular interpretation, Hosea is not instructed to marry a prostitute; and there is no indication in the following report that Gomer, the woman he did marry (v. 3), was ever a prostitute. Rather, he is to marry a "woman of *fornication[s]*." The abstract plural noun "*zenunim*" suggests multiple sexual acts and consequently a promiscuous disposition or nature. Applied to the children as well, it must have the same meaning. It appears here for the first time—possibly Hosea's creation—and is the same noun used in 4:12 in the expression "a spirit of *fornication[s]*." Here the reported sign-act is meant to reinforce the basic message that the *land* has committed grievous fornication against its husband/owner.[23] "Land" in Hebrew is feminine, and the symbolism is transparent: the children are the inhabitants. In the accusations that follow it is sometimes the mother, sometimes the children, sometimes the earth itself that is in view. But the dominant image, elaborated at great length in the allegory of chapter 2, is that of the wife who has abandoned her husband for other lovers (specified here as "the Baals," 2:13 [Heb. 15]; cf. 2:16–17 [Heb. 18–19]), who offer her bread and water, wine and oil, flax and wool. But the gifts, Hosea insists, are the LORD's, bestowed by the true "fertility god" and Israel's true husband/master.

The target of Hosea's accusations appears to be some kind of "fertility cult" that seeks the benefits of nature by propitiation of the storm god Baal (here belittled by pluralizing as "the Baals")—or by worship of YHWH as though he were Baal. And the charges in 4:11–14 suggest that sexual acts were part of the cult itself or at least thought to help secure the desired benefits. But we lack information about the actual practices, and it is impossible to determine how much of the description may simply be caricature of licentious practices at rural sanctuaries—analogous to the practices associated with convention centers and places of pilgrimage in other times and places. Moreover much of the detail may be generated by the simple choice of ZNH/fornication as the metaphorical language of denunciation—following common practice of using sexual slander to heighten an accusation. What is clear is that the prophet is not targeting simple prostitution as described in the texts examined earlier. On the other hand, the notion of "sacred prostitution" as ritual sex in the service of the cult is equally problematic, despite the hold it has gained in virtually every textbook and commentary.[24]

Hosea's use of the language of fornication to describe worship of other gods as "affairs" with other lovers depends on an underlying metaphor of the (covenant) bond between God and Israel as a marriage relationship.[25] And it seems to have been occasioned by practices at local sanctuaries of the Northern Kingdom that involved sexual activity of some sort. Thus Hosea's metaphorical usage remains close to the basic meaning of ZNH as it works multiple variations on the theme. Later authors developed these leads in a number of different ways. While Jeremiah and Ezekiel take up the metaphor of the promiscuous bride, the latter in two extended allegories (chaps. 16, 23), most of the other uses are confined to formulaic, summary accusations with a limited repertoire of expressions—and few of the accusations have any demonstrable relationship to sexual activity at all. To illustrate this two-fold development, I offer a sampling of the formulaic usage and then take a brief look at Ezekiel's exploitation of the language—which includes a specific comparison with the prostitute.

"Fornication" (ZNH) as Illicit Religious Practice or Political Alliance

In a number of passages in the Pentateuch (all recognized as exilic or postexilic) ZNH is used simply to describe the worship of other gods—not only by Israelites who may be induced to adopt the foreign practice but by their own devotes. Thus Exodus warns against making a covenant with the "inhabitants of the land " (34:15–16): "For they will *fornicate* [*wezanu*] after their gods and sacrifice to their gods, and invite you, and you will eat from their sacrifice. (16) And you will take wives from among their daughters for your sons, and their daughters will *fornicate* [*wezanu*] after their gods and will *make* your sons *fornicate* [*wehiznu*] after their gods." Here *"zanah,"* "to fornicate," is simply substituted for the verb "to walk" in the common expression for allegiance to a deity (or political leader), "to walk after" (that is, "to follow").[26] Leviticus 20: 5 condemns any Israelite who "*fornicates* after Molech" (a deity associated with child sacrifice). Deuteronomy 31:16 warns that after Moses' death the people will "*fornicate* after the strange gods of the land" into which they are entering, forsake the LORD, and break the covenant that he made with them. Judges 2:17 describes the cycle of apostasy that followed each act of deliverance by the judges whom the LORD had raised up: "They did not listen even to their judges; for they *fornicated* after other gods and bowed down to them." Judges 8:27 reports that all Israel "*fornicated* after" the ephod (cult object) that Gideon had made and set up in his city, and Judges 8:33 says that as soon as Gideon died, the Israelites again "*fornicated* after the Baals, and made Baal-berith their god."

Israel as a Fornicating Woman

In Jeremiah and Ezekiel, personification of Israel as a promiscuous woman (introduced by Hosea) is continued—with new elaborations. In Jeremiah 3:1 the prophet asks whether Israel, who has "*fornicated* with many companions," can return to the LORD. His reply underscores the impossibility by stressing the brazen and hardened nature of Israel's "fornication" as that of a common prostitute with no sense of shame (2–3): "Look up to the bare heights, and see! Where have you not been laid [K *shuggalt*; Q *shukkabt*]? By the roadsides you sat [waiting for lovers]. . . . You had the forehead of a *fornicator*-woman [*ishshah zonah*], you refuse to be ashamed." Jeremiah 3:6–9 picks up the language of Hosea 4 to summarize the LORD's indictment against the Northern Kingdom, comparing the divine judgment to divorce and condemning the Southern Kingdom for following the same path. The marriage metaphor is central here and the language of fornication is paired with that of adultery:

(6) The LORD said to me in the days of King Josiah: Have you seen what she did, that faithless one, Israel, how she went up on every high hill and under every green tree, and *fornicated* there? (7) And I thought, "After she has done all these things she will return to me;" but she did not return, and her false sister Judah saw it. (8) . . . Because Rebel Israel *had committed adultery,* I cast her off and gave her a bill of divorce; yet her false sister Judah did not fear, but she too went and *fornicated.* (9) Because she took her *fornication* [*zenutah*] so lightly, she polluted the land, *committing adultery* with stone and tree.[27]

Ezekiel 16 presents an elaborate allegory (in 63 verses!) of Jerusalem/ Israel as the LORD's unfaithful wife. From her origins as an unwanted child of mixed Amorite and Hittite parentage her history is traced. Abandoned at birth in an open field, she is spied by the LORD passing by, who says to her "Live!" (v. 6). Growing "like a sprout in the field," she arrives at full womanhood, "naked and bare" (v. 7). When the LORD passes by again, he sees that she is at the "time of love" ('et dodim), and so he "covers her nakedness," "pledges himself to her," and enters into a covenant with her (v. 8). Five verses then detail the LORD's adornment of his bride, her fine food, her beauty, and her fame among the nations, all as the LORD's gift. In verse 15 the accusation begins, employing the root ZNH some twenty-one times: "(15) But you trusted in your beauty, and *fornicated* because of your fame, and you poured out your *fornications* [taznutayik][28] on any passerby. (16) You took some of your garments, and made for yourself 'colorful shrines'[29] and *fornicated* on them. . . . (17) You also took your beautiful jewels of my gold and my silver that I had given you, and made for yourself male images [tsalme zakar] and *fornicated* with them." The accusation continues by detailing Israel's devotion of the fine garments and food that the LORD had given her as coverings for the images and as offerings and also charges her with child sacrifice (20-21). Further descriptions of cultic(?) transgressions follow (24-25): "You built yourself a platform [geb] and made yourself a lofty place [ramah] in every square; at the head of every street you built your lofty place and made your beauty an abomination, and spread your legs to every passer-by, and you multiplied your *fornications.*" The accusations now shift to the subject of political alliances and are expressed using the same "fornication" language (26-29): "You *fornicated* with the Egyptians, your lustful [literally, 'large-membered'] neighbors, multiplying your *fornications,* to provoke me to anger. . . . You *fornicated* with the Assyrians, because you were insatiable; you *fornicated* with them and were still not sated. You multiplied your *fornication* with Chaldea, the land of merchants; yet even with this you were not sated."

Finally, Ezekiel compares the promiscuous wife with an "ordinary" prostitute:

(30) How sick is your heart, says the Lord GOD, that you did all these things, the deeds of a brazen *fornicator*-woman [ishshah-zonah]; (31) building your platform at the head of every street and making your lofty place in every square! Yet you were not like the *fornicator* [zonah], because you spurned fees [etnan].

[You were like] the adulteress woman [*ha'ishshah hammena'apet*], who receives strangers [*zarim*] instead of her husband! (33) Gifts are given to all *fornicators* [*zonot*]; but you gave your gifts to all your lovers, bribing them to come to you from all around for your *fornications*. (34) So you were the opposite of other women; in your *fornications* you were not *solicited to fornicate* [*zunnah*]; you gave payment [*etnan*] when no payment [*etnan*] was given to you; you were different.

The LORD now pronounces judgment on Jerusalem, addressing her as a "*zonah*" (35) and summarizing her offenses in much the same language that precedes the judgment, with added references to her brazenness and nakedness (36). As punishment she will be handed over to all her past lovers and her nakedness exposed before them (37). Although the language of "fornicating" is used throughout this passage to characterize her offenses, the punishment is described in verse 38 as the punishment decreed for "*those* (f. pl) *who commit adultery* [*no'apot*] *and pour out blood* [i.e., 'murder']." The description of the punishment combines language of an enemy's assault and plunder of a city with the image of a woman being publicly abused (39–41):[30] "I will deliver you into their hands, and they shall throw down your platform and break down your lofty places; they shall strip you of your clothes and take your beautiful objects and leave you naked and bare. They shall bring up a mob against you, and they shall stone you and cut you to pieces with their swords. They shall burn your houses and execute judgments on you in the sight of many women; thus I will make you stop *fornicating* [*wehishbattik mizzonah*], and you shall also make no more payment [*etnan*]." The same language, with additional erotic/pornographic detail, is found in Ezekiel 23, which describes the "fornications" of the two sisters Oholah and Oholibah (representing Samaria and Jerusalem). Here the generalizing noun "*taznut*" meaning "fornication(s)" is used of the male lovers (translated as "lust" by NRSV and NJPS) as well as the promiscuous sisters. But here the accusations are entirely concerned with foreign relations: Samaria's "fornication" with the Assyrians (vv. 5–10) and Jerusalem's "fornication" with the Babylonian Chaldeans (vv. 11–31).

It is clear from these latter examples particularly, that the metaphor of the promiscuous bride of YHWH has developed a life of its own, generating new applications and associations, while continuing to feed on, and reinforce, current views of prostitutes and sexual promiscuity. Its afterlife can be traced through the New Testament and into Christian apologetics—but that is another world of religious rhetoric.

Notes

1. This secondary usage is often interpreted by reference to "sacred prostitution," a modern expression and construct, which in different periods and disciplines has been understood in quite different ways and used to interpret different, and often quite disparate, texts and traditions. There is as yet no adequate comprehensive treatment of the subject. Partial and specialized studies may be found in Beard and Henderson (1998), Bird (1996), Gruber (1986), Oden ([1987] 2000, 131–53), van der Toorn (1992), Wacker (1992), and Westenholz (1989). See my forthcoming monograph, *Sacred Prostitutes in Ancient Israel?*

2. Brown, Driver, and Briggs (1907, 275) adds "be a harlot," with reference to Amos 7:17. Cognate usage (Aramaic, Ethiopic, and Arabic) confirms the broad meaning of the root, especially evident in Arabic, where verbal and nominal forms are used of adultery and adulterers (of both sexes) as well as fornication and prostitution.

3. Hebrew lexicons identify families of related words by an abstracted sequence of consonants (typically three) called a *root*. Nouns and verbs are said to be "formed" from the root through different patterns of vocalization and the use of affixes. The Hebrew Bible contains 134 occurrences of words containing the root ZNH, 47 of which are in the book of Ezekiel (42 in chaps. 16 and 23) and 22 in Hosea. Verbal uses (overwhelmingly metaphorical) constitute 93 of these occurrences, and 3 abstract nouns (predominantly, if not exclusively metaphorical) account for 41 more. The feminine participle is used 32 times to designate the prostitute.

4. Although widowed and sent home to her father's house, Tamar has been promised to her husband's brother and thus has the status of a married or betrothed woman.

5. The participle may appear alone, as a substantive (*"zonah"* meaning "[female] fornicator") or as an attributive adjective modifying "woman" (*"ishshah zonah"* meaning "fornicating woman")—in apparently interchangeable use (cf. *"ishshah zonah"* in Joshua 2:1 and 6:22 and *"zonah"* in 6:25).

6. The KJV of 1611 appears to have restricted the language of "whoring" to extended and metaphorical uses of ZNH, employing "harlot" for literal references to prostitutes and prostitution. This contrasts with earlier versions, such as Wycliffe's (1382), which refers to the "tweyne *horis*" who appeared before Solomon (*OED* 2002, s.v. "whore," n.1.a.). "Whore" seems to have been the common term for a prostitute in early English usage, where it is attested as early as the twelfth century (derived from the same Indo-European root that appears in the Latin *"carus"* meaning "dear" [as in the English word "charity"], with cognates in various old Germanic languages [*OED* 2002, s.v. "whore," n.]). "Prostitute" is not attested as an English noun until 1613 (*OED* 2002, s.v. "prostitute," *ppl. A* and *ni.:* B. *n.1.a.*) and does not replace "harlot" in Bible translations until very recent times. It appears that "harlot" had been stamped by popular KJV usage as the "biblical" term.

7. In practice, a more complex semantic relationship probably obtained between the verbal and nominal uses of the root, with specialization of the feminine participle for "prostitute" influencing certain verbal uses.

8. In the following discussion, I use the term "prostitute" to refer to the class of persons designated by Hebrew "zonah" and "ishshah zonah," corresponding to contemporary English usage. In my translations of passages from the Hebrew Bible, however, I have attempted to duplicate the primacy of the verbal idea and the interconnections of the nominal and verbal forms by using "fornicate" and its derivatives for all occurrences of the root ZNH—thus "fornicating" (ptc. in verbal usage), "fornicator" (ptc. in nominal usage), and "fornication(s)" (three abstract nouns: "zenunim," "zenut," and "taznut"). In order to indicate the interchangeability of the nominative and attributive forms of the participle I use "fornicator" for both (thus "fornicator-woman" for "ishshah zonah," rather than "fornicating woman"). I have chosen "fornicate" over the more colloquial "whore" (the only other English term that allows both nominal and verbal uses without periphrastic constructions) because the latter has a history of its own and is generally perceived today as too coarse—or distinctly "biblical" (see n.6 above).

9. Unless otherwise indicated, all biblical translations are my own, based on the tradition of the RSV and NRSV. Cf. v. 14, where the chief priest may not marry a "widow or a divorced [woman] or a defiled [woman], a zonah" ("almah ugerushah wachalalah zonah").

10. Cf. Leviticus 19:29, which targets the complicity of fathers: "Do not defile [techallel] your daughter by causing her to fornicate [lehaznotah], so that the land will not fornicate [tizneh] and be full of depravity [zimmah]." The context of this passage, which refers to a variety of prohibited religious practices, and the application of ZNH to the land as well as the daughter suggest that an extended meaning may be intended.

11. Contemporary examples would include rape victims shunned or murdered by their dishonored kinsmen.

12. The nature of the comparison is not entirely clear owing to a difficult Hebrew text. Cf. NJPS: "The last loaf of bread will go for a harlot; A married woman will snare a person of honor."

13. Exhibited, for example, in the expression, "daughter-Zion" ("bat-tsiyyon," conventionally translated "daughter of Zion") (Isaiah 52:1-2 and 62:[4-5]11; Micah 4:8, 10, 13) and "virgin daughter Zion" ("betulat bat-tsiyyon," Isaiah 37:22; Lamentations 2:13); cf. "virgin daughter Babylon" (Isaiah 47:1 [2-9]).

14. He foils the Gazites plans to capture him at daybreak by arising at midnight—and pulling up the city gate (Judges 16:2-3).

15. In fact we have no evidence for Canaanite practice; sources from ancient Mesopotamia offer a richer portrait but a similar view of prostitutes as both honored and despised. See, e.g., Enkidu's curse and subsequent blessing of the prostitute who initiated him into the pleasures and griefs of civilized life (Gilgamesh 7, 3.6-22 and 4.1-10; see Bird [1997, 201-2] and Martha Roth's essay in this volume).

16. van der Toorn bases his argument on a highly problematic interpretation of Proverbs 7:6-23, which concerns adultery, not prostitution, and in which prostitution is only a ruse. See Berlinerblau (1996, 103-7, 141-44, and n.1 above).

17. A priest is identified in Hosea 4:4 as the target of the prophet's complaint, and some interpreters see the priestly class (or particular priests) as the subject of the continuing accusations.

18. The standard verbs for "sacrificing" *("zabach")* and "offering incense" *("hiqtir")* are used here in the Piel stem, in contrast to normal usage, producing an effect comparable to our use of quotation marks or inverted commas to signal a sense other than the normal or literal meaning.

19. "Daughters" and "daughters-in-law" are paired for purposes of poetic parallelism—and are to be understood as a single class: sexually mature young female dependents of the men who are under indictment (Bird 1997, 231–32).

20. In Hebrew, *"yeparedu."* Usually translated contextually: in NRSV it is given as "go aside" and in NJPS as "turn aside" (with a note stating "Meaning of Heb. uncertain").

21. It is possible to argue that all of the uses of ZNH in this passage are extended or metaphorical, but I believe that robs the accusation of some of its edge.

22. On Hosea's unique constructions "fornicate *from after"* (1:2)/*"from under"* (4:12)/*"from upon"* (9:1) YHWH, see Bird (1997, 229–31).

23. The common Hebrew term for "master"/"owner"/"husband" is *"ba'al,"* which is also the name (originally title) of the deity whom Hosea accuses Israel of serving instead of its true master, YHWH. Traditional renderings of the Hebrew divine name substituted another Hebrew term for "lord"/"master," *"adon,"* yielding *"adonay"* meaning "[my] LORD."

24. See van der Toorn (1992) and n.1 above.

25. Perhaps drawing on mythic conceptions of the union of earth and sky or the storm god's impregnating of earth's womb.

26. Cf. Hosea 2:7 and 1:2 cited above.

27. Apparent references to the "standing stones"/"pillars" *("mazzebot")* and "sacred poles" *("asherim"),* condemned by the Deuteronomic reformers along with other cultic items associated with the "former inhabitants of the land" (Deuteronomy 12:2–4).

28. The abstract noun *"taznut"* (usually plural) is unique to Ezekiel 16 and 23, which contain twenty occurrences.

29. In Hebrew, *"bamot telu'ot";* in NJPS, "tapestried platforms."

30. See Day (2000).

Heavenly Bodies

Monuments to Prostitutes in Greek Sanctuaries

CATHERINE KEESLING

References in Greek literature to monuments commemorating prostitutes habitually stress the extent to which they violate conventions governing public monuments. The thirteenth book of Athenaeus's *Deipnosophistae* offers a veritable treasure trove of references to such monuments, but the theme of monuments to prostitutes in Greek literature goes back much further, to Herodotus's account of the courtesan Rhodopis. The most obvious forms of transgression were their excessive size, prohibitive expense, and prominent location. Dicaearchus of Messene (as quoted by Athenaeus 13.594d–95a) remarked that the funerary monument of Pythionike was so physically imposing and so strategically sited along the road between Athens and Eleusis that the unsuspecting passerby would assume it to be a public monument to one of the great Athenian generals of the fifth century rather than a tomb erected by Harpalus for his dead mistress.[1] In the case of portraits of prostitutes, their very subject matter was considered transgressive of norms regulating the erection of public monuments by some ancient observers. According to Plutarch (*Moralia* 336d and 401a) and Athenaeus (13.591b), the Cynic philospher Crates called the portrait statue of Phryne at Delphi by the sculptor Praxiteles "a trophy to the incontinence of the

59

Greeks."[2] Even some modern commentators have been willing to impugn the Greeks for their monuments to prostitutes. In the unforgettable words of W. H. D. Rouse in his 1902 study of Greek votive offerings, by the end of the fourth century BCE in Greek sanctuaries, "licence becomes impiety in the golden image of Phryne; and Cottina of Sparta had the effrontery to dedicate her own image to Athena. Long before the Delphic oracle had not refused the offering of Rhodopis; but now so low had the gods sunk, that they could accept the image of a common strumpet" (373).

Leslie Kurke has rightly called attention to the importance of literary representations of prostitutes' monuments from Herodotus onward.[3] The task of verifying the authenticity of the representation of such monuments of any period proves to be impossible. Thus the primary aim of this paper is not to claim historical and archaeological authenticity for any Greek monuments to prostitutes. Instead, it is to reconsider the issue of deviation from the norms governing votive dedications within a specific context in which prostitutes' monuments were said to have appeared, that of Greek sanctuaries in the Archaic and Classical periods. Rhodopis and Phryne, arguably the two most famous prostitutes in Greek history, both are reported to have made prominent dedications in the sanctuary of Apollo at Delphi. These two dedications took very different forms, but both functioned as public memorials to prostitutes, memorials that were displayed within a straightforwardly religious context. Though Herodotus (2.135) claims that Rhodopis intended to dedicate a monument unlike any other by converting a tenth of her property into iron ox spits, recent commentators have sought to characterize Rhodopis's dedication as according well with the norms for sanctuary dedications in the Archaic period. As Sitta von Reden has remarked, Rhodopis's dedication was not unique and she "betrays hilarious ignorance" to think it is (1997, 173–74).[4] At the same time that Rhodopis's dedication has come to be characterized as conventional, lingering claims that Phryne's portrait statue does violate norms have yet to be systematically addressed. I would like to suggest in this paper that Rhodopis's monument actually does transgress contemporary Archaic norms for votive dedications in at least one important respect, but that, conversely, Phryne's fourth-century monument in the same sanctuary, conventionally viewed as transgressive in every respect, does conform to some contemporary Greek ideas about portraiture.

The Dedication of Rhodopis

Rhodopis's offering at Delphi has a greater claim to being authentic than most monuments associated with Greek prostitutes in literature, especially if we accept (as I believe we should) the restoration of Rhodopis's name on a small Archaic marble fragment found built into the walls of a church near the site. The votive dedication of Rhodopis, according to Herodotus (2.135), consisted of a pile of iron ox spits *(bouporoi obeloi)* constituting a tithe *(dekatê)* of her net worth.[5] Though fragmentary and reworked, the inscribed base (Delphi Museum inventory no. 7512= *SEG* XIII.364) does nothing to contradict what Herodotus implies about the monument's form, size, and appearance.[6] Though only five letters can be read on the stone, Mastrokostas's restoration "[ane-thê]ke Rhod[ôpis]" ("Rhodopis dedicated") should inspire confidence for two reasons: the ubiquity of the verb of dedication *"anethêke(n)"* on inscribed votive offerings, and the relative rarity of names and other words in Greek beginning in *"Rho-."* Furthermore, the word order of the inscription, in which the dedicator's name is given after the verb of dedication, allows us to reconstruct a metrical epigram, specifically a hexameter verse.[7] Herodotus's report that Rhodopis dedicated a *dekatê* or tithe could be based on the wording of the dedicatory inscription: in the Archaic period, *"dekatê"* hardly ever occurs in dedicatory inscriptions that are not metrical, and it can occur both in hexameter verses and in elegiac couplets.[8]

Mastrokostas's fragment belongs to the lower step of a base consisting of two steps. On the basis of other Archaic private dedications inscribed on stone, one can speculate that the complete inscribed dedicatory epigram may have consisted of a single hexameter, of two or more hexameters, or of a single elegiac couplet.[9] The height of the surviving letters of the inscription (between 0.05 and 0.07 meters) is large enough to suggest a base of substantial size even if the inscription consisted of a single hexameter verse inscribed around two, three, or all four sides of the monument.[10] Unfortunately, the top step of Rhodopis's monument, which would have provided evidence for how the *obeloi* were attached to the base and for how many *obeloi* there were, has not been preserved.

Herodotus would have us believe that the number of *obeloi* dedicated by Rhodopis was considerable and that in his own time these remained "piled up" *(sunneatai)* on their base behind the altar of the Chians near the entrance to the temple of Apollo. Collections of iron *obeloi* or spits have been found in numerous Greek sanctuaries.[11] The spectacular discovery in 1894 in the Argive Heraion of a bundle of ninety-six *obeloi* in front of the classical temple, found together with the lead soldering originally used to attach them to a lost stone base, has often been connected with literary sources saying that Pheidon of Argos commemorated his introduction of coinage by dedicating the *obeloi* that had previously been used as currency to Argive Hera.[12] Yet the absence of any inscription connected with the *obeloi* from the Heraion, combined with their uncertain date, call into question the association with Pheidon, though it does appear that these *obeloi*, like the ones dedicated by Rhodopis, were removed from use permanently when they were put on display. The parallels most often cited for Rhodopis's dedication at Delphi are three fragmentary limestone stelae from Perachora inscribed with metrical dedicatory epigrams, all of which should date somewhere between ca. 650 and ca. 550 BCE (*LSAG*[2] 131.7, 12, and 17= *CEG* 352, 353, and 354). Since the stelae seem to be comparable to one another in size and shape and since one of the epigrams begins "I am a drachma" (*"drachma egô"*), each has been plausibly restored as a holder for six *obeloi*, a drachma's worth of iron spits.[13] Apart from a lost and very questionably restored inscribed base from Crisa near Delphi (*CEG* 344), the stelae from Perachora are in fact the only examples from Greek sanctuaries in any period of *obeloi* attached to inscribed stone bases, the type of dedication made by Rhodopis at Delphi.[14]

In contrast to the *obeloi* dedicated by Rhodopis at Delphi, the votive *obeloi* in the sanctuary of Hera at Perachora seem to have been intended to remain in use as implements of sacrifice. In a reconstruction suggested first by H. T. Wade-Gery and followed by L. H. Jeffery, the *obeloi* were attached to the sides of their inscribed limestone holders by iron brackets; traces of one of these brackets survive on one of the three stelae, and another appears to have broken along the line of a similar bracket.[15] At some unknown point in the history of the sanctuary, the inscribed holders themselves were reused to line a sacrificial roasting pit located inside the so-called temple of Hera Limenia, reidentified as a *hestiatorion* (cult dining room) by R. A. Tomlinson (1977, esp. 199–200). What this means is that Rhodopis's dedication of *obeloi*, which involved their permanent display as part of an inscribed monument intended to serve as a memorial (in Herodotus's own words, a *mnêmosunon*) to its dedicator, with the removal of the *obeloi* from effective use that such a monument entailed, has no true parallel and may thus be unique as Herodotus implies.

The bundle of *obeloi* found in the Argive Heraion, like those of Rhodopis's dedication, were removed from use, but they were not accompanied by any dedicatory inscription; the *obeloi* originally attached to the three inscribed stelae from Perachora seem to have been intended to remain in use after their dedication. All of the other iron *obeloi* dedicated as offerings in Greek sanctuaries can be interpreted as implements used to roast the internal organs *(splanchna)* of sacrificial animals, a ritual described in the *Iliad* and the *Odyssey*.[16] Dedications of tripods, bowls, and other metal vessels are far more common than dedications of *obeloi*, and these too were used as sacrificial implements (though tripod dedications are most often associated with victories in Panhellenic games and choregic competitions, at least some of the tripods and bowls dedicated in Greek sanctuaries should be explained as sacrificial rather than agonistic in significance).[17] Some of the metal vessels and related implements dedicated in sanctuaries were intended to be used, others clearly were not: both tripods and other metal vessels were commonly attached to stone bases, both inscribed and uninscribed, in the Archaic period.[18]

The archaeological and epigraphical evidence available suggests *obeloi* were not normally treated in the same fashion. Anthony Snodgrass has made an important distinction between two types of offerings in Greek sanctuaries: raw offerings consisting of objects of everyday use such as fibulae and armor and converted offerings such as statues (1989–90).[19] Raw offerings were far more common in the Archaic period than they were subsequently. Apart from the bundle of *obeloi* from the Argive Heraion and Rhodopis's dedication at Delphi, all other offerings of *obeloi* we know of from Greek sanctuaries were raw in Snodgrass's terms. Rhodopis's monument straddles the normally clear dividing line between raw and converted. She took sacrificial implements of everyday use and transformed them into a monument to herself by attaching them permanently to an inscribed base. If I am right about the lack of parallels for Rhodopis's monument, the overt claim in Herodotus's text that she transgressed the norms for votive offerings could be accurate and not merely a facet of Herodotus's literary trivialization of Rhodopis and what she stands for. Rhodopis's dedication in the sanctuary at Delphi may truly have been something unique.[20]

Fictive Transgressions or Transgressive Fictions?

The type of transgression of norms I am claiming for the dedication of Rhodopis may appear to be too subtle; yet an examination of some

monuments to prostitutes in Greek sanctuaries attested solely by literary sources demonstrates that not all forms of transgression in the literary record are immediately obvious. Violation of the normal customs
governing votive dedications is a subtext, which has gone unrecognized
in the case of some of the monuments to prostitutes in Greek literature.
One case in point is the so-called portrait of Leaina on the Athenian
Acropolis. According to Pausanias (1.23.1–2), the Athenians of his own
time explained the bronze statue of a lioness standing at the entrance to
the acropolis beside a statue of Aphrodite as a monument commemorating Leaina ("Lioness"), a mistress of the tyrant-slayer Aristogeiton tortured and killed by Hippias after the assassination of Hipparchus in 514
BCE. Pliny (*Natural History* 34.72) and Plutarch (*Moralia* 505e) go Pausanias one better by adding the detail that the lion lacked a tongue because Leaina had refused to name her co-conspirators.

Though archaeologists have generally accepted the monument commemorating Leaina itself as authentic, the story of Leaina that became
attached to the statue of a lioness over the course of time is not; rather it
speaks to the development of an oral tradition responding to three aspects of this votive monument: its placement next to a statue of Aphrodite; its missing tongue, more likely a result of damage than an original
attribute; and, most obviously, the fact that Leaina, the supposed mistress of Aristogeiton, is named "Lioness."[21] Votive monuments normally
were not inscribed with the names of the subjects they represented or
specifics about the occasion motivating their dedication; oral traditions
tended to fill the gaps left by inscriptions, and in this case the connection
with Leaina effectively explained why there was a statue of a lioness
standing next to one of Aphrodite on the acropolis—herself a "visiting
god" there whose presence potentially called for some explanation—
and for this reason the tradition spread and endured.

When interpreted as a "portrait" of the courtesan Leaina, the bronze
lioness on the acropolis is transgressive in at least one respect. The lioness statue functions as a canting device, namely a representation of an
animal used as a pun on the name of the one being honored, just like the
marble lion set up over the tomb of Leonidas at Thermopylae (Herodotus 7.225.2). Yet, with the exception of one example on an Athenian state
document relief of the fourth century, all other known examples of
animals used as canting devices appear as funerary monuments, not
sanctuary dedications (see Ritti 1973–74 for examples and discussion).
Leaina's monument thus stands out in transgressing the normal generic

boundaries between funerary and votive commemoration in Archaic and Classical Athens. In this case, a transgressive interpretation unrelated to the original intent of a votive dedication attaches itself to it, recasting it as a "portrait" commemorating a prostitute.

It is possible to consider another monument associated with prostitutes by literary sources in a similar light. Athenaeus (13.573c–d), citing earlier sources, refers to a dedication made by the Corinthians in the temple of Aphrodite on Acrocorinth: this consisted of a votive plaque *(pinax)* on which the names of Corinthian *hetairai* were written, accompanied by an epigram attributed to Simonides. The epigram makes it clear that the occasion for the dedication was the supplication of Aphrodite by the *hetairai* of Corinth on the eve of the Persian invasion of mainland Greece in 480 BCE. Two other late sources, Pseudo-Plutarch *(Moralia* 871b) and a *scholion* on Pindar *(Olympian* 13.32b), change the women in question from *hetairai* into Corinthian citizen women and the dedication itself from a name list into either a group of bronze portrait statues (Pseudo-Plutarch) or a votive painting representing these women (Pindar).[22]

In spite of justifiable scholarly disagreement concerning the relative reliability of Athenaeus and the competing explanations of the Corinthian dedication, the dedicatory epigram as it has been transmitted by each of the sources identifies itself clearly as belonging to a representation of a group of women, either in the form of a catalogue of their names or an artistic representation.[23] Though the epigram is most likely authentic, the true nature of the votive dedication it accompanied has become impossible to recover. The dedicatory epigram itself is nonspecific, referring to the women in question only epideictically as "these women." An inscribed catalogue consisting of exclusively female names would have been anomalous in the fifth century BCE and would surely have called for some explanation even in the fourth century, the date of the sources Athenaeus cites as his authorities.[24] Representations of groups of women in votive sculpture and painting were also unusual both in the fifth century and in the fourth.[25] The fame in the Roman imperial period of both the temple prostitutes of Aphrodite and of legendary Corinthian courtesans such as Leaina, the mistress of Demetrius Poliorcetes, would have encouraged later observers to read the dedication and its accompanying epigram, both prominently displayed in the temple of Aphrodite on Acrocorinth, as a dedication commemorating prostitutes rather than ordinary Corinthian citizen women.

The Portrait Statue of Phryne at Delphi

According to Athenaeus (13.591b–c), citing the Hellenistic periegete Alcetas as his source, a golden portrait statue of the fourth-century courtesan Phryne stood atop a column base of Pentelic marble in the sanctuary of Apollo at Delphi. Phryne's statue is said by Athenaeus's source to have been made by her lover the sculptor Praxiteles and to have stood between portrait statues of King Archidamus III of Sparta and Philip II of Macedon; according to Athenaeus, it bore the inscribed name label "Phryne, daughter of Epikles, of Thespiai." Pausanias (10.15.1) describes Phryne's statue as gilded instead of solid gold; he claims that Phryne dedicated it herself, while Athenaeus's source attributes this dedication to "the neighbors" (periktiones)—perhaps a garbled reference either to the Delphic Amphictiony or to the polis of Delphi, both dedicators of portrait statues in the sanctuary.[26]

Despite the fact that neither the statue nor its inscribed base survives, there is no particular reason to doubt that Phryne's portrait did stand in the sanctuary at Delphi. If Phryne's portrait statue is indeed authentic, it raises obvious questions concerning the original intent of the dedication, especially if the Amphictions or the people of Delphi dedicated it. Here I would like to reevaluate specific aspects of Phryne's portrait statue which have been thought of as deviating from the norms regulating the fourth-century custom of dedicating portrait statues in Greek sanctuaries in the eyes of both ancient and modern viewers and to relate these alleged deviations to what we know about these norms.

Phryne's status as a prostitute opened her portrait to criticism by ancient observers. Yet, on the balance of the available evidence, the very fact of a portrait statue representing a woman by herself in the sanctuary of Apollo at Delphi in the fourth century was an anomaly. Phryne's statue can best be understood within the context of the fourth-century practice of erecting honorific portraits of living subjects in public places, chiefly sanctuaries and agoras. From the fourth century onward, far more men than women were commemorated with portraits, both official ones commissioned by public bodies such as the Delphic Amphictiony and private dedications in Greek sanctuaries. Even in the Hellenistic period, only a few well-defined categories of female subjects were honored with portrait statues on their own, that is, not as part of aristocratic family portrait groups. Apart from Phryne and Cottina of Sparta (Athenaeus 13.574c–d), we know from literary and epigraphical sources of portraits in Greek sanctuaries representing female civic benefactors, female victors in Panhellenic contests, Hellenistic queens, priestesses, lesser sacred personnel such as the Athenian *arrhephoroi* and *kanephoroi,* and Eleusinian initiates.[27] At Delphi before the Roman period, Phryne's is the only female portrait attested by literary and epigraphical sources that did not form part of a mixed male-and-female family group. Hers may also be the earliest female portrait, with the possible exception of the statue of Hydna, who together with her father Scyllis was honored by the Delphic Amphictiony with a bronze portrait statue for helping to defeat the Persians at Salamis (Pausanias 10.19.1).[28]

Priestesses on occasion dedicated their own portraits, as did Cynisca, a Spartan woman whose chariot won first prize in the Olympic games; otherwise, what few female portraits we do know of in Greek sanctuaries were dedicated by others (Pausanias 6.1.6 and *CEG* 2.820). Statue dedications of any type in sanctuaries by women were surprisingly uncommon: in the Archaic period and the fifth century, they account for fewer than 10 percent of the statue dedications on the Athenian Acropolis, and at Delphi from the Archaic period through the Hellenistic period we know of only a handful of statues or statue groups dedicated by women.[29] Could Phryne's portrait at Delphi have been dedicated by either the Delphic Amphictiony or the polis of Delphi as Athenaeus seems to say it was? The earliest known inscribed bases for honorific portrait statues dedicated by both the Amphictiony and the Delphians date to the third century rather than the fourth, but the statue of Philip II near Phryne's portrait, if not also the statue of Archidamus III, is likely to have been dedicated by the Amphictiony in the fourth century, specifically between the end of the Third Sacred War (346 BCE) and Philip's death in 336 BCE. This period overlaps with Praxiteles' attested sculptural activity in the middle of the fourth century.[30] The portraits of Scyllis and his daughter Hydna mentioned above, even if they were not dedicated immediately after the Persian Wars, might still predate the statue of Phryne.[31]

We learn from Pausanias that Phryne's portrait was made of gilded bronze rather than solid gold, and he is almost certainly correct (Jacquemin 1999, 166–67 and 238; Arafat 2000, 196–97). Pausanias as a rule mentions very few portraits of women in Greek sanctuaries and reports the materials of somewhat less than 30 percent of the statues he mentions; the use of gilding was no doubt one of the features that attracted his attention to Phryne's portrait. The only three gilded bronze portraits we know of before the Hellenistic period all stood in the sanctuary of Apollo at Delphi, and two of these predate the statue of Phryne.

Alexander I of Macedon dedicated a gilded portrait of himself in front of the temple of Apollo after the Persian Wars (Herodotus 8.121.2), and the sophist Gorgias of Leontini dedicated his own portrait in gilded bronze at Delphi (Pausanias 10.18.7) early in the fourth century.[32] From the literary and epigraphical sources, it appears that gilded portraits became far more common in the Hellenistic and Roman periods, though they were still criticized as excessive (see especially Whitehorne 1975 and Mattusch 1996, 28–29 and 121–29). Gilding was unquestionably appropriate for divine images, but since bronze statues of any kind are scarce we have no way of knowing exactly how common gilded bronzes representing either gods or human subjects were before the Hellenistic period. Suffice it to say that gilding went a step beyond the norm for bronze portraits in the fourth century, and that it may have evoked more common golden images of the gods.[33]

Athenaeus reports that the base for Phryne's portrait was inscribed with her name, her father's name, and the ethnic of her home city, Thespiae. The sequence used here (name+patronymic+ethnic) calls to mind the form of reference preferred by the citizens of Greek city-states in the fourth century. By quoting the name in full Athenaeus may intend to emphasize the anomaly of Phryne's portrait in the midst of a sanctuary in which most of the honorific portraits on display represented men (and a few women) of aristocratic status. Similarly, Athenaeus's anecdote that Phryne offered to rebuild the walls of Thebes but only if the walls were inscribed "Alexander destroyed it, but Phryne the *hetaira* restored it" (13.591d) plays on both the incongruous juxtaposition of Phryne and Alexander the Great and the legendary opposition of the Greeks to individuals taking full credit for collective public works in inscriptions.[34] The names inscribed on sanctuary dedications reflect the self-evaluation of their dedicators rather than an externally determined social status; all the same, the inclusion of Phryne's patronymic and ethnic on the base of her portrait statue, like the use of gilding, appears to signal a self-evaluation at odds with her status as a prostitute.[35]

Athenaeus places Phryne's statue between two others, the portraits of Archedamus III of Sparta and of Philip II. Pausanias says that it stood next to statues of Apollo dedicated by the Epidaurians and the Megarians. No inscribed bases belonging to any of these statues have yet been discovered. Plutarch at one point (*Moralia* 400f–401b) describes Phryne's portrait as being surrounded by portraits of "generals and kings" and at another point (*Moralia* 753f) refers to its placement "amidst kings and queens." By doing so, he effectively characterizes her statue as an interloper among portraits representing more worthy subjects.[36] The dedication Pausanias mentions just before Phryne's statue is a bronze wolf dedicated by the Delphians that stood near the altar of the Chians, east of the entrance to the temple of Apollo. After Phryne and the two Apollo statues, Pausanias mentions a bronze ox dedicated by the people of Plataea: this statue probably also stood near the temple entrance where other monuments commemorating the Persian Wars—among them the Serpent Column of Plataea and a colossal bronze Apollo dedicated from the spoils of Salamis—were located. If Phryne's portrait statue also stood somewhere near the entrance to the temple, then Plutarch's references to portraits of kings might be to the gilded statue of Alexander I of Macedon, which Herodotus places near the Apollo of Salamis, and to portraits of Prusias II of Bithynia, Attalus I, and Eumenes II that postdate Phryne's portrait. Like the statue of Phryne, the latter three stood atop tall pillar or column bases (for the locations of these statues, see Jacquemin 1999, 178, 250–51, and 260). If we are correct in placing the portrait of Phryne east of the entrance to the temple of Apollo, then its location within the sanctuary was particularly prominent. Perhaps more significantly, Phryne's statue must not have been far from the dedication of Rhodopis, which Herodotus locates between the altar of the Chians and the temple entrance.

Phryne's portrait statue, as Athenaeus describes it, appears to have no justification at all according to the norms for statue dedications of its time in Greek sanctuaries. Did she herself, or did the Amphictions or the Delphians, intend to dedicate something exceptional that deviated from the norms of the fourth century, as I have suggested earlier that Rhodopis did in the sixth century when she dedicated her own monument? The precedent of Rhodopis's monument in the same sanctuary may have helped to justify Phryne's even if we fail to identify any plausible occasion behind the dedication of Phryne's portrait (Jacquemin 1999, 83–84). There were already at least two precedents for the dedication of gilded portraits in the sanctuary at Delphi in the mid-fourth century when Phryne's portrait was set up. Furthermore, even if we agree in the end that Phryne's portrait statue really was exceptional owing to its subject matter, I would suggest that it does bear some affinities with contemporary portraits of other subjects, which Athenaeus and the other literary sources omit, since these sources seek uniformly to characterize Phryne's portrait as transgressive.

Though at first glance portrait statues of prostitutes such as Phryne appear to be a complete anomaly when compared with honorific statues of priestesses and other women in sacred service, the same religious justification may have informed portraits of both subjects. Portrait statues of both priests and priestesses are well-attested in the first half of the fourth century and seem to go back as far as the second half of the fifth.[37] Some priestesses dedicated their own portraits; others had their portraits dedicated in sanctuaries by family members or by public bodies. Portrait statues of lesser priestly personnel such as processional basket bearers *(kanephoroi)*—and in Athens the *arrhephoroi* who served Athena on the acropolis and the children who became "hearth initiates" at Eleusis—are first attested in the fourth century, though they did not become common until the late Hellenistic and Roman imperial periods.[38] Dedicatory inscriptions allude directly to the function of portraits of priestly personnel as decoration *(kosmos)* for the sanctuary.[39] In the case of *kanephoroi* especially, physical beauty constituted an important criterion for selection, and the statues that represented these young female votaries in effect perpetuated the spectacle of the sacrificial procession: statues of beautiful women, like the actual women in sacred service, decorated the sanctuary and made it more pleasing to the recipient deity.[40]

Another, related aspect of Greek portraiture, the theme of commensurability with a god or a perceived resemblance to the god, appears in the *Palatine Anthology*. In one of several epigrams playing on this theme (13.2), a man named Callistratus dedicates a portrait of himself to Hermes, calling it "an image common in form and age" to the god himself.[41] In the case of Aristeas of Proconnesus in the fifth century BCE, a close association with the god Apollo, as evidenced by a series of miracles and confirmed by the Delphic oracle, led to the placement of his portrait next to the statue of Apollo in the agora of Metapontum (Herodotus 4.13-15). A second votive dedication associated with Phryne could be relevant in this context. In the sanctuary of Eros in Thespiai, Phryne's home city, a marble statue of Eros by Praxiteles was accompanied by two others, also attributed to Praxiteles, representing Aphrodite and Phryne. In the Roman period all three statues were reputed to have been dedicated there by Phryne herself, as their location in Thespiae would imply.[42] The stock literary traditions that Phryne modeled for her lover Praxiteles' Aphrodite of Knidos and the painter Apelles' Aphrodite Anadyomene (Athenaeus 13. 590f-91a) support the premise of a perceived resemblance between Phryne and Aphrodite herself. Phryne's dedication of her own portrait together with a statue of Aphrodite asserts a connection with the goddess that may have been justified by her great beauty; it could also provide the basis for the tradition that Phryne was a votary or servant of Aphrodite.[43] We can speculate that either her perceived association with Aphrodite or her piety as the dedicator of divine images at Thespiae may have motivated Phryne herself or the sanctuary authorities at Delphi to dedicate a gilded portrait statue in the sanctuary of Apollo near the monument to an earlier courtesan, Rhodopis.

Conclusion

The history of monuments to prostitutes in Greek sanctuaries goes back to Rhodopis's dedication in the Archaic period; the literary discourse characterizing these monuments as transgressive of the norms governing sanctuary dedications originates from the same source. I have suggested here that, when viewed within the context of contemporary dedications in Greek sanctuaries, at least some of these monuments, including Rhodopis's famous *obeloi* at Delphi, do transgress the norms, but in more subtle and less obvious ways than Harpalus' grandiose funerary monument for his mistress Pythionike. At the same time, the fourth-century portrait statue of Phryne at Delphi, the monument most often singled out as violating conventions by literary sources, may to some extent have been misrepresented by the literary tradition. The precedent of Phryne's portrait statues at Delphi and Thespiae prefigures the cultic assimilation of Hellenistic prostitutes to Aphrodite, in which we find several examples of royal mistresses being depicted in portraits, and even worshipped, in the guise of the goddess (see Scholl 1994, 266–71; Havelock 1995, 126–31; Ogden 1999, 262–66). She thus inaugurates a period apparently marked by far more grandiose public monuments dedicated by and in honor of prostitutes and helps to illuminate their ancestry within the traditions of Greek votive religion. Monuments to prostitutes in Greek sanctuaries, whether fictive or authentic, remain deeply embedded within the rich Greek and Roman literary discourse on prostitution. Further work is called for to study the relationships between these monumental realia and the claims found in the literature that they transgressed norms.[44]

Appendix: Monuments to Prostitutes in
Athenaeus *Deipnosophistae*, Book 13

572f: statue of Aphrodite on Samos dedicated from work earnings by the Athenian *hetairai*, who accompanied the army of Pericles [439 BCE].
573a–b: Gyges of Lydia set up a monument to his *hetaira* so tall it was visible to all the inhabitants of Lydia.

573d-e: *pinax* in Corinth with the names of the *hetairai* who were suppliants of Aphrodite before the battle of Salamis, epigram by Simonides (also discussed in [Plutarch] *Moralia* 871a-b and *scholion* to Pindar *Olympian* 13.32).

574c-d: Cottina of Sparta dedicated a statue *(eikonion)* of herself and a small bronze cow to Athena Chalkioikos.

576f: monument of Stratonike near Eleusis. Portraits of Kleino, cupbearer of Ptolemy, set up in Alexandria, wearing only a tunic and holding a drinking horn.

577c: Lamia built a Stoa Poikile for the Sikyonians.

586c and 595c: Harpalus set up a bronze portrait of his mistress Glykera at Rhossos in Syria beside his own and Alexander's portraits.

589b: tomb of Laïs in Thessaly beside the Peneius river with a stone hydria and epigram.

591b: Eros dedicated by Phryne at Thespiae (also discussed in Pausanias 1.20.1 and 9.27.3-5).

591b: golden portrait statue of Phryne at Delphi with name inscription (also discussed in Pausanias 10.15.1; Plutarch *Moralia* 336d, 401a [Mnasarete], and 753f; Aelian *Varia Historia* 9.32; and [Dio Chrysotom] *Oration* 37.28).

591d: Phryne promised to rebuild the walls of Thebes with inscription.

594d-95a: Harpalus's funerary monument for Pythionike on the Sacred Way to Eleusis.

595a-c: two funerary monuments for Pythionike in Babylon costing more than two hundred talents.

595c: temple and altar of Aphrodite Pythionike.

596c: dedication of *obeliskous* at Delphi by Rhodopis/Doriche (also discussed in Herodotus 2.135).

605a-d: dedications at Delphi inscribed with the names of their dedicators stolen by the Phocians and given to their male and female favorites.

Notes

1. Remains of this tomb have been found (Scholl 1994, 254–61); on the passage in Athenaeus, see Kurke (2002, 27–29).

2. Diogenes Laertius (6.60) attributes the same remark to the Cynic Diogenes. See also [Dio Chrysostom] *Oration* 37.28: one might argue that neither Gorgias of Leontini nor Phryne deserved to be represented by portraits in the sanctuary.

3. See especially Kurke (1999, 175–246).

4. Lloyd (1988, 86–87) and Kurke (1999, 223–24) also treat Rhodopis's dedication of *oboloi* at Delphi as one example of a common offering type.

5. Cf. Athenaeus (13.596c), who calls Rhodopis "Doriche" and the objects she dedicated *obeliskous* ("small spits").

6. For a full description and illustrations, see Mastrokostas (1953, esp. 635–42 and figs. 2 and 3 [photographs]); *LSAG*[2] 102–3, 7 and pl. 12.7 (drawing). Jeffery (1988) dates the inscription to ca. 530? BCE on the basis of its letter forms.

7. Mastrokostas (1953) placed the two surviving words *"anethêke Rhodôpis"* in the middle of a hexameter verse (as in *CEG* 190, 195, 202, and 243 from the

Athenian Acropolis), but they could also belong to the end of a hexameter; for *"anethêke"* in this metrical position, see *CEG* 188 and 205, also from the acropolis.

8. On *"dekatê"* in metrical dedications of the Archaic period, see, e.g., *CEG* 203, 217, 218, 250 (hexameters) and 179, 190, 194, 200, and 202 (elegiac couplets), all from the Athenian Acropolis. For another *dekatê* dedication by a woman, see *CEG* 395, a small bronze statuette or figural mirror support from Paestum dedicated by Phillo, daughter of Charmylidas, to Athena (described by Kron [1996, 199, 159–60]; she dates the dedication to ca. 500–475 BCE).

9. Single hexameter: *CEG* 188, 191, and 209; two hexameters: *CEG* 189, 225, and 227; elegiac couplet: *CEG* 190 (ca. 530–520?), 194, 197, 202, and 205.

10. For stepped bases, see Kissas (2000, 13–15, 42–69, and 90–106). For a base of the same date inscribed on three sides, see *CEG* 302 (rectangular capital for a bronze tripod dedicated in the Ptoön in Boeotia by the Athenian Alkmeonides ca. 540?). *CEG* 425 (ca. 550–530?), a rectangular pillar capital inscribed with the name of the Chian sculptor Archermus from Delos, may have featured three hexameters inscribed across two adjoining sides.

11. For lists of examples, see Lazzarini (1982) and Strom (1992).

12. On Pheidon of Argos, see *Etymologicum magnum,* s.v. *"obeliskos."* With respect to *obeloi* as protomonetary currency, see Plutarch *Lysander* 17.1–3. Argive Heraion *obeloi* are described and illustrated in Waldstein (1902, 61–63 and fig. 31) and identified as Pheidon's dedication in Wade-Gery (1940, 258–61) and Courbin (1983).

13. For a full description of the stelae and their inscriptions, see Wade-Gery (1940, 256–67 and pls. 36 and 132).

14. A drawing of the Crisa base (ca. 600–550? BCE) first published soon after its discovery in 1848 is the only source of information about it. The dedicatory inscription is almost entirely preserved, as are two large round cuttings for metal bowls on the top of the base and a small hole between and in front of them. Raubitschek (1950) read the name of the objects dedicated as "drachmas" and suggested that the small hole held a drachma's worth of *obeloi;* but Hansen (*CEG* 344 [= *LSAG*² 103.1 and pl. 12.1]) points out that the word must instead be *"draweous,"* an otherwise unattested but plausible name for the metal vessels attached to the top of the inscribed base. In the drawing the small hole does not appear to be large or deep enough to hold a bundle of *obeloi.*

15. Wade-Gery (1940, 257–58 and pls. 36 and 132) and *LSAG*² pls. 18.7, 19.12, and 20.17. Wade-Gery considered it more likely that the spits were attached to the inscribed stelae vertically, but also mentioned the possibility that each stele originally lay flat with its inscription on top and "with two metal stanchions let into it (like fire-dogs) across which the bundle of iron spits lay" (257–58).

16. E.g. Homer *Iliad* 1.464–66; for a collection of the evidence, see van Straten (1995, 118–41). *Bouporoi obeloi* were *obeloi* suitable for roasting the *splanchna* of sacrificial oxen and as such they may have been particularly large (cf. Richardson 1961, 56–57). See also the smaller *obeliskoi* listed in temple inventories from the Athenian Acropolis and Delos (Lazzarini 1982, nn.31 and 32).

17. For a sacrificial interpretation of votive *obeloi,* see Furtwängler (1980). For a sacrificial interpretation of votive tripods, see Herrmann (1979, 6–7). A series of more than fifty inscribed bronze vessels were dedicated on the Athenian

Acropolis by private individuals, including several women, in the sixth and fifth centuries (*IG* 1³ 550–83ff).

18. For an example of votive vessels remaining in use, see *LSAG*² 371.35 (stele from the Samian Heraion commemorating the dedication of a silver *phiale* and a bronze lampstand). For examples attached to bases from the Athenian Acropolis, see *IG* 1³ 690, 597 (agonistic), 591, 757 (agonistic), and 831, and Kissas (2000, nos. B156, B166, and B180).

19. A small bronze statuette from the Ptoön in Boeotia bearing the inscription "I am the *obelos* of—anios" is one such "converted" offering: it was evidently paid for by the sale of an *obelos* (Lazzarini 1982).

20. Cf. the dedications to Aphrodite of "tools of the trade" on retirement attributed to prostitutes in the *Palatine Anthology* (e.g., 6.1, 6.133, and 6.208), a parodic twist on a genre of modest votive offering (Rouse 1975, 70–74).

21. See, e.g., Fuchs (1995, 74–75), who takes the "portrait" of Leaina literally and Boardman (1986), who reconstructs it as an authentic Archaic votive monument.

22. The term *"pinax"* can refer both to inscribed tablets and to panel paintings, and it is not possible to tell in many cases which type of *pinax* is meant. Wilhelm (1909, 325–26) suggested that a decree prohibiting the attachment of *pinakes* to the woodwork of a stoa in the sanctuary of Apollo Delphinios at Miletos (*LSCG suppl.* 123) refers to "tablets" (*"Schrifttafeln"*); the *pinax* in the Erechtheion on the acropolis showing the succession of priests of Poseidon (Plutarch *Lycurgus* 843e–f), though usually interpreted as a painting by Ismenias of Chalkis, might in fact have been a name list written or compiled by Ismenias (Jeffery 1988, 126 and Löhr 2000, 163). See Faraone's essay in this volume for further discussion.

23. For the epigram and the problem of its interpretation, see especially Page (1981, 207–11), Kurke (1996, 64–66 and nn.36–38), and Faraone's essay in this volume.

24. Inscribed lists of exclusively female names occur in the fourth-century inventories of garments dedicated to Artemis Brauronia found on the Athenian Acropolis (*IG* 2² 1514–31, discussed by Linders [1972]). A Hellenistic public subscription list from Tanagra, discussed by Migeotte (1992, 75–81, no. 28 [*SEG*.XLIII.212]), consists exclusively of female names; for a discussion of women's participation in public subscriptions, see Migeotte (1992, 371–76).

25. See the catalogue of the names of the Athenian dead inscribed on a monument together with a series of epigrams soon after the Persian Wars (*IG* 1³ 503/504) and the epigram accompanying weapons dedicated collectively by Corinthian sailors after the battle of Salamis (Page 1981, 206–7). The only "group portraits" of women in Pausanias are statues of priestesses dedicated at different times but grouped together within sanctuaries (e.g., 7.25.7), and statues of women and children in the agora of Troezen purported to represent the most important of the Athenians who took refuge there during the Persian invasion of 480 BCE (2.31.10).

26. For dedications by the Amphictiony and the Delphic polis, see Jacquemin (1999, 11–18, 309–12, and 321–27). Cf. Aelian (*VH* 9.32), who claims that Phryne's portrait was dedicated by "the Greeks."

27. For priestesses, sacred personnel, and Eleusinian initiates, see below. Portraits of female civic benefactors, like those of royal women, belong primarily to the late Hellenistic period: Gauthier (1985, 74–75). See in general Kron (1996, 171–82), van Bremen (1996), and *SEG* XXXIII.1035–41: Archippe of Kyme was honored with both a colossal bronze portrait and a golden portrait in return for her benefactions (discussed by van Bremen [1996, 13–19]). On Kos in the late Hellenistic and early imperial periods, inscribed statue bases show that men were honored with portrait statues three times as often as women (Höghammar 1997).

28. For portraits of women at Delphi, see Kron (1996, 168–69) and Jacquemin (1999, 77 and 205–7). For the portraits of Scyllis and Hydna, see Jacquemin (1999, 47, 95, 198, and no. 054).

29. For these statistics, see Kron (1996, 160–61).

30. For the problem of Praxiteles' date, see most recently Ajootian (1996).

31. See Jacquemin (1999, 60, 132, 204–5, and no. 464 [Phryne]; 39 and no. 498 [Archidamus III]; 47 and no. 510 [Philip II]).

32. On Alexander I of Macedon see Jacquemin (1999, 167, 204, 251, and no. 347). On Gorgias of Leontini, see Jacquemin (1999, 71, 87, 204, and no. 334). Gorgias's grandnephew dedicated another portrait of him at Olympia; the inscription on the base (*CEG* 2.830) asserts that the justification for the offering was Gorgias's piety (*eusebeia*).

33. For further discussion of the significance of gold and gilded portrait statues, see the article by Ralf Krumeich in Peter Schultz and Ralf von den Hoff, eds., *Early Hellenistic Portraiture: Image, Style, Context* (forthcoming).

34. For a discussion of Phryne's name and the anecdote, see Rosenmeyer (2001, 243–48). Alexander the Great reportedly offered to pay for the completion of the temple of Artemis at Ephesus if he could have his name inscribed on it; he was rebuffed by the Ephesians (Strabo 14.1.22), but the people of Priene seem to have accepted a similar offer judging by the inscription on the temple of Athena there (Carter 1983, 26–31). When the Athenian *dêmos* complained about the expense of the Periclean building program on the acropolis, Pericles reportedly threatened to have his own name inscribed on the buildings (Plutarch *Life of Pericles* 14.1). Umholtz (2002) argues that inscribing dedications by individuals on buildings was not considered inappropriate in the Archaic and Classical periods; what *was* inappropriate was taking credit for a dedication one did not pay for oneself, as in Herodotus 1.51.

35. For name forms on votive dedications, see in general the remarks of Stewart (1979, 109–11), Aleshire (1992, 85–92), and Kron (1996, 165–66).

36. A similarly anomalous juxtaposition was created by Harpalus when he set up a bronze portrait of his mistress Glykera beside portraits of Alexander and of himself at Rhossos in Syria (Athenaeus 13.586c).

37. For a convenient synthesis of the evidence, see Kron (1996, 140–55). The earliest known portrait of a priestess on the Athenian Acropolis represented Lysimache, priestess of Athena Polias for sixty-four years (*CEG* 2.757, ca. 360? BCE).

38. The evidence is summarized by Geagan (1994) and Donnay (1997, 180–83).

39. The dedicatory inscription accompanying the bronze portraits dedicated by a priestess of Aphrodite Pandemus and her family reads in part, "we decorate [kosmoumen] this [monument] with our portraits" (CEG 2.775 [from Athens], discussed by Kron (1996, 154–55; she dates the inscription to ca. 350–320 BCE). Cf. the inscription on a portrait statue of herself dedicated by a priestess of Dionysus in the late fourth or early third century from Erythrae: "Timo, the wife of Zoilos and the daughter of Pankratides, set this up to Dionysus, a portrait [eikon] of her form [morphes] and token of excellence and wealth, an immortal remembrance for her children and descendants" (CEG 2.858).

40. See especially Garland (1995, 63–65) on requirements of physical perfection and Kavoulaki (1999, 298–306) on processions. In the 330s BCE, the Athenian statesman Lycurgus initiated a program to provide new precious metal vessels and jewelry to adorn the kanephoroi in the Panathenaia (Parker 1996, 244–45).

41. E.g. Palatine Anthology 6.269 (dedication to Artemis by Arista her attendant) and 16.100 (epigram on the resemblance between a statue of Lysimachos and Herakles). Cf. the fourth- or third century BCE dedication from Athens (inscribed on a marble stele) by a woman named Athenagora of a sculpted or painted representation of her own face (prosôpon) to Aphrodite (Meritt 1941, 60, no. 24 and van Straten 1981, 115, no. 4.1).

42. For a synopsis of the literary sources, see Marcadé (1957, 119–20). For Phryne as the dedicator, see Athenaeus 13.591b (Eros statue only) and Strabo 9.2.25 (Phryne called Glykera). Alciphron, in his fictional letter from Phryne to Praxiteles (4.1), makes Praxiteles the dedicator (discussed by Rosenmeyer [2001]). Pausanias (9.27.3–5) does not name the dedicator of the statues, but the story (1.20.1) about Phryne's trick to get Praxiteles to reveal his favorite works implies that she dedicated the Eros. Plutarch (Moralia 753f) calls Phryne the sunnaos of Eros: the placement of her portrait next to a divine image in a temple would have implied deification in the late Hellenistic and Roman periods, but not yet in the fourth century BCE (Nock 1972).

43. On Phryne as votary of Aphrodite, see Athenaeus 13.590d–e, discussed by Havelock (1995, 42–47). Of course, this could also work the other way around: the portraits of Phryne at Delphi and at Thespiae may have been viewed in retrospect as evidence of her resemblance to Aphrodite, and as support for the story that she modeled for Praxiteles' Knidian Aphrodite.

44. I would like to thank the organizers of the Madison conference "Prostitution in the Ancient World," Laura McClure and Christopher A. Faraone, for their generous help and warm hospitality. They and several participants in the conference, including Patricia Rosenmeyer, contributed toward the improvement of the published version of this paper, as did Eran Lupu, Aileen Ajootian, and Chris Pfaff.

Sacred Prostitution in the First Person

STEPHANIE L. BUDIN

This paper reconsiders the evidence for sacred prostitution in the classical corpus. It takes as a departure point the recent Near Eastern scholarship that shows that sacred prostitution never existed in the ancient Near East but rather was a fabricated idea based on allegations made by classical authors and mistranslation by scholars of cultic terminology. Rather than seeing sacred prostitution as an historical reality, I consider Biblical scholar Robert Oden's suggestion that it was an accusation, a literary motif used by one society to denigrate another, and test this suggestion against the notion of firsthand accounts of sacred prostitution, whereby a society recounts the existence of sacred prostitution in its own time and culture; thus, sacred prostitution in the "first person." If a society freely claims sacred prostitution as one of its own cultural institutions, the hypothesis of accusatorial, literary motif must be abandoned. However, as the evidence will show, there are, in fact, no known firsthand accounts of sacred prostitution in the ancient world. Those apparent examples from the classical world are either misinterpretations of classical authors, or, as with the Near Eastern evidence, mistranslations of certain terminology. In the end the evidence supports the idea that sacred prostitution never existed in the ancient world.

What Is "Sacred Prostitution"?

As it is currently understood, sacred prostitution in the ancient world was the sale of a person's body for sexual purposes where some portion (if not all) of the money received for this transaction went to a deity. In the Near East, this deity is usually understood to have been Ishtar or Astarte; in Greece, it was Aphrodite. At least three separate types of sacred prostitution are recorded in the classical sources. One is a onetime prostitution or sale of virginity in honor of a goddess. Our earliest testimonial of such a practice is recorded in Herodotus 1.199:

The most shameful of the customs among the Babylonians is this: it is necessary for every local woman to sit in the sanctuary of Aphrodite once in her life and "mingle" with a foreign man. But many, thinking highly of themselves because of their wealth do not deign to interact with the others, and they set themselves before the sanctuary, having arrived in covered chariots, with many a maidservant in tow. But the majority act thus: in the *temenos* of Aphrodite many women sit wearing a garland of string about their heads. Some come forward, others remain in the background. The foreigners have straight passages in all directions through the women, by which they might pass through and make their selection. Once a woman sits there, she may not return home until one of the foreigners tossing money into her lap should mingle with her outside the sanctuary. And in tossing he must say thus: "I summon you by the goddess Mylitta." The Assyrians call Aphrodite Mylitta. The money may be of any amount; it may not be rejected: it is not their custom, for the money is sacred. The woman follows the first man who tossed her money; she may not reject anyone. When she should have mingled, having discharged her obligation to the goddess, she leaves for home, and after this time no one might take her, no matter how great the gifts might be that he offers. Those who are attractive and tall go home quickly, while those who are homely wait about a long time, being unable to fulfill the law—some among them wait about for three or four years. And in some areas of Cyprus the custom is similar to this.[1]

A second type of sacred prostitution involves women (and men?) who are professional prostitutes and who are owned by a deity or a deity's sanctuary. Thus Strabo (6.2.6) says of Eryx: "Inhabited also is Eryx, a lofty hill, possessing a highly honored sanctuary of Aphrodite in times of old replete with female hierodules whom many from Sicily and elsewhere dedicated in fulfillment of vows. But now, just as the settlement itself so too the sanctuary is depopulated, and most of the holy bodies have left."[2] Finally, there are references to a temporary type of sacred prostitution, where the women (and men?) are either prostitutes for a limited period of time before being married or only prostitute themselves during certain rituals. An example of the former comes from Strabo (11.14.16): "The Medes and Armenians very much revere all the sacred customs of the Persians, and the Armenians especially those of [the goddess] Anaïtis, dedicating temples in various regions and especially Akilisenê. There they dedicate male and female slaves. This is nothing remarkable, but the most illustrious people dedicate even maiden daughters, for whom it is the custom, having been prostitutes (*kataporneutheisais*) a long time in the goddess's presence, to be given marriage, no one disdaining to live with them in marriage." An example of the latter is recorded in Lucian (*De dea Syria* 6): "[The women of Byblos] shave their heads, as do the Egyptians when Apis dies. The women who refuse to shave pay this penalty: for a single day they stand offering their beauty for sale. The market, however, is open to foreigners only and the payment becomes an offering to Aphrodite."[3]

Theories beyond merely the economic one have come to be associated with the concept of sacred prostitution, theories often involving notions of fertility or a sacred marriage. Thus wrote McKenzie in his study of sacred prostitution in the Bible: "The practice of prostitution in the ancient Near East seems to have been under no moral censure whatever and was common. A peculiar feature of the Mesopotamian and Canaanite culture was ritual prostitution. To the temple of the goddess of fertility (Inanna, Ishtar, Astarte) were attached bordellos served by consecrated women who represented the goddess, the female principle of fertility" (1965, 700). Nevertheless, the simplest definition of sacred prostitution which I use here is the economic one whereby a deity would receive the money paid to buy or rent the prostitute's body.

The Nature of the Evidence

The evidence for sacred prostitution can be divided into two separate categories—direct references to the institution in the classical corpus and implied references in the Near Eastern corpus. The direct, classical references, like the examples above, unambiguously refer to women who sell their bodies for sex, who are either "sacred' or who hand over the money they earn to a deity. The words used to describe them are *hetairai* (courtesans), *scorta* (whores), and *kataporneuo* (to prostitute). In short, their occupation(s) are expressed clearly in the texts.

The implied references in the Near Eastern corpus are more difficult to analyze, as the claims to the existence of sacred prostitutes depend on the translation of words that are not as blatant as *hetaira*. The individuals most commonly referred to as sacred prostitutes are the *qedeš* and *qedešah* of the Bible; in the cuneiform corpus female functionaries identified as sacred prostitutes include the *ēntum, nadītum, qadištum, ištarītum, kulmašītum,* and the *kezertu* and male functionaries so labeled are the *kalbu, assinnu kurgarru,* and *kulu'u* (Hooks 1985, 3). In short, almost every recognizable female cult functionary in Mesopotamia has been branded as a sacred prostitute, including those priestesses whose masculine equivalents have *not* been recognized as having a sexual function (no one, for example, has ever accused the *en*-priest of prostitution). From here, it was a short step until, in the words of Beatrice Brooks, writing in 1941: "It was noticeable that a number of terms in Akkadian texts were arbitrarily translated, 'eunuch,' 'harlot,' 'whore,' 'hierodule,' or 'prostitute,' until it seemed that an improbable percent of the population must have been either secular or religious prostitutes of some sort" (Brooks 1941, 231 in Assante 1998, 5).

Reassessment of the Near Eastern Data

In his 1985 dissertation "Sacred Prostitution in Israel and the Ancient Near East," Stephen Hooks reconsidered the evidence for these various cult functionaries to ascertain if the terms designating them could be translated in such a way as to support the idea of sacred prostitution. What he discovered was that not a single reference to the functions or laws associated with these women or men in any way indicated a sexual component to their religious duties. Quite to the contrary, there were specific limits placed on their sexuality.

To offer only a couple of examples (the reader might look to Hooks [1985] and Roth in this volume for further reading): *"nadītum,"* translated as "sacred prostitute," literally means "woman who lies fallow," from the verb *"nadû,"* "of field 'fallow'; of building, city, region 'deserted, abandoned'"* (Black, George, and Postgate 2000, 230). The cult texts specify no sexual component to her duties. She is not allowed to bear children, but she is permitted to adopt a child, which strongly suggests that she is specifically not allowed to reproduce sexually. This is emphasized in the Law Code of Hammurabi 144–46, where the *nadītum* who marries is obliged to provide her husband with a second wife to bear him heirs. All of the available evidence concerning the functions of the *nadītum* show her to be a nonsexual(ized) individual, whose function actually seems to emphasize her chastity, even in marriage (Hooks 1985, 14–15).

Similar evidence appears in the case of the *qadištum*. While the functions and associations of this official changed over the long course of Mesopotamian history, two aspects of her office remained fairly constant. One is her association with the cult of the weather god Adad, at least in the Middle Babylonian and Assyrian periods. Her duties included performing purification rituals, singing with the *sanga* priest before the deity, and participating in sacrifices (Hooks 1985, 15; Westenholz 1989, 253–55). Second, she is strongly associated with childbirth and wet nursing. The *Atrahasis* legend states: "let the midwife rejoice in the house of the *qadištu*-woman where the pregnant wife gives birth" (Westenholz 1989, 252). Furthermore, the *qadištum* could marry, as is evident in the Middle Assyrian law (*MAL* A 40) which specifies that she might wear a veil if married, but she must not veil herself in public if unwed. Likewise, a legal training exercise records the case of a man who: "took a *qadištum* in from the street. Because of his love for her, he married her even though she was a *qadištu*-woman. This *qadištu*-woman took in a child from the street. At the breast with human milk [she nursed him]" (Westenholz 1989, 251). While the woman's status as "from the street" and the suggestion of low status conveyed by the phrase "even though she was a *qadištum*" were originally used as arguments that this woman was some manner of prostitute, it is now generally accepted that "from the street" means that the woman was without family and that the qualification "even though she was a *qadištum*" means she was not supposed to bear the man children on account of her office. In this instance, as in others, adoption was a common practice for the *qadištu*. Once again, the fact that this woman could marry but was not expected to bear children suggests her sexuality was strictly controlled, in sharp contrast to that of a prostitute, sacred or otherwise.

Hooks went through this process of analysis with every term in the Mesopotamian corpus and found only one functionary, the *kezertum*, whose duties include a reference to prostitution *(harīmūtu)*.[4] However, these cult functionaries were also married, and current research by Julia Assante is now bringing into question whether the word *"harīmtu"* itself should be translated as "prostitute" or, more likely, "single, fatherless woman" (1998, passim). It would appear, then, that there are no sacred prostitutes to be found in the cuneiform sources.

To date, the only word that still suggests a sacred-sexual function is the biblical *"qedeš"* (m.)/*"qedešah"* (f.). The triradicals q-d-š in Hebrew (and in most Semitic languages) usually refer to something that is "set apart," usually in the sense of "holy"; in the Bible they are often used to refer to God himself (Hooks 1985, 152–56). However, there are about eight places in the Bible where the term "*qedešah*" is used as an apparent synonym for the word "*zonah*," which refers to a woman who has un-regulated sex, either an adulteress or, more likely, a prostitute (see Bird in this volume).

This parallel usage is clearest in Genesis 38, when Judah encounters his daughter-in-law Tamar on the road. Not recognizing her, he takes her for a *zonah* and accepts her favors, pledging to send her a young goat in payment once he manages to get back home. Judah sends his servant to find the woman to offer her payment and the servant asks the men in the region if they have seen the *qedešah* who was at Enaim by the roadside. They reply that they have seen no *qedešah*. The parallel use here seems to imply that *zonah* and *qedešah* are roughly interchangeable terms that mean a "woman of the streets." This usage appears yet again in Deuteronomy 23:18-19 ("You shall not bring the hire of a whore [*zonah*] or the wages of a dog into the house of the Lord your God in payment for any vow; for both of these are an abomination to the Lord your God. There shall be no *qedešah* of the daughters of Israel, neither shall there be a *qedeš* of the sons of Israel"), in Hosea 4:14 ("I shall not punish your daughters when they play the harlot [*tiznenah*] nor your brides when they commit adultery; for they [the priests] themselves go apart with harlots [*hazzonôt*] and sacrifice with *qedešôt* [pl. of *qedešah*], and a people without understanding will come to ruin") and finally, with respect to males, in 2 Kings 23 ("And he broke down the houses of the *qedešîm* (pl. of *qedeš*) which were in the house of the Lord, where the women wove hangings for Asherah").[5] The fact that the *qedešôt* are present at sacrifices with the priests of Israel, and the fact that the radicals of the word refer to sacredness gave rise to the idea that a *qedeš/qedešah* was specifically a sacred prostitute, probably associated with the Canaanite cults of Astarte or Asherah.

Various theories have been put forth to explain the presence of the *qedešôt* in these texts, theories that maintain that they are sacred prostitutes, that they are votaries of unacceptable cults (especially condemned by the prophets), or that the meaning of the *q-d-š* radicals as something set apart for God ("holy") refers in this instance to something set apart as profane ("dirty")—thus, they are whores, but not sacred whores (Gruber 1986, passim).

There is little likelihood that these women and men were sacred prostitutes. There are no deities in either the Hebrew or Canaanite pantheons who are specifically sexual. Astarte, contrary to the later, classical opinions of her, was not a goddess of sex, nor was she sexual in her own persona. Likewise Asherah, here understood as her cognate Ugaritic Athirat, was pointedly married to the chief deity El. She was a sexual (as well as maternal) goddess, but her sexuality was of a distinctively regulated kind, a kind that stressed marriage and procreation (Budin 2002, 218–24).[6] As such, there are no deities in the Hebrew Bible to whom sacred prostitution can be attached, as might be argued it could be to Ishtar in the east or Aphrodite in the west. I think it possible that the terms *"qedeš"* and *"qedešah"* may have at one time referred to Canaanite cult functionaries who later were condemned by the Yahwistic cults of Israel. They then came to be redefined as prostitutes, as in the story of Judah and Tamar, possibly because prostitutes stood in the same place that the former functionaries did—before the temple. One might liken this to the term "streetwalker," which has no literal sexual connotations and could, in a literal sense, just as easily refer to a police officer who "walks the beat." This, however, is the topic of future research.

This very brief survey of the Near Eastern materials shows how little solid evidence exists for the practice of sacred prostitution. The conclusion that it is present in the Near Eastern texts can only be awkwardly derived by extremely circular reasoning. Having been told by the classical authors that sacred prostitution existed in the Near East, Biblical scholars and Assyriologists skewed their vocabulary so as to create sacred prostitutes (*nadītum, qadištum,* etc.). Once one piece of evidence was so "discovered," it was used to strengthen other pieces of so-called evidence. For example, in his 1966 essay "Tamar the Hierodule," Michael Astour "proved" that the definition of *"qedešah"* was "sacred prostitute" through analogy with the Mesopotamian term *"qadištum,"* forgetting, apparently, that it was on the basis of the Hebrew *qedešah* that the *qadištum* was originally identified as a sacred prostitute (1966, 191–92).

Reassessment of the Classical Data

The new data force a reconsideration of sacred prostitution in the ancient world. Up to the present day, the assumption has been that sacred prostitution was an aspect of Near Eastern religion, often associated with the cults of Ishtar and Astarte, which spread to those parts of the classical world that had close affinities with the Near East, especially Phoenicia. Thus the general belief in the sacred prostitutes of ancient Corinth, or Italian Locris, or Sicilian Eryx. However, when faced with the fact that sacred prostitution never existed in the Near East, we simply must reassess our opinions about its existence in the classical world. Certain inevitable questions come to the fore: if sacred prostitution did not exist in the Near East, did it nonetheless exist in the classical world? If not, what were Herodotus, Strabo, and even the early Church Fathers writing about? And, perhaps most importantly, what is the origin of our modern understanding of sacred prostitution?

It is Robert Oden, in his book *The Bible without Theology,* who may have hit on the beginnings of the answer to these questions. He suggests that sacred prostitution was, in fact, not an historical reality, but an accusation, the sort that one society makes against another so as to show off the "barbarity" and inferiority of that other group. Thus it falls into the same category as accusations of bestiality and baby-eating ([1987] 2000, 131–53).

It is an intriguing notion. It must be noted that a grand majority of sources for sacred prostitution in the ancient world claim that it occurred in a distant land and/or a distant time ("A long time ago in Eryx . . ."; "Way far away in Egypt . . ."). Our earliest evidence for sacred prostitution in the classical world—the writings of Herodotus (see above)— suggests as much, as do the writings of the church fathers.

However, there is one category of evidence that could undermine the plausibility of Oden's hypothesis—firsthand accounts of sacred prostitution. If the literature records an "us" committing barbaric acts, the accusation hypothesis can no longer really be considered tenable.

But, are there *any* firsthand accounts of sacred prostitution in the ancient repertoire? The recent scholarship argues against this notion in the Near East, but there are a number documents in the classical repertoire that, to this day, have been accepted as firsthand accounts.

The most famous of these is Pindar fragment 122, preserved in 13.573 e–13.574 b of Athenaeus's *Deipnosophistai,* written around 200 CE. It, plus Athenaeus's surrounding commentary, reads:

Athenaeus:
Even the private citizens vow that they will bring courtesans to the goddess once their prayers have been fulfilled. Such a custom belonging to the deity, Xenophon the Corinthian, going to Olympia for the games, himself vowed to bring the goddess courtesans upon his victory. And Pindar, first writing in his honor the *enkomion* that begins:
    "Praising a house thrice victorious at Olympia . . ."
later also sang the *skolion* at the sacred festival, in which, at the very beginning, he addressed the courtesans who joined in the sacrifice to Aphrodite when Xenophon was present and sacrificing. Thus he spoke:

Pindar:

> "O Mistress of Cyprus, here to your grove
> a hundred-limbed herd of grazing girls
> Xenophon has led, rejoicing in vows fulfilled."

Athenaeus: But the song itself begins:

Pindar:

> "Young ones welcoming many strangers,
> handmaids of Persuasion in wealthy Corinth,
> who burn amber tears, shoots of frankincense,
> often flying up to the heavenly mother of loves
> in thought, to Aphrodite.
> For you without blame she destined,
> O children, to cull the fruit of soft youth
> in amorous beds.
> With necessity all is lovely
>
> . . . .
>
> But I wonder what they will say of me,
> the masters of the isthmus, devising such a
> beginning for the honey-minded skolion,
> joining myself with common women.

Athenaeus:

For it is clear that in addressing himself to these courtesans he was concerned how the affair would appear to the Corinthians.

It certainly appears that Pindar is discussing sacred prostitution. The "grove" in question (*"alsos"* in Greek) is usually understood to be a sanctuary of Aphrodite, probably on Acrocorinth, or possibly that of Aphrodite Melanis outside the city walls. Xenophon claims to have "led" them there, much as one would a hecatomb or the first fruits to Demeter (*IG* 1^3 76.75). Thus we have come to understand this poem as a reference to sacred prostitution, the dedication to Aphrodite occurring at the sacrifice after the games, as Athenaeus tells it.

But there is a problem with this interpretation. Pindar himself refers to this poem as a *skolion,* a drinking song. *Skolia* are not sung in sanctuaries during "proper" religious rituals (just as one would not recite obscene limericks in church, especially if one were at the pulpit at the time); they are sung at drinking parties.

Furthermore, as Leslie Kurke has noted, in this poem Pindar makes a consistent practice of animalizing the women in question. They are a "hundred-limbed herd" (*hekatogguion*). They "graze" (*"phorbadon"*) (Kurke 1996, passim). It is perfectly reasonable to accept that the "grove of Aphrodite" in this instance refers not to a sanctuary (precluded by the nature of the piece), but the *andron*, the men's drinking room, where enough debauchery generally occurred to justify the euphemism "grove of Aphrodite." What is really happening in the poem, then? Xenophon, perhaps after his sacrifice of thanksgiving, had a huge party at his residence and invited twenty-five odd prostitutes for entertainment and revelry; Pindar wrote about Xenophon's "generosity" to his friends. There is prostitution involved, but not "sacred" prostitution. The prostitutes are not dedicated to Aphrodite as a permanent offering, and there is no evidence that the goddess receives any share of their pay.

Where, then, does the idea of "sacred" prostitution come into play here? Pindar *himself* does not tell us that the Corinthians made a practice of dedicating courtesans to Aphrodite. *Athenaeus*, writing in the third century CE, makes this statement, leading us to *interpret* Pindar's poem as referring to sacred prostitution.[7] It is not a fifth-century BCE primary source, but a third-century CE interpretive/contextual source. And, as over half a millennium separates the poem from Athenaeus, it really is not possible to consider Athenaeus as a primary source for the interpretation or contextualization of Pindar, much less of society and culture in fifth-century BCE Corinth. So, instead of a firsthand account by a fifth-century BCE poet, we are left with a third-century CE account of what occurred long ago in far away Corinth. Pindar's fragment must be removed from the list of firsthand accounts of sacred prostitution, leaving us with no primary evidence or first-person accounts from classical Greece.

The second two supposed firsthand accounts of sacred prostitution in the classical world are a pair of inscriptions from Roman Tralles in Caria, Turkey.[8] These two inscriptions were most recently published by F. B. Poljakov in his work *Die Inschriften von Tralleis und Nysa* (1989, nos. 6 and 7 with full bibliography). The first of the two (no. 6 in Poljakov), was inscribed on a small marble basis with a circular depression at the top for the *anathema* (Ramsay 1883, 276). Ramsay records that the item, then in the possession of one Mr. Purser, was from Aidin, probably originally from the sanctuary of Zeus Larasios (1883, 276; Robert 1970, 406). The text reads as follows: "Good Fortune. L. Aurelia Aimilia from an ancestry of concubines [*pallakidôn*] and those with unwashed feet, daughter of L. Aur. Secundus Seius,[9] having been a concubine [*pallakeusasa*] and according to an oracle. To Zeus."[10] The second inscription (no. 7 in Poljakov), also from Aidin, was discovered in a house on the slope of the plateau of Tralles, and, according to L. Robert, must have been dedicated at the same sanctuary (1970, 407). The text is: "Meltine Moscha,

Concubine [*pallakê*], of the mother Paulina, of Valerianus Philtate, who was a concubine [*pallakeusasês*] consecutively during two five-year periods [*pentaetêrisi*], from an ancestry of concubines [*pallakidôn*]. To Zeus." The critical word in both inscriptions is *"pallakê."* In the second, Meltine Moscha clearly states that she herself was a *pallakê* and that her mother was also a *pallakê* (*"pallakeusasês,"* aorist feminine participle in the genitive case). In the first text L. Aurelia Aimilia also claims to have set up her *anathema* after a period of *pallakê*-ship (*"pallakeusasa,"* aorist feminine participle in the nominative case). Both claim to come from "an ancestry of *pallakidôn"* (either *ek progonôn* or *apo genous).* The critical issue, then, is the appropriate definition of the term *"pallakê."*

When Ramsay published the first text in 1883, he took the term *"pallakê"* to mean "sacred prostitute," suggesting that Aurelia Aimilia "belonged to a family in which the ancient custom was retained that the women should in their youth be *hetairai* in the service of the temple . . . : she acted as a hierodoule like her ancestors in obedience to an order from the oracle" (1883, 276–77). Ramsay originally based his interpretation on his own belief in the practice of sacred prostitution in Asia Minor, as presented in two passages of Strabo, one referring to the sacred prostitutes of Comana on the Black Sea (12.3.36), and one referring to the Egyptian institution of the *palladê* (17.1.46) (see below). Believing that he had found evidence of sacred prostitutes in Anatolia and that the term *"pallakê"* might be used in connection with sacred prostitution, Ramsay concluded that Aurelia was a sacred prostitute as well. Robert accepted this interpretation, referring to the dedication as "émanant d'une prostituée sacrée" (1970, 406).

Based on the proposed definition of *"pallakê"* in the Aurelia Aimilia inscription, Robert imposed a similar meaning on the second inscription: "La mère et la fille ont rempli les mêmes fonctions sacrées. . . . J'entends que la prostitution s'exerçait seulement au moment de la fête pentaétérique de Zeus Larasios, quand la panégyrie faisait affluer les pélerins au sanctuaire" (1970, 407). Robert likens the sacred prostitution of Meltine and her mother (and, presumably, Aurelia?) to a specific style of sacred prostitution practiced in Byblos as recounted by Lucian (*De dea Syria* 6, see above). The implication would be that Meltine, Paulina, and Aurelia (?) were not long-term or quotidian sacred prostitutes, but that they merely prostituted themselves during isolated religious festivals, perhaps only occurring once every four or five years (*pentaetêrisi).*

Liddell and Scott clearly accepted the sacred prostitute definition, and gave "concubine for ritual purposes" as the first possible definition

of *"pallakis/pallakê"* in the *Greek-English Lexicon* and "of ritual prostitution" at the end, referring specifically to the first Tralles inscription. As
recently as 1992, MacLachlan (1992, 151) maintained this definition,
claiming that Aurelia "boasts that she became a temple-prostitute at the
command of an oracle, and that her female ancestors had done the
same." And Rebecca Anne Strong, in her 1997 dissertation "The Most
Shameful Practice: Temple Prostitution in the Ancient Greek World" offers a similar interpretation (169–71).

That the word *"pallakê/pallakis"* might denote a sacred prostitute in
these two inscriptions is highly unlikely. As mentioned above, Ramsay
originally based his interpretation on two passages of Strabo (17.1.46
and 12.3.36). In the first the word *"pallakê/palladê"* is used of an Egyptian
girl of high birth who is dedicated to Zeus until the "natural cleansing of
her body": "But for Zeus, whom they [the Egyptians] honor most, a
most beautiful maiden of most illustrious family serves as priestess,
[girls] whom the Greeks call *'pallades'*; and she 'concubines' [*pallakeue*]
herself, and has sex [*synestin*] with whomever she wishes until the natural cleansing of her body; and after her cleansing she is given to a man;
but before she is given, a rite of mourning is celebrated for her after the
time of her concubinage [*pallakeias*]." The word *"pallas/pallades"* is not
the same as *"pallakê/pallakai,"* although Strabo certainly tries to make it
appear so by using alternate forms of the word *"pallakeuein"* in this section and especially by combining the verbs *"pallakeuein"* and *"syneinai."*
But the word *"pallas"* itself refers to a "maiden-priestess" according to
Liddell and Scott, or at least to a younger cult functionary (*"pallax"*
means "young man," so *"pallas"* means "young female"?). As such, it
would be eminently plausible to offer a "nonsexualized" translation of
the passage as follows: "But for Zeus, whom they [the Egyptians] honor
most, a most beautiful maiden of most illustrious family serves as priestess, [girls] whom the Greeks call *'pallades'*; and she serves as a handmaiden and accompanies whomever/attends whatever [rites?] she
wishes until the natural cleansing of her body; and after her cleansing
she is given to a man/husband; but before she is given, a rite of mourning is celebrated for her after the time of her handmaiden service."

The priestess-hood Strabo is describing here may be either the Divine
Votaress, often held by the daughter of the High Priest of Amun; the
heneret—the female musicians of the temple; or the "Wife of Amun"
whose importance as a cult functionary increased dramatically during
the New Kingdom. The confusion of the *heneret* with prostitutes and/or
concubines was not peculiar to Strabo. According to Lesko, even

modern Egyptologists have identified these women, mistakenly, as "concubines of the god," probably in reference to their service to Amun in his role as ithyphallic fertility deity. As the role of these women was to please this god with their music and dancing, the assumption was that their service increased the god's fertility by way of divine sexual stimulation. Thus, the "stimulators" of the fertility god were, in a sense, his "concubines." However, as Lesko (2002) notes, the term *"heneret"* is consistent in its orthography and usage whether in the context of a god's or goddess's cult, or even a funeral. Thus, these functionaries are not specifically associated with Amun's sexual life, and the translation "(divine) concubine" is not accurate (Lesko 2002, "Women and Religion in the New Kingdom" section).

Traditionally, the "Wife of Amun" position belonged to either the sister or daughter of the Pharaoh himself, thus "most illustrious family." The title "Wife of Amun" could easily be translated into the Greek language and cultural understanding as "Concubine of Zeus," and several classical authors make frequent reference to "concubines of the god," by which they appear to mean the female royal cult functionaries (for example, there is a reference to their pyramids in Diodorus Siculus 1.47.1).[11] These extremely high-ranking priestesses certainly did not "concubine themselves and have sex with whomever they wished" but were reserved for god and husband, and they had children within the familial context (Teeter 1999, 25). If we assume that Strabo actually understood the function of the Wife of Amun, even if he was wrong about the age of the priestess, it may be preferable to consider the non-sexualized translation of this passage as the correct one and to suggest that the sexualization was imposed on it by later translators and editors.

Whichever of the above-mentioned cult functionaries Strabo was referring to, there is no reason to associate the Egyptian *pallades* with sacred prostitutes. None of the possible Egyptian referents were concubines or prostitutes: it is only later (classical or modern) commentators who mistakenly ascribe a sexual role to their functions. As the Egyptian *pallades* did not function as "sacred prostitutes," there is no reason to suggest that the Tralles *pallakai* did.

Ramsay considered a second passage from Strabo in his analysis of the inscription in which the geographer claimed that the city of Comana on the Black Sea, not far from Tralles, was also famous for its "sacred bodies" taken to mean sacred prostitutes (12.3.36): "And the inhabitants live luxuriously, and all their properties have vineyards. And a number of women earn their living from their bodies, the majority of whom are sacred. For indeed the city is like a little Corinth." There is no explicit use of the word *"pallakê"* here. By contrast, the comparison with Corinth would suggest that the word for "sacred prostitute" would be *"hetaira"* or possibly *"hierodoulos,"* as per Strabo's own reference to the city in this regard (8.6.20): "And the sanctuary of Aphrodite started out so rich that it possessed more than a thousand hierodule courtesans, whom both men and women dedicated to the deity. And because of these the city became populous and grew rich. For shipmasters easily overindulged, and thus the saying: 'Not for every man is the trip to Corinth.'" Furthermore, in contrast to the institution of sacred prostitution as it was understood to occur in Corinth, and so presumably Comana, the Tralles dedications associate the *pallakai* with Zeus, not Aphrodite.[12] Even if we assume that sacred prostitution existed in Comana, Strabo uses different terminology to describe it, and the deity associated with Tralles is not the same as the one associated with Comana. Thus, this Strabo passage does not make a good foil for the Tralles inscriptions, eliminating the second possible support for Ramsay's argument that the Tralles *pallakai* are sacred prostitutes.

In contrast to this one alleged case of the word *"pallakê"* meaning "sacred prostitute," all other references to it and its derivatives in the classical corpus are to some manner of nurse or handmaiden, as is evident in [Demosthenes] 59.122: "We have courtesans [*hetairai*] for pleasure, concubines [*pallakai*] to take care of our day-to-day bodily needs, and wives to bear us legitimate children and to be the loyal guardians of our households" (Blundell 1995, 121–22). Or it refers to a concubine or mistress, as was the case with Aspasia and Perikles. There are no inherent implications of prostitution, sacred or secular, in any use of this word so far known in the ancient Greek language. The Tralles inscriptions do not refer to sacred prostitution, and they must be eliminated from our list of firsthand accounts of the institution.

Conclusions

With the elimination of these inscriptions from our list of sources for sacred prostitution, we are left with *no* firsthand accounts of this practice in the classical repertoire. What we are left with is a heap of quotes from classical authors telling us how distant societies, the Babylonians, the Egyptians, the Lydians, the Phoenicians, the ancient Corinthians, practiced sacred prostitution. Oden's hypothesis is certainly supported by such data. But, I would go beyond Oden's hypothesis and argue that misrepresentation and confusion also had their parts to play in the rise of the sacred prostitution myth. The majority of our supposed documentation of sacred prostitution comes from Strabo, whose account of the Babylonian practice mirrors Herodotus', as his account of the practice in Corinth (8.6.20) seems dependent on a (mis-)understanding of Pindar. Perhaps Strabo was less than vigorous in checking his sources and thus repeated misinformation in his own work. Furthermore, as previously discussed in the section on the Egyptian *pallades*, there do appear to be places where translations and interpretations of Strabo have been over-sexualized, thus presenting so-called evidence of sacred prostitution where there in fact was none. The early Church Fathers, only too happy to have reasons to condemn their pagan predecessors, seized the opportunity to use this so-called evidence to condemn the heathens who sold their daughters' bodies in front of idols before being "civilized" and "saved" through Christian conversion. So did the element of accusation emerge.

In the end, we are confronted with some long-standing methodological problems that have plagued the study of sacred prostitution. One is the problem of defining primary sources. We have been far too blithe in accepting what classical authors have told us about far-off, long-gone societies without considering the actual evidence from those societies themselves. This is especially problematic in classical studies of ancient Near Eastern sacred prostitution, but can be just as daunting when seeing what classical authors, like Athenaeus, say about other classical authors, such as Pindar. A further, and far more pernicious, problem is that of circular reasoning. Much like the Assyriologists and Biblical scholars of early last century, many scholars are not only uncritically accepting of documents supposedly referring to sacred prostitution, but they are quick to put sacred prostitution into contexts where there really is no evidence for it, such as Ramsay and Liddell and Scott did with the Tralles inscriptions. Finally, there is the problem of parochialism. Sacred prostitution cannot truly be understood as a reality, an accusation, a literary topos, or a piece of propaganda, without considering all regions implicated in the debate and the full history of the problem across all disciplines. Only when Greek, Roman, Near Eastern, and Biblical scholarship are considered together do we really discover that sacred prostitution was not an historical reality, but a myth that came to take on a life of its own.

Notes

1. The translations throughout the essay from Herodotus's *Histories* are mine.

2. The translations throughout the essay from Strabo's *Geography* are mine.

3. Translation mine.

4. See also Gallery (1980) passim.

5. All translations from the RSV.

6. There is continued debate concerning the presence, identification, and interpretation of the Biblical *asherah*. Since the sacred prostitutes in question are associated with the Canaanite religion, it seems appropriate here to consider the Ugaritic goddess as a possible patroness in that cultic system.

7. That Athenaeus' account seems to agree with that of Strabo in chapter 8.6.20 of his *Geographies* may indicate an early misrepresentation of the poem, possibly devised by one of Pindar's Hellenistic biographers, such as Chameleon of Heraclea Pontica. As such, this interpretation may be as old as the third century BCE, but still well removed in time from Pindar himself.

8. For additional information on these inscriptions, see Budin (2003, passim).

9. Robert (1970, 406) has "[i] (?)-." The family name Seius is attested in the Roman prosopography, and is possibly of Etruscan origin. See Schulze (1904, 93).

10. Once again, probably Zeus Larasios specifically, to whom the city of Tralles was sacred. See Laumonier (1958, 505).

11. Because these women were specifically seen to have royal tombs, I suggest here that the confusion in terminology was with the "Wife of Amun" rather than the aforementioned *"heneret."*

12. As Rouse (1975) notes, such dedications are traditionally made to the deity whom the cult functionary served.

Legal and Moral Discourses on Prostitution

Free and Unfree Sexual Work

An Economic Analysis of Athenian Prostitution

EDWARD E. COHEN

"It's Greek to Me"—Difficulties in Defining Prostitution

Modern languages use the word "prostitution" (and its foreign equivalents) inexactly to cover a multitude of conflicting meanings denoting a variety of physical, commercial, and social arrangements.[1] Although scholars have long sought to differentiate commercial sex from other erotic arrangements, emphasizing factors like payment, promiscuity, and emotional attachment (or indifference), the defining line—if any—between modern prostitution and other forms of sexual exchange remains unclear:[2] even marriage has sometimes been characterized as "legal prostitution."[3] Ultimately, and in frustration, it is sometimes asserted that "the meaning of 'prostitution' is self-evident" (Pateman 1988, 195).

But for modern historians of ancient Greece there is little "self-evident" about the meaning of the two principal clusters of ancient Greek words relating to "prostitution"—those cognate to *"pernanai"* ("sell") and those cognate to *"hetairein"* ("be a companion").[4] Our comprehension of these terms is impeded by the limited number and nature of our sources, our imperfect knowledge of Athenian social and economic

95

institutions, and the absence of native informants who might illuminate nuances of usage and contexts of behavior. Although these generic difficulties constrict our understanding of virtually all ancient Hellenic institutions, "Athenian prostitution" provides yet a further exegetical challenge—the unusual complexity (noted by ancient sources) of Athenian attitudes to both sex and business. Sexually, in Plato's concise summary, "in other *poleis* erotic conventions are easy to understand and well defined, but at Athens they are *poikilos*"—"complex," "intricate," "many-hued" (*Symposium* 182a7–9).[5] Commercially, Athens was a thriving entrepreneurial megalopolis—in fact, in the fourth century the dominant commercial center of the eastern Mediterranean—but she nevertheless harbored a conservative side that objected to all profit-making endeavor,[6] including that relating to sex. Xenophon, for example, finds the commercialization of *erôs* no less disgusting than charging for education (*Memorabilia* 1.6.13).[7] But Athens was not monolithic, and such views had to coexist with the reality of a "city [that] lived entirely by cash transactions" (Humphreys 1978, 148), producing a culture "fraught with ambivalence, ambiguity and conflict" (D. Cohen 1991a, 21; cf. Larmour, Miller, and Platter 1998, 27) in which legislative disincentives to "citizen" prostitution paralleled the widespread, lawful purchase of sex from "citizen" prostitutes. Athenian commercial life was rife with a "multiplicity of narratives" (Dougherty 1996, 251), reflecting the discontinuities, contradictions and deviations that rendered the definition or explanation of few Athenian institutions "self-evident."[8]

But one aspect of Athenian prostitution *is* self-evident—the fact (but not the significance) of the dual use of the words *"pernanai"* (and cognates) and of *"hetairein"* (and cognates) for what in modern Western societies is a single, albeit intractably undefinable, concept of prostitution. This Greek binomialism reflects the Hellenic tendency to understand and to organize phenomena not (as we do) through definitional focus on a specific subject in isolation, but through contrast, preferably antithesis.[9] Where modern Western thought generally posits a broad spectrum of possibilities and seeks to differentiate a multitude of slightly varying entities,[10] ancient Greek assumed not a medley of separate forms, but only a counterpoised opposition, complementary alternatives occupying in mutual tension the entire relevant cognitive universe. For modern thinkers, opposites are mutually exclusive; for the Greeks, antitheses were complementary (and thus tended to be inclusive). Greek commercial institutions accordingly tend to derive their meaning from their binomial interrelationships with their putative opposites.[11] Thus, interest (*tokos*, literally "yield") is either "maritime" (*"nautikos"*) or "landed" (*"eggeios"*): there is no alternative.[12] Where Anglo-American law easily contrasts "real property" and "personal property" but still allows for items sharing certain characteristics of both ("fixtures"), for the Greeks all property is either "visible" (*"phanera ousia"*) or "invisible" (*"aphanês ousia"*):[13] even the differentiation between realty and personalty tends to be expressed through this antithesis.[14] And so it is not surprising that every manifestation of commercial sex had to be encompassed within the antithesis of *pernanai* ("sell"), and its cognates, and *hetairein* ("be a companion"), and its cognates.

Modern scholars have generally recognized the fundamental importance of this dualism to an understanding of Greek prostitution but have uniformly ignored the business context within which prostitution occurred and the cognitive processes of antithesis through which Athenians described this activity. Instead they have typically sought to differentiate the *hetairos (-a)* from the *pornos (-ê)*[15] by identifying, impressionistically, characteristics seemingly common to one term or the other. Some scholars accordingly argue that "in general" promiscuity is the key: a *pornos* is a man "who constantly sells his body to different men, whereas a *hetairos* has a more long-term relationship with one partner" (MacDowell 2000, 14); a *hetaira* engaged in relationships that were "not merely occasional" (Cantarella 1987, 50; cf. Dover 1984, 147). For other commentators, "emotional attitude" supposedly identifies a *pornos (-ê)* as "a common prostitute," while a *hetairos (-a)* is "nearer to 'mistress' than to 'prostitute'" (Dover [1978] 1989, 20–21; cf. Lentakis 1999, 162). But for most analysts, neither promiscuity nor affection but "status" has been the differentiating characteristic: social position is believed to separate the high-class *hetairos (-a)* from the street or brothel *pornos (-ê)*.[16] In fact, Greek literature is replete with tales of glamorous and brilliant women who allegedly made important contributions to Athenian civilization and politics, while supporting themselves magnificently by providing sexual services to important male leaders.[17] Yet many scholars reject outright—as mere myth and romanticization—the very concept of prostitutes of high status: the "refined hetaira" is "a fabrication of the male mind" (Keuls 1985, 199). For these classicists, *"hetaira"* and *"pornê"* are for the Greeks merely two words covering a single form of exploitation.[18] And for those scholars who (following Hesiod) see marriage as the functional equivalent of prostitution, the *hetaira* is an "ersatzfrau" (Reinsberg 1989, 87), indistinguishable in her nullity from a wife.[19] Even advocates of the idea that there is a clear differentiation between *"hetaira"* and *"pornê"* concede that "the distinction" between the two terms "is not always sharp" (MacDowell 2000, 14).

Comic writers actually seem to fuse the two categories. Anaxilas describes the same women indiscriminately as both *"hetairai"* and *"pornai,"* while Aristophanes conflates the grouping of *hetairai* and *pornoi* (frag. 22 [K-A], lines 1, 22, 31).[20] Athenian legislation prohibiting male prostitutes' participation in political life, instead of distinguishing or defining the groups, treats them as a couplet, applying the law explicitly, but without differentiation, to both *pornoi* and *hetairoi* (Aeschines 1.29). In court presentations, a single person is sometimes referred to indiscriminately in a single forensic speech by both terms.[21] The single word *"hetaira"* sometimes encompasses all aspects of female prostitution (from the most dependently debased to the most independently magnificent),[22] while the word *"pornê"* is occasionally used to describe a woman clearly in a long-time relationship (see Lysias 4.19; [Demosthenes] 59.30). Such inconsistencies strongly suggest the uselessness of an impressionistic search for distinguishing characteristics inherent in the specific terms, increasingly causing scholars to despair of identifying meaningful distinctions in the actual usage of words that seem often interchangeable.[23]

In contrast, modern discursive analysis avoids an exclusively philological approach, focusing instead on the antithetical nature of the two terms and finding the differentiation, in Kurke's words (paraphrasing Davidson), "constituted along the axis of gift- vs. commodity-exchange, identified with the *hetaira* and the *pornê* respectively."[24] But this approach also presents evidentiary difficulties. Dover, for example, in his detailed study of "popular morality," concludes that for the Greeks "submission in gratitude for gifts, services or help is not so different in kind from submission in return for an agreed fee" (1984, 152). For this reason, perhaps, Kurke's *hetaira* is sometimes a chameleon: "the pressure and anxieties of the male participants occasionally refashion her as a *pornê*" (1997, 145–46), and in certain contexts Kurke is even compelled to acknowledge *"hetaira* and *pornê* as interchangeable terms"* (1997, 219 n.110).[25]

Ultimately, however, whether unitary, binary or diverse—whether definable or impervious to definition, whether a commodity or a gift—prostitution involves payment for sex. And so, in what follows, I will explore the labor context in which Athenians provided erotic services. Philologically, my thesis is that since the Greeks did not consistently differentiate *"pernanai"* (and related terms) from *"hetairein"* (and related

terms), an author's choice between one or the other of these two group-
ings does not reflect an objective and consistent inherent distinction
between the two clusters. Rather since *"pornos"* and its cognates tended
to be derogatory, and *"hetairos"* euphemistic—reflective, at least in part,
of their differing economic functions (as set forth below)—actual usage
corresponded to the way a speaker wanted to characterize a person in
immediate context. Economically, my thesis is that certain baffling historical phenomena (such as the predilection of wool workers to "moon-
light" as prostitutes, the disclosure by the *phialai exeleutherikai* inscriptions that at Athens "women seem just as likely to have jobs as do men"
[Todd 1997, 122], and the insistence of male and female *hetairoi, -ai* on
working pursuant to written contract) reflect an obsessive Athenian
concern not with the inherent morality of an occupation like prostitution, but with the extent of a worker's freedom from another person's
control or supervision—in Greek terms, the relative degree to which a
working individual appears to be *eleutheros* (free) or *doulos (-ê)* (slave).

Work Ethics Governing the Sale of Sexual Services

In the modern world, prostitution is, of course, not "just another job":
contemporary societies in general reject commercial sex as morally de-
generate and humanly exploitative.[26] Labor laws deny sexual workers
rights available to others. Prostitutional arrangements are denied recognition as legitimate contracts of employment.[27] In most countries, prostitutes are even branded as criminals.[28] Modern scholars often insist that
prostitution likewise aroused Athenian antagonism or contempt[29]—
sometimes citing as evidence remarks by unrepresentative theorists opposed to all forms of commercial endeavor or erotic expression,[30] but
usually simply assuming the universality of negative attitudes toward
sellers of sex.[31] In fact, at Athens prostitution was lawful and pervasive
(see Xenophon *Memorabilia* 2.2.4, for example, which notes that prostitutes were available everywhere).[32] Lauded by comic poets as a democratic and ethically desirable alternative to other forms of nonmarital
sex (Eubulus frag. 67 and frag. 82 [K-A]; Philemon frag. 3 [K-A]), prostitution gained social legitimacy from its association with the goddess
Aphrodite,[33] who was believed to aid *hetairai* in securing wealthy clients and whose cult sites (outside Attica) sometimes offered "sacred
prostitutes."[34] The shrine of Aphrodite Pandemus, in Attica near the
acropolis,[35] was said to have been built from the proceeds of one of
Solon's innovations, the state's purchase and employment of female

slaves as prostitutes. Despite the doubtful historicity of this tale,[36] the laudatory connection of democracy's founder with the foundation of brothels does provide startling insight into a fourth-century Athens that treated prostitution as a " 'democratic' reform" (Kurke 1999, 199), "as an intrinsic element of the democracy" (Halperin 1990, 100). And through its "tax on prostitution" (pornikon telos), Athens—which never did restrict "victimless sexual conduct" (Wallace 1997, 151-52)[37]—was an active accessory to the sexual labors of its residents (Aeschines 1.119).[38] Even the city's goddess, Athena, titular deity of crafts, listed prostitutes among her benefactors (Harris 1995, 144-49), and a monument honoring a famed hetaira stood on the Athenian acropolis next to a statue of Aphrodite (Pausanias 1.23.2).

Another form of labor, however, did evoke moral outrage. Athenians uniformly disapproved of free persons engaging in work that required regular and repetitive service for a single employer on an ongoing basis over a continuing period—what we would term a "job." For free Athenians, a pervasive moral tenet was "the obligation to maintain an independence of occupation . . . and at all costs to avoid seeming to work in a 'slavish' way for another" (Fisher 1998a, 70).[39] In Aristotle's words, "the nature of the free man prevents his living under the control of another" (Rhetoric 1367a33).[40] Isocrates (14.48) equates hired employment (thêteia) with slavery (see also Aristotle Rhetoric 1367a30-32). Isaeus laments the free men, and Demosthenes the free women, compelled by a "lack of necessities" to labor for pay: free people "should be pitied" if economic necessity forces them into "slavish" (doulika) employment (Isaeus 5.39; see also Demosthenes 57.45 and Martini 1997, 49). Receipt of a salary (misthophoria) was the hallmark of a slave. When the Athenian state required coin testers and mint workers to perform services on an ongoing basis, legislation explicitly provided for the payment of misthophoriai to the skilled public slaves (dêmosioi) who supplied these services (and for their punishment in the event of absenteeism) (SEG 26.72, lines 49-55).[41] Even lucrative managerial positions were disdained by free persons: most supervisors accordingly were slaves,[42] even on large estates where high compensation would have been required to motivate free but highly skilled individuals (see Xenophon Oeconomicus 12.3). Thus, in Xenophon's Memorabilia (2.8), Socrates proposes permanent employment as an estate supervisor to Eutheros, an impoverished free man. Such epitropoi, Socrates notes, were well compensated (6) for even routine services (3). But Eutheros curtly rejects the suggestion: managing an employer's property was only appropriate for a slave (4).

Athenian morality, in short, focused on the structure of work relationships, and not on the actual nature of the labor undertaken. Confounding modern expectations, the same labor functions might be performed indiscriminately by slave workers or by free "foreign residents" ("*metics*") or by "citizens" ("*politai*").[43] (In fact, the shoes for the public slaves working at Eleusis were made by a cobbler who was a *politês*! [*IG* 2².1672.190; see also lines 70–71].) In the Athenian navy, *politai, metics* and slaves served together as crew members without differentiation of status or work assignment: a master and his slave even appear often to have been rowers on the same trireme.[44] Within Athenian households, free women worked alongside domestic slaves at many tasks.[45] Yet the willingness of Athenian "citizens" to do the same work as foreigners or slaves was accompanied by a scrupulous effort to avoid even the appearance of being "employed" at a job. Service outside the Athenian household by free persons was usually for a single specific task or for a limited period of time and seldom exclusive to a single employer: we typically encounter Athenian businessmen working on their own for a variety of customers, or agents undertaking a limited task for an individual client.[46] Even slaves attempted to avoid the appearance of "slavish employment": the Athenian institution of "servants living independently" ("*douloi khôris oikountes*") permitted unfree persons to conduct their own businesses, establish their own households, and sometimes even to own their own slaves[47]—without much contact with, and most importantly, virtually without supervision from, their owners.[48] The presence, or absence, of supervision and control was a critical, perhaps the central, factor in Athenian evaluation of work situations.

Weaving the Web of Dependence

Athenian aversion to the dependence inherent in salaried employment meant that in principal providing sex in brothels was appropriate only for slaves. In actual practice, numerous opportunities for self-employment of free persons in craft or trade,[49] and the wide availability of paid public positions,[50] left only slaves (and family members) as potential employees for the many Athenian businesses (workshops, stores, brothels, banks, and numerous other *ergasiai*) that needed the labor of individuals over a continuing period of time.[51] "Nowhere in the sources do we hear of private establishments employing a staff of hired workers as their normal operation" (Finley 1981, 262–63 n.6). Athenians assumed, correctly, that persons performing repetitive functions in a commercial context—whether bank staff[52] or sexual workers—were likely to be slaves.[53] At Kolonos Agoraios, the site of Athens' incipient version of a labor market,[54] *douloi* constituted virtually all of those standing for hire (Pherecrates frag. 142 [K-A]).[55]

Most slaves, however, worked "at home," that is, within the household *(oikos)* with which virtually all persons at Athens, both free and unfree, were affiliated (Aristotle *Politics* 1253b6-7). As an entity encompassing the physical attributes of a residence, the complement of members now (or in some cases previously) living in that residence, and the assets and business activities relating to those members,[56] the *oikos* was the physical location of virtually all retail establishments, workshops, and craft and trade activities (see Demosthenes 47.56; Menander *Woman from Samos* 234-36; Pollux 1.80).[57] Even the permanent physical premises of an Athenian bank were usually coextensive with the personal residence of the *trapeza's* proprietor (Demosthenes 49.22; 52.8; 52.14). As a result, at Athens, " 'firm' and private household" were, in Moses Finley's words, "one and the same" (1981, 69; cf. Plácido 1997),[58] and so, for those slaves working in brothels, their *oikos* was likely to be both their place of work and their residence.[59] Aeschines actually describes a single house that was used in turn as a business place and home by a doctor, smith, fuller, and carpenter and also as a brothel (1.124; cf. Herodas 2.36 with Cunningham 1971, 88).

Substantial ancient evidence shows that "the prostitution of slaves was paradigmatically based in brothels" *(porneia)* (Flemming 1999, 43; cf. Davidson 1997, 90-99; Kapparis 1999, 228-29) and that *pornai*—in contrast to the predominantly free *hetairoi* and *hetairai* chronicled in the literary tradition[60]—were predominantly slaves *(doulai)*. Aeschines makes explicit the contrast between free *hetairoi* and slave *pornoi* when he urges Timarchus, charged with prostitution, to respond to the accusations not as a *pornos*, but as a prostitute who is a free man (1.123). Demosthenes warns that if Athenian juries do not uphold laws relating to citizenship, the work of *pornai* will fall to the daughters of "citizens," but that *hetairai* will be indistinguishable from (other) free women (59.113). Menander sets the *pornê* in direct antithesis to a free woman. The abject slave whore of *The Arbitration*, working for a *pornoboskos* who has hired her out for twelve drachmas, is a *pornê* (see lines 136-37, 430-31, and 646); in the *Woman from Samos*, the confident sex mate of the wealthy Demeas, is a free *hetaira* (cf. lines 30-31, 748-49).[61] For Menander there is a natural conflict between the free woman and the slave *pornê*: the slave is more manipulative and in her knavery knows no

shame (see, for example, *Arbitration* frag. 7). Herodas likewise assumes
that *pornai* are slaves: to protect his *pornai*, Battaros invokes a law dealing with *doulai* (2:30, 36–37, and 46–48). Indeed, the words *"pornê"* and
"doulê" occur together so commonly that a study by the Italian scholar
Citti has concluded that mention of the term *"pornê"* in ancient Greek
necessarily evokes the mental image of a *doulê:* the two words form
"una coppia nominale," "a verbal coupling" (1997, 92).[62] Thus the defendant in Lysias 4, seeking to have a woman give evidence under torture,
refers to her not merely as a "slave"[63] but as a "slave *pornê*" (in Greek
"doulê pornê" [4.19]). In fact, her characterization as a *"doulê"* is based
only on the defendant's characterization of her as a *pornê:* the plaintiff
insists that she is free (4.12 and 14), and no evidence (other than her
characterization as a *doulê*) suggests that she is enslaved. Theopompus,
the fourth-century historian, emphasizes the linkage between the two
terms in describing a certain Pythionike, a slave who had belonged to
three separate owners, and was therefore "thrice a *doulê* and thrice a
pornê" *("tri-doulon kai tri-pornon")* (Athenaeus 13.595a [= *FGrH* 115 F
253]). A scholiast explains a passage in Demosthenes by offering the example of *"douloi* and sons of *pornai"* (Dilts 1986, 274, Scholion 69). Libanius, in a rhetorical critique, brands Aeschines as an individual born
of a father who was a *doulos* and a mother who was a *pornê* (Foerster
1903–27, 8.301–2). And, as one might expect, the fullest examples of this
verbal combination are to be found in patristic works (see John Chrysostom, *PG* 59.165.23 and 63.554.12).

Within their brothels, Athenian prostitutes—like other slaves—
would have received instruction in the provision of sexual services.
Athenian society functioned through an enormous network of hundreds of distinct occupations, most unrelated to agriculture.[64] To maintain this diverse specialization in the many fields requiring knowledge
and skill *(tekhnai)* (see Xenophon *Oeconomicus* 1.1; Pollux 4.7 and 22)[65]—
handicraft, catering, and medicine, for example—*douloi* and *doulai* normally received substantial training,[66] vocational education that free
persons often lacked.[67] Slaves working in *trapezai* were taught the intri-
cacies of finance and accounting,[68] and slaves working as prostitutes
are known to have received specialized training, sometimes starting in
childhood.[69] Yet even the best educated and most highly skilled *douloi*
generally also performed domestic labor within the household.[70] Thus
slaves working as doctors or doctors' assistants are known to have devoted part of their time to household duties (Garlan 1988, 68; cf. Kudlien 1968; Joly 1969). (Aeschines, charging Timarchus with betraying his

free status by acting in a slavish fashion, specifically accuses him of combining work as a prostitute with a purported pursuit of training in medicine [1.40]).

This pattern of having more than one assigned task provides the context for a division of labor in which some female slaves worked as both prostitutes and wool workers.[71] Brothel prostitution and wool working were important Athenian businesses in which women's services were dominant. Female *pornai*, believed to be more numerous than male *pornoi* (Davidson 1997, 77),[72] typically worked under a senior woman who "knew how to run her business . . . and how to keep the women under strict control" (Kapparis 1999, 207; cf. Carey 1992, 94). Similarly wool working—"the characteristic area of feminine expertise normally cited by ancient authors" (Brock 1994, 338)[73]—was entirely dependent on female labor.[74] Although many free women were skilled in this craft and often supervised or even worked along with their slaves,[75] the actual production and servicing of textiles were almost entirely the work of unfree women.[76] Aristotle, in defending slavery as natural and necessary, focuses on this *tekhnê* and its slave workers: so long as shuttles could not spin by themselves, owners would have need for slaves (*Politics* 1253b33–54a1). Even under the sting of unwonted poverty, the Athenian Aristarchus only reluctantly put his free female dependents to work producing wool, and even then he himself refused personally to be involved in the labor (Xenophon *Memorabilia* 2.7.12). With good reason: because wool working was identified as a strictly female activity, a man so engaged was *ipso facto* marked as effeminate (see Midas [Athenaeus 516b], Sardanapalos [Diodorus Siculus 2.23], and Kallon [Diodorus Siculus 32.11).

Reflecting such factors as slaves' personal characteristics, owners' economic situations, and numerous other elements of chance and opportunity, the actual work assignments of unfree persons would have varied greatly. Many *pornai* would likely have had no involvement in textile work, and many wool workers, no involvement in commercial sex—but substantial evidence suggests that numerous female slaves functioned both as wool workers and as brothel prostitutes (Rodenwaldt 1932; Keuls 1983; Neils 2000).[77] Athena (as goddess of female crafts) joined Aphrodite in receiving the real-life offerings of Athenian prostitutes[78]—and was portrayed in literature as the recipient of dedications by wool workers who were also working as or hoped to work as prostitutes. Surviving Athenian vases offer a number of scenes linking female erotic and textile labor, including depictions of young men bringing gifts or moneybags to women working with wool[79] and scenes of women with names appropriate to prostitutes (Aphrodisia and Obole) putting aside their wool while male customers approach or wait.[80] A water jar depicts a naked woman spinning wool before a clothed seated woman, "clearly the madam who forces her *pornai* to work during the off hours" (Neils 2000, 209).[81] Material culture provides the evidence of more than a hundred loom weights found (along with hundreds of drinking vessels) in virtually every room in the classical levels of a labyrinthine building that has been identified as a *porneion*.[82]

This involvement of individual women in both erotic and wool-working commerce explains a series of dedications that have baffled scholars. The *phialai exeleutherikai* tablets—our prime source of information on the manumission of Athenian slaves—document the freeing (in the 320s) of approximately 375 slaves,[83] each of whom offers a hundred-drachma silver bowl *(phialê)* after his or her acquittal in formalistic (i.e., fictitious) actions *(dikai apostasiou)* brought by exowners.[84] In these inscriptions, occupations are recorded for 52 of 86 exslaves who are probably or certainly female, but for only 62 of 110 probable or certain males.[85] For scholars accustomed to thinking of Athenian women, and especially slave women, as hapless objects of male domination locked away in the interior of society, consigned to ignorance and reserved for exploitation,[86] this information—showing manumitted slave women as more likely than slave men to have had an occupation—is "most surprising" and "too straightforward an inference" (Todd 1997, 122). As a result, scholars have resorted to a "corrective approach" in an effort to make the ancient evidence conform to modern expectation.[87] Todd dismisses the testimony of the *phialai exeleutherikai* as an "illusion" (1997, 122). Rosivach (1989), noting that a majority (29) of the 52 working women are designated as *talasiourgoi* ("wool workers"), finds a simple solution: the standard Liddell-Scott *Greek-English Lexicon* must be corrected. He insists that the word *"talasiourgos"* here does not mean "wool worker" as the lexicon (1996 supplement) claims:[88] with a "diagnostic reading," *"talasiourgos"* actually means "housewife."[89] So "corrected," the inscriptions would report just the opposite of the actual texts: relatively few Athenian freedwomen would have had occupations. With this alteration, however, the inscriptions would now present what even Todd sees as "a curious omission" the absence of "female household slaves" (Todd 1997, 23).

But scholars need not manufacture such a "curious omission" through "corrective" mutilation of the texts. In my opinion, the "plain meaning" of the inscriptions—interpreted in the context of the linkage between prostitution and wool working—makes good sense without "corrective" interpretation:

Researchers have long conjectured that slaves obtaining manumission at Athens were likely to be disproportionately those who had special access to a free person's support and/or possessed skills that produced relatively high compensation—a portion of which (termed *apophora*) slaves often retained,[90] thus providing funds for the purchase of a slave's freedom or, at the least, offering a source of repayment of monies advanced by others (see Faraguna 1999, 72 and Finley 1985, 104–5).[91] But enslaved wool workers would have had virtually no opportunity to earn or accumulate personal funds or to gain access to possible benefactors: they generally toiled in anonymity at repetitive chores in a supervised process requiring the joint labor of a number of workers,[92] often producing goods intended not for the market (and the generation of cash) but for the *oikos* itself (Rosivach 1989, 366–67).[93] Lucian (*Dialogues of the Courtesans* 6) contrasts the meager wages of wool work with the anticipated prosperity of prostitution, while elegiac literature records the complaints of women relegated to the famished poverty of wool work (see *Palatine Anthology* 6.283–85). Prostitutes, however, might earn enormous fees, and were (obviously) in a position to establish a "personal relationship" with the payers of those fees. Loomis, in an exhaustive survey of prices charged for the services of ancient Greek prostitutes (1998, 166–85, 309–12, 334–35, and passim),[94] has shown that "a high-class and socially acceptable" prostitute might earn as much as a thousand drachmas in a single extended liaison (perhaps fifty to one hundred thousand dollars in purchasing power equivalence),[95] and not less than two drachmas per individual servicing, "depending on her age, attractions, mood at the moment, and the resources and urgency of the customer" (1998, 185). Typical fees for an "average prostitute" were not less than one-half drachma per act (185). Surviving material even explains in detail how Neaira, an alleged slave prostitute, bought her freedom through a combination of her own earnings and assistance from several of her "lovers," who had developed an emotional relationship with her.[96] This contrast between the impoverished wool worker and the potentially high-earning prostitute (and the linkage between the two pursuits) is confirmed by a number of Hellenistic epigrams that describe dedications to Athena or to Aphrodite offered by women aspiring to abandon the impoverishment of wool working in order to devote themselves entirely to sexual commerce.[97]

In a clever ditty by Nicarchus, a woman has placed spindles and other equipment connected with Athena on a raging fire. For this woman, wool working is an impoverished ("famished") occupation appropriate only for "base females" ("*kakôn gynaikôn*" [*Palatine Anthology* 6.285.5–6]). In contrast, prostitution offers a "pleasured life" ("*terpnon bioton*") of festivals, revelry, and music in which Aphrodite, freeing her from wool working, and "sharing in the [new] labor," will be her 10-percent partner (lines 7–10). In another epigram, a woman named Bitto dedicates to Athena the textile apparatus of the work she hates, "the tools of impoverished enterprise": emulating Paris, she's casting her vote for Aphrodite's labor instead (*Palatine Anthology* 6.48). Yet another woman—whose sexual labors have reaped finery through lucrative assignations—would choose now entirely to abandon wool working (6.284), an option not available to the subject of a further epigram, an aging female who in contrast has had to abandon lucrative prostitution and is now left only with the impoverished yields of wool working (6.283).

The unexpurgated texts of the *phialai exeleutherikai*—showing that "women seem just as likely to have jobs as do men" (Todd 1997, 122)—thus make good sense: slaves working in wool can be properly described as *talasiourgoi* ("wool workers"). They need not be denominated by modern scholars as "housewives." Earnings from prostitution—and useful relationships developed from this métier—would have provided a financial and/or personal mechanism for obtaining freedom, and slaves who commanded earnings from prostitution would likely have figured prominently among those gaining manumission. Not surprisingly, therefore, some of the freed slaves carry names that are typical Athenian designations for sex workers—Glykera ("Sweetie") and Malthake ("Softie"). Others—like the musicians (a flute girl, a harpist) who "entertained" at male social functions—are recorded under callings that are known frequently to have been coupled with the provision of sexual services.[98] But, most explicitly, the *phialai exeleutherikai* inscriptions record a relatively large number of freed persons (both male and female) who are termed *"pais"* (or *"paidion,"* diminutive of *pais*). (Of the 185 persons for whom occupations are recorded, 16 are so denominated, of whom 3 are definitely female, 2 certainly male, and the others of uncertain sex.) This term—although often carrying the meaning of "slave" or "child"—frequently refers to persons engaging in sexual activity at the behest of an importuning male who offers something of value.[99] Appearing in a formulaic list of occupations, "prostitute"—as

Todd (1997, 123) notes—is an appropriate possible translation. In contrast, neither *pornai (-oi)* or *hetairai (-oi)* would be suitable designations for these newly liberated persons: *pornê (-os)*—as we have seen— was a virtual synonym for "slave," an incongruous appellation for a dedication attesting to free status; *hetaira (-os)*—as we shall see—was a term scrupulously trumpeted as the calling of a free person, a perhaps overly ostentatious honorific for a formerly enslaved worker. Of course, many females are recorded in these inscriptions as *talasiourgoi*. Were they women whose identity was primarily as wool workers but whose freedom was owed to the wages of sex, or were they persons now retired from compensated sexual activity? Or were some of these *talasiourgoi* part of the small minority of highly skilled (and possibly highly compensated) specialist producers of exquisite textile products crafted to meet market demand?[100] We will never know. The extraordinarily elliptical language of the inscriptions, the highly fragmentary state in which they have survived, our ignorance of their social and legal context leave us unable to determine even whether the choice of occupation attributed to each worker was made by the newly freed persons, by their former owners, by some *polis* official—or perhaps even by the stone cutter(s).[101] Yet these lists of *paides* and *talasiourgoi* and other freed persons, evidence for a process of manumission otherwise unknown, do offer a context for the situations portrayed in epigrammatic literature. They help explain a paradox otherwise inexplicable, a mystery raised by the anonymous poet of the *Palatine Anthology* and, I think, answered by our discussion—of how Philainion, the wool worker, made herself a gray coat sleeping in the embrace of Agamedes (6.284).

"Free" Love: Market Morality and Sexual Contracts

Antagonism to the idea of working under a master should not be confused with antipathy to labor itself.[102] Numerous Athenians were self-employed in a great variety of pursuits. According to Xenophon, in addition to farmers, the Athenian Assembly was full of clothes cleaners, leather workers, metalworkers, craftsmen, traders and merchants (*Memorabilia* 3.7.6).[103] Many free residents followed entrepreneurial pursuits (see Thompson 1983; Garnsey 1980),[104] and many others pursued specialized callings, including prostitution (Harris 2002).[105] Harris (2002, 70) has estimated that about half of all *politai* (perhaps ten thousand citizens) pursued nonagricultural work in hundreds of individual métiers. For extended relationships in all these areas, Athenian morality mandated clear manifestations of egalitarian independence of occupation. Sexual labor was no exception.

Free Athenian purveyors of *erôs* sought carefully to avoid all
suggestion of dependence, and sought to manifest their autonomy
through elaborate, sometimes seemingly recherché, mechanisms.[106]
Thus, among the *hetairoi* of Athens, contractual arrangements for sexual services—whether directly explicit, as in Lysias 3 (see above), or constructed with greater complexity, as in Hyperides 5 (see E. E. Cohen,
forthcoming)—were the norm. References to such contractual arrangements were so commonplace that the phrase "whoring under contract"
("*sungraphê*")—a usage popularized by a prominent *politês* who had
worked as a prostitute—had become idiomatic in local discourse (Aeschines 1.165). Requests were routinely anticipated in court proceedings
for written confirmation of commercial sexual acts (Aeschines 1.160).
Reminiscent of the special probative value given in Athenian legal actions to bankers' entries (see Gernet 1955, 176 n.2; Bogaert 1968, 382
n.461), Demosthenes attributes to these prostitutional contracts an evidentiary superiority to oral testimony or other possible forms of evidence (22.22–23; see De Brauw and Miner, 2004). As with written agreements for other commercial undertakings, contracts for sexual services
appear on occasion even to have been deposited for safeguarding with
third persons (Aeschines 1.165),[107] and prostitutional obligations, as was
the case with other contractual arrangements, were undertaken with a
panoply of witnesses to confirm the agreements (Aeschines 1.125).[108]

Even female prostitutes are known to have entered into elaborate
contractual commitments. In Plautus's *Asinaria,* an adaptation of a Hellenic original,[109] there is presented, in comic form but at considerable
length, a contract in writing (termed "*syngraphus,*" the Latin rendering
of the Greek "*sungraphê*"), providing for Philaenium, daughter of Cleareta, to spend her time exclusively with the Athenian Diabolus for a period of one year at a price of two thousand drachmas, a "gift" paid in
advance.[110] The contract contains extended provisions of humorous
paranoia—for example, Philaenium is not even to gaze upon another
man and must swear only by female deities. Similar Greek contractual
arrangements with courtesans are alluded to in a number of other Plautine comedies and in a work of Turpilius (who also seems often to have
adapted plays from Menander).[111] In Menander's own *Woman from
Samos,* the wealthy Athenian Demeas seeks in anger to end his "live-in"
relationship with the free *hetaira* Chrysis. But the property settlement

that he proposes (through which Chrysis will retain not only "her own property" but additional maidservants and other valuables [lines 381–82]) is suggestive of a detailed prior understanding. Similarly, Lucian's Philinna refuses to have sex with her lover after he violates their agreement ("contratto" [Sirugo 1995, 158, n.15]) on mutual intimate exclusivity (Dialogues 3.3). From legal sources we know directly of the complex financial arrangements made by a hetaira in Corinth with the Athenian Phrynion—and with Timanoridas the Corinthian, Eukrates of Leukas, and other of her "lovers" ([Demosthenes] 59.29–32). The same woman later, acting on her own behalf in a private arbitration proceeding at Athens, reached agreement with two Athenian patrons requiring mutual consent for any alteration in the terms governing allocations of property and obligations of maintenance undertaken in exchange for her provision of sexual services to both men (59. 45–46).

For prostitutes, however, formal contracts were not the sole indicia of a labor relationship compatible with the work ethics of free Athenians. Other manifestations included control over one's physical and familial surroundings, including the ownership of valuable personal property[112] (the antithesis of servile confinement in a brothel), the freedom to choose the clients with whom one associated (the antithesis of compulsory sexual submission to any would-be purchaser), the provision of reciprocated largess to one's lovers, the appearance of leisurely dedication to cultural and social activities,[113] and the pursuit of work not merely as an economic necessity but also as a mechanism of self-definition.[114]

Such signs of independence are found frequently in the Dialogues of the Courtesans of Lucian, comic vignettes adumbrating the life and values of the hetairai of the fourth century BCE (material preserved, most improbably, through the anachronistic tales of a Roman imperial writer).[115] These hetairai retain for themselves the option of accepting (or rejecting) individual customers, and they exercise control (sometimes ostentatiously) over their professional and personal surroundings. Often disdaining narrow considerations of economic gain (kerdos), on occasion they instead valorize humanistic concerns. In practice, their own access to valuable compensation is sometimes offset by excessively generous largess to their lovers. Within (because of ?) this congeries of values, Athenian hetairai assert the freedom to suffer the jealousies,[116] plot the vengeances,[117] and experience the triumphs and denigrations of erotic affection and sexual passion.[118]

To these courtesans, monetary incentives are often unpersuasive if acceptance is conditioned on acquiescence to male effronteries to their

persona: the element of self-definition central to the Hellenic conceptualization of free labor tends to preclude sacrifice of self-image
through nonreciprocal cash transactions. Thus Philinna—despite her
financial dependence on Diphilus—refuses to sleep with him after he
violates their understanding regarding mutual sexual exclusivity, re-
ducing Diphilus to tears of mortification, and leading her mother to
remind her of the proverb, "don't kill the golden goose!" (*Dialogues* 3.3).
Tryphaina insists that she would not have accepted an assignation had
she known that its overarching purpose was to make another woman
jealous (*Dialogues* 9.2). Hymnis, espousing Athenian concepts of human-
ism,[119] objects to the soldier Leontichus's boasting of his war crimes: a
bloody butcher and mutilator of the vanquished will not share her bed
even at double the usual rate (*Dialogues* 13.4). Rejecting lucrative relationships with wealthy would-be clients, Mousarion insists on giving
gifts to her lover, who is unable, or unwilling, to pay her anything (*Dialogues* 7.1 and 3).

Yet narrow, and sound, commercial calculations did govern the
actions of some of Lucian's *hetairai*. Pannychis, for example, is determined to accommodate a former lover newly returned with wealth
from war booty—but also seeks to retain her present patron who has already paid much but has promised much more (*Dialogues* 9.2). When
Charmides is unable readily to pay Philemation's suggested fee, she
"shuts him out" and receives Moskhion in his place (*Dialogues* 11.3). Although customers generally seem to have accepted the *hetaira*'s right to
bestow services as she (or he) wished (see, for example, *Dialogues of the
Courtesans* 9.5), a few clients did respond with indignation or even with
violence, sometimes to their own grave harm. Krokale, for example, refused even to see Dinomachus after his failure to pay her the daunting
sum of two talents, the suggested cost of an exclusive relationship.
Dinomachus in anger then broke down Krokale's outer door, and pro-
ceeded through her house to inflict life-threatening injuries on the
wealthy farmer Gorgos, a new client, with whom she had been drinking and dancing. The happy ending (from a prostitutional rights' perspective): Krokale escapes unharmed to a neighbor's home, but Dinomachus winds up dealing with a posse of citizens seeking his arrest
(*Dialogues* 15.1–2). While Krokale's experience is presumably fictitious,
the assault on Gorgos resembles the real-life experience of the male
prostitute Theodotus, who likewise escaped harm when Simon, a dismissed would-be lover whom he had come to dislike (Lysias 3.31), at-
tacked Theodotus and his new patron (6 and 12). In this case, however,

Theodotus, pursuant to a formal contractual commitment of sex for money, had actually received three hundred drachmas from Simon, but preferred the foreign travel and other enticements offered by Simon's wealthy rival (Lysias 3.22.). His opponent denies the existence, but not the plausibility, of any such contractual arrangement (Lysias 3.26).

Like the *oikoi* (households) through which other businesses were conducted, the households of Lucian's courtesans functioned dually as seats of home and of business—replete with servants expediting sales and services,[120] with mothers proffering advice and demands (see especially *Dialogues* 3, 6 and 7), and sometimes even with children about to be born (2). The *hetaira* (or her mother) was clearly in control, securely ensconced behind doors and gates,[121] barriers that could be closed to, or even on, rejected would-be customers/lovers. Myrtale's former lover, for example, is left weeping at his exclusion, unable to gain admittance to Myrtale's quarters—which are being paid for by another (wealthier) patron (*Dialogues* 14.1, 3).

Menander similarly portrays *hetairai* living in their own homes as self-assertive, confident, and prosperous. Thus the free *hetaira* Chrysis in Menander's *Woman from Samos* is presented as sumptuously garbed,[122] commanding personal servant(s) (373), and disposing of substantial personal possessions (381). She is so confident of her situation—correctly, as the play's dénouement demonstrates—that she is willing to offend her lover Demeas by pretending to have given birth to a child, seemingly by another man, and then to have kept the child without Demeas's consent—a manifestation of the considerable power that she yields within the household (lines 80ff.). Now upset with her for a further (mis)perceived outrage, Demeas threatens to deprive her of his financial support. Then, he claims, she will experience the life of an ordinary *hetaira* (390 and 392–94): working in town, attending parties, having to accept mere ten-drachma fees (perhaps five hundred to a thousand dollars calculated on purchasing power equivalence). Not so bad by modern Western standards, or even by Athenian. Demeas, however, adds a foreboding warning, devastating to a free Athenian (albeit a threat that for us reflects an ordinary, unremarkable aspect of earning a living): Chrysis would have to follow directions. "If she didn't do as instructed happily and quickly, she'd die of starvation" (394–95). But not to worry. It's only comedy—not real life—and the play has a happy, and (by Athenian standards) true-to-life ending: Chrysis remains Demeas's *hetaira*—presumably now more independent than ever before.[123]

The occupational ethics of a free Athenian prostitute, however, are perhaps displayed most compellingly in Xenophon's description of Socrates' meeting with the *hetaira* Theodote as "a woman of the sort who sleeps with men who are persuasive"—emphasizing her freedom of selection—whose livelihood comes from the benefactions of men who have become "friends" (*Memorabilia* 3.11), an indication of the extent to which her relationships have been elevated from the master/servant or customer/commodity variety to one in which she possesses the independence inherent in personalized reciprocity.[124] Socrates is awed by the domestic world she controls: like Chrysis, Theodote lives in luxurious surroundings, apparently with her mother, in a home furnished sumptuously in every way; she dresses and adorns herself consummately, and is accompanied by a retinue of finely outfitted and attractive maidservants (3.11.4–5). Exploring the sources of her prosperity, Socrates' queries ("do you own land? rental property? craftsmen?" [3.11.4]) assume that she herself might be a citizen *(politis)* whose possessions include real estate and slaves. When Theodote asserts total indifference to Socrates' efforts to help her increase her income from her "friends" through systematic pursuit of "fine and wealthy" benefactors (3.11.9), they each are playing appropriate roles. Xenophon, seeking to refute the charge that Socrates was a deleterious "destroyer" of the young (1.1.1 and 2.7.1), offers in these *Memorabilia* examples of how the sage was in fact a practical dispenser of sound ideas,[125] including business advice, such as the suggestions that brought prosperity to Aristarchus and his female relatives in the wool business. But Theodote in her turn is careful to manifest the values of "free" Athenian labor. She herself has no desire or capacity to implement Socrates' schemes to maximize profit (3.11.10), but she is willing to let *him* work for *her* (3.11.15). She spends her time posing for artists, forcing potential customers like Socrates and his friends to wait (3.11.2–3). Whatever the reality of her situation,[126] here Xenophon, as so often, presents a portrait of shimmering but unconfirmable verisimilitude, highly seasoned with Socratean irony: Theodote, providing services in a manner and context appropriate to a free person, is the reification of the Athenian *imaginaire* (self-image):[127] she works for her living but can plausibly claim that she does so to her own benefit and that of her "friends." By modern Western standards, she is at best a pretentious sexual worker earning a fine living from a dubious occupation, but in Athenian context she is a practitioner of a liberal profession, an erotic métier appropriate to a free person. For Athenians such independence was, morally, infinitely more commendable than the slavish conditions of brothel labor.

Notes

1. But "the disagreement on what constitutes prostitution" may be "merely a surface manifestation of a disagreement over the fundamental categories to be used in describing social activities" (Jaggar 1985, 349). A further difficulty: "prostitution" in one culture may describe an activity utterly different from the phenomenon evoked by the equivalent term in another society. Studies of "prostitution" in ancient Babylon, colonial Kenya, medieval Occitania, and modern Nepal suggest that "these comparable behavioral forms reflect incommensurable beliefs and values" (Shrage 1994, 100). Cf. White (1990, 10-21) and Karras (1996, 10).

2. See, for example, Flemming (1999, 38-39); Palmer and Humphrey (1990, 150); McGinn (1998c, 17-18); Bloch (1912, 7). Cf. Jaggar (1985) and Shrage (1994, 99-119).

3. See, for example, Wollstonecraft (1983, 247); Hamilton ([1909] 1981, 37); Goldman (1969, 179); Beauvoir (1974, 619).

4. For the etymology of "pernanai," see Benveniste (1973, 112); Chantraine ([1968-70] 1999, 888) defines porné as "franchement different (et plus péjorative) de hetaira." For "hetairein," see Chantraine ([1968-70] 1999, 380-81).

5. All translations are mine unless otherwise noted.

6. "[T]he trade of Athens [in the fifth century], its monetary commercialism, its naval policy, and its democratic tendencies . . . were hated by the oligarchic parties of Athens" (Popper 1950, 173).

7. For the causes and some manifestations of aristocratic disdain for commerce, including prostitution, see E. E. Cohen (1992, 4-8) and (2000, 186-91).

8. For the social and economic dissonance to be expected in dynamic and complex societies, see Keiser (1986); Rueschemeyer (1984) 134; Bourdieu (1977, 98).

9. On this dualistic opposition so central to Hellenic culture that it has been said to have "dominated Greek thought" (Garner 1987, 76), see Lloyd (1987, 15-85) and E. E. Cohen (1992, 46-52, 191-94).

10. For the present tendency "to divide each difficulty into as many parts as necessary the better to solve it," extolled by Descartes, see Lévi-Strauss and Eribon (1991, 112).

11. Differing contexts yield differing antitheses. As Davidson (1997, xxv) notes, "the Greeks often talked about the world in binary terms as polarized extremes . . . [but] the terms of the opposition might change all the time."

12. By modern Western criteria, attributions to one or the other category frequently seem arbitrary. A loan secured by land may be characterized as a "maritime" loan because its traits as a whole seem to a speaker to fit the "maritime" grouping rather than the "landed" category. See E. E. Cohen (1990); Lipsius ([1905-15] 1966, 721); Harrison (1968, 228 n.3); Korver (1934, 125-30).

13. Modern scholars have again been entirely unsuccessful in abstract efforts to find distinct qualities inherent in specific objects that would render

them predictably either "invisible" or "visible." See Gabrielsen (1986, esp. 101 n.7); Bongenaar (1933, 234–39); Koutorga (1859, 6–11); Schodorf (1905, 90ff.); Weiss (1923, 173, 464, and 491); Schuhl (1953).

14. Harpocration, s.v.: *"aphanês ousia kai phanera"*; Lysias frag. 79; Demosthenes 5.8.

15. *"Pornos"* (plural *"pornoi"*) and *"hetairos"* (plural *"hetairoi"*), Greek terms for male prostitutes, are paralleled by *"pornê"* (plural *"pornai"*) and *"hetaira"* (plural *"hetairai"*), Greek terms for female prostitutes.

16. Cf. Hauschild (1933, 7–9); Herter (1957, 1154 and 1181–82); Herter (1985, 83); Peschel (1987, 19–20); Harvey (1988, 249); Calame (1989, 103–4).

17. See, for example, Plato *Menexenus* 236b5; Xenophon *Oeconomicus* 3.14; Plutarch *Pericles* 24; Alciphron 4.19; Athenaeus 13. Cf. Brulé (2001, 230–31); Garrison (2000, 29 n.28); Mossé (1983, 63–66); Dimakis (1988); Henry (1985, passim).

18. See Just (1989, 5 and 141) who notes that all women other than "wives" or "potential wives" constitute a single group "open to free sexual exploitation." See also P. Brown (1990, 248–49) and Keuls (1985, 153–54 and 199–202).

19. Cf. Henry (1986, 147) who states that "The difference between wife and harlot is not absolute" and Davidson (1997, 125) who notes that "Hetaeras are closer to wives than (to) prostitutes." Hesiod assumes marriage to involve—to the male's potential detriment—an exchange of women's sexual services for economic benefits (*Works and Days* 373–75).

20. He uses *"hetairai"* at the beginning and end, but *"pornai"* in the middle. Aristophanes (*Wealth* 149–55) describes Corinthian *hetairai* and *pornai* as acting in exactly the same fashion.

21. See [Demosthenes] 48.53, 56 and Aeschines 1 passim. Cf. Demosthenes 22.56 and [Demosthenes] 59.116.

22. See, e.g., [Demosthenes] 59.122, where the term "encompasses all forms of prostitution . . . from expensive courtesans to common prostitutes established in brothels" (Kapparis 1999, 422–23).

23. Kapparis (1999, 408) and Davidson (1997, 74); regarding Greek-speaking areas of the Roman Empire, see Flemming (1999, 47).

24. Kurke (1999, 179). Cf. Kurke (1997, 145); Davidson (1994, 141–42; 1997, 117–27); Reinsberg (1989, 80–86).

25. Kurke is speaking here of their relation to "the sacralized public space identified with the Basilinna."

26. Some seventy percent of Americans believe that "prostitution involving adults" should be illegal (Gallup poll, 5/96). In a majority of European countries, "prostitution is seen as a moral evil, undermining the family and family values. . . . [A]ccording to this view the prostitute should not be penalized—she is the victim—but all other aspects of prostitution are considered criminal activities" (Wijers 1998, 73). The French Law on Internal Security (*loi sur la sécurité intérieure*), adopted in March 2003, now explicitly criminalizes "soliciting" (*"racolage"*).

27. Pateman (1988, 191); Richards (1982, 115, 121); Ericcson (1980, 335–66); McIntosh (1978, 54).

28. More than ninety thousand arrests are made in the United States annually under statutes prohibiting prostitution (and an additional indeterminable

number of prostitutes are apprehended under laws forbidding disorderly conduct or loitering). See Weitzer (2000, 159–65). For European prosecution of prostitution-related activities, see above, n. 26.

29. See, for example, Kapparis (1999, 5); Pierce (1997, 166); Davidson (1997, 89); Brock (1994, 338 and 341); D. Cohen (1991b, 179); Henry (1986); Seltman (1953, 115).

30. For philosophers' proposed constraints on sex, see Plato *Republic* 458d–61b and *Laws* 840d–41e and Aristotle *Politics* 1334b29–35b37, 1335b38–36a2. For traditional abhorrence of "money-making" activities, see E. E. Cohen (2000, 187–90) and Balot (2001, 22–43).

31. Irrelevant evidence is sometimes carelessly adduced, supposedly confirming negative Athenian attitudes toward prostitution. Thus, for example, Krenkel, in his encyclopedia article on prostitution in Greece and Rome (1988, 1293), claims that "prostitution . . . according to Plato (*Laws* 841a–e) . . . jeopardized familial ties, public health, morality and the birth of offspring required for maintaining the community." Yet Plato in this passage actually censures every manifestation of nonmarital sex as damaging to public welfare—but seems to accept "purchased" sex as the least harmful alternative to marriage, provided that it occur clandestinely (841d5–e2). Cf. Morrow (1993, 441).

32. Harrison (1968, 37) infers from the charges set forth in Aeschines 1 the existence of a *graphê hetairêseôs*, effectively prohibiting prostitution by male citizens. But there is no allusion in the speech to any such statute (despite Aeschines' invocation of a host of other proscriptions). Lipsius ([1905–15] 1966, 436) correctly dismisses the possibility of even an unenforced legal ban on prostitution.

33. "*Hetairai* in ancient Athens prayed and made offerings to their patron deity Aphrodite, just as wives and pregnant women worshipped Hera and Artemis respectively" (Neils 2000, 216). Cf. Thornton (1997, 152). At Corinth supplicants to Aphrodite actively sought prostitutes' help (Athenaeus 13.573c). On the perceived power of Aphrodite in human affairs ("les puissances de l'amour en Grèce antique"), see Calame (1996, 11–20).

34. On aid in obtaining customers, see Athenaeus 13.588c. On "sacred prostitution," see Wake (1932) and Legras (1997, 250–58), who (250 n.5) provides references to earlier literature; see also Beard and Henderson (1997); Lentakis (1998, 321–44); Kurke (1999, 220–46). In the last decade or so, many scholars have moved to a consensus that "sacred prostitution" is a confused, problematic, and probably mistaken modern construction. For a full bibliography, see in this volume the essays of Roth (for the Near East), Bird n. 1 (for the Hebrew Bible and more generally), and Budin passim.

35. For the temple of Athena Pandemus (located immediately below that of Athena Nike at the Propylaia), see Pausanias 1.22.3 and Beschi (1967–68); for Aphrodite's temple on the Sacred Way, see Travlos (1937) and *IG* 2^2.4570, 4574–85.

36. Athenaeus 13.569d–f (Philemon frag. 3 [K-A]) and Nicander of Colophon *FGrH* 271/2 F 9. *Pace* Herter (1985, 73) and Pellizer (1995, 9), most scholars dismiss the report as unfounded: see Halperin (1990, 100–101).

37. Attic law mandated the recognition of "whatever arrangements either party willingly agreed upon with the other" (Demosthenes 56.2). See also

Demosthenes 42.12, 47.77; Hypereides 5.13; Dinarchus 3.4; Plato *Symposium* 196c. For occasional limitations on other personal freedoms, see, however, Wallace (1993, 1994a, and 1994b).

38. Cf. Pollux 7.202, 9.29; Lentakis (1998, 130–54); Pirenne-Delforge (1994, 117). There was a similar tax at Cos (Reinach 1892; Khatzibasileiou 1981, 8.55–56).

39. See also Cartledge (1993, 148–49) and Fisher (1993).

40. Jameson (1997–78, 100) notes free persons' "reluctance to admit to the need of working for someone else." Cf. Humphreys ([1983] 1993, 10); Finley (1981, 122).

41. See Figueira (1998, 536–47); Alessandri (1984); Stumpf (1986). Cf. *IG* 2².1492.137 and *IG* 2².1388.61–62.

42. As employees, unfree labor fell into two categories: "management slaves" (*"epitropoi"*) and workers (*ergatai*): see [Aristotle] *Oeconomicus* A.5.1.

43. Osborne (1995, 30); Hopper (1979, 140); Finley (1981, 99); Ehrenberg (1962, 162, 183, and 185); Loomis (1998, 236–39). This concurrence is especially well-attested to in the construction trades: Randall (1953); Burford (1972); E. E. Cohen (2000, 134–35, 187).

44. See *IG* 1³.1032 and Thucydides 7.13.2, which together confirm that "slaves regularly formed a substantial proportion of the rowers on Athenian triremes, and their masters included fellow oarsmen" (Graham 1998, 110). Cf. Graham (1992) and Welwei (1974). See the discussion of Isocrates 8.48 in Burke (1992, 218).

45. See, for example, Ischomachus's wife at Xenophon *Oeconomicus* 7.6. The wife's role, however, was often essentially managerial: see E. E. Cohen (2000, 37–38).

46. For example, the maritime entrepreneur who introduces a client to the bank of Heraclides in Demosthenes 33.7; Agyrrhios who serves Pasion as a representative in litigational matters (Isocrates 17.31–32; cf. Stroud [1998, 22] and Strauss [1987, 142); Archestratus who provided the bond for Pasion (Isocrates 17.43); Stephanus's relationship with the banker Aristolochus at Demosthenes 45.64.

47. See E. E. Cohen (2000, 145–54); Hervagault and Mactoux (1974); Perotti (1974). For the banking *oikoi* of slaves and former slaves, see E. E. Cohen (1992, chap. 4).

48. The *douloi* Xenon, Euphron, Euphraios and Kallistratos—while still enslaved—as principals operated the largest bank in Athens, that of Pasion. Their only involvement with their owners appears to have been annual payment of lease obligations (Demosthenes 36.14, 43, 46, and 48). See also Meidas, a slave who ran a substantial perfume business but provided his owner with reports only monthly and again subject only to a fixed payment (Hyperides 5.9).

49. See my discussion below, pp. 108–9.

50. The Athenian state offered paid service in the armed forces and compensation for frequent jury duty and assembly meetings; for "incapacitated" *politai* of limited means, there were outright public grants ([Aristotle] *Constitution of the Athenians* 49.4). See Lysias 24.6 where an Athenian unable to work easily at his own business but too poor to buy a slave doesn't even consider the possibility of hiring a free man to work for him: instead he seeks public assistance.

51. For the complex commercialization of the fourth-century Athenian economy, see Shipton (1997). Cf. Theokharês (1983, 100–14); Gophas (1994); Kanellopoulos (1987, 19–22).

52. For example, in questioning whether collateral security had actually been delivered, a creditor would have assumed that a bank's workers would be exclusively servile (Demosthenes 49.51).

53. A few free persons—motivated by abject circumstance or financial incentives—might occasionally have accepted paid employment (see above p. 100).

54. Marx believed that the formation of a labor market necessarily meant the introduction of "wage slavery," a precursor to classical capitalism (1970–72, vol. 1, 170); cf. Lane (1991, 310–11). But this proposition is not confirmed by the continued dominance of the Athenian economy by household-based businesses primarily utilizing household members.

55. See also Fuks (1951, 171–73) and Garlan (1980, 8–9). The prime ancient Greek term for "slave" was *"doulos"* (masculine plural *"douloi,"* feminine singular *"doulê,"* feminine plural *"doulai"*). On the multiplicity of unfree statuses in ancient Greece, and the corresponding multitude of descriptive terms, see Gschnitzer (1964, 1283–1310); Carrière-Hervagault (1973, 45–79); Mactoux (1980, 21–124). Cf. Faraguna (1999, 58–59) and E. E. Cohen (1992, 74 n.63).

56. Although "the different senses of the word" can be studied separately (as MacDowell [1989] does)—and in context a particular aspect may be emphasized (as with the physical premises in Antiphon 2d.8)—the unique significance of the term lies in its denotation of an *entity*. For each of the separate notations of physical place, the human beings associated with that place, and assets of value belonging to those persons, Greek offers a plenitude of alternative terms, most particularly *"oikia"* for the physical house, *"klêros"* for the assets, and *"agkhisteia"* for a circle of related persons.

57. See Nevett (1999, 66–67, 88); Jameson (2002, 168–69); E. E. Cohen (2000, 42–43).

58. Identity of firm and household appears to have been widespread in antiquity: for the ancient Near East, see Silver (1995, 50–54).

59. Kapparis (1999, 228) notes that "prostitutes working in brothels lived on the premises"). Cf. Bettalli (1985); Jameson (1990, 185); Pesando (1987, 47–55).

60. "Ces hétaïres étaient en fait les seules femmes vraiment libres de l'Athènes classique" (Mossé 1983, 63). Cf. Klees (1998, 147 n.16).

61. On Chrysis's self-assured decision-making, see, for example, lines 137–45.

62. Citti sees the two terms as virtually synonymous: "uno dei due termini comportasse l'altro" (1997, 95). Cf. Marzi (1979, 29).

63. Only unfree persons were putatively subject to examination under torture in private disputes. But—despite much surviving rhetorical posturing—no slave is known to have actually given testimony under torture in private disputes. Todd (1990, 33–34) summarizes: "on forty-two occasions in the orators we find the challenge, either 'torture my slaves for evidence' or 'let me torture yours.' Forty times this challenge was flatly rejected; twice (Isocrates 17.15–16 and Demosthenes 37.42) it was accepted but not carried through." Various

explanations have been proffered for this pattern: see Gagarin (2001); Mirhady (2000); Allen (2000b, 365–66 n.14).

64. For a survey of "the extensive horizontal specialization in the Athenian economy," and the resultant profusion of discrete labor functions, see Harris (2002).

65. On prostitution as a *tekhnê*, see [Demosthenes] 59.18.

66. Cf. Xenophon *Oeconomicus* 7.41, 12.4; [Aristotle] *Oeconomicus* 1344a27–29 and passim. On the training of artisans and caterers, see, for example, Demosthenes 45.71. On medicine, see Klees (1998, 96–100) and Sigerist (1970, 74).

67. Aristarchus contrasts the vocationally useless "liberal education" of free persons with slaves' training in *tekhnai* (crafts or trades requiring knowledge and skill (Xenophon *Oeconomicus* 1.1; Pollux 4.7.22); his female relatives lack the knowledge and skills of slaves (*Memorabilia* 2.7.4).

68. With regard to the great *trapezitês* Phormion who entered banking as a slave, see Demosthenes 45.72. See also the slaves who as principals operated the largest bank in Athens (n. 48) above.

69. See, for example, [Demosthenes] 59.18, concerning Nicarete. Kapparis (1999, 207) comments: "she knew how to educate them to become commercially successful courtesans." See Alciphron 4 passim; Lucian *Dialogues of the Courtesans* 4.3 and 10.4. Cf. Vanoyeke (1990, 33–35).

70. Garlan (1988, 62) notes that "domestic slaves devoted part of their time" to "strictly productive work," although "slaves were, in most cases, simply general 'dogsbodies.'" Cf. Jameson (2002, 168–70).

71. In the modern world, prostitution is often a part-time pursuit: "in few cases are women and men engaged full-time . . . sex work is commonly just one of the multiple activities employed for generating income" (Kempadoo 1998, 3–4). Modern prostitutes often find additional employment in retail trade, office occupations, domestic service, and in street activities such as shoe-shining. Cf. Azize, Kempadoo, and Cordero (1996); Senior (1992); Kane (1993); Bolles (1992).

72. *Pornoi* generally provided sex in smallish individual rooms (*oikêmata*) accessible from the street (see Isaeus 6.19, Aeschines 1.74, and Athenaeus 220d), not in the imposing domestic establishments, where *pornai* are portrayed as gathered in large central halls for presentation to customers (Xenarchus frag. 4 [K-A] and Eubulus frags. 67 and 82 [K-A]).

73. Cf. Plato *Alcibiades* 126e, *Lysis* 208d–e, and *Laws* 805e–6a and Xenophon *Memorabilia* 3.9.11 and *Constitution of the Lacedaimonians* 1.3.

74. "Una delle attività di competenza esclusiva delle donne" (Faraguna 1999, 70). Market trade seems to have been centered in the *himatiopôlis agora* (Pollux 7.78); see Wycherley (1957, 200, no. 663 and 187–88, no. 614). Clothing for slaves seems to have been an important retail product (Bettalli 1982, 264 and 271–72).

75. Aristophanes *Frogs* 1349–51, *Lysistrata* 519–20, 536–37, 728–30, and *Clouds* 53–55; Plato *Republic* 455c; Xenophon *Oeconomicus* 7.6, 21, 36; Plutarch *Moralia* 830c (citing Crates the Cynic).

76. For dyeing, see Eupolis frag. 434 and Aristophanes, *Ecclesiazusae* 215. For weaving, see *SEG* 18.36 B2. For linen-working, see Aeschines 1.97, Alexis frag. 36. For sewing, see *IG* 2².1556.28, Antiphanes *Alestria* frags. 21–24, Jordan

(1985, n.72). For wool-working, see scenes on Attic vases (Webster 1973, chaps. 16 and 17). The best treatment of "l'importanza della mandopera servile nella manifattura tessile" is Faraguna (1999, 72–79). Cf. Jameson (1977–78, 134 n.63).

77. Davidson (1997, 89) summarizes: "a large group of women . . . were forced (or chose)" to work at both pursuits.

78. On Parthenon dedications to Athena from *hetairai*, see Harris (1995, 244–49). For Aphrodite as patron goddess of prostitutes, see n. 33 above.

79. See, for example: *ARV²* 101.3 (= Robert 1919, 125–29; 557.123; 795.100) and Heidelberg 64/5 (a kalpis by the Nausikaa Painter). Cf. *ARV²* 276.70, discussed in Meyer (1988). For other examples, see von Reden (1995, 206–9).

80. In the collection of Paul Zanker, Munich, Münzen und Medaillen AG, *Auktion* 51 (Basel 1975), discussed in Williams (1983, 96–97). Cf. *ARV²* 189.72.1632 and 275.50.

81. The vase is in Copenhagen (National Musuem 153 [= *ARV²* 1131.161] and Williams 1983, 96, fig. 7.4). Cf. *ARV²* 795.10294-7.

82. So-called Building Z located by the city wall at the Sacred Gate, in an area long identified as one of the red-light districts of ancient Athens. Among the remains was an amulet depicting Aphrodite Ourania riding a goat across the night sky. For the site, structure, excavation and contents of this building, see Lind (1988); Knigge (1988, esp. 88–94); Lentakis (1998, 64–65).

83. These documents have been published in *IG* 2².1553-78 and republished (in part) by Lewis in (1959) and (1968), who incorporates additional finds from the Athenian Agora excavations. See Kränzlein (1975) for a survey of scholarly work on these texts. For early treatments of the original nineteenth-century fragments, see Calderini ([1908] 1965, 424–34).

84. On the *dikê apostasiou*, see Klees (1998, 348–54) and Todd (1993, 190–92).

85. I follow calculations made by Todd, who produced, as he notes, "deliberately conservative figures" (1997, 121). For example, he disregards twelve *talasiourgoi* as being of "uncertain sex," even though five of the twelve have names that are typically feminine, and wool-working seems to have been an exclusively female pursuit (see above). As apparent confirmation of the undercounting by Todd of female *talasiourgoi*, there is not a single *talasiourgos* among the 110 slaves who (by Todd's reckoning) are "probably" or "certainly" male (1997, 121–22). Of the total of 375, Todd found 179 to be of "uncertain sex" (meaning that without regard to other possible indicia of sex, their names were not followed by the formulaic language *oikôn* [male]/*oikousa* [female] or *apophugôn* [male]/*apophugousa* [female]). (Many of these omissions, however, reflect the fragmentary nature of the surviving inscribed materials.)

86. According to Schaps (1979, 96), Athenian society was "an extremely patriarchal one in theory, not only legal theory but the generally accepted social understanding of the people." In practice, Athenian patriarchy was supposedly yet more "severe and crass" than that of modern "patriarchal industrial societies" (Keuls 1985, 12). Cf. Joshel and Murnaghan (1998, 3); Wright ([1923] 1969, 1); Keuls (1989, 26); Vidal-Naquet (1986, 206–7); Cantarella (1987, 38); Schuller (1985, passim). Recently, such views have been yielding to more nuanced interpretations: see Sourvinou-Inwood (1995); E. E. Cohen (2000, 30–48).

87. In French terms, "documentation 'surdéterminée'" requires "une lecture 'symptomale'" (Garlan 1982, 31). "Diagnostic reading," a popular tool of francophone methodology, is viewed as merely a defensive response to the inevitable subjectivity of those espousing objective pretensions: "very few of the apparently purely scholarly debates on [Greek slavery] avoid, in one way or another, consciously or unconsciously, adopting a particular ideological perspective" (Garlan 1988, 23). For decades, scholars dismissed the evidence that Building Z (see n. 82 above) was a brothel and denied that the sale of sex had some coherent relationship to the many scenes on vases showing young men bringing gifts or moneybags to women working with wool (see Davidson 1997, 85–90).

88. Even Rosivach (1989, 365) concedes that the word in all other ancient citations means "wool-worker." "*Talasiourgia*" ("wool-working") sometimes refers only to the process of spinning wool into thread but often encompasses the entire process, including weaving.

89. Although Rosivach sometimes substitutes "home-maker" for "housewife," he generally uses "wife" in its literal sense, even trying to identify de facto husbands. But this interpretation is impossible: on Lewis's "Great Inscription," two *talasiourgoi* are grouped with a single man (1959, side B, col. 1, lines 253–66).

90. See, for example, Andocides 1.38; Aeschines 1.97; Menander *Arbitration* 380; Xenophon *Constitution of the Athenians* 1.10–11. For *apophora* in the construction trade, see Randall (1953) and Burford (1963); for it in workshops, see Francotte (1900, 12) and Bolkestein (1958, 63); for it in the pottery trade, see Webster (1973). For slaves operating retail establishments and banks, see n. 48 above.

91. Lenders (operating as groups of *eranistai*) appear with frequency on the *phialai exeleutherikai* inscriptions. See IG 2².1553.7–10, 20–23; 1556 B27–29; 1557 B105–7; 1558 A37–43; 1559 A 2 26–31; 1566 A27–29; 1568 B18–23; 1569 A 3 18–21; 1570.24–26, 57–62, 82–84; 1571.8–13; and 1572.8–11; Lewis (1959, face A, lines 141–42 and 566–67, face B, lines 2 and 153); Lewis (1968, 368, line 8). The silver bowls themselves are generally believed to have been paid for by the freed persons. This again would have required considerable funds. (We have no reliable information on prices paid to owners at Athens in connection with manumissions.)

92. See Xenophon *Oeconomicus* 2.7 and Timokles frag. 33 (K-A): *sunerithoi Attikoi, sunuphainousai Hellênes.*

93. But there were some workers of high skill producing specialized product for sale in the market, such as the craftswoman expert in lace making described at Aeschines 1.97. An otherwise ordinary female slave skilled at woolworking might be worth twice the price of an untrained *doulê* (Xenophon *Oeconomicus* 7.41).

94. Cf. Halperin (1990, 107–12) and Schneider (1913, 1343–44). Loomis (1998, 185) disregards reports of prices that are "pretty clearly an exaggeration."

95. On comparative monetary values, see E. E. Cohen (1992, xiv and 22 n.92) and Gallo (1987, esp. 57–63).

96. See [Demosthenes] 59.29–32 and the discussion in Kapparis (1999, 227–35).

97. For a survey of these poems and similar material, see Davidson (1997, 87–88).

98. These musicians "might also be called on to provide sexual entertainment" (Rhodes 1981, 574). See Metagenes frag. 4 (K-A); Adespota 1025.1 (K-A); Aristophanes *Acharnians* 551; Theopompus *FGrH* 115 F 290. Cf. Krenkel (1988, 1294) and Herter (1960, 86 n.290).

99. According to Dover ([1979] 1989, 16), in (homo)sexual relationships, "the passive partner is called 'pais,' ('boy'), a word also used for 'child,' 'girl' 'son,' 'daughter,' and 'slave.'" "Pais" frequently appears on vases as a denomination for attractive young men or women. For male and female *paides* identified as objects of sexual desire, see Plato *Laws* 836a7.

100. See n. 93 above.

101. "The truth of the matter is that our evidence is inadequate" (Lewis 1959, 238).

102. For the distinction, and an analysis of its historical basis, see Wood (1988, 126–45, esp. 139). Some Athenians, however, did tend to view work as essentially the obligation of unfree persons (*Peri Hedones,* quoted in Athenaeus 512b4–6). See Wehrli (1969, frag. 55) and Vernant (1983).

103. See also Plato *Prôtagoras* 319d. Cf. Humphreys (1978, 148).

104. For the significance of such activities in the ancient world, see Goody (1986, 177–84).

105. See E. Harris (2002). For the male and female "citizens" known to have been prostitutes, see E. E. Cohen (2000, 167–77).

106. Among the Athenian *hetairoi* and *hetairai* who became notorious for accomplishment and/or wealth, there is virtually no indication of personal enslavement, or of slave-like brothel dependence. "Unter der Gruppe der renommierten Hetären, die als Spitzenverdienerinnen galten *(megalomisthoi)* (Athenaeus 570b; 558a-e), waren Sklavinnen kaum anzutreffen" (Klees 1998, 147 n.16). Cf. n. 17 above.

107. For safekeeping of maritime loan agreements, for example, see Demosthenes 34.6 and 56.15.

108. Without witnesses, even written agreements were unrecognized and unenforceable until very late in the fourth century. See Thomas (1989, 41–45) and Pringsheim (1955).

109. For the validity of the use of Roman comic material as evidence for Athenian legal and social practices, see Scafuro (1997, 16–19) and Paoli (1976, 76–77).

110. Lines 751–54 read "Diabolus Glauci filius Clearetae / lenae dedit dono argenti viginti minas, | Philaenium ut secum esset noctes et dies / hunc annum totum." See Sharon James's essay in this volume for an extended quotation and analysis of this scene. For analysis of Athenian prostitution "along the axis of gift- vs. commodity-exchange" (Kurke 1999, 179), see Kurke (1997, 145); Davidson (1994, 141–42 and 1997, 117–27); Reinsberg (1989, 80–86).

111. See Plautus *Mercator* 536ff.; *Bacchides* frag. 10 and 896ff.; Turpilius *Comici fragmenta* 112; Ribbeck *Leucadia.* Cf. Schonbeck (1981, 150–51 and 203 n.73) and Herter (1960, 81 nn.193 and 194).

112. Courtesans' luxurious possessions are frequently mentioned in Athenian literature. See, for example, Lucian *Dialogues of the Courtesans* 4.1. See the sumptuous lifestyles and impressive property attributed to Chrysis in Menander's *Samia* (see my discussion below) and to Theodote in Xenophon's *Memorabilia* (see my discussion below). On the Athenian conceptualization of "ownership," see Aristotle *Rhetoric* 1361a (1.5.7), Foxhall (1989), and Sealey (1990, 45–49).

113. For the Athenian elite idealization of such pursuits, see Fisher (1998b) 84–86; Stocks (1936); Ste. Croix (1981, 114–17).

114. On the Athenians' tendency to idealize labor not as a form of production but as "cultural self-definition" *("kulturellen Selbstdefinition")* see von Reden (1992); Loraux (1995) 44–58. Cf. Schwimmer (1979).

115. Lucian was consciously seeking to recreate, linguistically and historically, the world of classical Athens. His *Dialogues of the Courtesans* "look back to fourth-century comedy" (Davidson 1997, 332), offering a setting "vaguely Hellenistic" (Jones 1986, 158). For the appropriateness of using this text in a synchronic analysis of Athenian prostitution (focused on the fourth century and the years immediately before and after that period), see E. E. Cohen (forthcoming).

116. See especially *Dialogues of the Courtesans* 1.1. Prostitutes' jealousy *(zêlotypia)* is also an animating theme of *Satires* 2, 11, and 14. For men, jealousy was seen as a fundamental element of purchased *erôs:* a lover not painfully possessive was not really a lover (*Dialogues of the Courtesans* 8.1).

117. See, in particular, *Dialogues of the Courtesans* 4, in which Bacchis uses magical spells to steal back a customer from a rival prostitute. Cf. Faraone (1999, 150–52).

118. In *Dialogues of the Courtesans* 11, for example, Tryphaina, although well-paid (11.1), is affronted by her client Charmides' yearning for Philemation (11.3).

119. Athenian concepts of *philanthrôpia* (a word that translates as "kindliness," "benevolence") encompassed concern for vulnerable or helpless persons: see Fisher (1995).

120. See, for example, *Dialogues of the Courtesans* 2 (false report from the servant Doris upsets the *hetaira* Myrtion); 4.3 and 10.2 (dispatch of servants to investigate disturbing reports); 9.1 (Dorkas reports to Pannychis, her "owner" [*"kektêmenê"*]); 13.4 (Hymnis gives direction to Grammis); 15.2 (Parthenis hired by Krokale to play music at intimate party). At 6.2–3 Crobyle dangles before her newly mature daughter, Corinna, a novice prostitute, a future profuse with attendants (and other accoutrements of wealth)—provided she follows her mother's advice.

121. Athenian residences, especially those also functioning as business locations, often encompassed substantial security features. See Young (1956, 122–46); Osborne (1985, 31–4 and 63–7).

122. A late mosaic from the so-called "House of Menander" at Mytilene on Lesbos depicts Chrysis richly adorned in a multicolored tunic and gown. See Webster (1995, 1.93 [XZ 31] and 2.469 [6DM 2.2]).

123. Because Chrysis remains a courtesan, modern scholars, however, tend to be unhappy with the play's ending: see Jacques (1989, xli–xliii).

124. Athenians generally felt an obligation to help their friends and on so doing expected to receive gratitude (and future reciprocity). See Millett (1991, 24–52). For the "fundamental difference between the social consequences of exchange based on coinage on the one hand and on gift exchange on the other" (von Reden 1997, 154), see Kurke (1994, 42) and Seaford (1994, 199). Cf. Seaford (1998); von Reden (1998); Steiner (1994); Kurke (1989).

125. Socrates explains how she might acquire clients and maximize their contributions to her (3.11.9, 12, and 14).

126. Cartledge (2002, 159–60) offers an economic, Goldhill (1998) a cultural, interpretation of this vignette. For further discussion of this scene, see the end of Faraone's essay in this volume.

127. The French "l'imaginaire" (originally popularized by Sartre and Lacan) has penetrated history from its origins in French psychoanalysis (where it has functioned as a flexible rendering of Freud's "fantasy"). Transposed into social theory as the equivalent of the "social imaginary," it has come to mean, when applied to Athenian history, "the city's 'self-image,' how it sees itself in fantasy, with a large element of idealization and wish fulfillment" (Levine in Loraux 1993, 3).

The Bad Girls of Athens

The Image and Function of Hetairai *in Judicial Oratory*

ALLISON GLAZEBROOK

In a climactic moment of the epilogue of [Demosthenes] 59, Apollodorus makes the following appeal to his audience (114):

So let each one of you believe that he is casting his vote, one in defence of his wife, another his daughter, another his mother, another the city and its laws and religion, so that those women are not seen to be held in equal esteem with this whore [*pornê*], and that women reared by their kinsmen with great and proper decency [*sôphrosunê*] and care and given in marriage according to the laws [*kata tous nomous*] are not shown to have equal rights with a woman who has been with many men many times each day, in many lascivious ways [*meta pollôn kai aselgôn tropôn*], as each man wished. (Carey 1992, 77)

In the course of this appeal, Apollodorus presents an obscene and debased description of the *hetaira* Neaira[1]—he calls her a "whore" (*"pornê"*), and makes her availability and sexual expertise explicit. Absent is a popular modern image of the ancient prostitute as witty, cultured, and educated—more like an intellectual companion than a sexual partner (Licht [1932] 1956, 339 and Seltman 1956, 115).[2] Instead, Apollodorus distinguishes the law-abiding, decent woman from her inferior, the prostitute. He erects a boundary, perhaps more ideological

125

than real, between women eligible for marriage and women available for pleasure. This description, contrasting with the frequent references labeling Neaira a *"hetaira,"* actually blurs any boundaries between categories of prostitutes. In general, scholars distinguish between *pornai* and *hetairai.* They view the former as low-class prostitutes and the latter as sophisticated courtesans. Apollodorus's dissolution of categories complicates attempts to interpret the image of Neaira and to define the status of various prostitutes, rendering the focus on a taxonomy of prostitution misplaced.

Recent scholarship demonstrates that context is important to the understanding of images and terms relating to prostitution and reveals that attitudes toward the sex worker in the ancient world were complex. The work of David Halperin (1991) and Leslie Kurke (1997) reveals that ancient writers created and manipulated images of the prostitute for social and political purposes. Madeleine Henry (1985 and 1987) points to evidence of contradictory attitudes toward such women in ancient Greek comedy. Together, these scholars demonstrate the importance of genre, date, and context of the sources to studies on prostitution. Utilizing such a method, Kapparis (1999, 408–9) concludes that Apollodorus, most frequently labeling Neaira a *"hetaira,"* clearly intends his reference to her as a *"pornê"* in his epilogue to be insulting and not an indication of a change in her status. As Kapparis demonstrates, knowledge of rhetorical technique is key to interpreting characterizations of women in judicial oratory. By examining the representation of prostitutes in such texts, I aim to show that invocation of the image of the *hetaira* is part of an orator's strategy against an opponent. Rather than Neaira, my focus is on how orators construct and manipulate images of *hetairai* to their own advantage and on what the genre of judicial oratory tells us about Athenian attitudes toward *hetairai.*

Hetaira as Constructed Image

An adverse attitude toward *hetairai* exists in judicial oratory, where rhetorical strategies, sexual stereotypes, and social reality shape the image of the *hetaira.* She is often a sign of an opponent's extravagance and corrupt nature. Aeschines describes Timarchus as "being slave to the most shameful pleasures: gourmet foods and expensive dinners, flute-girls and *hetairai,* dice, and other pursuits that must not have power over a noble and free man (1.42)." He further accuses Timarchus of having squandered his patrimony on such habits and then of prostituting himself as a way to earn money to meet these needs. Callistratus argues that Olympiodorus never married and instead wastes inheritance money on a *hetaira* while his sister and niece live in poverty ([Demosthenes] 48.53). He intends the *hetaira* to serve as a sign of Olympiodorus's extravagance and corrupted nature. Furthermore, Demosthenes reproaches Apollodorus for freeing *hetairai* (36.45), and the speaker of Isaeus 3 relates how young men who cannot control their passion for such women bring themselves to ruin (17). Clearly, Athenians look down on excessive desire for *hetairai* and those who waste money on such women.

The orators also present an image of the *hetaira* herself as extravagant, promiscuous, available to anyone, requiring payment, excessive in her behavior, scheming, and arrogant. Neaira, in [Demosthenes] 59, fits this portrait perfectly. She adorns herself in fine clothes and gold jewelry and has two female slaves to attend to her personal needs (35). She cannot make enough money in Megara to maintain her household, but Apollodorus attributes this to her expensive tastes. He calls her "extravagant" (*"polutelês"*) (36). In addition, Neaira is available for sex with anyone who wants her *(boulomenos)*, as long as he can pay. The speaker emphasizes this sexual availability both when Neaira is working for Nicarete and when she is living with Stephanus in Athens (19, 23, and 41). He regularly refers to her as working for pay *(mistharnousa)* and as costing a lot of money (20, 22, 23, 28, 29, and 41). Apollodorus also emphasizes her excessiveness. We see that she gets drunk at parties and even has intercourse with slaves (33). With the help of Stephanus, she comes up with a scheme to blackmail naive rich foreigners. Neaira accepts them as clients, but Stephanus accuses them of adultery and extorts a large sum of money (41). Finally, the speakers describe her as impious *(asebousa)* with respect to the gods, insolent *(hubrizousa)* in her behavior toward the city, and contemptuous *(kataphronousa)* of the laws (12, 107).

Other detailed portraits of *hetairai* are similar. Callistratus emphasizes the extravagance and arrogance of Olympiodorus's *hetaira*. She struts her stuff around town: gold jewelry, finery, and a train of servants accompany her wherever she goes ([Demosthenes] 48.35). The speaker uses *hubrizousa* to convey her arrogant deportment. He also claims she has unnatural influence over Olympiodorus (53). The speaker of Isaeus 3 stresses the availability and excessiveness of Phile's mother, labeled a *hetaira*. He repeats more than once that she is available to whoever wants her *(boulomenos)* (11, 13, 15 16, 77). He makes the emphatic claim

that to name all her lovers would be no small task and attributes the ri-
otous company and frequent wild parties at Pyrrhus's house to the
presence of Phile's mother (11, 13). She appears to have joined fully in
the revelry of Pyrrhus and his friends. To top it off, he refers to her behavior as licentiousness (aselgeia).[3] In a last example, in Isaeus 6, Alce
represents the scheming and arrogant prostitute. She gains control of
her lover Euctemon, a man with a family of daughters and sons (21, 48).
She then convinces Euctemon to introduce a boy to his phratry under
his own name, despite, as alleged by the speaker, the boy not being
Euctemon's son (21–24). The speaker also claims his opponents came
under Alce's influence and plotted with her to gain control of Euctemon's wealth by convincing the old man to cancel his will and sell off
part of his property (29–30, 38). Finally, she is insolent (hubrizein), treats
Euctemon's family and the city with contempt (kataphronein), and
showed her daring (tolman) when she unlawfully participated in the
Thesmophoria (a festival in honor of Demeter; 48, 50).

Speakers identify Neaira, the woman with Olympiodorus, Phile's
mother, and Alce as prostitutes, in three cases labeling them "hetaira."
Not one, however, is portrayed as the cultured and witty woman described by Licht, or solely in a way that reflects a more recent understanding of the hetaira as a woman who accepts gifts, rather than payment, and sleeps with whom she prefers, rather than with whoever
wants her.[4] The character of the hetaira in judicial oratory is further note-
worthy on account of its opposition to the image of the ideal wife, the
sôphrôn gunê. Helen North constructs a portrait of the sôphrôn gunê for
the Archaic and Classical periods as chaste, faithful, dutiful, obedient,
modest, and a productive member of her household (1977, 36–38). Penel-
ope and Andromache become the model for such wives for the Classical
period. In contrast, the hetaira in oratory provides sex to anyone who can
pay, is excessive in her behavior, and often arrogant and impious. She is
also a drain on a man's oikos on account of her extravagance and cost.[5]

Orators intentionally emphasize an antithesis between the hetaira
and the sôphrôn gunê in their portraits of prostitutes by openly contrasting hetairai with an ideal of the sôphrôn gunê. In descriptions of hetairai,
references to such wives are never far off. For example, the description
of Olympiodorus's extravagant hetaira contrasts sharply with the description of other women in the same passage. Callistratus emphasizes
their official status as his wife and daughter, and as the sister and niece
of Olympiodorus. Then he opposes their poverty to her extravagance
([Demosthenes] 48.53–55). Clearly he wants the jurors to question why

a *hetaira* is being treated better than an Athenian's female relatives. In the midst of describing the behavior of Phile's mother, the speaker states that married women are not seen at symposia, and that men do not dare to carouse with such women (Isaeus 3.14). In this way, the speaker emphasizes the contrast between *hetairai* and *gunaikes* and thus between Phile's mother and the wives of the jurors. In Isaeus 6, the speaker mentions a law forbidding slaves, prostitutes, and women caught in adultery from participating in the *Thesmophoria* (48).[6] He then states that Alce, although she was a slave who lived a shameful life *(aischrôs biousa)*, entered the temple and viewed the sacred rites performed there.[7] In addition, she joined in the procession of a sacrifice in honor of Demeter and Persephone and witnessed what she had no right to witness (49–50). The *Boulê* (the Athenian council) appears to have responded to her actions with some sort of decree (50).[8] The speaker's prime purpose in quoting the law and the decree is to inform his listeners about Alce's character: her unlawful participation in the *Thesmophoria* and the emphasis on her status and behavior create an antithesis between her nature and that of a *sôphrôn gunê*, who could rightfully attend the *Thesmophoria*.[9]

In the epilogue of [Demosthenes] 59, Apollodorus contrasts Neaira's behavior with that expected of married women in general and emphasizes that Neaira is the opposite of the wives, mothers, and daughters of the jurors. First, he stresses the opposition through a question: "Will you decide that a woman of her character who is known for certain by all to have plied her trade over the breadth of the world is a woman eligible for marriage with a citizen?" (108).[10] Second, he manufactures a dialogue between the jurors and their wives, daughters, and mothers that highlights the difference between them and Neaira (110–11).

And what could each of you actually say when he goes home to his own wife or daughter or mother after acquitting this woman, when she asks you: 'Where were you?' and you say 'we were trying a case.' 'Whom?' she will ask at once. 'Neaira' you will say, of course (what else?) 'because though she is an alien she is living in marriage with a citizen against the law, and because she gave in marriage to Theogenes who served as King-Archon her daughter who had been caught in adultery.' . . . And they on hearing this will ask: 'So what did you do?' and you will say: 'We have acquitted her'. (Carey 1992, 75)

Switching back to narrative, Apollodorus informs the jurors that the most decent of the women *(sôphronestatai tôn gunaikôn)* will be furious because the men have treated Neaira as their equal (111). Thus he suggests to the jurors that their wives, daughters, and mothers will view Neaira as distinct from themselves. He uses *sôphrôn* to emphasize that, in addition to having a different status, they are distinct in reputation.

The climax of Apollodorus's comparison appears in the quote at the beginning of this chapter. "Those women" (meaning wives, daughters and mothers) contrast with "whore," while "women reared by their kinsmen with great and proper decency [*sôphrosunê*] and care and given in marriage according to the laws" contrast with "a woman who has been with many men many times each day, in many lascivious ways, as each man wished." (114; Carey 1992, 77). Here again, *sôphrosunê* is what distinguishes these women from Neaira. Marriage characterizes their sexual relationships with men, while Neaira is not only promiscuous, but regularly performs indecent sex acts. Thus, orators contrast the *hetaira* with the *sôphrôn gunê,* emphasizing the negative traits of the prostitute to ensure that the difference between these women is made crystal clear. In reality, however, the differences may not always have been so apparent. After all, Apollodorus claims Stephanus has been passing Neaira off as his wife.

Unraveling the Image

It is no coincidence that the women discussed in [Demosthenes] 59 and 48, and Isaeus 3 and 6 are women associated with the speakers' opponent. Just as they speak ill of their male adversary, orators attempt to malign the woman associated with such an opponent.[11] Calling a woman a *hetaira* in itself is not necessarily enough to criticize a woman and arouse the disapproval of the jurors, since prostitution was common place. Speakers must ensure that the woman's character will not be likeable. The emphasis on her overt promiscuity, offensive and dangerous behavior, as well as her scheming nature accomplishes this. The orators further demonstrate that the woman has overstepped certain bounds by wrongfully claiming a specific status, or undeservedly enjoying particular privileges. The details and the repetition of details, most notable in the case of Neaira, confirm that speakers appeal to a negative stereotype of the *hetaira* as part of a strategy to arouse the *pathos* of the jurors, in this case anger, hatred and fear. For example, who of the jurors would not be annoyed when they consider the charge that Stephanus tried to pass a woman like Neaira as his wife and allowed her the privilege of such status?

Orators even appear to apply this negative characterization of the *hetaira* regardless of the actual status of the woman under scrutiny.[12] Phano, also characterized by Apollodorus in [Demosthenes] 59, and Plangon, discussed by Mantitheos in Demosthenes 39 and [Demosthenes] 40, are victims of such a strategy. Phano, for example, was arguably a legal wife, since she was twice married to an Athenian (50, 72).[13] In addition, although Apollodorus disputes the status of her child, he never confirms that her first husband failed to register the son in his *genos* and phratry (55–63).[14] Despite her status and circumstances, Apollodorus associates Phano with the habits and traits typical of *hetairai* in oratory, and at times even directly alludes to her role as a prostitute. Phano is a drain on the household on account of her extravagance—she is described as unable to live in accordance with the penny-pinching ways of her first husband (50). After he sends her away, she makes herself sexually available to a lover (64–71). According to Apollodorus, she even receives payment from Epainetos, the lover, who claims he spent a great deal of money on her and the rest of the household (67). Stephanus, in turn, later convinces him to contribute one thousand drachmas to Phano's marriage, citing the fact that Epainetos has been using her sexually and so owes her a good turn (70–71). Apollodorus further argues that when charged with adultery, Epainetos defended himself on the grounds that Phano was a practicing prostitute (67). Apollodorus, however, never formally substantiates the accusation of prostitution.[15] The mere suggestion, combined with his detailed description of her behavior, is likely enough to anger the jurors when they recall her marriages, and cause them to suspect her status.

Plangon, in the second example, was the daughter of the Athenian Pamphilos of Keiriadai, and was likely the first wife of the speaker's father, Mantias.[16] In the case of this woman, the speaker Mantitheos ignores the past marital relationship between her and his father, and instead emphasizes the contact between them, when they were no longer married. He comes close to stating that it was a prostitute-client relationship but tempers his remarks: "with Plangon, the mother of these men, [my father] consorted [*eplêsiazen*] in some way or other at one time, but it is not my place to say" (40.8) "*Plêsiazein*" ("to have a relationship with") is the common term orators use to refer to the sexual relationship between a *hetaira* and her client, and it appears numerous times in Isaeus 3 and [Demosthenes] 59.[17] Its appearance here means the speaker wishes to imply that Plangon is similar to a prostitute, although he feigns reluctance to be more specific about her relationship with his father. He goes on to use this verb two more times in a similar context (40.27). Furthermore, he emphasizes that Plangon lives extravagantly *(polutelôs)*—a complaint leveled against the others. For example, he describes her as keeping many personal female slaves, and he lets his audience know that she cost Mantitheos's father great expense (40.51). This last charge also implies that she was paid like a *hetaira*. Finally, Mantitheos emphasizes her scheming nature, recalling how she tricked and double-crossed his father when she swore before the public arbitrator that he was the father of both her sons (40.10–11; 39.3–4). Although the orator is not intending to prove Plangon's status as a *hetaira*, associating her with such women influences the jurors' opinion about her, undermines their sympathy for her, and makes them question Plangon's reputation and position in the community. Furthermore, the portrait of Plangon hints at the illegitimate status of the speaker's opponent, her son, and thus insults the opponent.[18] Although legitimacy is not the main issue of the conflict, the speaker obscures her relationship with Mantias, and questions Mantias' recognition of her sons.

In addition to influencing the opinion of the jurors and arousing their anger, vilifying a woman by attributing to her the negative traits associated with the *hetaira* can be an important element of the orator's argument for winning a case. Orators use this unflattering picture of the *hetaira* and its opposition to the vision of the chaste wife to challenge an opponent's claim to inheritance and question the status of his household. Of the speeches referred to, Isaeus 3 and Isaeus 6 stem from arguments over familial status and the right of inheritance. Both discredit claimants on the grounds that their mothers were *hetairai* and not married women. Isaeus 3 is an accusation of perjury against an Athenian who swore in a previous trial that his sister was the legitimate wife of Pyrrhus (4–7). The relationship between this woman and Pyrrhus is of prime importance because if they were legally married, the daughter Phile has the status of an *epiklêros*.[19] Pyrrhus's adoption of a son and the fact that many of the events described occurred at least twenty years earlier complicate the case (1). On the death of the adopted son, who also died without issue, two families claimed the estate: Pyrrhus's sister (also the mother of the adopted son) and Phile's husband (2–3). The speaker recounts his argument, which he had made at a previous trial, stating that it was unlikely Pyrrhus would have married a woman who acted as Phile's mother did (11–16). Thus, he claims that Phile's mother was a *hetaira* and not the wife of Pyrrhus, making Phile the daughter of a prostitute and her status as *epiklêros* impossible.[20] Isaeus 6, in turn, concerns the rightful heir of Euctemon. In this case, the adopted son of Euctemon's deceased son Philoctemon claims the estate but is opposed by Euctemon's kinsman Androcles on the grounds that Euctemon has two surviving sons, with the eldest recognized by his phratry as being legitimate (3, 10, 24). These two sons are not by Euctemon's wife (the wife identified by the speaker), but, as Androcles appears to claim, a second wife (13). The speaker, however, argues that both sons are illegitimate, and that neither is a son of Euctemon. He claims they are the offspring of the prostitute Alce and the freedman Dion, and that Euctemon is the victim of her schemes (18–37). Thus, the speaker's key argument associates sons, recognized by Euctemon and in one case his phratry, with a prostitute in order to discredit their claims to inheritance.

[Demosthenes] 59 centers on Stephanus's household and the nature of his association with Neaira. This trial is the last of a series of disputes between Apollodorus and Stephanus, the motivation for which is political.[21] In the current case, Apollodorus accuses Stephanus of treating Neaira as his wife, when she is an alien and not eligible for marriage with a citizen. Apollodorus's main strategy consists in detailing Neaira's life as a *hetaira*—almost a third of the speech is devoted to this purpose (18–48)—to convince the jurors of her status as foreigner *(xenê)*. If successful, Stephanus will have to pay one thousand drachmas in penalty and Neaira will be sold into slavery (16). Apollodorus further associates the daughter of Stephanus's household with Neaira. If the jury is convinced that Phano is not his daughter, then Stephanus will suffer an even greater penalty: *atimia* (loss of citizenship rights) and confiscation of his property because he married Phano to Athenian citizens, representing her as his own (52). In this case, Apollodorus emphasizes Phano's behavior, showing how it is like a prostitute's, to convince the jurors she is the daughter of Neaira and not Stephanus (50–70). A winning conviction could bring the status of Stephanus's sons into question as well (Patterson 1994, 203). Thus, Apollodorus uses the women associated with Stephanus and descriptions of their behavior to place the entire *oikos* of Stephanus in jeopardy. In all of these trials, the status of the women and/or the nature of their relationship to particular men, oftentimes the opponent himself, are part of the speaker's attack on the opponent and part of his strategy for winning the case.

Emphasizing the negative image of a *hetaira*, characterizing a woman as a *hetaira*, and/or associating opponents with *hetairai* in disputes concerned with the status of individuals or households were effective strategies for two reasons. First, there was no permanent record of a female's status (see Cole 1984, 237 n.25). Instead, women were dependent on individual witnesses who could attest to parentage and to a history of participation in traditional and communal events.[22] Very little of the ritual designed to assimilate a child to private and public groups, however, applied to females. Those that did exist were mostly private ceremonies with invited guests as witnesses. In the ceremony known as the *amphidromia,* the father recognized a child, whether male or female, as an official member of the family and worthy to be brought up. Then at the *dekatê* (tenth-day ceremony), the father gave the infant a name. Marriage with betrothal *(enguê)* further indicated a woman's status in the community. Betrothal included, but did not require, the provision of a dowry, which was additional evidence of marriage status (Wyse [1904] 1967, 308). For example, women of poor families would not always have dowries to attest to their status as married.[23] Public recognition was rare and infrequent, most common for elite women whose husbands possessed some wealth.[24] A newlywed husband might hold a sacrifice and marriage feast *(gamêlia)* for his phratry.[25] Husbands of the liturgical class were expected to finance a festival, such as the *Thesmophoria,* on behalf of their wives. Members of this elite and wealthy class, however, represented only a small fraction of the population. Thus, proof of a woman's social standing was primarily dependent on individual witnesses, making women's status vulnerable to attack.

Secondly, Pericles' citizenship law strengthened the categorization of women into two groups. Enacted in 451/0 BCE, this law redefined *astai* (women eligible for marriage with citizens) and distinguished them from non-Attic women by requiring that both parents of Athenian citizens be *astoi.*[26] Thus, being a wife took on special distinction with specific requirements. Non-Attic women included slaves, freedwomen, and foreign women *(xenai),* and Athenians did not recognize their children as *astoi.* To most Athenians, *hetaira* would imply slave, freedwoman, or *xenê*—a woman who was clearly non-Attic—because *astai* who became prostitutes in Classical Athens seem to have been rare.[27] Being a *hetaira* meant the male client would not recognize any of her offspring as his responsibility and that the *polis* would not recognize them as Athenians. The lifestyle of the *hetaira* was also unique in that she regularly interacted with males, attended symposia, and had a reputation for extravagance. Labeling women as *hetairai* indicates a certain reputation and lifestyle and brings the paternity of any children into question. Thus, the contrast between *hetairai* and *astai* becomes an exploitable polarization for the orator in cases centering on a woman's status, inheritance, or the status of a household. By equating women associated with the opponent with *hetairai,* orators not only malign women connected to opponents but effectively distinguish them from *astai.*

Conclusion

My examination of orators' use of a negative characterization of *hetaira* and their use of antithesis shows that orators manipulate images of women to their own advantage. Thus, images of women associated with the opponent are constructed and serve a rhetorical function. Recognizing portraits of women in forensic oratory as artfully constructed enriches our interpretation of these representations. Narratives involving women associated with the opponent are neither historically correct representations of women's lives nor accurate representations of historical individuals. Such narratives present a stock character that the orator uses to cast doubt on the status and/or respectability of his target. They are intended to vilify women, insult the opponent, and arouse the *odium* and *indignatio* of the listeners. Furthermore, they act to destroy an opponent's claim to inheritance, question the status of his household, or even his own status. The use of an image of the *hetaira* in portraits of women of varying status indicates a double standard of sorts. Athenian society approves of female prostitution, but orators use an image of the prostitute and sexuality associated with the prostitute to judge and abuse various types of women. The use of such images in judicial oratory would have had a significant impact on the individual lives of ancient women. Whether or not the opponent prevailed was immaterial to the woman under scrutiny. Her reputation, now sullied, entered the public domain.

Notes

1. *"Hetaira"* (pl. *"hetairai"*) refers to a type of prostitute in classical Athens. The term's first use in reference to female prostitution appears in Herodotus 2.134–35. The best translation is "sexual companion." I avoid using "courtesan," a popular rendering in English, because it carries connotations for the modern reader not appropriate in the current context.

2. For more recent scholars holding this same view of the *hetaira* see Cantarella (1987, 49–50) and Blundell (1995, 148). Keuls (1985, 188–200) and Reinsberg (1989, 80–86, 88–89) critique this view of the *hetaira* as an idealization and draw few distinctions between *hetairai* and *pornai.*

3. More such details likely emerged in the discussion of the mother's status as *hetaira* in a previous trial, alluded to by the speaker (Isaeus 3.11–12), but unfortunately the earlier speech does not survive.

4. See p. 125 and n. 2 and Davidson (1997, 120–26).

5. Cox (1998, 168–89) discusses *hetairai* as a strain on the household.

6. The law is not included in the text, but Isaeus 3.80 restricts participation to married women. Also see Wyse ([1904] 1967, 536–37) on the likely nature of the law.

7. Note that Alce is in fact a freedwoman, not a slave, but according to Wyse ([1904] 1967, 537) "to call a freedwoman a 'slave' is a pardonable license" in oratory.

8. The *Boulê* reviewed the celebration of festivals to ensure that participants observed the necessary piety. For example, the speaker of Andocides 1.111 reports that the *Boulê* met after the celebration of the Mysteries and received a report regarding the conduct of the festival. No record exists of a special session after the *Thesmophoria*, but in all likelihood the Archon-Basileus could report disturbances or acts of impiety at a regular meeting of the *Boulê*, where a course of action could be decided upon and a decision made about whether or not to punish the offenders. See Wyse ([1904] 1967, 538).

9. See De Brauw (2001–02, 162–76) on citing law as a way to portray character.

10. Translaton adapted from Carey (1992, 75). I translate *"astê"* as "a woman eligible for marriage with a citizen" rather than simply "citizen" to emphasize that men and women had different rights in Athens. Athenian males had full citizen rights, whereas Athenian women only had partial rights. This translation also highlights the difference between the Athenian woman and other women in the *polis*. Only she was eligible for marriage with a citizen and able to bear children of Athenian status in such a marriage.

11. Although a surprise to the modern reader, attacking the character of the opponent was a typical strategy of the orators. Aristotle includes this strategy in his discussion of artful proofs and encourages the orator to add details that convey the wickedness *(kakia)* of the opponent (*Rh.* 1417^{a}3–8). In practice, orators extend their character assassination to family and friends associated with the opponent. See Carey (1994, 32). For information on typical accusations against the character of a male opponent see Hunter (1994, 101–10, 118–19).

12. Some scholars remain unconvinced by orators who label women as prostitutes. Hunter (1994, 113) hints that Phile's mother was in fact a legal wife, not a *hetaira*. Compare with Patterson (1990, 71–73). Foxhall (1996, 151) questions the status of Olympiodorus' *hetaira*, suggesting the identification may be "a slanderous attack on a legitimate wife." Perhaps the status of Neaira as a prostitute is also questionable since the events used to prove such status date back twenty or thirty years. See Glazebrook ([2005] 162, 182–83).

13. See Kapparis (1999, 35–36). Patterson (1994, 207–9) claims that Phano must be the legitimate daughter of Stephanus.

14. See Kapparis (1999, 36, 282–84).

15. According to Apollodorus, Stephanus accused Epainetos with adultery, and Epainetos defended himself against the charge by claiming that Phano was a practicing prostitute (59.64–71). Scafuro (1997, 112) points out that claiming

prostitution was a possible defence against adultery, especially if gifts were accepted. Formal proof of Phano's prostitution is not provided. Kapparis (1999, 313) argues this charge would have been difficult to prove. In the end, Epainetos accepts the compromise of contributing to Phano's dowry. According to Kapparis (1999, 38) the dowry indicates that Phano was not a prostitute, or treated as a prostitute by Stephanus, but a legitimate daughter and treated as such. Thus, Apollodorus is simply exploiting an uncomfortable situation.

16. Boeotus claims his mother was married to Mantias with a dowry, but Mantitheos obscures the relationship between his father and Plangon. See Demosthenes 39.23 and [Demosthenes] 40.14–15, 20, 22.

17. See Isaeus 3.10, 15 and [Demosthenes] 59.9, 20, 37, 41. Notably, this verb also describes the relationship between Epainetos and Phano ([Demosthenes] 59.67).

18. Demosthenes also draws on the negative characteristics of the prostitute in a brief reference to Aeschines's mother as a way to insult Aeschines. The description here, however, is less subtle and much more obscene—in addition to labeling her a prostitute, he comments that she would perform any sexual act and undertake all sexual requests (De corona 129–30). For a discussion of the larger context see Harding (1987, 30–31).

19. An epiklêros is the surviving daughter of a deceased father with no sons. Her closest male relative on her father's side was obliged to marry her and the resulting son became the rightful heir. Harrison (1998, 132–38).

20. See n. 12 on the possible status of Phile's mother as wife.

21. Theomnestus outlines the disputes in the opening of the speech (59.6–11).

22. See Patterson (1998, 108–14) on the lack of legal recognition for the state of matrimony and Scafuro (1994) on the importance of witnesses in determining an individual's status. Scafuro (1994, 157–63) emphasizes that there are different proofs for males and females and a summary of those for females follows in the main text. Also see Hunter (1994, 112).

23. According to [Demosthenes] 59.113, the state tried to provide dowries for girls who were poor, but we have no knowledge of the frequency or amount of such dowries.

24. There is debate about whether the birth of girls was announced to the phratry at the offering of the meion as well. The only text to suggest this is Isaeus 3, but it may be a special circumstance since the girl Phile may be an epiklêros. For a discussion and summary of the arguments on this issue see Cole (1984, 233 n.2 and 235–36 and n.19).

25. Cole (1984, 236–37) emphasizes marriage and the gamêlia as indicative of a woman's status as astê. Scafuro (1994, 163) mentions that a son recognized and accepted by the father's phratry and deme indicated his mother's legitimacy since a woman's status as astê was required before the son was accepted, but I do not consider this to be proof in a court of law since the questioning of her status was often a way to bring the status of the son into question.

26. For the law see [Aristotle] Constitution of the Athenians 26.4 and Plutarch Life of Pericles 37.3. Scholars generally agree Pericles' citizenship law lapsed (or was ignored) for a short period in the second half of the fifth century BCE, but was definitely in effect for the fourth century after its reenactment by Nicomenes

in 403/02 BCE. See Patterson (1981, 140–50). On the implications of the term *"astai"* resulting from the law and the distinction between them and other women see Patterson (1981, 161–67, especially 162 and n.31); also Patterson (1987, 57 and 63). For a possible explanation for the implementation of this law see Boegehold (1994, 57–66).

27. Based on Isaeus 3, it is possible that *astai* could sometimes become *hetairai*, but this was likely uncommon (Wyse [1904] 1967, 318–19). Also see Cox (1998, 173–75). Cohen (2000 and his essay in this volume) convincingly demonstrates that the idea that *astai* could not be prostitutes is a myth, but regardless of the reality, there seems to exist a belief (or convenient lie) among ancient Athenians that this does not happen. See [Demosthenes] 59.112–13, where Apollodorus suggests the jurors would not acknowledge that *astai* could become prostitutes and reminds them that the state provides girls from poor families with dowries to ensure their marriageability.

The Psychology of Prostitution in Aeschines' Speech against Timarchus

SUSAN LAPE

The Regulation of Morals in Classical Athens

In 346/5 BCE Aeschines successfully prosecuted Timarchus for violating a law that prohibited any man who had mistreated his parents, been derelict in his military duty, squandered an inheritance, prostituted himself, or otherwise acted as an "escort," from political activity in the democratic city (28–32). According to Aeschines, Solon, the author of the law, excluded prostitutes from citizenship for political reasons, believing that the man who sold himself for sexual services would be likely to betray the state (29). This explanation for the ban on citizen prostitutes is consistent with the recently emerging consensus that Athenian law regulated the sexual conduct of citizens only when it was perceived to endanger the civic community and its values rather than for either moral or paternalistic reasons (D. Cohen 1991a, Wallace 1995 and 1996).

The language of extant Athenian laws certainly supports this interpretation. Yet, although Athenian laws do not explicitly regulate sexual behavior for moral reasons, from the mid-fourth century onward

Athenian litigants argued that they did. The discrepancy between the actual laws as we know them and the moral interpretations offered by litigants is often explained by appealing to the interested position from which litigants spoke. Although speakers may have offered self-serving and highly idiosyncratic interpretations of Athenian law, it does not necessarily follow that these interpretations carried no legal or social force. It was obviously in the interests of litigants to make claims that resonated with the intuitions and expectations of jurors. More important, the meaning of law always depends on someone's interpretation. The key question then, is whose interpretation counts.

There were no professional lawyers or judges in democratic Athens and no compilations of case law to guide judicial interpretation. Rather, the meaning of the law as it was applied in particular cases was principally determined by the arguments of litigants, especially those in the prosecutorial role, and by the verdicts of democratic juror-judges. In fact, the meaning of a law could change—even if the actual words of a law did not—as the result of a trial outcome. For this reason, prosecutors urged jurors to consider themselves actual lawmakers rather than simply judges of a single case (Lycurgus 1.9, Lysias 14. 4). This is not to claim that jury verdicts changed or created law by setting formal legal precedents: they certainly did not. Rather, litigants speak of jury verdicts as establishing informal but nonetheless authoritative *social* precedents. The outcome of trials was thought to articulate the practical meaning of law, including the social values and practices the laws embodied or endorsed. For example, Aeschines claims that a conviction for Timarchus will inculcate morality (*eukosmia*) in the city's youth (191-92).[1] Yet, it is sometimes argued that there were two moralities in democratic Athens: one for private citizens and one for the politically active like Timarchus.[2] In fact, however, the difference is not that politicians were held to a higher moral standard per se but rather that their public lives made them more judicially vulnerable. Thus, trial outcomes in cases involving public figures were thought to be exemplary for all citizens—regardless of whether they were politically active or not (Dinarchus 1.27).[3]

Although the explicit content of Athenian laws is not moral in emphasis, Aeschines successfully argued that the laws were intended to promote and protect the morality of democratic citizens: Timarchus was convicted and punished with *atimia*, the loss of his citizen "rights."[4] In this study I consider the ways in which Aeschines presents Timarchus's alleged offenses as specifically moral problems. How did

Aeschines convince the jurors that their laws were intended to regulate morality despite the apparent value neutrality of the laws themselves? His success stems in part from his rhetorical strategy. By portraying Timarchus as the ultimate bad citizen, as disgusting, shameless, licentious, and incontinent, Aeschines simultaneously emphasizes the moral virtues of ordinary democratic citizens: *sôphrosunê* (continence or self-control), *eukosmia* (good order), *aretê* (virtue) and *enkrateia* (temperance). While this strategy seems to have been highly effective, it was not unproblematic. Aeschines' valorization of morality echoed certain ideas associated with the philosophical and elite traditions—traditions generally thought to be critical of democratic culture.[5] To avoid incurring the rancor of democratic jurors, Aeschines transforms the elite moral critique of democracy into a traditional if not inherent feature of democratic citizenship and ideology.[6] The advantage of this tactic was that it allowed Aeschines to present the supposed immorality of Timarchus and citizens like him as an alternative explanation for Philip of Macedon's rise to power and Athens' attendant decline in military stature. In other words, Aeschines' history of democratic morality (like his history of sexuality) is inextricably linked to the contemporary domestic and international political environments.[7]

Acting Out: The Psychological "Motive"

One of the most striking features of the Timarchus case is Aeschines' complete lack of evidence for the charge that Timarchus prostituted himself. It is true that Aeschines was also prosecuting Timarchus for wasting his inheritance, an accusation he supports by cataloging the liquidation of his estate. Yet, he clearly regards prostitution as the more serious offense and it is the charge he is most at pains to prove. In part, Aeschines bypasses the legal and logical difficulties of his case by seeking to evoke the jurors' negative emotions, characterizing Timarchus as shameless and disgusting.[8] He repeatedly points to Timarchus's supposedly disgusting physical condition as if to summon his guilty body as a witness.

While this physiognomic strategy might seem imprecise if not circular, the Athenians routinely grounded moral and political judgments in a person's physical appearance. Although Athenian citizenship was based on age and birth requirements, the Athenians did not keep marriage or birth records. Instead, candidates for citizenship were paraded naked before members of their demes who visually inspected them to assess whether or not they met these requirements.[9] In other words, the candidate for citizenship was primarily evaluated on the basis of whether he looked Athenian or not.

This system was obviously not foolproof, as the recurrent complaints and fears about fraudulent citizens in the sources attest.[10] A hint of this anxiety about the integrity and purity of the citizen body can be detected in the Timarchus case. In the year before the trial, the Athenians voted to hold a special scrutiny *(diapsêphisis)* to check the status of every citizen.[11] This extraordinary measure was reportedly passed due to a widespread belief that aliens were buying their way onto the deme registers (Demosthenes 57.49). To weed out the presumed aliens, every citizen was required to present himself to his deme and to submit to a vote to determine whether he was a genuine citizen or not. Citizens who failed the scrutiny had the opportunity to appeal their expulsion in court. Aeschines explicitly appeals to this scrutiny and its aftermath in the courts to assist the jurors in making their decision about Timarchus.

Consider the matter, if you would, on the basis of parallels from political affairs, too, and especially matters with which you are currently dealing. Ballots have taken place in the demes, and each of you has submitted himself to the vote, to see who of us is truly Athenian and who is not. And when I personally find myself in the courtroom and listen to the litigants, I see that the same factor is always influential with you. Whenever the accuser says: "Jurors, the demesmen with their vote rejected this man on oath, though nobody in the world accused him or bore witness against him; they voted on the basis of their own knowledge," and without hesitation, I think, you make a commotion, convinced that the man on trial has no claim to citizen rights. For your view, I think, is that you need no further discussion or testimony in matters that a man knows himself for certain. Come now, if Timarchus had been compelled to submit to a vote on his way of life just like on the birth qualifications, to determine whether he is guilty or not, and the issue was being decided in court, and was being brought before you as now . . . how would you have voted? I know full well that you would have convicted him. (77–79)[12]

Aeschines encourages the jurors to view their task of determining whether or not Timarchus engaged in certain unseen sex acts as no more than what they ordinarily do in evaluating citizens. Although the parallel is apt and neatly neutralizes the question of evidence, Aeschines had an additional difficulty to overcome in presenting his argument. Midway through the speech, he reports that Demosthenes was planning to defend Timarchus by impugning the coherence of the charges, claiming that prostitution was a crime of youth, while the squandering of an estate was the offense of a man (94). Demosthenes was likely going to question why a wealthy citizen like Timarchus would have needed to sell his body in the first place, forfeiting the bodily autonomy that traditionally separated freemen from slaves.[13] Accordingly, to answer this question, Aeschines introduces a "psychological" explanation for Timarchus's deviance.

The appeal to psychological factors first appears in the narrative of Timarchus's involvement with Misgolas:

This man [Misgolas] perceiving the reason for Timarchus' spending his time at the doctor's house, paid a sum of money in advance and moved Timarchus and set him up in his own house, well-developed, young, and disgusting and ready for the acts that Misgolas was eager to perform and Timarchus to have done to him. Timarchus had no inhibition but submitted to it, although he did not lack the resources for all his reasonable needs. For his father had left him a very large estate, which he has consumed, as I shall show later in my speech. No, he did all this because he is a slave to the most disgraceful pleasures [*douleuôn tais aiskhistais hêdonais*, gluttony and expensive eating and flute girls and courtesans and dice and the other activities that should never have power over a noble and freeborn man (41–42).

According to Aeschines, Timarchus works as a prostitute because he is enslaved on the inside, literally mastered by the most "shameful pleasures."[14] By claiming that Timarchus is "enslaved," Aeschines rules out the possibility that Timarchus is simply a hedonist, a person who has chosen rightly or wrongly to pursue a life of pleasure. The problem is not that Timarchus has erred in his choices, but rather that he is incapable of making moral or rational choices at all. Aeschines pushes the jurors to interpret Timarchus's prostitution as an acting out of his psychic life. In his concluding remarks to the jurors, Aeschines draws a direct correlation between a person's intrapsychic condition and his behavior. He explains that the source of wrongdoing stems from men's immorality (*aselgeia*) rather than from the gods, and that impious men are not driven and punished by the Furies (*Poinai*), as they are in the tragedies (190–91). Aeschines goes on to redefine the Fury as a person's insatiable desire, rejecting the personified Furies of tragedy, thereby presenting a view of "human beings" (citizens at any rate) as driven by internal psychological forces.[15]

Elsewhere in the speech, Aeschines attributes Timarchus's prostitution and prodigality to his disgusting and unholy nature (*phusis* [95]). However, Aeschines goes further, rendering the "natural" a function of the psychological.[16] He clarifies that Timarchus's nature is deformed by a psychological condition: excessive *akrasia*.[17] This appeal to *akrasia* or incontinence to account for a citizen's deviance is unparalleled in extant Athenian oratory.[18] It was the philosophers, rather than the orators, who explicitly formulated a theory of *akrasia* to explain how a person could be "overcome" by desire.[19]

The Soul's Testimony

According to Aeschines, the psychological explanation of Timarchus's behavior can be empirically confirmed. For by acting out his diseased moral psychology, Timarchus also embodies it, or so Aeschines would have the jurors believe:

> Who among you is unfamiliar with the disgusting conduct [*bdeluria*] of Timarchus? In the case of people who exercise, even if we don't attend the *gymnasia*, we can recognize them from a glance at their fit condition [*euhexias*]. In the same way we recognize men who have worked as prostitutes from their shameless and impudent manner and from their general behavior even if we're not present at their activities. For the man who has shown contempt for the laws and *sôphrosunê* on the most important issues comes to be in a state of soul [*hexis tês psuchês*] that is clearly revealed by the disorder of his character (189).

In comparing the prostitute and the athlete, Aeschines employs a sleight of hand. When the jurors look at an athlete, they see the legacy of his training, the good condition of his body, or his overall *euhexia*. By contrast, when they look at Timarchus, the prostitute, they *see* his disreputable behavior from the condition of his soul (*hexis tês psuchês*) (189). By using the same term to refer to the condition (*hexis*) of Timarchus's body and his soul, Aeschines papers over his transition from the physical to the psychological. There was need for this subtlety, if not subterfuge, because democratic justice was traditionally oriented to the citizen's *sôma* (body) rather than his *psuchê* (soul).

Aeschines' Moral Turn

Aeschines' concern for the souls of citizens is rare in extant democratic oratory. So too is his overriding concern for morality. He goes so far as to encourage the jurors to imitate Spartan virtue, making a demand on a democratic jury that would have been unthinkable fifty years before (180–81). In calling attention to Aeschines' exceptional emphasis on morals, I am not claiming that democratic civic identity lacked a moral component prior to the prosecution of Timarchus.[20] Ideals of moderation and self-control were long associated with the public discourse of democratic citizenship. The speech against Timarchus is exceptional, however, for its characterization of morality as the dominant component of democratic civic identity. In other words, although morality may traditionally have been an element of democratic citizenship, in the Timarchus speech it assumes a new priority as the privileged axis on which democratic citizen identity is defined.

The moral emphasis in Aeschines' speech is especially remarkable because it echoes language and ideas more commonly found in elite writers like Plato, Isocrates, Xenophon, and Aristotle. These writers not only valorized morality as the key to good citizenship but they also explicitly faulted democratic states like Athens for failing to attend to civic morality. They claimed that democratic freedom *(eleutheria)* was not a political ideal at all but rather a euphemistic alibi for "license" or immorality.[21] The lack of regulatory infrastructure in democratic states, they argued, led to the production of citizens with a corresponding lack of psychic infrastructure.[22] As an antidote to the perceived immorality of democratic states, elite writers advocated an ethics and politics of self-mastery. The ethical demand to be sovereign over oneself and one's pleasures in critical writing was less a prescription for ordinary citizens than a justification for a paternalist politics headed by either a small ruling class or a monarch.[23]

In the *Republic*, Socrates complains that democratic states are arrogant because they neglect provisions for education. Democratic states, he claims, care nothing about the habits of their political leaders (558b). Whether or not Aeschines has read the *Republic*, he directly refutes this charge, asserting that the lawgiver (i.e., Solon) believed that only a citizen who was properly raised from childhood would make a useful citizen and politician (11). Thus, Aeschines draws on elite criticisms of democracy, but he employs them for democratic ends. Aeschines does not indict the entire *dêmos* for recklessly seeking freedom to indulge their desires but rather only a select few: Timarchus and the members of a dissolute "aristocracy" (34, 194). By targeting a small group of moral degenerates for disfranchisement, Aeschines simultaneously emphasizes and commends the morality of ordinary citizens. In this way, Aeschines employs a moral discourse originally articulated in opposition to democracy as a potent democratizing and collectivizing force.

It is in this context that Aeschines' remarkable rendering of prostitution and *hetairesis* as acts of hubris against one's own body should be seen.[24] In democratic discourse, hubris was a violation of another person's status, usually committed for the perpetrator's narcissistic ends (Demosthenes 21.158–9 and passim). Because an act of hubris asserted a hierarchical relationship in the context of an egalitarian political culture, hubris came to be viewed as the paradigmatic antidemocratic offense.[25] This sense of the term, however, demands at least two participants, an offender and a victim or victims. Although Timarchus is said to have colluded in his clients' commission of acts of hubris against his person, he is also repeatedly described as having committed hubris against his own body (29, 108, see also 116, 185, 188). With this usage, Aeschines effectively moralizes the democratic concept of hubris: if Timarchus's prostitution is an acting out of his diseased moral psychology, and prostitution is equivalent to a self-inflicted act of hubris, then acts of hubris, quintessential antidemocratic offenses, can also be attributed to a diseased moral psychology (see 137 and 141).

Making Moral Citizens

Although Aeschines employs an innovative moral discourse to discredit and disfranchise Timarchus, he seeks to represent it as traditional by insisting on its Solonian origin. He claims that Solon, the democracy's traditional founder, made moral standing the only politically salient feature of a citizen's social identity (27–8, 31). I want to turn now to the reading of the laws on which this claim rests. For although modern commentators often dismiss Aeschines' jurisprudential claims, these claims are at the heart of his effort to redefine democratic civic identity in moral terms by replacing distinctions based on class and status with an overarching distinction between the moral and immoral.[26] And in addition, Aeschines' moral interpretation of Athenian legislation importantly answers to the elite charge that that democratic states (meaning primarily Athens) failed to provide a moral education for their citizens.

Aeschines introduces Solon's moral legislation to enable the jurors to compare their laws with the character and habits of Timarchus (8).[27] This is a key point: Aeschines assumes that Athenian law articulates moral norms that shape both the practices and characters of democratic citizens. He begins by elaborating the laws pertaining to the morals, habits, and education of freeborn children (7). The laws he cites, however, contain no information about what the substantive content of this education ought to be. Rather, they define and regulate the contact that teachers, trainers, and slaves may have with boys and youths (9–12).[28] For instance, one law forbids teachers and gymnastic trainers to open their schools before sunrise or to keep them open after sunset because, according to Aeschines, the lawgiver did not trust them enough to leave them alone or in the dark with children (10). After discussing the laws purportedly pertaining to education, Aeschines cites several laws supposedly intended to prohibit sexual offenses against children: the law prohibiting acts of hubris or outrage against all inhabitants of the polis, and the laws prohibiting the pandering and selling of freeborn children (13–19). Again, Aeschines emphasizes that the laws are targeted at adults rather than children: only the adults who bought and sold children could be held legally responsible (13).

Although it is clear enough that these laws safeguard children from the improper desires and advances of adults, it might be less obvious how they moralize or instill moral norms in the children whom they protect. We need to remember that children were both thought to have an undeveloped capacity for moral and intellectual judgment and, at the same time, to be especially susceptible to desire.[29] Since indulging desires was considered the royal road to habit and addiction, safeguarding the young from inappropriate sexual conduct was a necessary ingredient in a proper upbringing. Viewed from this perspective, Aeschines is emphasizing that the laws are oriented to protect children from their own desires and vulnerabilities as much as from the machinations of possibly predatory parents, teachers, and authority figures. In other words, the central point for Aeschines is that the laws enable children to emerge unscathed from the perils of childhood (11). At the same time, however, Aeschines argues that the laws make it possible for the externally regulated child to develop into an internally regulating adult. The laws ensure that upon reaching the age of consent—which is also the age of citizenship—the new citizen will have the capacity to distinguish between right and wrong or between the noble and the base (18–9, 139). According to Aeschines' logic, the repeated performance of the law's prohibitions not only protects the child's eventual capacity for consent, but it also shapes that consent by encouraging the young citizen-in-the-making to internalize the physical boundaries enshrined in the laws as moral norms. Thus, for Aeschines there is no need for the external regulation of the citizen's behavior, as elite critics maintained, because the boundaries enshrined in the city's laws prepare the citizen to be a self-regulating adult. Moreover, it precisely the absence of formal regulations that allows the citizen to demonstrate that he has internalized the moral demeanor appropriate to a "free" democratic citizen.

The Laws of Desire

The notion that citizens received moral education through a process of internalizing the principles and practices encoded in democratic laws is the lynchpin in Aeschines' moralization of democratic identity. It provides the point of reference from which Timarchus's deviance can be marked as well as a basis for the collective identity of the citizen group. It is also crucial to Aeschines' own defense. Later in the speech, in a kind of "trial within the trial," Aeschines reports another one of the defense strategies. In addition to having Demosthenes as his defense speaker, Timarchus was also going to have an unnamed general speak on his behalf. The general was allegedly planning to undermine the prosecution by putting Aeschines' sexual history on trial, thereby implicating him in the very practices for which he was condemning Timarchus.

In part, Aeschines discredits the general by satirizing his aristocratic cultural pretensions, making fun of his arrogant posturing and affected familiarity with the wrestling grounds (132). More cunning yet, he turns the general's patronizing tone back on the general himself, making his valorization of aristocratic culture hinge on a shallow fetishization of physical beauty.

[A]nd he will eulogize beauty, as though it had not long been celebrated as a blessed thing, if it happens to be combined with moral self-control [sophrosunê]. If, he says, certain men slander bodily attractiveness, and thereby make it a misfortune to those who possess it, the result will be that you contradict in your public vote what you say in your private prayers. It would seem to him to be very bizarre, if you, when you are about to have children, all pray that your unborn sons may be fair and noble in appearance [kalous kagathous tas ideas] and worthy of the city, yet those that have been born, in whom the city may well take pride, if they are exceptional in beauty and youthful charm and if they arouse desires of some men and become the objects of fights because of erotic passion, you are then to disfranchise them, on the persuasion of Aeschines (133–34).

Aeschines discredits the general by having him condescendingly insinuate that the Athenians were so in thrall of aristocratic culture that they harbored not so secret desires to bear children endowed with "aristocratic" beauty.[30] By reminding the Athenians of their supposed love of beauty, Aeschines' general seeks to elicit support for his claim that Timarchus is being victimized simply because he is too beautiful.

Aeschines responds by correcting the general's view of beauty, claiming that everyone already knows that beauty is good thing, provided that it is coupled with morality *(sôphrosunê)*.[31] In other words, Aeschines—and the jurors—are too sophisticated to value surface appearances in the absence of moral depth.[32] With this strategy, Aeschines clears a space in which to defend his own activities, courting young men at the exercise grounds and composing erotic poetry for them, as both moral and democratic.

Aeschines admits to participating in a form of love between males according to which an older man, an *erastês* or lover, educated a younger man, the *erômenos* or beloved, in exchange for favoring of some kind.[33] What he denies, of course, is the parallel between his own love of beautiful young men and Timarchus's disgraceful sale of his body for profit and perhaps pleasure. In addition to distinguishing his own behavior from Timarchus's, he also had to avert the perception that he was laying claim to a superior or special status. To be successful in the democratic courts, litigants had to mold their rhetoric so that it would conform with the sensibilities of juries composed of predominantly middling citizens. Aeschines' preferred activities, hanging out at gymnasia and having relationships with men, were traditionally associated with aristocratic and elite culture. Although it is not clear to what extent these practices retained an aristocratic stamp in the mid-fourth century, Aeschines' haughty general was reportedly going to emphasize their aristocratic province, and in so doing, to characterize Aeschines as an ardent admirer of aristocratic culture.[34]

Aeschines diffuses any opprobrium his habits might have given rise to in the democratic court by refuting the general's association of pederasty and athletics with high culture. To this end, he implicitly combines his own defense with a defense of the democracy's "sexual" history. According to Aeschines, the general was going to remind the jurors that the foundation of the democracy was owed to Harmodius and Aristogeiton:

He will attempt to discredit the whole basis of the dispute, maintaining that I have initiated not so much a prosecution as the start of an appalling decline in our cultural education. He will cite first of all those benefactors of yours [*tous euergetas tous humeterous*], Harmodius and Aristogeiton, describing their mutual loyalty [*pistis*], and the good their relationship did for the city (132).

According to Athenian tradition, Harmodius and Aristogeiton were lovers who together plotted to overthrow the Pisistradid tyranny at the end of the sixth century. Although they failed to end the tyranny, later tradition venerated them as tyrannicides and credited them with founding the democracy.[35] The general's purpose in citing the tyrannicides is twofold. First, he assimilates Timarchus's love relationships to the relationship between Harmodius and Aristogeiton, thereby making it difficult to criticize Timarchus for doing no more than imitating the quintessential democratic heroes. Second, he claims their relationship for aristocratic culture—as his distancing and patronizing reference to Harmodius and Aristogeiton as "those benefactors of yours" makes clear. By emphasizing that it was their fidelity (pistis) and relationship that benefited the polis, the general seeks to engender a sense of obligation in the democratic jurors, implying that they owe Timarchus an acquittal because he is a practitioner of the very erotics that enabled Harmodius and Aristogeiton to benefit the democratic state.

Aeschines does not, as might be expected, refute the general's parallel between the tyrannicides and Timarchus, although such a refutation is implicit in the defense of his own erotic life. Instead, he focuses on dissolving the obligation and awe the general's narrative is calculated to evoke. This is the context in which he offers his second exposition of Solonian law. He reminds the jurors of two Solonian laws, one law forbidding slaves to exercise in the gymnasia, and another one forbidding slaves to become the lovers of freeborn boys (138; see also Plutarch Life of Solon 1.3–4). According to Aeschines, the legal restrictions on the activities of slaves contain tacit injunctions or corollaries encouraging free men to engage in the very activities forbidden to slaves, namely to take exercise and lovers. He explains the tacit logic of these provisions as follows:

But he [Solon] did not forbid the free man from being a boy's lover or associating with him and following him, and he envisaged not that this would prove harmful to the boy but that it would be testimony to his sôphrosunê. But since the boy is at this stage not responsible, and is unable to distinguish between real and false affection, it is the lover he disciplines, and he postpones talk of love to the age of reason, when the boy is older. And he considered that following and watching over a boy was the most effective way of securing and protecting his chastity. In this way the city's benefactors [tous tês poleôs euergetas], Harmodius and Aristogeiton, those men of outstanding virtues, were so educated by that chaste and lawful feeling [ho sôphrôn kai ennomos]—call it love [erôs] or what you will—to be men of such merit that when their deeds are praised the panegyrics seem inadequate to their achievements (139–40).

Just as in his introductory legal exposition, Aeschines accounts for the productive power of law by positing a developmental process whereby the repeated performance of the law's prohibitions trains boys and young men to internalize the implicit principles of the city's laws. In this case, the restrictions and tacit injunctions contained in the laws cause the lover and the beloved to internalize the city's laws as laws of desire. According to this procedure, the law (or legislator) teaches the lover to be *sôphrôn* by making him wait until the beloved boy comes of age to begin a relationship. At the same time, the laws pave the way for the beloved to exercise *sôphrosunê* by protecting him from the advances of older men until such time as his reason matures (139, see also 18–19). In this way, the laws regulating the contacts between lovers serve to make men into self-regulating citizens whose desires operate in accordance with the laws of the state. For this reason, Aeschines describes love as lawful and legitimate, literally begotten by law (*ennomos erôs* [140], *erôta dikaion* [136]).[36]

By embedding pederasty into the Solonian foundations of the democracy, Aeschines is able to present his own erotic activities as democratic and, equally important, to refute the general's appropriation of Harmodius and Aristogeiton for aristocratic culture. In Aeschines' version of events, the tyrannicides were educated and made moral by Solonian law, not aristocratic cultural tradition. Accordingly, he refers to them as "benefactors of the polis," revising the general's attempt to render them representatives of a narrow elite to whom the *dêmos* was forever indebted. Yet, it should be noted that Aeschines' appropriation of pederastic pedagogy for democratic culture along with its frankly hierarchical structure is tied to his patent preference for hierarchy in politics. Aeschines is our only source for a Solonian law of *"eukosmia"* giving older men the right to speak first in the Assembly (1.22–3; 3.2–4). The extraordinary valorization of this law enables Aeschines to construct an isomorphism between the political and the erotic.[37] In each domain, as Aeschines would have it, participation depends on a man's moral standing and his age (19–21, 27–31). And, in politics as in pederasty, age and moral standing are the sole basis for hierarchy and deference: age distinguishes the dominant from the subordinate and those who speak from those who are spoken to. Thus, Aeschines' insertion of a hierarchical educational bond into the practices and laws of the democratic polis goes hand in hand with his call (perhaps nostalgic, perhaps elitist), for a form of political hierarchy.

Democratic Reproduction and the Enemies Within

Aeschines not only had to ward off the perception that he was leaning too heavily on aristocratic and elite culture, but he also had to distance himself from the philosophical discourse to which he was so indebted. To this end, he repeatedly refers to Demosthenes as a sophist, displacing onto his opponent any suspicions his own philosophically tinged arguments might have elicited (125, 175, see also 119, 164, 166, 170). To make sure that the jurors get the point, Aeschines offers an exemplary narrative in which Demosthenes' sophistry leads to a perversion of pederasty and politics. Demosthenes reportedly seduced the young Aristarchus, son of Moschus, for the sake of his legacy rather than love (170-72). Although Demosthenes promised to make him the foremost orator in Athens, as Aeschines tells the story he schooled Aristarchus only in the arts of murder, convincing him to gouge out the eyes and cut out the tongue of a political enemy, one Nicodemus of Aphidna.[38] In concluding the anecdote, Aeschines asks the jurors: "So then, men of Athens, you put Socrates the sophist to death, because it was found that he had taught Critias, one of the Thirty who overthrew the democracy; yet is Demosthenes to get his comrades off in your court, this man who has exacted such terrible revenge from ordinary men loyal to the democracy for exercising their equal right to political speech?" (173). After offering the jurors an example of precisely how Demosthenes corrupts the city's youth, political institutions, and most cherished principles, Aeschines cites this famous precedent—the conviction and execution of Socrates in 399—to guide the jurors in casting their vote against Demosthenes and his client. However the rhetorical power of the precedent works on another level as well. Aeschines not only likens Demosthenes to Socrates and the jurors in the present trial to those in Socrates' trial, but he also strategically evokes a precise historical milieu. Socrates was convicted and condemned on charges of impiety and corrupting the youth. Aeschines, however, translates these charges into their "real" political meaning: his Socrates was put to death because he was the teacher of one of Thirty tyrants, the corrupt oligarchic regime that ruled Athens at the close of the Peloponnesian War and committed numerous outrages and atrocities against citizens and noncitizens alike. By referring to Socrates as the teacher of one of the notorious Thirty, Aeschines strategically summons this historical context, reminding the jurors that in the aftermath of the Peloponnesian War they suffered more from the brutality of their fellow citizens than from their enemies in war.[39] And, by addressing the jurors in Timarchus's trial as though they were the very same jurors who convicted Socrates, Aeschines collapses the temporal distance between "then and now," lending the present prosecution the urgency of the past.

Elsewhere, Aeschines more explicitly links Demosthenes' sophistry to national and international affairs. He anticipates that Demosthenes will harp on what he deems irrelevant matters, Philip of Macedon, his son Alexander, and the Phocians, to scare the jurors and cloud the real issues at stake (166, 175). This claim is, of course, both clever and disingenuous on Aeschines' part because without Philip, there would have been no trial against Timarchus, no concern for the national morality, and no dire predictions about the consequences of Demosthenes' sophistry. In the year before the trial, the Athenians agreed to end their long-standing but futile war with Philip—but on peace terms that excluded their Phocian allies.[40] Although Demosthenes was one of the ambassadors who negotiated the peace, he immediately began to undermine it by impugning Philip's intentions in settling the Third Sacred War in which the Phocian cities were involved. Shortly after the Athenians approved the peace, Demosthenes and Timarchus decided to prosecute Aeschines for committing treason on the fateful embassies, claiming that he had accepted Philip's bribes. In the actual settlement, which occurred just after the Athenians approved the peace, Philip disbanded the Phocian cities, destroying them as military powers.[41]

The power and prestige Philip won by settling the Sacred War, coupled with the corresponding deterioration of Athens' position, lent new credibility to Demosthenes' accusations against Philip and, more important, to his allegations against Aeschines. Given these circumstances, Aeschines decided to strike first: he launched the prosecution against Timarchus specifically to eliminate one of his own prosecutors, and so to better his chances in court. Nevertheless, Aeschines needed to ensure that Demosthenes would not be able to reintroduce the Macedonian question on his own terms or reduce the prosecution of Timarchus to a debate concerning the pro- or anti-Macedonian sentiments of the parties involved. On a rhetorical level, his preemptive banishing of Philip and Alexander secures precisely this end while simultaneously supplying him with an opportunity to defend his Macedonian policy in a way that seemed not to be defensive.

Aeschines had to show that Philip was not the dangerous enemy Demosthenes and others alleged him to be. To this end, he reframes the Macedonian question, presenting Demosthenes' "foolish," "untimely," and "uneducated" talk about Philip, rather than Philip himself, as the real problem and embarrassment for Athens (166-67). To illustrate precisely how Demosthenes' language was harming the city's reputation, he cites the shameful sexual innuendoes Demosthenes reportedly made about Alexander, Philip's young son, in a meeting of the Athenian council (167-68).[42] By portraying Demosthenes as publicly passing on malicious gossip about Alexander—Philip's eleven-year-old son—Aeschines closes the gap between the Athenian jurors and the Macedonian king. It leads to an emphasis on Philip's status as the father of a young boy whose morals and reputation require guarding and protecting rather than his standing as a Macedonian monarch, which thus renders him as rather more like than unlike Athenian citizens and fathers. Although other writers and speakers depicted Philip as a polygamous barbarian despot with a court populated by degenerates of all types, Aeschines incorporates Philip into his vision of a moral collective in which adherence to shared moral norms subordinates differences of class, social status, and in Philip's case, of ethnic and political position as well.[43]

Although Aeschines strategically neutralizes the Macedonian threat, he could hardly disguise the discrepancy between recent Macedonian and Athenian military fortunes. Whereas Athens continued to lose allies and possessions from 357 onward, Philip's influence was correspondingly growing in the same period. If, as Aeschines maintained, Philip and his bribes were not behind recent Athenian setbacks and the corresponding Macedonian successes, who or what was? Instead of blaming the Macedonians, Aeschines directs the jurors' attention to the immoral citizens in their midst, to Demosthenes, Timarchus, and their associates. His narrative of Timarchus's exploits as a male prostitute is interwoven with a tale of his equally scandalous political career.[44] So too his story of Demosthenes' venal sophistry also doubles as a parable of political subversion. In fact, the interconnection between personal immorality and political corruption is a logical consequence of Aeschines' implicit presumption that intrapsychic states are unavoidably acted out. The rhetorical force of Aeschines' prosecution stems precisely from this economy of explanation: the same logic that explains Timarchus's prostitution also explains Athenian policy setbacks. Whereas Demosthenes scarcely missed an opportunity to castigate the *dêmos* for its failure either to appreciate or meet the threat Philip posed, Aeschines offered a face-saving explanation, attributing Athens' waning power to its immoral leaders, men whose diseased moral psychology was externalized in political affairs (125, 175, see also 119, 164, 166).

Here again Aeschines' strategy is indebted to the philosophical tradition he professes to disavow. In fact, he frames the prosecution with reference to the paradigmatic political problem as formulated by the philosophers and critical writers. Plato, Isocrates, and Aristotle assume that the task of political theory and practical politics is to ward off the chronic threat of *stasis* or internal instability.[45] Although Plato's *Republic* and *Laws* are cognizant of the need to defend the state against external threats, each work is dedicated to designing a state impervious to internal sources of instability and so to change itself. In his opening exegesis on constitutional forms, Aeschines also begins from the premise that states weaken from the inside out:

I am well aware, men of Athens, that you will certainly have heard already from others what I am going to say at the outset; but I think it appropriate that I, too, should now make the same statement to you. It is agreed that there are three kinds of constitution in the world, tyranny, oligarchy, and democracy, and tyrannies and oligarchies are governed by the temperament of those in power, but democratic cities are governed by established laws. You are aware, men of Athens, that in a democracy the persons of citizens and the constitution are protected by the laws, while tyrants and oligarchs are protected by distrust and armed guards. Oligarchs and all who run a constitution based on inequality must be on guard against people who attempt to overthrow the constitution by force; but you, and all who have a constitution based on equality and law, must watch out for people whose words and way of life contravene the laws. For your real strength is when you are ruled by law [*eunomêsthe*] and not overthrown by the lawless (4–5).

Although Aeschines claims to be iterating the common wisdom, a trope that everyone has already heard before, there is no parallel for the actual distinction Aeschines draws among constitutional forms.[46] It may be precisely the pretense of appealing to what everyone already knows that allows Aeschines to adapt commonplace constitutional rhetoric to suit his own argumentative needs. Yet, there is a sense in which Aeschines is drawing on traditional philosophical ideas, despite the fact that some commentators rule out Platonic influence on this passage because Plato's *Republic* identifies five legitimate constitutional forms, in contrast to Aeschines' three, and because it does not count tyranny as a legitimate form at all.[47] For Aeschines is not seeking to classify or enumerate constitutional forms but rather to explain how democracies, oligarchies, and tyrannies sustain and reproduce themselves, namely, by means of armed guards or by safeguarding the law. In other words, like the philosophers, Aeschines assumes that all states are continually menaced from within and must struggle to suppress the internal sources of revolution and unrest (5, 190). By emphasizing the need for internal stability and claiming that the most dangerous enemies to that stability, and hence to the reproduction of the state, are the lawless debauchees harbored within, Aeschines offers a new agenda for politics, effectively diminishing the significance of foreign affairs and war. In this respect, it is no accident that Aeschines' prosecution of a citizen prostitute is also a discourse on and prescription for civic education, that is, for the production of citizens fit to reproduce the democratic state. To a polis weary of fighting, of endless levying and expeditions, Aeschines' reconceptualization of the political problem and its solution must have seemed infinitely—albeit temporarily—more appealing than Demosthenes' constant haranguing about the need to defend against the enemy without and the energetic military response required to do so.

Notes

An early version of this study was delivered at the annual meeting of the Association of Ancient Historians in Madison, Wisconsin, April 2000. I would like to thank participants at the history conference and participants at the prostitution conference in Madison (2002) for helpful criticism and suggestions. Unfortunately, I did not know A. Lanni's 2004 study when writing this study.

1. Elsewhere, Aeschines characterizes the prosecution as an exhortation of the citizens to *aretê* and *sôphrosunê* (1.11); see also Aeschines 2.180–81.

2. For the stricter moral standards to which speakers and generals were supposedly held accountable, see, e.g., Demosthenes 10.70, Ober (1989, 108–12), Winkler (1990, 55–64).

3. See also Lysias 14.12–13 and Aeschines 1.186, which emphasize the shared moral standards for all citizens, regardless of their political activity.

4. For the outcome of the trial, see Demosthenes 19.284, 285, and 287.

5. In emphasizing the elite and philosophical origins of Aeschines' arguments, I am not claiming that Aeschines meant to convey philosophical ideas *per se* or that he studied in any particular school. Rather, my purpose is to show how Aeschines deploys concepts and ideals that, before the speech against Timarchus, are found primarily in philosophical writing, and how he reshapes them to suit the democratic environment. It is worth mentioning, however, that a late tradition identifies Aeschines as a student of both Isocrates and Plato, see [Plutarch] *Moralia* 840b. Aeschines' characterization of Timarchus along the lines of Plato's tyrannical man has been well discussed by Davidson (1997, 301); for Platonic elements in the speech, see also Sissa (1999, 153) and Fisher (2001, 350–51) and the additional references cited in them. For the cross-fertilization of philosophical and democratic discourse in the fourth century, see Ober (1998, 369–72) and Allen (2000a).

6. According to cultural theorist Sonya Rose, moral discourses are central to the continual processes of creating and sustaining imagined unities and collectivities like the nation. Moral discourses allow communities to define themselves by identifying what their members condone and what they condemn, what they value and what they abhor. Paraphrasing Richard Rorty, Rose describes morality as a matter of "we-intentions" with the core meaning of an immoral action being "the sort of thing *we* don't do" (1999, 231).

7. This analysis of the speech against Timarchus is part of a larger diachronic history of the citizen in ancient Greece. Due to limitations of space, I cannot here examine all of the cultural and political processes informing the increased importance attached to morality in fourth- century discussions of Athenian citizen identity.

8. For the rhetorical force of Aeschines' emotionally charged descriptions of Timarchus, see further Sissa (1999).

9. On the scrutiny *(dokimasia)* for citizenship, see [Aristotle] *Constitution of the Athenians* 42.1–2, with Whitehead (1986), Scafuro (1994), Robertson (2000).

10. See esp. Demosthenes 57 and Whitehead (1986, 292–301).

11. See Demosthenes 57, with Libanius' hypothesis, Aeschines 1.77–8, 86, 114 and 2.182, the scholiast on Aeschines 1.77 (for which see Dilts 1992, 33), Isaeus 12, Harpocration, s.v. *diapsêphisis* (= *FGrH* 324 F 52), Whitehead (1986, 106–9), and Scafuro (1994).

12. Translations of Aeschines 1 are adapted from Carey (2000).

13. For Timarchus's family wealth see 1.101, 42.

14. Although Aeschines does not actually include Timarchus's prostitution in the catalogue of his shameful addictions, its inclusion therein may follow from his claim that Timarchus went to live with Misgolas for their mutual pleasure rather than for a compelling economic reason.

15. For the uses of tragedy in fourth-century oratory, see P. Wilson (1996).

16. In the *Timarchus* speech, Aeschines employs the concept of nature to refer to innate disposition (49, 185) and disposition as it is formed by education, training, and habit (11). In 185, Aeschines notes the contradiction that would arise if the Athenians were to get angry with an unmarried woman who allowed herself to be seduced, thus making a mistake in accordance with nature, while allowing Timarchus, a man who has committed *hubris* against his own body—contrary to nature—to serve as a policy advisor. The language of nature in this passage pertains to the male's natural capacity for self-control (if developed) and the female's assumed natural incapacity for such control, contra Sissa (1999, 156). This passage may intimate that appeals to moral psychology may have originated in the democratic need to justify and rationalize the denial of political rights to women. Thus, the philosophers may have transformed and adapted traditional "democratic" ideas in theorizing *akrasia*. I discuss the gendered genealogy of moral psychology in more detail in my project on the history of the citizen.

17. This is clarified at 95: "But there came a time when these resources had been squandered, diced away, and gobbled up, and the defendant was getting past his youthful bloom, and no one, reasonably, would give him anything; but this man's revolting and unholy nature still longed for the same pleasures, and

in his excess of uncontrolled desire [*huperbolên akrasias*] he kept making demand upon demand, and was carried back to his daily habits." For *akrasia,* see also 141–42, 160.

18. Prior to the *Timarchus* speech, the only use of the term *"akrasia"* in an extant democratic oratorical context occurs in Demosthenes' second Olynthiac speech where he attributes an incontinent life to Philip of Macedon (2.18).

19. For the philosophical debate about *akrasia,* see, e.g., Plato *Protagoras* 352 and *Republic* 430e–31a.

20. The good citizen was long idealized as a *metrios* or "middling man" (see Morris (1996, 22, Foucault 1985, 63–77), and Winkler 1990, 48–50). It should be noted, however, that before Aeschines' speeches, the term *"metrios"* is not generally employed to designate "keeping one's appetites under control," that is, it is not equated with *sôphrosunê* and / or *enkrateia;* see however Demosthenes 54.17. For the specific moral sense of *"metrios"* in Aeschines, see 2.181 and 3.170, 218.

21. Plato *Republic* 557b–58c, Isocrates 12.131, 7.20, Aristotle *Politics* 1310a26–33, 1317 a40–b17. For the "license" of slaves and metics in democratic states, see [Xenophon] *Constitution of the Athenians* 1.10 and Plato *Republic* 563b–c.

22. On the need for exacting laws and provisions to produce good citizens, see, e.g., Plato *Republic* 558b. By contrast, in the *Areopagiticus,* Isocrates argues that civic conduct should be regulated by the Areopagus Council, rather than through an excess of written legislation (7.39–40). I have found Lear's (1992) discussion of the city-soul analogy in the *Republic* particularly helpful in clarifying the correlation between intrapsychic states and political structures in Greek thought.

23. Xenophon *Memorabilia* 1.5–1.6.10, Isocrates 2.29, Plato *Gorgias* 491d; see also Hunt (1998, 146–53) and Foucault (1984, 341).

24. Previous commentators have faulted Aeschines for his "specious" and "strange" use of the term *"hubris";* see, e.g., Dover ([1979] 1989, 38) and Hindley (1991, 171).

25. For the democratic ideology of *hubris,* see Halperin (1990a, 88–112) and Ober (1996). For *hubris* more generally, see Fisher (1992) and Cairns (1996).

26. On the accuracy, or lack thereof, of Aeschines' citation and interpretation of Athenian law generally, see Dover ([1979] 1989, 23–39), Winkler (1990, 59), Hindley (1991), Lane Fox (1994, 147–55), and Fisher (2001, 127–28). For present purposes, I am interested in the logic and rhetorical strategies underlying Aeschines' interpretative legal citations rather than in empirical considerations. For a similar "literary" approach to law in the speech against Timarchus, see Ford (1999).

27. Aeschines' framing of his legislative review has a distinctively Isocratean ring; compare Aeschines 1.7–8 with Isocrates 7.37.

28. For the authenticity of the laws cited in speech against Timarchus, see Fisher (2001, 129–35 and references cited there).

29. Dover (1974, 102–4) and Golden (1984, 309 and 1990, 4–7 and passim).

30. The phrase Aeschines employs to describe beautiful children, *"kalos kagathos,"* was an aristocratic ideal appropriated by the democracy to characterize the presumed excellence of the citizens (Ober 1989). The transvaluation, however, was never total, and hence its ideological inflection is context dependent.

For Aeschines' use of this phrase, see Bourriot (1995, 435–47 with lines 445–46 in Aeschines 1.134).

31. The distinction between beauty valued for its own sake (the general's view) and beauty valued only if tethered to morality (Aeschines' view) is crucial to the ideological moves Aeschines is making in this section. Aeschines does not agree with the general (contra Fisher [1998a] 100) but rather discredits his valorization of beautiful appearances.

32. With this argument, Aeschines undermines the general's aristocratic ideology by appropriating the classic Platonic critique of superficial love based only on bodily beauty—targeted at aristocratic and democratic culture in the *Symposium*—for the *dêmos* and for himself. See Dover (1964, 31–42) and Hindley (1991, 133) for a discussion of some of the parallels between Aeschines' conception of *erôs* and the arguments advanced in Plato's *Symposium*.

33. For the protocols of pederasty, see Dover ([1979] 1989) and Halperin (1990a, 130–37). For a critique of this view, see Davidson (1997, 167–82).

34. For some recent discussions of the origins and class politics of this form of pederasty, see Dover ([1979] 1989, 148–53), Halperin (1990a, 91), Hubbard (1998), Sissa (1999, 156–57), Wohl (1999, 355–57), and Fisher (2001, 27, 34–36). For the status of athletics and the gymnasia in the democratic period, see Golden (1998, 158–59) and Fisher (1998a).

35. For Harmodius and Aristogeiton as democratic founders, see Thomas (1989, 238–82). For the tyrannicide legend in general, see Monoson (2000, 21–50 and references cited there).

36. Dover ([1979] 1989, 46) maintains that *erôs* in Aeschines' works always carries the sense of *"dikaios"* or "legitimate" and that consequently the word *"dikaios"* is pleonastic in the expression *"dikaios erôs."* Although Aeschines builds the notion of "legitimacy" or "justice" into his conception of eros, "legitimate" is not a redundant adjective but rather identifies the source of *erôs*. In praising "legitimate desire," Aeschines is approving an eros that has been produced, disciplined, educated, or made *dikaios* by democratic law.

37. Lane Fox (1994, 148–49) assembles evidence for the law's disuse and questions whether it ever existed at all; see also Kapparis (1998). The historicity of the law is perhaps supported by the democratic tendency to award special privileges to older citizens (Golden 1984, 312 with n.20 and Ober 1989, 14 with n.23).

38. On the murder of Nicodemus, see also Aeschines 2.148, 166, Demosthenes 21.103–4, and Dinarchus 1.30, 47.

39. On the reign of the Thirty and the civil war, see Wolpert (2002, 3–28).

40. There is a large literature on the complex events leading to the Peace of Philocrates; see Montgomery (1983), Buckler (2000), and Harris (1995) on Aeschines' involvement in the negotiations.

41. For the Amphictyonic Council's punishment of the Phocian cities, with Philip's backing, see Diodorus Siculus 16.60.1–3. On the settlement of the Third Sacred War and Philip's motives, see Ellis (1976).

42. This interpretation of Aeschines 1.167–8 differs from that of Fisher (2001, 313) and Carey (2000, 79). In this passage, Aeschines recalls that Demosthenes told the council a story about Alexander's lyre playing and his *"antikrouseis"*

against another boy. The meaning of the rare word *"antikrousis"* ("abrupt close," "hindrance," "check" [LSJ]) is not certain here, and hence translations vary widely: Fisher (2001) gives "sallies," Carey (2000) gives "debates," C. D. Adams (1919) "thrusts," and the standard Greek lexicon suggests "repartee." What is at stake is whether the term has a sexual connotation in this passage. Fisher (2001, 313) does not think so; he suggests instead that it refers to "brief, sharp, debating points made by Alexander to a mate." However the fact that Aeschines introduces the anecdote by stating that Demosthenes has been insinuating shameful suspicions against the boy with contrived metaphors seems to call for a sexual or any rate double reading of the term *"antikrouseis"* here. In addition, Aeschines shows an exaggerated concern for Alexander's morals and reputation, adding to the likelihood that he was defending Philip's son against Demosthenes' sexual intimations about his behavior.

43. For Macedonian polygamy, see Ogden (1999); for sexual scandal at Philip's court, see Theopompus *FGrH* 115 F 224 and F 225 (= Athenaeus 166f–67c and 260d–61a) and Demosthenes 2.18.

44. For this point, see Davidson (1997, 260–63).

45. On the problem of stasis in Greek political thought, see, e.g., Isocrates 7.13–4, D. Cohen (1995, 25–34), and Loraux (2002).

46. Lane Fox (1994, 144) suggests that Aeschines has appropriated his constitutional rhetoric from Demosthenes 24.75–6. The Demosthenic passage does not, however, parallel what Aeschines is claiming in the passage quoted in the text. Demosthenes distinguishes democracies from oligarchies on the basis of the durability and force of law in the former and the lack thereof in the latter, whereas Aeschines describes how democracies, tyrannies, and oligarchies *preserve* themselves.

47. See the scholiast on Aeschines 1.4 in Dilts (1992, 13–14).

Zoning Shame in the Roman City

THOMAS MCGINN

tonsor, copo, cocus, lanius sua limina servant.
nunc Roma est, nuper magna taberna fuit.
          Martial 7.61.9–10

Brothels at Pompeii

In recent years the idea that there were around thirty-five brothels in ancient Pompeii has occasioned disquiet among scholars.[1] How could a city with a population of, say, ten thousand people support so many? Even more shocking perhaps is the possibility that thirty-five may be too *low* an estimate.

Whatever their precise number, one thing seems clear, simply that a great deal of uncertainty surrounds the number and location of brothels at Pompeii. They seem to have been situated in a variety of places all over town, near gates, upper-class houses, baths, hotels, and snack bars, a promiscuous arrangement of space that can seem even more strange to a modern sensibility than a high number might by itself. My purpose is to investigate Roman ideas or the lack thereof on segregating prostitution. Where does the idea of zoning shame, which seems so obvious to us, whatever we might think of it, come from?

Here, in a nutshell, is my argument. The uncertainty over the sheer number of Pompeian brothels makes it difficult to agree with recent views that the Romans practiced a kind of moral zoning, keeping brothels in certain areas and out of others.[2] Ray Laurence, for example, holds that the concern was to restrict the sale of sex to parts of the city not frequented by elite women and children, thereby rendering it invisible to them (1994, 73). Andrew Wallace-Hadrill posits a more general purpose, arguing that the aim was to purify one area of the town center by displacing and concentrating "impure activities in another inconspicuous and hidden, but nevertheless central area" (1995, 51). He supports this contention by reference to the location of "the definite brothels," by which he means the Purpose-Built Brothel and the *cellae meretriciae* (54).[3]

Moral Geography

What is striking about the topography of Roman prostitution, however, is the complete absence of any evidence for such moral zoning. First, to turn the argument about "definite brothels" on its head, it is difficult to be certain that many of the establishments scholars have posited as such and questioned by Wallace-Hadrill were not in fact brothels, though some may seem more likely candidates than others. At a certain point in the analysis the problem of identifying individual brothels is less important than the conclusion that Pompeii knew a number of brothels, which were scattered throughout the city.[4] This means that what we should focus on are the probable, or even possible, venues for the sale of sex in Pompeii, if we want to argue for the segregation of prostitution in that city.

It is, moreover, a bit misleading to concentrate on brothels and not prostitutes.[5] Public buildings and elite townhouses may have squeezed the former, but not the latter, out of some areas, to judge from the fairly abundant evidence, which shows a wide pattern both of public solicitation and nonbrothel prostitution in places of public entertainment such as circuses, temples, and baths. In other words you do not need a brothel to sell sex any more than you need a McDonald's to sell hamburgers, though I would not care to push this analogy one bit further.

The Vicus Sobrius at Rome may be relevant to the argument. According to the grammarian Festus,[6] the Romans called one street "Sober," because it had no *tabernae* or *cauponae*. One may doubt that it was the only such street, but the point militates against the assumption that the Romans practiced moral zoning. Brothels, including what would be termed, on a somewhat narrow definition, strictly nonbrothel venues such as *cauponae* and *popinae* where sex was sold, tended to blend in with a city's lower-class housing stock in a manner that might render them invisible to many elite Romans and, unfortunately, to us as well.[7] While most scholars would not assume that every *caupona*, *popina*, and *deversorium* offered sex for sale, it is far from certain which ones did and which ones did not, a point that also holds for baths. For this reason, perhaps, the well-explored Roman port city of Ostia, for example, turns up not one certain example of a brothel, and not many good candidates at that.

A further point to make is that brothels were often not located at any great distance from upper-class dwellings.[8] The houses of the Roman elite were not distributed evenly throughout their cities, but neither were they packed together, isolated from the rest of urban society. A pattern of limited clustering, rather than strict segregation, is what emerges from recent studies of places such as Roman Britain (Clarke [1993, 56] finds some quite disparate patterns, to be sure [63, 65]), Egypt (Alston and Alston 1997, 211–16; Alston 2002, esp. 172 and 183–84), Pompeii,[9] and Rome itself (Ramage 1983, 86–88; Kardos 2001, 397 [on the Esquiline]), where the highest concentration of senatorial houses is found in areas of the city (*Regiones* Three and Four) in which the Subura, commonly regarded by moderns as a brothel district, is located (Eck 1997, 177, 181, and 183).[10]

If Roman cities were relatively socially homogeneous, in terms of topography,[11] there is simply no plausible rationale supporting the theory of moral zoning. Without officially segregated prostitution districts, one expects brothels to be distributed throughout the city, with some clustering in those areas that presented the right mix of residential and commercial elements, especially a good share of lower-class housing, in what we might describe as the "Subura-effect."[12]

Even where Roman authors appear to suggest a different pattern, that is, the existence of a clear distinction between wealthy and poor districts, an alternative reading is often possible and perhaps to be preferred. For example, when Ovid writes in the first book of the *Metamorphoses* of the heavenly Palatine, almost certainly in reference to the Rome of his own day, that "the common people live elsewhere" (*"plebs habitat diversa locis"*), the obvious meaning is that the rich had made that hill exclusively their own, but a covert reference to imperial usurpation of prime urban real estate seems even more plausible, at least to me.[13] In any event, the point is that literary topography—topography on the page— is not always coterminous with material topography—topography on the ground—though scholars will inevitably disagree on how precisely to reconcile these different maps of the ancient Roman city.[14]

Comparing Brothels

In an important sense, this should end the question. If there is no evidence for any rules, legal or administrative,[15] enforcing the geographic segregation of brothels and the location of such establishments is uncertain and quite possibly widespread, the argument for moral zoning fails. The difficulty is, however, that the thesis advanced by Ray Laurence and Andrew Wallace-Hadrill, even in the absence of evidence to support it, remains somewhat compelling, at least from a modern perspective, and so deserves greater consideration.

Just how compelling this modern perspective can seem is well illustrated by the dire problems facing Nevada's legalized brothels in 2001. Nevada is famously the only state in the union to permit these institutions. Ten of its seventeen counties have allowed them since 1971, though the tradition of prostitution in that area dates back to the "Gold Rush" days in the nineteenth century.[16] While legal, these brothels are nevertheless heavily regulated. They are for the most part permitted only in a few rural areas, in contrast to the much more common urban setting especially characteristic of prostitution that is illegal and unregulated. Advertising is not permitted, nor public solicitation in any form.

The prostitutes who work in such places are not strictly employees of the brothels but independent contractors who are required to pay for weekly examinations to check for sexually transmitted diseases. The brothels themselves pay hefty registration and licensing fees to their local communities. They prefer to call themselves "ranches" and most retain the same 1970s decor that they opened with three decades ago. In fact, when a brothel owner in Pahrump, about sixty miles west of Las Vegas, announced a plan to convert his "ranch" into a major resort facility with a golf course, casino, and steakhouse, the proposal rocked the entire state's prostitution industry, for which publicity of any kind is something akin to poison.[17]

The paradoxical situation of Nevada's brothel business shows how deeply rooted the assumption is in our culture that prostitution should be, and often actually is, hidden away from public view. The barriers to thinking outside of this box are uncomfortably high. It also serves as an example of the false promise held out by some of the comparative evidence available on the subject of prostitution.

Given the lack of ancient evidence for zoning, however, it is difficult, if not impossible, to raise the issue without resort to comparison with other cultures. A useful example lies in attempting to see a link between official approaches toward brothels on the one hand and sewers on the other. Wallace-Hadrill draws a connection between keeping the streets and sewers clean and controlling prostitution that is reminiscent of much nineteenth-century discourse on venal sex, above all that of the famous Alexandre Parent-Duchâtelet (Wallace-Hadrill 1995, 50–51).[18] The key question of course is whether such a connection exists in Roman policy on prostitution. This is not a simple matter of anachronism, but an issue of just what kind of comparative evidence is most likely to shed light on ancient Rome given that past cultures demonstrate a wide range of experience with respect to prostitution.

Christian Topography

As far as I am able to discover, a policy aiming at the segregation of venal sex from respectable elements of the population has every appearance of being a phenomenon that postdated the rise of Christianity.[19] It may be relevant that, despite a longstanding association between brothels and filth, and a "special relationship" between the sewer and the moral criticism of satire (a genre quite familiar with the brothel),[20] the first ancient to identify brothel with sewer appears to have been precisely Cyprian, Bishop of Carthage, who writes of a putative follower of his opponent Novatian: "having entered a brothel, the location of the sewer and the slimy black hole of the rabble, he has befouled his own sanctified body, God's temple, with hateful filth."[21] By itself, however, this account cannot explain an inclination to zone brothels so that they were kept away from respectable establishments. Cyprian's concern with squalor and the horrors of class mixing are very old hat from a Roman elite perspective and, importantly, do not necessarily range beyond the walls of the brothel in their consequences. From what he writes, it does not appear that he believes a person would be implicated in the evils of the brothel without actually setting foot in one.

As for segregation itself, the first well-attested example is a text that attributes to Constantine the establishment, in his new city of Constantinople, of a large brothel in the Zeugma district, complete with a statue of Aphrodite outside on a stone pillar (a nice touch). This establishment was supposed to be the only brothel, indeed the only place where prostitutes worked, in the entire city (*Patria of Constantinople* 2.65 [= Preger

1975, 185–87]).[22] One is inclined to distrust this report as representing yet another effort in the long campaign to make Constantine appear more Christian than he ever was in actual fact.[23] This particular instance appears to rely on wholesale invention or, more probably, represents the recounting of a popular legend. At any rate, the notion that this pragmatist emperor attempted to limit prostitution in his new capital to a single venue defies belief. Nevertheless, it must stand as an example of what some Christians thought a Christian emperor ought to do. This is where its true value as evidence lies.

I hasten to point out that even a Christian might shrink from such an attribution. In establishing a brothel as an act of public policy, Constantine would seem to join the distinguished, if at the same time dubious, company of ruler-pimps such as Solon and Caligula.[24] Some Christians, perhaps of a more fundamentalist stripe, might not be inclined to view the attempted "paganification" of the brothel site through the alleged installation of the statue of Aphrodite as a saving grace. At all events let us not saddle emperor Constantine with more credit—or blame—than the sources allow, as one scholar risks doing in stating, "[i]t is characteristic of his pragmatic approach to prostitution that Constantine designated a section of his new capital city, Constantinople, as an official red-light district and required all of the city's harlots to remain within its confines" (Brundage 1987, 105; no source cited). So one brothel morphs into a red-light district in the tradition of scholarship. The legend lives on.

A more likely candidate for the first Christian intervention of this kind is perhaps seen, albeit indirectly, in the *Historia Augusta*, which reports that the emperor Tacitus "outlawed brothels in the capital, a measure which, to be sure, could not hold for long" ("meritoria intra urbem stare vetuit, quod quidem diu tenere non potuit" [*Historia Augusta Tacitus* 10.2]). The author is almost certainly making fun of Christian antiprostitution legislation rather than reporting an action that can be reliably attributed to the third-century emperor, and my best guess would be some initiative of the Theodosian dynasty lost to us at least in part because of its swift and manifest failure.[25] Even if one credits the report about Constantine's Zeugma brothel, a similar conclusion is inevitable, namely that the policy of zoning failed. Brothels in Constantinople, as in other Byzantine cities, were located where the customers were to be found, at the harbors, near the holy shrines, and, where we might expect the administrative heirs of the classical aediles to be the busiest, in the heart of the city center.[26]

From where did these Christian ideas about zoning prostitution arise? Before attempting an answer to this question, I must first confront a difficulty in my argument. If it is indeed possible to show, or simply to suggest strongly, that the impetus to segregate venal sex within cities originates with Christianity, this does not render the argument that there was zoning at Pompeii somehow automatically anachronistic. Far from it. Such an argument in fact opens the door to the suggestion that the Christians, as with a number of aspects of their teaching on sexual matters or morality in general, took some elements of the various moral traditions that predated them in the Mediterranean world and made them their own.[27] This is what might fairly be described as the dominant opinion in the field, which is not to say that there are not some notable exceptions to the general trend.

What makes the difficulty particularly acute in the matter of segregating prostitution is that there is nothing about Christian moral teaching in antiquity that in any sense predestines it to favor a policy of zoning over others. It is a peculiar fact about Christian moral teaching that over the centuries it has shown itself remarkably supple in accommodating itself to any number of policies regarding the sale of sex, ranging from repression, to regulation, to tolerance, or any of the various mixing and matching of two or more of these approaches contained in the historical record.[28]

Augustinian Policy

A useful demonstration of this point is provided by a text of St. Augustine, which has been of monumental importance in the formation of public policy on prostitution in the Christian West and beyond, not to speak of its significance in the historical understanding of these developments, *De ordine* 2.12 (= *CCSL* 29.114): "Remove prostitutes from human societies and you will throw everything into confusion through lusts" ("Aufer meretrices de rebus humanis, turbaveris omnia libidinibus"). By itself, this text is polyvalent. By itself, all it really amounts to is an argument against the repression of prostitution rather than a case for regulation or tolerance. This fact has left the door open to various interpretations of the passage as justifying tolerance, regulation, or some mixed policy. The historical—and historiographical—record in fact is full of such varied interpretations, rendering the search for Augustine's meaning that much more difficult.[29]

Of course the approach Augustine is implicitly criticizing—the elimination of prostitution from human society—in the *De ordine* was not characteristic of pre-Christian Roman policies on prostitution, at least, not in the drastic form he presupposes. In other words, this too is a Christianizing policy. Evidence of Christian hostility toward prostitution is not far to seek.[30] The Roman practice of punishing Christian women, mentioned by Tertullian, among others, by interning them in brothels may have helped sour them on the profession (Tertullian *Apologia* 50.12 [= CCSL 1.171]). But the disfavor is much older than that, based in no small measure on a text of Paul that appears to exclude both prostitute and client from the Christian Church (1 Corinthians 6.15–16: below).

One may reasonably question whether all of this evidence is inevitably linked to the repression of prostitution, since disapproval of the practice can notably coexist with other official approaches, though admittedly is unlikely to be found alongside sheer tolerance. At all events, one does find various repressive measures launched by Christian emperors, albeit partial in nature, and in most cases directed at pimping rather than prostitutes or prostitution itself.[31] This evidence does encourage an inference to be drawn. What we seem to have in this passage by Augustine is the outline, bare as it is, of a debate among Christians about the optimal public policy on prostitution.

Can we be any more precise about Augustine's own position? The context of the sentence quoted above suggests that this is perhaps possible. The future bishop is grappling with the problem of the place of evil in God's creation.[32] Does it show the limits of His power or, worse, suggest that He endorses evil?[33] With that context in mind, it is not surprising to find that, immediately before introducing the problem of prostitution in this passage, Augustine cites the need to tolerate the existence of the marginal and socially despised figure of the executioner in a well-ordered society *(bene moderata civitas)*. Here is the full passage concerning prostitution :

What can be said to be baser, more worthless, more laden with humiliation and disgrace [*dedecoris et turpitudinis plenius*] than prostitutes, pimps, and the other vermin of this type? Remove prostitutes from human society and you will throw everything into confusion through lusts. Confer on them the status of respectable women [*matronarum*], and you will only disgrace the latter through blot and humiliation. So instead this kind of person is rendered most foul in terms of lifestyle by their conduct, and lowest in social status by the laws of the universal order [*ordo*]. Are there not, in the bodies of living creatures, certain parts, which if you should pay attention only to them, you would not be able to pay attention? Nevertheless, the natural, universal order [*naturae ordo*] did not wish them to be lacking, since they are necessary, nor did it allow them to stand out, because they are ugly. These misshapen elements, all the same, by retaining their own contexts, yield a better place to the better parts. What has been more pleasant to us, what entertainment more appropriate for field and farm, than that combat and contestation of barnyard-bred cocks, of which we spoke in the preceding book? All the same, what have we seen that is more cast down than the defacement of the one who is defeated? And yet it is through that very defacement that the beauty of this same competition had emerged as more perfect. (2.12 [= *CCSL* 29.114])

First, it must be noted that much of this passage is woven simply from the more or less whole cloth of traditional Roman male upper-class attitudes about prostitutes and prostitution. The use of the language of social disgrace and sexual shame (*dedecus, turpitudo*, e.g.) in characterizing prostitutes is very familiar,[34] as is the contrast between the status of respectable women (*matronae*) and that of prostitutes, which had been, after all, a fundamental premise of the Augustan law on adultery (McGinn 1998c, 147–71). The same statute assumed that prostitutes ideally served to distract male lust from respectable women, and so exempted them from its penalties, as well as exempted those males who had sexual relations with them (McGinn 1998c, 194–202). One can easily see that the idea, which we would locate in a kind of biological determinism, that prostitutes functioned—or should function—as a safety valve for male sexual desire is central to Augustine's thinking in this passage. As far as his using the map of the human body to help chart the coordinates of the body politic, this too has an excellent classical pedigree, traceable for example to Livy's Menenius Agrippa, whose fable of the body politic in the second book of the history has the revolt of the other parts against the stomach function as a cautionary tale for the plebeians in the Struggle of the Orders and potential rebels everywhere (2.32.9–12).[35]

The Body and the City

A closer examination, however, suggests that Augustine's stress on the precise *location* of the parts in his version of the fable of the body finds only very limited precedent in the tradition. The degree of emphasis he lends this one aspect is far, far greater. The difference is essential, then, for understanding the nature of his own particular contribution to this discourse. Livy, in his account of Menenius' fable, mentions merely in passing that the stomach is found *in medio* (2.32.9). Most of the other authors who trade in the tale of the parts of the body, too numerous to list here, are silent on this point.[36]

Notably, it is St. Paul, in a passage from 1 Corinthians analogizing the Body of Christ to the human body, who offers the closest precedent to Augustine's thought in the *De ordine,* though perhaps not in any straightforward sense. Paul argues that the different elements of the body ideally exist in concord with one another, declaring that Christians bestow greater honor on those parts that are deemed less honorable, just as those less seemly among them are accorded greater decorum, while the more seemly have no need of such recognition (12.12–31; the crucial lines are at 12.23–24). Paul seems less concerned with location of body parts than with matters of social, moral, and even aesthetic hierarchy, but we are getting close to the heart of the matter of zoning, as we shall soon see.

These issues are obviously of central concern to Augustine as well, though he presents them in a very different manner. For one thing, Paul appears to question or even subvert the social hierarchy in 1 Corinthians, while Augustine is evidently concerned to shore up and defend that hierarchy.[37] He is surely more "Roman" in this sense than is Paul.

Many commentators, pointing to the language of honor and shame that Paul deploys in this key passage from 1 Corinthians, are almost certainly right to insist that he refers to the sexual organs and their veiling,[38] a suggestion that at the very least gets us closer to the idea of zoning on a metaphorical plane. This helps clarify, to an extent, Augustine's possible reliance on a line of thought that in other respects seems very different from his own.

What does seem reasonably clear at minimum is that Augustine has taken up this tradition of the human body as a metaphor for human society as found in Cicero, Livy, Paul and the rest, and utterly transformed it. The disparate elements of these varied discourses on the construction of the body stress its decorum, its relation to the cosmos, including the social order, and above all its role as a metaphor for the universal hierarchy of things. With Augustine there is something very new. His purpose is to explain what for him is only apparently a paradox in God's providential design. Evil is not simply an inconvenience in this; it is part of its deep structure, the DNA or source code, of the universal order.

What the passage from *De ordine* offers us, in brief, is the Christian rationale for zoning prostitution. Just as the human body segregates certain elements, so a well-ordered society isolates and renders as inconspicuous as possible the sale of sex.[39] By displacing and concentrating this "impurity" in a hidden, though nevertheless central, area, it concedes and guarantees a purity to the rest. The social order is confirmed, with respectable women *(matronae)* at the top; the natural order is also ratified, with prostitutes at the bottom. Unlike Paul, apparently, Augustine does concede prostitutes a place, however humble, in society, even Christian society. They are necessary for a desirable social order, in the same way that for Augustine and his audience the splendor of a cock fight was dependent on the harm wrought on its vanquished opponent.

Prostitution for Augustine was an evil, and some fellow Christians evidently thought that it should be prohibited. Few if any would have advocated a policy of tolerance. This in itself suggests that the apparently polyvalent argument against repression of prostitution functions as a somewhat veiled, if unmistakable, case for regulation, precisely to be accomplished through the device of zoning. Augustine argues that the sale of sex should be allowed only under certain conditions that permit the social order to be preserved. The most obvious, and most important, condition to emerge in this passage is that its practice should be limited to certain inconspicuous places. One might at most concede an element of ambivalence, or indifference, over the precise role of the state in overseeing this result, parallel to Augustine's notorious unconcern even with the basic form that a government should take.[40] At any rate, in political matters he was no utopian (Taylor 1998, 290).

As suggested above, few of Augustine's readers have viewed the passage from *De ordine*, above all the brief statement against the repression of prostitution, as ambiguous. One can easily see how a late-fourth- or even very early-fifth-century emperor might have been tempted to translate what could appear to be no more than Christian common sense into action.[41] Segregating brothels might have seemed both more practical and palatable than the alternative of repression, which we know to have been tried at this time.[42] It was certainly more acceptable than tolerance, which would have led to more (and louder) complaints about the urban distribution of brothels from this period of the sort registered above. It may be that the experiment of Constantine's Zeugma brothel, if the story has any small kernel of truth to it, dates to this period, that is, the late fourth or very early fifth centuries, and did not last very long.[43] Unfortunately, if enacted, such a measure has disappeared without a trace, but for the satire of its failure preserved in the *Historia Augusta*.

I admit that the evidence for Christianizing segregation of brothels in late antiquity is not as strong as I would like it to be. The entire argument remains far from proven. The important point, however, is simply that it is so much stronger than anything we have for the classical period. In any case, the real impact of Augustine's thought on prostitution policy was not felt until centuries later. One decisive moment was its reception by Thomas Aquinas in the thirteenth century. Another appears to have been the interlinear gloss on Augustine, nearly contemporaneous with Aquinas, that introduced the famous metaphor of palace and sewer to describe the ideal place of the prostitute in human society.[44] This was to mesmerize and confuse later ages and authorities, from sixteenth-century Spanish clerics to the great Alexandre Parent-Duchâtelet, down until our own time.

Christianizing and post-Christianizing policies to "zone" prostitution both out of and within cities were founded on a concern with moral, if not also medical, contagion, as well as in some cases with public disorder. They were a hallmark of the medieval and early modern periods—where they managed to survive a new campaign of repression in the latter, they were generally toughened considerably.[45] All the same, they reached their zenith in the nineteenth and early twentieth centuries, when concern with moral pollution and social instability was—if only partially—subsumed into a fear of sexually transmitted disease.[46] The Romans themselves appear to have been utter strangers to this apprehension of contagion both medical and moral. Lack of concern over the spread of disease might be explained by reference to the existence among them of less virulent forms of STDs and/or inadequate medical knowledge. But what is the reason for their apparent indifference to what any of us might regard, with justice, as the moral challenge of brothels and prostitutes? That is a discourse for another time.[47]

Notes

1. This essay grows out of an argument developed in the context of my 2002 study of Pompeian brothels. My thanks to John Humphrey for allowing me to reuse some of its material. See now McGinn (2004, 78–111).

2. I note that a similar view is more assumed than argued by Chauvin (1983, 17–18).

3. The views of Laurence and Wallace-Hadrill on moral geography have been criticized by Kellum (1999, 291) and DeFelice (2001, 129–40). I agree in substance with Kellum's brief statement, while I find DeFelice's argument problematic in many respects.

4. Cf. Jongman (1988, 252) for a similar argument regarding onomastics, where (un)certainty over individual cases yields to a possible statistical application.

5. Cf. DeFelice (2001, 101 and 136). Much more could be said about Pompeian prostitutes than is possible here: for a partial list, see Evans (1991, 218). See also the discussion in Savunen (1997, 109–18). See now McGinn (2004, 295–302).

6. Festus 382L. See Kleberg (1957, 60). Martial 7.61 also suggests retailers were ubiquitous in Rome, not only before imperial intervention, but afterward as well: Domitian seems only to have aimed at clearing the streets; see also 1.41 (Spano 1920, 62–64).

7. All types of shops are integrated into the context of urban housing (Gassner 1986, 84, 88).

8. See Stansell (1987, 174–75), Corbin (1990, 141), Gilfoyle (1992, 47), and Hill (1993, 178, 195, and 378) for evidence from nineteenth-century Paris and New York. In fourteenth-century London, the phenomenon generated complaints (Hanawalt 1998, 116). Cf. the mix of respectable and nonrespectable commerce in 1880s London (Walkowitz 1992, 129). For a pattern of mixed residence in Renaissance Rome, see E. S. Cohen (1991, 205).

9. That Pompeii had no social zoning is the dominant thesis (apart from the question of brothel-location, evidently): see Laurence (1994, 121); Wallace-Hadrill (1994, 65–90); Laurence 1995, 65); Parkins (1997, 87); Robinson (1997, 142)—more sources are cited in McGinn (2002, 17 n.91). Despite the arguments of Grahame (1999, 574) and Parslow (1999, 341), it is not clear to me how Robinson's reliance on Fiorelli's *Regiones* vitiates his analysis; any modern topographical scheme is bound to be somewhat arbitrary, while for Robinson to invent his own would have raised suspicions of a *petitio principii*.

10. Cf. Guilhembet (1996, esp. 15): aristocratic houses were in all parts of the city though clustering in certain areas. Eck, to be sure, locates these dwellings on the hills. For a clearer, and utterly convincing, presentation of the Subura as a locus of elite as well as lower-class housing, see Welch (1999, 382) (I thank Andrew Wallace-Hadrill for this reference). For literary representations of the Subura, see Kardos (2001, 393) (Martial and Juvenal suggest a decidedly mixed use in this area).

11. For a general statement in support of this thesis, see Storey (1997, 969).

12. For an important parallel from nineteenth-century New York City, see Hill (1993, 95).

13. Ovid *Metamorphoses* 1.173. For the first interpretation, see Wallace-Hadrill (2001, 134). On the matter of sensitivity over the issue of imperial appropriation of property, especially in the first century, see McGinn (1998a).

14. For a similar point regarding the poet Martial's use of topography, see Kardos (2001, 389).

15. The aedilician regulations cited by Laurence (1994, 80–81) and Wallace-Hadrill (1995, 45, and 50–51) are irrelevant.

16. On prostitution in nineteenth-century Nevada, see Goldman (1981).

17. For these details, see Nieves (2001). Note also the hostile reaction of brothel owners to the appearance of a consumer-oriented website (Albert 2001, 240).

18. Cf. Harsin (1985, 96–130); Bernheimer (1989, esp. 6–33); Corbin (1990, 3–8). For an anticipation of the theory of "moral geography," see the argument of the sociologist Robert Park in 1915 (in Connelly 1980, 11) that it was in the very nature of urbanization for a city to develop "moral regions."

19. One might try to evade the problem of the "brothel next door" posed by Roman Comedy by citing dramatic convention, Greek influence, etc. But the truth is that no such problem existed for the Romans.

20. On this special relationship, see Gowers (1995, 30–32).

21. Cyprian Epistles 55.26 (= CCSL 3.1.289): "lupanar ingressus ad cloacam et caenosam voraginem vulgi sanctificatum corpus et dei templum detestabili conluvione violaverit." See Gowers (1995, 27 with n.42).

22. On this work of c. 995 CE, see Kazhdan (1991).

23. For some—other—examples of Christian spin on Constantine's actions, see McGinn (1999, esp. 70–71).

24. For Solon, knowledge of whose brothel we owe to the evidence of fourth-century comic poets, see Kurke (1999, 196–97), who is rightly skeptical about the historicity of the anecdote. McGinn (1998a) is inclined to credit Caligula with actual pimping, though this may be a case of the exception that proves the rule.

25. See McGinn (1998c, 269–74) for a discussion of the anti-Christian disposition of the author of the Historia Augusta. Christian sensitivity to the problem at this time is suggested by the evidence of Macarii Aegyptii, Macarii Alexandrini acta 1 (=PG 34.221A), if this is correctly dated to the late fourth century.

26. Macarii Aegyptii, Macarii Alexandrini acta 1 (= PG 34.221A); Iustinianus Novella 14 (a. 535); Procopius De aedificiis 1.9.2–4 with Leontsini (1989, 63–65), who accepts the tradition on Constantine's brothel, arguing the utter failure of the policy behind it.

27. For an elegant presentation of this question regarding the particular aspect of sexual renunciation, see Brown (1988).

28. See McGinn (1994). Cf. Chauvin (1983, 27, 52, 68–71, 85, 93, and 96) whose argument cannot be accepted on many points of detail.

29. See Chauvin (1983, 60) for the general point; Harsin (1985, 110) for the point that Alexandre Parent-Duchâtelet relied on Augustine as justification for his work, which laid the foundation for French nineteenth-century regulationism); L. L. Otis (1985, 12) and Rossiaud (1988, 80–81) for the point that Augustine was of critical importance for the medieval intellectual position on fornication; Brundage (1987, 106) for the idea that Augustine advocates the toleration of prostitution; Perry (1990, 46–47) for the point that authorities in sixteenth-century Spain used Augustine to prove that prostitution was a necessary evil; Guy (1991, 13, 50, 181, 200, and 202) for the fact that both Catholics and anticlerics cited Augustine to justify regulating prostitution instead of repressing it in late nineteenth- and early twentieth-century Buenos Aires and discussion of at least one important objection against this position; and Karras (1996, 6) for the

point that Augustine was critical in the development of the medieval version of the hydraulic thesis of male sexuality.

30. See, for example, Justin Martyr *Apologia* 1.27 (= Munier 1995, 70–72); Tertullian *Apologia* 15.7 (= CCSL 1.114), 50.12 (= CCSL 1.171), *De cultu feminarum* 2.12.1 (= CCSL 1.367), *De pallio* 4.9 (= CCSL 2.745); Minucius Felix 25.11 (= Kytzler 1992, 24).

31. For example, those of Valentinian II, Theodosius I, and Arcadius in *Collatio* 5.3 (a. 390) and of Theodosisu II in *Novella Theodosii* 18 (a. 439): the latter is certainly more accurately to be described as a measure repressing pimps. For more references and discussion, see McGinn (1998c, 305 n.84 and 2004, 96, 97 and 229).

32. The dialogue *De ordine* is one of Augustine's earliest surviving works, dated to December of 386 CE by Brown (2000, 64).

33. The dilemma is laid out at Augustine *De ordine* 1.1 (= CCSL 29.89).

34. Such language also plays an important role in moral discourse about *decorum*, in particular that which concerns the body. See Doignon (1997, 347), who cites Cicero *De officiis* 1.126 (see also 127) and 3.85, and see my discussion below.

35. For discussion of this passage and its parallels, see Ogilvie (1970, 312–13), R. P. Martin (1984, 22–23), and Collins (1999, 458–61). Dionysius of Halicarnassus 6.86 also has Menenius use the fable of the body, which the historian says was based on Aesop (6.83.2).

36. See, e.g., Xenophon *Memorabilia* 2.3.18 and Cicero *De officiis* 3.22–23, 26–27, 32.

37. On Paul as a questioner or subverter of hierarchy, at minimum of that of the Christian Church at Corinth, see for example R. P. Martin (1984, 28–29); D. Martin (1995, 94–95); Witherington (1995, 258–61); Collins (1999, 464–65); Schrage (1999, 226–28 and 242). It is obvious enough that Augustine is asserting the claims of social hierarchy, a hierarchy that even in its most immediate implications for a Christian society reaches far beyond the conception of Paul.

38. See, for example, R. P. Martin (1984, 28); D. A. Carson (1987, 48–49), though Carson goes too far, I believe, in denying sociological import to the passage; D. Martin (1995, 92–96), who is good on the subject of social status; Witherington (1995, 258–61), who is also helpful on social status; Collins (1999, 464–65), who usefully invokes Mikhail Bakhtin's concept of "heteroglossia" or polyvalent vocabulary); Schrage (1999, 226–27); and Soards (1999, 265).

39. Augustine prepares us for this discussion in the passage immediately preceding at *De ordine* 2.11 (= CCSL 29.113), where he says, regarding the way of life of the imprudent (*vita stultorum*), which is embraced in the order of things (*rerum ordo*) by Divine Providence, "and, just as certain places are arranged by that ineffable and eternal law, it is in no way allowed to be where it ought not to be" ("et quasi quibusdam locis illa ineffabili et sempiterna lege dispositis nullo modo esse sinitur, ubi esse non debet").

40. On the latter, see Fortin (1994, esp. vii, xiv–xv, xxii–xxvi) and Taylor (1998, esp. 293–94, 300–302).

41. The *Historia Augusta*, often dated to c. 395, might have been composed just a bit later; see the discussion with bibliography in McGinn (1998c, 270–73).

42. Chauvin (1983, 29–30) traces the experience of Justinian in attempting to repress prostitution.

43. It seems unlikely to have been in force in 418–20 CE, when Augustine asserts that there was no law regulating brothels (*City of God* 14.18 [= *CCSL* 48.440–41]).

44. See Chauvin (1983, 21); Rossiaud (1988, 80–81 with n.17).

45. The generalization made in the text should not obscure the fact that these concerns gave rise to some quite varied policies. See Pavan (1980, 242–45 and 250–51); Trexler (1981, 990); Chauvin (1983, 22 and 64–65); L. L. Otis (1985, 17–18, 25–26, 31–32, 35, 41, 56, 77–78, 95–97, and 104); Perry (1985, 142, 148, and 156–57); Brundage (1987, 524–25); Rossiaud (1988, 4–5 and 9); Schuster (1995, 26, 45, 52, 56, 67, 71–79, 88–102, 131, 181–82, 215–23, 262, 305–15, 342–50, 352, 358–95, 399–404, and 411–19); and Karras (1996, 15, 18–20, and 32–33).

46. Here too there is no uniform approach to segregation of prostitution. See for example Goldman (1981, 59–63 and 147–48); Corbin (1990, 54–60, 84–86, 205, 317, 322–25, and 333); Mahood (1990, 18 and 116); Clayson (1991, 15); Gilfoyle (1992, 313–14); and Gibson (1999, 136–37 and 240 n.93; notes informal clustering of brothels, much like the Roman model).

47. See McGinn 2004.

The Politics of Prostitution

Clodia, Cicero, and Social Order in the Late Roman Republic

MARSHA MCCOY

Cicero's scathing attack on Clodia in his speech defending M. Caelius Rufus in the spring of 56 BCE has usually been seen as the result of the complex political situation of the time and Cicero's desire to take revenge on her brother Clodius for his role in Cicero's exile in 58 BCE.[1] It certainly served the latter purpose since Caelius' acquittal on all charges against him seems to have resulted in the complete disappearance of Clodia from public life (Austin 1960, viii). But the unusual virulence of Cicero's public attack on the private behavior of an elite Roman woman, in particular his accusation that Clodia was a *meretrix*, a prostitute, finds no parallel in other criminal trials of the period (see discussions of prostitutes and criminal trials in McGinn [1998] and Alexander [1990]). Indeed, the use of the word *"meretrix"* to describe a Roman woman of elite standing is unprecedented in Latin literature; even Catullus at his worst never actually calls Lesbia a *meretrix*.[2] Erich Gruen has shown that by the late republic political struggles among the elites had moved into the law courts where they were fought out in rounds of charges and countercharges of criminal behavior (Gruen 1974, 260–357; Gruen 1968). In this paper I argue that Cicero in his defense of Caelius was building on his prosecution of Verres fourteen years before in the hope of turning the law courts into an arena for critiquing and shaping social behavior; this strategy was part of his more general efforts to reform Roman civil society in order to prevent its collapse.

Use of the Term *"Meretrix"*

No Latin authors employ the word *"meretrix"* more often than Cicero except writers of comedy and literary criticism. Plautus uses the word 72 times, Seneca the Elder 85 times, and Quintilian employs it 114 times, some in passages quoting from Cicero himself to comment on them. The bulk of Cicero's usages (34) are in the *Verrine Orations* (13) and the *Pro caelio* (9); the rest are found in six other works.[3] Cicero always uses the term in his orations to disparage the subject he is attacking, but only in the *Verrine Orations* and the *Pro caelio* does he make sustained references to specific individuals to build an argument of larger significance.[4]

The Prosecution of Verres

In 70 BCE Cicero was approached by prominent citizens of Sicily to bring a prosecution before the *quaestio de pecuniis repetundis*, the court for monetary restitution, against Gaius Verres, who had served as governor of Sicily for the previous three years. The charge was gross extortion of the provincials during Verres's years of absolute power in the province, and Cicero embraced the opportunity to enhance his relationship with an important group of provincials whose affection he had originally earned while serving as quaestor in western Sicily in 75. The case also gave Cicero a critical opportunity to test his forensic skills against those of the most prominent advocate of his day, Quintus Hortensius, and, in the event, best him at his own game and replace him as the foremost forensic orator in Rome for the next two decades. Scholars have usually attributed Cicero's hyperbole and vehemence in the Verres prosecution solely to the threat that the criminal courts, in the hands of senatorial juries since the reforms of Sulla in 80 BCE, would be returned to the partial control of the *equites* if the senators would not convict one of their own so evidently guilty.[5] Gruen, however, has argued persuasively that the *lex Aurelia iudiciaria* (which did restore partial control of the courts to the *equites*) promulgated by the praetor Cotta in 70 BCE shortly after the conclusion of the Verres trial (Broughton 1952, 127) was clearly under consideration as early as the year before: Pompey mentioned it at his *contio* while consul-elect in 71.[6] In fact, the *lex Aurelia* was not opposed, and perhaps was even supported, by the Sullan senate. So Gruen argues that the prosecution of Verres probably had minimal impact on the passage of the law a month after the trial (1974, 28–46). Gruen's view therefore supports my argument that Cicero's excessive rhetoric about Verres's misbehavior and its reflection on the senate of which Verres was a member was not due to immediate political considerations relating to the *lex Aurelia iudiciaria*. Instead, Cicero's flamboyant language and images convey his view that the law courts were the appropriate arena for an elite jury to pass judgment on the social behavior of one of its own: "Today the eyes of the world are upon us, waiting to see how far the conduct of each man among us will be marked by obedience to his conscience and by observance of the law. . . . It is the present trial in which, even as you will pass your verdict upon the prisoner, so the people of Rome will pass its verdict upon yourselves. It is this man's case that will determine whether, with a court composed of Senators, the condemnation of a very guilty and very rich man can possibly occur" (1.46–47).[7]

Cicero's criticism of Verres's activities covers both public and private misdeeds; he focuses on Verres's *meretrices* to show how Verres has turned private behavior into public misbehavior:[8] "For my own part the rest of Verres' robberies and villainies stir my heart no further than to make me feel that they call for denunciation; but this one afflicts me with such intense pain that I feel that nothing more shameful, nothing more intolerable could come to pass. Shall Verres take the memorials of Scipio Africanus to adorn his own house, a house full of lust and wickedness and foulness? Shall Verres take this memorial of a wholly temperate and upright man, this image of Diana the virgin goddess, and set it up in a house defiled without ceasing by the debauches of prostitutes and pimps?" (2.4.83).

Cicero emphasizes his point by focusing on one *meretrix* by name. A certain Chelidon was so notorious that prominent citizens were forced to become acquainted with her name, habits, and home in order to negotiate at all with Verres in his public capacity:[9]

The guardians, perceiving the difficulty of making any appeals to him [Verres], and finding every pathway of approach steep, not to say completely blocked, since he was a man with whom neither law nor equity nor compassion, neither the arguments of a relative nor the wishes of a friend nor anyone's influence or goodwill, counted for anything at all—the guardians decided that their best course (and the idea would have occurred to anyone) was to ask the help of

Chelidon, the woman who, so long as Verres was praetor, not only controlled
the civil law and all the private controversies of the nation, but also dominated
in all these matters of maintenance contracts. . . . They went, as I have said, to
see Chelidon. Her house was full: decisions, judgments, methods of procedure—
none ever heard of before—were being applied for: "make him give me possession," "don't let him take it from me," "don't let him pronounce against me,"
"get him to award me the property." Some were paying her cash, others were
signing promissory notes: the house was filled, not with a prostitute's visitors,
but with the crowd that attends a praetor's court. (2.1.136–37)

His degrading intimacy with Chelidon is confirmed by the fact that on
her death her will made him her heir, and further tainted any claims he
might have even to the pleasures of civil society: "It was not that the
Cupid felt any yearning for the house of this pimp or for the society of
his prostitutes. He . . . had no wish to belong to the heir of a prostitute"
(2.4.7).[10] The fact that the association with Chelidon took place in Rome
while Verres was *praetor urbanus* in 74 BCE, the year before he took
up the governorship of Sicily, only adds, in Cicero's estimation, to the
overwhelming depravity and obvious guilt of Verres later on. The Cupid
he refers to above was a statue Cicero claims Verres stole while governor from the chapel of the prominent Heius family in the town of
Messana in northeastern Sicily (*Verrine Orations* 2.4.3–8).

And this is only a single example of Verres's overarching abuse of his
civic responsibilities as governor of Sicily that Cicero traces directly
back to his misuse of Chelidon in Rome: "So far from forbidding Chelidon your house during your year of office, you transferred your office
bodily to the house of Chelidon. Then came your provincial government, during which it never crossed your mind that those rods and
axes, that crushing weight of authority, that position of majestic splendor, were not given you in order that you might use their force and their
authority to break through every barrier of decency or duty, or that you
might treat all men's property as your prey, or that it might be impossible for anyone's possessions to be safe, anyone's house secure, anyone's life defended, or anyone's chastity guarded, against your cupid-
ity and your unscrupulous wickedness (2.5.38–39).

The well-documented use of humor in late Roman republican politics (Corbeill 1996), and in particular the use of sexual humor in public
life (Richlin 1992), is reflected in the *Verrine Orations* too. In the first passage on Chelidon for example, the choice of the verb "dominated" (*"do-
minata est"*) surely refers deliberately to Chelidon as "dominatrix" in
Verres's public life. The double entendres of the speaker pile up, as

Chelidon's premises are transformed from a place of sexual supplication into a place of legal supplication. Cicero's shocked comment at the end of the passage doubtless must have amused his listeners as they reflected that the "prostitute's visitors" and the "crowd" in a "praetor's court" were in fact surely one and the same group of men. In the second passage, in describing the repulsion even a statue of the son of Venus has for the house of Verres, Cicero draws comic attention to the sexual depravities he is assailing. In the third passage, the ironic image of Verres's bodily conveying his praetorship to Chelidon's house along with himself humorously emphasizes the way Verres has debased one of Rome's highest civic offices. This strategy of using political and sexual humor to underscore the social inversions that Cicero is attacking also shows up later in Cicero's assault on Clodia.[11]

With his prosecution of Verres, then, Cicero argues that the senate as represented in Verres's jury desperately needs to maintain social order and display its integrity by disowning publicly one of its own who has so debased the institution with his misuse of public office and, in particular, his misuse of *meretrices*.

The Defense of Caelius

M. Caelius Rufus, early protégé of Cicero and lover of Clodia, made his name in 59 BCE while still a young man by prosecuting C. Antonius on a charge of *repetundae* for crimes allegedly committed while he was governor of Macedonia. Ironically, Antonius's defense lawyer was none other than Cicero himself, whose colleague he had been as consul in 63 BCE and who had given Antonius his proconsular province of Macedonia in return for Antonius's support of Cicero against Catiline. Even more ironically, Caelius, later to be hailed as a master of invective (Quintilian 4.2.123), won this case against Cicero, his former mentor and, now, opposing counsel, and Antonius went into exile. Perhaps hoping to use this conviction of an exconsul and this victory over the master orator to reenact Cicero's upset of Hortensius eleven years earlier, Caelius, never a modest man, decided to move up in the world. He moved to the Palatine, Rome's most exclusive quarter, took up with his aristocratic neighbor Clodia (Catullus addressed several bitter poems to him upon being supplanted by him in Clodia's affections [Catullus 58, 77]) and, early in 56 BCE, initiated a prosecution of L. Calpurnius Bestia on a charge of *ambitus* (bribery), with Cicero, once again, as the opposing counsel. However, things did not go so well for Caelius this time

round. Not only did he lose the case to Cicero, but in revenge for his
father's prosecution, Bestia's son, L. Sempronius Atratinus, brought a
charge of *vis* (illegal use of armed force) against Caelius. Cicero graciously agreed to defend Caelius against this charge, quite a comeup-
pance for the still relatively young upstart, now twenty-six, and no
doubt it pleased Cicero to rescue his would-be usurper with his superior forensic skills. Moreover, the participation in the prosecution of
Caelius's by-now former lover Clodia, the sister of Cicero's bitter political enemy Clodius, provided Cicero with added incentives to take on
Caelius's defense.[12]

But as with the trial of Verres, Cicero's virulent attack on Clodia in
his defense of Caelius is attributable to more than immediate political
and personal considerations. Cicero expands dramatically the argument he laid out in the prosecution of Verres. He accused Verres of mis-
using *meretrices;* here he accuses Clodia of blurring and distorting the
lines of social order so radically that a complete social inversion has
taken place. What should be private behavior has been made egre-
giously public: "Does public rumor, does Baiae itself say nothing? Yes,
Baiae does not merely talk, but even cries aloud that there is one woman
whose amorous passions are so degraded that, far from seeking privacy
and darkness and the usual screens for vice, she revels in her degraded
lusts amid the most open publicity and in the broadest daylight" (47).[13]
A member of the elite herself has actually become a *meretrix:*[14]

Caelius' case is quite without difficulty. For what charge could there be on
which he would not find it easy to defend himself? I am not now saying anything against that woman [Clodia], but suppose it were someone quite unlike
her—a woman who made herself common to all, who openly had some special
lover every day, into whose grounds, house and place at Baiae every rake had a
right of free entry, who even supported young men, and made their fathers'
stinginess bearable at her own expense; if a widow were casting off restraints, a
frisky widow living frivolously, a rich widow living extravagantly, an amorous
widow living like a prostitute, should I regard any man guilty of misconduct if
he had been somewhat free in his attentions to her? (38)

If there was no stigma attached to elite men privately visiting *meretrices,* as we know there wasn't from numerous passages in Roman literature,[15] there was obviously a great stigma attached to elite women
publicly becoming *meretrices:*[16]

If there existed such a woman as I painted a short while ago, one quite unlike
you, with the life and manners of a prostitute—would you think it very shameful

or disgraceful that such a young man should have had some dealing with such a woman? If you are not this woman, as I prefer to think, for what have the accusers to reproach Caelius? But if they will have it that *you* are such a person, why should we be afraid of this accusation, if you despise it? Then it is for you to show us our way and method of defense; for either your sense of propriety will disprove any vicious behavior by Caelius, or your utter impropriety will afford both him and the rest a fine opportunity for self-defense. (50)

In fact Cicero suggests that Clodia has so distorted the normal social order and debased the elite by taking on the behavior of a *meretrix*, that her entire household is inverted, with bizarre activities taking place and slaves who are no longer slaves acting at will:

Lastly, in whom did he [Caelius] confide, whom did he have to assist him, who was his partner, his accomplice, to whom did he entrust so great a crime, entrust himself, entrust his own life? To the slaves of this woman? For this has been alleged against him. . . . But, I ask, what kind of slaves? This very point is most important. Were they slaves whom he knew not as subject to the ordinary conditions of servitude, but as living a life of more licence, liberty, and intimacy with their mistress? For who does not see, gentlemen, or who is ignorant that in a house of that kind, in which the mistress lives the life of a prostitute, in which nothing is done which is fit to be published abroad, in which strange lusts, profligacy, in fact, all unheard-of vices and immoralities, are rife—who does not know that in such a house those slaves are slaves no longer? (57)

In this passage and in the passage in which he compares Verres extremely unfavorably to Scipio Africanus, Cicero uses invective to great effect, as he does in all of his forensic speeches (Braund 2002, 92–93). As with humor, Cicero employs invective as a rhetorical strategy for accomplishing his larger goal of presenting Clodia as well as Verres to the jury as social perversions worthy of expulsion from elite civil society.

Conclusion

Recent research on the late Roman republic has often characterized republican politics as taking the form of discussions about, and contestations over, the nature of the common social good in response to the decay of republican institutions.[17] Cicero's own efforts centered on appeals to *concordia ordinum* and attempts to establish consensus among the senatorial and equestrian elites as a means of restoring Roman social and political order. In the trials of Verres and then more explicitly Caelius, Cicero is aiming his attacks at elite individuals who are using or becoming *meretrices* in a dangerous inversion of the social order, one that threatens the entire community (Edwards 1997; 1993; Stallybrass and White 1986). The law courts were the arena Cicero chose as the most appropriate civic setting in which to demand, from the senatorial elite and then from the senatorial and equestrian elite, the repudiation and expulsion of Verres and Clodia from civil society. The response was clear: Verres fled before his trial ended, and Clodia vanished, never to be heard of again in the public sphere.[18] By emphasizing more than had ever been done before the (mis)placement of *meretrices* in the Roman social order, Cicero achieved a small but significant portion of his program to restore republican civil society.[19]

Notes

1. See most recently Tatum (1999) and the critical bibliographical article by Fezzi (1999); see also Gruen (1974, 305–9), Stockton (1971, 213), and Austin (1960, 154).

2. Although admittedly there are several poems where he describes her very disparagingly, with language certainly suggesting whore-like behavior, e.g., 11, 37, and 58.

3. In three orations (*De domo sua* 111.2; 112.6; 112.8, *De haruspicum responsis* 33.5, and *Philippicae* 2.44.10) and in three rhetorical or philosophical treatises (*De inventione* 2.118.8; 2.118.10; 2.118.12; 2.118.12; *De finibus* 2.12.2, and *De natura deorum* 1.14.1; 1.93.3).

4. In the passages in *De domo sua* and *De haruspicum responsis* Cicero is disparaging Clodia's brothers, Appius and Publius Clodius; in the passage in the *Philippicae* Cicero is attacking Marcus Antonius.

5. See, e.g., the summary in Greenwood ([1928] 1959, x–xiv) and also, most recently, the account in Mitchell (1979).

6. *Verrine Orations* 1.45: "In fact, when Gnaeus Pompeius himself, as consul-elect, for the first time addressed a public meeting near the city, and, in accordance with what appeared to be a very general expectation, declared his intention of restoring the powers of the tribunes, his words elicited a murmuring noise of grateful approval from the assembly: but when he observed, in the course of the same speech, that our provinces had been wasted and laid desolate, that our law-courts were behaving scandalously and wickedly, and that he meant to take steps to deal with this evil—then it was with no mere murmur, but with a mighty roar, that the people of Rome showed their satisfaction" (tr. Greenwood [1928] 1959).

7. The translations of the Verrine Orations are from Greenwood ([1928] 1959); in some cases, I have modified them.

8. See the commentary on this passage in Mitchell (1986). See also *Verrine Orations* 2.1.101; 2.3.6; 2.3.83; 2.4.7; 2.4.83; 2.4.123.

9. See also *Verrine Orations* 2.5.34.

10. See *Verrine Orations* 2.2.116 for evidence that the prostitute referred to here is Chelidon.

11. For humor in the *Pro caelio* specifically, see Geffcken (1973).

12. See Mitchell (1991), the chapter on "The Trial of Caelius" in Wiseman (1985), and Classen (1973) for a fuller account of the background of the *Pro caelio,* as well as the introduction and commentary of Austin (1960). Dorey (1958) discusses Clodia's actual role in the case against Caelius; it was not as important as Cicero claims, but this reveals Cicero's hostility to her (as Dorey points out) and, I would argue, reinforces my claim that Cicero views the law courts as a place to contest social values as well as litigate particular charges.

13. The translations of *Pro caelio* are from Gardner (1970); in some cases, I have modified them.

14. Cf. *Pro caelio* 1, 37.

15. This is the assumption throughout the *Pro caelio,* and it is stated explicitly at 49 and elsewhere; see also Horace *Satires* 1.2.31 and Austin (1960, 110).

16. Cf. *Pro caelio* 48, 49.

17. Millar (1998; 1995a; 1995b); Beard and Crawford (1985); Mitchell (1984); Nicolet (1980); Gruen (1974).

18. Cicero, in searching for suburban property near Rome on which to build a shrine to Tullia after her death in February 45 BCE, discusses with Atticus the possibility of buying a property from Clodia (through an intermediary) for that purpose; this is almost certainly the Clodia of the *Pro caelio* (Shackelton Bailey [1965] 1999, 345 n.5). See Cicero *Letters to Atticus* 279.2; 282.1; 283.3; 284.3; 285.3; 286.1; 288.1–2; 294.2; 300.2 (all from May 45 BCE). But she had surely dropped out of public life after Caelius' trial, to judge from Cicero's silence about her after the trial (compared to his many disparaging comments about her in his letters beginning in 60 BCE, culminating in his vicious portrayal of her in the *Pro caelio*). See also Wiseman (1985).

19. Versions of this paper have been read at the University of Wisconsin–Madison, and at Yale University. I would like to thank Professors Victor Bers, Susanna Morton Braund, Bentley Layton, Thomas McGinn, and Susan Treggiari for their very helpful comments, and particularly Professors Christopher Faraone and Laura McClure for inviting me to participate in the very stimulating conference "Prostitution in the Ancient World" at the University of Wisconsin–Madison in April 2002. All errors that remain are my own.

Matrona and Whore

Clothing and Definition in Roman Antiquity

KELLY OLSON

Clothing is an important part of the sign system of every society, a central aspect of its visual language.[1] Clothing has the power to express rank, communicate status, wealth, and power, symbolize the relation between the sexes, reflect values, exemplify anxieties. The sartorial behavior of any society involves gestures, sexuality, hygiene, economics, rituals, signs, morality, and law. Clothing therefore embodies social structure and is important to a society's sense of itself.

Philippe Perrot has noted that clothing in the ancien régime in France (prior to 1789) served as a code with its own language and purpose: to define and render visible the social hierarchy (1994, 8–10 and 16). Clothing was therefore an important tool of social regulation since it was a system of signs that reflected and even helped construct the social order (8, 10, and 15). Is what Perrot says in regard to clothing in the ancien régime also applicable to Roman antiquity?

Clothing's socio-political function in other preindustrial societies had the effect of defining and reinforcing the social hierarchy in them and symbolized "self-affirmation for some and subordination for others, freezing everyone in their place by guaranteeing the place of everyone" (Perrot 1994, 10). At first glance this also appears true of Roman antiquity. But although Roman clothing was at once the sign and the generator of rank and status, such symbols in a highly mobile society (within particular boundaries) like that of Rome did not render the social structure immobile. The present study recognizes that there was usurpation of the clothing of different ranks in Roman antiquity—this is common knowledge to historians of Roman male clothing and symbols of status—but also suggests that the deliberate omission of the distinctive garments that marked one's own rank might be more common than previously suspected (contra, e.g., Garnsey and Saller 1987, 116–17).[2] In addition, there was enough overlap among sartorial boundaries that clothing distinctions were probably not as immutable and as steadfast as authors (ancient and modern) would have us believe. This blurring of vestimentary (and consequently social) definition is especially evident in an examination of female dress in Roman antiquity; specifically the dress of the married woman (*matrona*) and the prostitute.

I have tried to restrict the spatial and temporal parameters of this article to the women of Italy, mainly (but not exclusively) those in Rome itself, during the central period in Roman history; that is, roughly 200 BCE to 200 CE (Bradley 1994, xi and 6; Brunt 1988, 9–12). Space precludes any detailed study of the women of the provinces. The problems that the male-authored literary sources present for the study of ancient women are well known; and, as one author has stated, "even these elite voices are somewhat disparate in their distribution in time and space" (Flemming 1999, 40). Also, when the historian speaks of "Rome" and "Roman society," s/he refers "at one extreme to a single city in Italy and at the other extreme to the whole of the empire. The shift is one of a geographical to a cultural designation, from the city in a narrow sense to wherever the city's culture came to impose itself" (Bradley 1994, 6). Thus I have used as "Roman" evidence a number of distinct sources that I believe reflect something of the social history and cultural mores of this period: the predictable satirists and epigrammatists, but also moralists, historians, later lexicographers and antiquarians, even Greek romances written in the Roman period. Most certainly follow the expected conventions of their particular genre: Ovid the love poet tends to encourage women to adorn themselves, for instance; Seneca the moralist tends to oppose it. Where the sources intrigue and attract the scholar is in their lines of intersection and correlation, in their points of consensus concerning female clothing and the adorned woman.

Naturally, any study of Roman clothing and ancient responses to clothing will want to make use of the wealth of artistic material available. While the nature of Roman art is certainly "public and status-oriented" (Stone 1994, 21) and never merely a snapshot of every-day life, this type of evidence may still prove useful for the historian. The ideals of costume present in Roman literature often are not those that the visual sources offer (and vice versa)—an interesting disjunction, if one may assume Roman art reflects the way Romans wished to be perceived.

Clothing and Roman Social Hierarchies

Roman male clothing was especially intended to indicate the social hierarchy, and there were specific sartorial signals meant to designate each order (senators, knights, the free poor, and slaves). Usurpation of status symbols most frequently occurred in relation to the rank of *eques* or knight, because equestrian rank was personal, not hereditary (Reinhold 1971, 281 and 285).[3] But in addition to instances where symbols of rank not one's own were usurped, there were other, more significant instances of deviance from ideal or expected appearance in Roman antiquity, in which symbols of status or rank were discarded entirely (surprising in such an apparently status-conscious society). The mark of the male citizen was supposedly the toga, but poorer men, free and freed, would not necessarily have owned one, since the toga was expensive, hard to care for, hot, and cumbersome: Tacitus refers to the plebs contemptuously as "the tunic-clad populace." Augustus had to legislate in order to ensure that the upper classes wore the toga, and Martial and Juvenal both testify to the garment's unpopularity.[4] Leaving off the toga may have led to a certain amount of sartorial confusion. There was, for instance, a natural correlation between the clothing of the slave and his low social position, but no clothes associated with slavery particularly. K. R. Bradley points out that because the toga was assumed by free men mainly on formal occasions, and because slaves at Rome had no special racial characteristics, the appearance of the toga-less poor (or even middling) free was likely to be confused with that of slaves.[5]

So, although male clothing offered a series of signs that indicated the social order, it did not necessarily strengthen that order: sartorial signs were illicitly usurped or even tacitly omitted, and there were gaps between rank and the vestimentary signs of rank. Because it was hard to enforce legislation concerning status symbols, and because many of them were a function of wealth, vestimentary and other signs served to visualize the social hierarchy but not necessarily to reinforce it. It has been said that restrictions on the usurpation of status symbols particular to a class are an attempt to enforce social boundaries; however, legislation designed to stop this practice in Rome "was simply not enforced systematically" (Reinhold 1971, 276). Thus dress at Rome could confuse, rather than define, social boundaries.

Nonetheless, rank was conceived by the Romans as including the right to wear certain articles of clothing (as is evident in cases of usurpation of equestrian and senatorial status symbols), whether or not these articles were actually assumed: often an article of clothing or ornament came to symbolize the office or legal status of those intended to wear it and the power of that office or status, whatever the sartorial reality. The Latin language thus employed the outward sign of status or rank, such as an article of clothing, to stand in for the status or rank itself. For instance, the right to stand for office was termed the right of the *latus clavus* (the wide stripe on a magistrate's toga) and incorporation into the rank of *eques* the *"ius anuli aurei"* (the "right of the gold ring"). Even the phrase *"calceos mutare"* ("to change into shoeboots") meant "to become a senator."[6]

That clothing was viewed by the Romans as part of a moral as well as external system of defining rank is not a new discovery and is in fact the main focus of much recent scholarship on ancient clothing.[7] Since the Romans equated oddities in dress with oddities of behavior, Quintilian (for instance) has many cautions and recommendations on the proper cut and draping of an orator's toga: improper draping could harm a career (Stone 1994, 17).

Female dress was equally supposed to indicate a woman's rank, status, and morality. The sources present more difficulties for the study of female clothing, inasmuch as the ancient authors tend to mention male (rather than female) clothing when they mention it at all. Still, some useful information may be gleaned from literary references. *Matronae*, the wives of Roman citizens, are said to wear the *stola* (a long slip-like garment worn over the underdress or tunic). The *stola* first and foremost indicated that the wearer was married in a *iustum matrimonium* (a legal marriage between two citizens) and it was therefore a mark of honor, a way to distinguish sexual and social rank in broad fashion. Literary sources also tell us that Roman women wore the *palla* or mantle, which was drawn over the head when out of doors, and bound their hair with woolen bands or fillets.[8] This description is offered by several modern scholars as that of the everyday clothing of the Roman *matrona*.[9]

Close inspection of both literary sources and the visual record, however, shows that women apparently did not always assume these signs

of rank and status. For example, according to one (admittedly not entirely trustworthy) source, by the second half of the second century
BCE women of the upper classes were increasingly tempted to abandon
the stola[10] (wives of the poorest citizens likely would not have worn the
stola since, like the toga, it would have been an uncomfortable hindrance to manual labor—this is perhaps another instance of the omission of a status symbol). The stola seems to have had a relatively short
lifespan in comparison its male counterpart, the toga: the earliest artistic portrayal of a woman in a stola is dated to the early first century BCE,
but the overwhelming majority of stolate busts and statues are Julio-
Claudian, and stolae do not appear to be in evidence after the time of
Faustina Minor (d. 175 CE).[11] The toga, in comparison, existed as a garment (albeit largely ceremonial) until the fifth century CE (Stone 1994,
38). Nor does every woman in the artistic record wear a stola, which we
would expect if the garment was the essential and quotidian status
symbol the literary sources describe. As for the palla, the vast majority
of female portrait busts we possess show the woman with an unveiled
head (probably in order to display her elaborate hairstyle to the
viewer).[12] It is difficult to see how most of these architectural hairstyles
could have withstood a mantle being laid on top—it would have
crushed the rows of curls and braids. Even in the procession depicted
on the Ara Pacis (fig. 1), an outdoor and public scene and one of Augustan date, where we would expect to find all the women with the palla
drawn up around their heads,[13] some are veiled, and some are not: apparently it was a decision left to the discretion of a woman. And although mentioned a few times in the literary sources, except for busts
of Vestal Virgins, and some representations of women sacrificing, there
are not many portraits extant in which the woman's hair is tied in fillets. It is clear that not every woman wore them, or perhaps they wore
them only on religious or ceremonial occasions.[14] Again, it is hard to see
what place fillets could occupy on the head if the woman chose to wear
an elaborate hairstyle.

There is some disjunction, then, between the literary and the artistic sources for the costume of the Roman woman. The combination of
stola, palla, and fillets, by no means ubiquitous in portrait busts, statues,
and reliefs, was very strongly linked with the appearance of the honorable married woman in literary sources: "be far from here, you signs of
purity, thin vittae and long stola [instita] that covers the feet," says Ovid
(Ars amatoria 1.31–32).[15] These "signs of purity" are seldom found in
the visual record, very likely because much of what we read in ancient

Figure 1. Procession, south side, Ara Pacis (DAI neg. 72.2403).

literature about women's clothing seems to be prescriptive. The literary record describes what the *matrona* should look like and how her clothing should embody her moral stance; she seems to be described in terms of exemplary (not actual) appearance. Martial, for instance, instead of employing a long phrase that delineates a specific social rank and accompanying moral probity, simply names articles of clothing: "whoever he be, despiser of *stola* or purple, that has assailed with verses those whom he ought to respect." A woman clearly did not have to wear these vestimentary signs in order to be associated with them (10.5.1–2).[16]

It is not my intention to give a description of every garment in Roman society that was designed to indicate rank or status and to speculate whether (or on which occasions) such a garment was actually assumed. I will state again, however, that literary description of sartorial boundaries seems to represent ideal or prescribed costume, and that the omission of signs of rank and status, as opposed to the assumption of signs of a status not one's own by law, may have been more common than scholars have supposed. Rome was a finely graded society in which there was much social mobility within particular boundaries; thus our elite authors display a fierce concern with *insignia dignitatis* and the regulation of symbols of rank. But clothing and status did not always necessarily correspond: what authors in general describe is an ideal sartorial situation, in which all citizens wear the toga, all *equites* the gold ring, all married women the *stola*, no one ornaments himself above his status, and the social order is both immediately apparent and, ultimately, immutable.

The Prostitute

In Roman antiquity prostitutes and adulteresses too were presumably immediately identifiable from their clothing: both wore the toga. By this "exclusion" from the sartorial distinctions of the chaste *matronae*, such women could ideally be identified as those who rejected the moral code bound up in those clothes. Specific passages on the *togate* woman are few, and may be quoted here.[17]

The following authors link the toga with an adulteress or a woman whose status is uncertain:

1. Horace mentions a *togata* (possibly an *ancilla togata*) and elsewhere states the *togata* has the advantage over the *matrona* when it comes to satisfying sexual urges, as there is no husband to fear. There is, however, no specification as to the social status of the *togata* (*Satires* 1.2.63).[18]
2. Martial berates a friend for giving a notorious adulteress (*famosa moecha*) dresses of purple and scarlet. "Do you want to give her the present she has deserved? Send her the toga" (*Epigrams* 2.39; see McGinn 1998c, 163; Courtney 1980, 133).
3. Martial elsewhere bestows the epithet "*damnata moecha*" (possibly "a convicted [?] adulteress") on the eunuch Thelys, who wears a toga (*Epigrams* 10.52; McGinn 1998c, 163).
4. Juvenal complains of an effeminate advocate's gauzy toga: "Fabulla is an adulteress; condemn Carfinia of the same crime if you wish; but however guilty, she would never wear such a gown as yours" (*Satires* 2.68–70; McGinn 1998c, 164). Possibly, too, one or both women are convicted adulteresses (hence the adjective "*damnata*").
5. Martial criticizes a man as being the son of a woman who wore the toga— "*mater togata*"—there is no specification otherwise as to her status (*Epigrams* 6.64.4; Courtney 1980, 133).
6. Porphyrio wrote that "women who were convicted of having committed adultery were forced to go out in public *togate*" (Acro *Scholia Horatiana* to *Satires* at 1.2.63).

There are a few authors who associate the toga specifically with the whore:

1. Cicero says to Antony "you assumed the toga *virilis* and at once turned it into the toga of a woman [*muliebrem togam*]. At first you were a common whore [*scortum*], with a fixed price for your favours, nor was it small" (*Philippics* 2.44; Dyck 2001, 127).
2. Sulpicia bemoans the fact that Cerinthus is unfaithful to her, and with a prostitute: "you attend rather to the toga and to the whore loaded with a wool basket than to Sulpicia[,] daughter of Servius" (Tibullus 3.16.3-5; Dalby 2000, 264).
3. Nonius quotes the comic writer Titinius who also emphatically names the toga as the garment of the whore. "Even shelter can be described as a toga. Titinius in his *Gemina*: 'if he decides to head out of town with the whore, I want the keys hidden immediately, so that there be no chance for him of any undercover business in the country;' that is, no chance of shelter" (653L, translated by McGinn 1998c, 158).
4. Acro reports: "Matrons who have been repudiated by their husbands on account of adultery lay aside the *stola* and wear the toga on account of disgrace; the toga of a prostitute is apt. For thus they are accustomed to stand forth in dark togas only, so as to be distinguished from matrons; and for that reason those women who were convicted of adultery wear this garment. In other words, women[,] because of [a conviction for] adultery[,] are said to go out in public *togate*. Others call a freedwoman *togate*, because previously freedwomen wore the toga, but matrons wore the *stola*" (Acro *Scholia Horatiana* to *Satires* 1.2.63).[19]

There are two problems here quite apart from the question of the normal dress of the whore. The first is the status of the woman referred to by the adjective "*togata*."[20] In these passages, Martial and Juvenal speak specifically of the *togate* adulteress, Cicero, Nonius, Sulpicia [Tibullus], and Acro of the *togate* prostitute, but it is often unclear whether in fact a convicted adulteress or a whore is actually being referred to. When Martial calls an enemy "the son of a *mater togata*," for instance, does he mean a whore or an adulteress? Horace's *togata*, again, wears transparent Coan silk and shows her body off to viewers—but the status of the woman is not specified (*pace* McGinn 1998b, 160).[21] It seems possible that in many cases *moecha* (adulteress) or *meretrix* (whore) is not indicated perhaps because they are the same type of woman in our authors' minds (i.e., sexually licentious: an adulteress was presumably generous with her sexual favors) and thus they felt that they did not need to be distinguished absolutely (see Adams 1983, 350-51). An adulteress *was* a whore; this is brought out clearly in Augustus's legislation on prostitutes and adulteresses. If he did not prosecute her for adultery, the husband of a guilty wife could himself be prosecuted for pimping (McGinn 1998c, 156–93; Gardner 1986, 127–32).

Secondly, there is no specific evidence in these passages that the adulteress or the prostitute was "compelled" to wear the toga, as is often asserted by modern authors (Balsdon 1962, 252; Courtney 1980, 133; McGinn 1998c, 156, 166, and 168). The presence of *damnata* in Martial Epigrams 10.52 and Juvenal, and *convicta* in the scholiasts on Horace does hint at this, but there is no extant Roman law stating that assumption of the toga was part of the penalty for a matrona's conviction of prostitution. Nor is there any edict that states that a common whore had to wear the toga, even if she registered with the aediles as such (presumably such a regulation, if it existed, would have been enforced with the help of interested third parties).[22] Nor (contra Acro) is there any evidence in classical literature that associates the toga with freedwomen or that states prostitutes were accustomed to wearing dark togas.[23]

It is one contention of this study the toga was not that in fact the "normal" dress of the whore, but only one of many types of dress prostitutes could adopt. Although Thomas McGinn has made the point,[24] he doesn't provide a comprehensive account of the descriptive details of prostitute clothing. There are many passages in classical literature in which whores, depending on their station, appear in everything from expensive clothing down to little (or no) clothing at all, that is, passages in which the toga is not named as their distinctive dress. Agorastocles in Plautus's *Poenulus* wants to delight his eyes with the "elegance of the prostitutes." Another Plautine character admires a harlot's appearance: "but the way she was dressed, bejewelled, ornamented—so charmingly, so tastefully, so stylishly!" (191–92). Seneca makes reference to a harlot "adorned for the public" and "dressed in the clothes her pimp had provided." He also speaks of "whores' colors" (probably referring to makeup or bright clothing) and then says that these would not be worn by decent women. He does not mention the toga. Tacitus too described the clothing of whores as colorful; again, the toga, the prostitute's supposed identifying mark, is not named (*Epidicus* 222).[25]

Nonius states that in olden times (*apud veteres*) whores wore short tunics which were "girded up from below" and cites Afranius for an instance in which prostitutes would don long dresses: "'A prostitute in a long gown? When they find themselves in a strange place they tend to wear it for self-protection'" (868L).[26] Isidore states (*Origines* 19.25.5) that the clothing of a prostitute is in fact the *amiculum* or linen *pallium* (possibly a mantle that could be draped around the body). He also states that "in olden days" (*"apud veteres"*) adulterous matrons would wear this garment instead of a *stola;* but in his own Spain the *pallium* is conversely the mark of respectability. His vagueness is unhelpful for the study of prostitute clothing but "may be taken as a sign that the woman's toga had long since disappeared from the scene" (McGinn 1998c, 167 with notes).

Evanthius mentions a saffron-colored *pallium* as the distinguishing mark of a prostitute in comedy (*Commentum Terenti* 8.6; McGinn 1998c, 159). In the Greek novel of Xenophon of Ephesus, the slave girl Anthia is forced to exhibit herself in front of the brothel keeper's establishment wearing beautiful clothing and loaded with gold jewelry (*Ephesiaca* 5.7). Some prostitutes would wear foreign headgear such as turbans to make themselves stand out and thus attract a customer's interest. Messalina gilded her nipples and wore a blond wig on her nightly shifts in the brothel (Juvenal 3.66; 6.120–24). Well-dressed harlots could even travel in sedans, and some would dye or perfume their hair as well, to add to their allure (Juvenal 3.135–36).[27] Whores may not always have worn the *strophium* or breastband (an undergarment): one of Catullus's prostitutes suddenly bares her naked breasts to a passerby, surely indicating she was not dressed in one (55.11–12).[28]

Nudity was the marker of the lowest whore, a woman who was said to be ready for every kind of lust. The whores in a squalid brothel would also be naked, and Juvenal describes this sort of harlot as "the whore that stands naked in a reeking archway."[29] But there were apparently different categories of "nudity": Cicero, in claiming that Anthony was seen in public *nudus,* means he was simply going about bare-chested. This raises the possibility that Rome's streetwalkers and brothel workers were not entirely naked but merely wore clothing that did not cover them completely.[30]

Tertullian and Ulpian, two sources who speak of prostitutes, do not name the toga as the whore's distinctive garment (McGinn 1998c, 163). Unfortunately, there is to my knowledge no visual evidence for the dress of the Roman prostitute,[31] but the literary sources present us with a range of clothing (from rich accoutrements all the way down to nothing), which seem to have varied according to the woman's station within a hierarchy of prostitutes. None of these sources mentions the toga. Why not?

Roman male clothing, as we have seen, had a legal basis: symbols of rank were incorporated into garments, and therefore dress was supposed to be an act of political and social signification. Ideally, social role and status could be read instantly in dress. Also, the Latin language often employed the term for the outward sign. Thus, the *matrona* and her moral stance were frequently specified simply by the words "*stola*" or "*stolata*" or "*vittae.*" Although *stola, palla,* and *vittae* do not always appear in the visual record, the *matrona* nonetheless continues to be identified in ancient literature in terms of her ideal appearance, both because the authors do not describe but prescribe, and because such brief designations function as literary shorthand.

Likewise, it seems possible that the word "*togata*" was employed not to designate common social practice but as metonomy for the sexually licentious woman. The adulteress or whore can be designated as "*togata*" whether or not she is actually *togate:* it is not a tangible piece of clothing that is indicated by the adjective, but a moral system. The device of naming an outward sign of status was employed instead of a description of that status: "*togata*" described in one word a woman whose sexual morals were questionable, just as "*stolata*" described in one word the woman who possessed a high degree of exemplary virtue. At some point in Rome's past (unfortunately now irretrievable) whores probably did wear the toga: thus its reputation as the dress of the whore. But the sources demonstrate that there was a range of prostitute clothing, and although several ancient authors mention the toga as the distinctive garment of the whore, there is sufficient evidence to state that this was only one garment that whores could adopt. Thus the use of the word "*togata*" to describe a woman of easy morals may not necessarily have been a token of its currency (*pace* McGinn 1998c, 163). Stereotypes had, as today, only a limited basis in reality.

Matron and Whore

If they did not always wear the toga, how were prostitutes visually defined? Ancient authors from all periods and genres are adamant that whores and matrons were sartorially distinct and immediately distinguishable from one another. When one of Plautus's prostitutes is required to disguise herself as a *matrona,* for instance, she is ordered to be "dressed in the matron's way, with hair combed and tied with woolen bands so that she can pretend to be your wife" (*Miles gloriosus* 790–93). Approximately two hundred years later, Ovid distinguishes between the dress of Latin brides and mothers (*vittae* and the long gown) and that of you (*vos*), others, who do not wear these garments. Martial asks, "who brings garments into Flora's festival and permits prostitutes the modesty of the *stola?*" (1.35.8–9).[32] M. Antistius Labeo (d. 10–22 CE) suggests that a woman dressed as a whore or slave laid herself open to being harassed: "If someone accosts virgins, even those in slaves' garb [*ancillari veste vestitas*], his offense is regarded as venial, even more so if women are in prostitutes' dress [*meretricia veste*] and not that of matrons [*matrum familiarum vestitae*]. Still, if a woman is not in the dress of a matron and someone accosts her or abducts her attendant, he will be liable to the action for insult" (*Digest of Justinian* 47.10.15.15). These passages indicate that matrons and whores were supposed to be sartorially distinct from one another but also strongly imply that such was not always the case. And, for what it is worth, Labeo was a lawyer of the Augustan era, a time in which old-fashioned clothing distinctions were supposedly of great importance and even he does not specifically mention the toga as a prostitute's garment.[33] He also incidentally implies that not every matron wore the dress of a matron and that confusion results when social and sartorial definitions are muddled.

There were other ways in which the supposedly clear vestimentary signs of matron and whore were confused: we read in the literary sources that some kinds of ornament were common to both types of women. Both whores and matrons used cosmetics, for example.[34] The use of makeup in early nineteenth-century America conventionally marked two extreme social boundaries: prostitutes and rich noblewomen. Whores tended to set trends in fashion and makeup that were often carefully toned down and employed by American women of the upper classes.[35] Women of the upper classes in antiquity may also have aped prostitute fashion: "You have not been perverted by the imitation of worse women that leads even the virtuous into pitfalls," says Seneca to his mother (this passage occurs in the section in which he is speaking of female adornment [*Ad Helviam matrem* 16.316.3]).[36] In addition to makeup, both whores and matrons wore colorful clothing.[37] A popular fabric for both classes of women was the daring Coan silk (or some imitation of it), a diaphanous stuff that apparently left little to the viewer's imagination. The color and weight of a woman's clothing was ideally a reflection of her morality, and the fashion among upper-class women for Coan silk, whether truly transparent or simply an extremely thin material that outlined the body,[38] confused sartorial and therefore moral and social definitions. It put a woman's body on display, an act that, as we will see below, was equated with prostitution.

It seems therefore that comparable kinds of feminine adornment could be worn both by noblewomen and whores, at least in varying degrees (although ancient authors do not acknowledge as much). According to moralists, cosmetics and other adornment made a woman look seductive and served merely to invite male attention. The face of such a woman, states Seneca, was proof of her shamelessness (*Controversiae* 2.7.4). Because for the ancients, clothing *and* adornment functioned as part of a moral system, and because *matronae* and prostitutes employed similar types of ornament, authors assert that they are often unable to tell the difference between a whore and a respectable woman.

The Christian Tertullian claimed that in the late second-century CE noblewomen were going about in public without the *stola* for the purposes of practicing prostitution more easily (*De pallio* 4.9).[39] Tertullian regarded these garments as "the indices and guardians of *dignitas*," although whether of husband or wife is not specified, and asserted that matrons discarded them to indulge in lower-class pleasures, to walk abroad, to see and be seen, and to field sexual advances. He maintained that a woman cast off her modesty along with the *stola*, and thus men would approach her more easily. As noted above, however, the *stola* had probably fallen out of favor before Tertullian's time; since it must have been, like the toga, long, hot, and cumbersome, women likely discarded it for reasons of comfort rather than sexual licentiousness. He also claimed, more fantastically, that prostitutes in turn were adopting the clothing and markers of the upper-class woman. Clothing, stated Tertullian, preannounced character; therefore the clothing of the whores was all the more disturbing. They were women who "some laws formerly restrained from [the use of] matrimonial and matronly decoration; but now, the daily increasing depravity of the age has raised [these whores] to so nearly an equality with the most honorable women, that the difficulty is to distinguish between them" (*De pallio* 4.9; *De cultu feminarum* 2.12.3).[40] It is unclear why wearing chaste clothing would be good for a whore's business, particularly since Tertullian had previously claimed that wearing a *stola* makes men afraid to approach a woman. Certainly he is exaggerating for the rhetorical purpose of exhorting Christian women to leave off overadorning and may be saying too that all women are lustful and shameless or perhaps merely implying that the signs of chastity were also the signs of the upper class, which is what led the whores to adopt them. Tertullian, like Seneca before him, displays profound anxiety because he imagines that *matronae* cannot be distinguished whores: for him the traditional social classes are in confusion and flux; noblewoman and prostitute have been assimilated into one category.

We have seen that the hierarchy of moral behavior was thought to correspond directly with how much or what type of clothing the woman was wearing. Since a woman's clothing made visible her moral position, a woman laid aside her modesty along with her clothing: naked or scantily clad whores would satisfy any lust. And clothing that marked a woman excessively, like Coan silk, was censured because of the perceived moral implications. "For a woman, in fact, the one glory is chastity; so she must take care to be chaste—and to be seen to be chaste," wrote Seneca (*Controversiae* 2.7.9). Women gave advance warning of their shamelessness by dress, talk, walk, and appearance (*Controversiae* 2.7.4), and clothing therefore constructed a social identity for the wearer at the same time as it signified that wearer's identity. The outward signs that were supposed to visualize the social order for Tertullian (and Seneca) instead perverted it; the disturbing truth was that clothing could insinuate things about the wearer that were half-truths or outright lies.

We need not posit a moral breakdown of Roman society in the late second century CE, however, in order to account for the confusion of vestimentary signs. The different styles of clothing for each class of women (the *stola* for matrons and the toga for whores), which were supposedly employed to define rank and status, as stated, were prescription. The seeming confusion concerning the clothing of *matronae* and whores in the sources may in part stem from the fact that the adorned woman who made herself conspicuous in society and wanted to put her body on show for the visual delectation of others was often likened to a prostitute. The adorned woman ran the risk of being accosted, at the very least: "a married woman who wants to be safe from the lust of the seducer must go out dressed up [*ornata*] only so far as to avoid unkemptness [*inmunda*]" (Seneca *Controversiae* 2.7.3)[41] More importantly, blatant and purposeful display of the self, however clothed, led to a dwindling of female modesty, and for a woman to be seen and a man to see promoted the desire for sexual relations on the part of both (Propertius 3.21.3; Ovid *Amores* 2.2.3-4, 3.2.34, and 2.19.19; Tertullian *De spectaculis* 25).[42] Women supposedly became sexually excited when they put themselves on display: chastity was eroded by being seen. Therefore, the adorned woman who ornamented herself for public display was no better than a prostitute. The prostitute was often described as "wheedling," "cajoling," or "coaxing" ("*blanda*") or taught to coax (*docetur blanditias*); she showed herself off in public; a notice was put above the door of the *cella* of the brothel whore advertising her body;

she welcomed all comers (Seneca *Controversiae* 1.2.5; Ovid *Amores* 1.15.18, 1.2.5, 1.2.12).[43] A whore was also taught to "make all kinds of movement with her body" to entice men (Seneca *Controversiae* 1.2.5). The dressed woman was considered to do all these things on a visual level: she put herself on public display to coax attention through appearance, was thought to welcome the gaze and hence the desire of men, visually advertised her willingness for sex, and used her body to attract.

Conclusions

Meyer Reinhold wrote in 1971: "The institutionalization of distinctive modes of dress as status symbols of class gradations, common in many cultures, did not characterize Roman society in the first few centuries of the empire, despite the intensity of class consciousness. There was never any serious intention of establishing a 'hierarchy of clothing' during the Principate, not merely because of the force of tradition but also because of fear of arousing class friction" (282). As many scholars have noted, however, distinctive modes of dress were indeed characterized as status symbols in Roman antiquity (the gold ring and narrow stripe on the tunic of the *eques* are obvious examples), and despite the fact that there was no established legal hierarchy of clothing, there was an unofficial system of sartorial signs that was understood and acknowledged. Male clothing in Roman society was supposed to define clearly the social rank and status of each of its members. *Iusti equites* wore the narrow purple stripe, and citizens the toga. But what the ancient authors describe is an ideal vestimentary situation that corresponds to an ideal static social situation, and we can identify instances of deviance from expected appearance (the usurpation of the gold ring of the *eques*, for example, or even, more unexpectedly, the omission of the toga). The system rather encouraged the usurpation of sartorial signs and the resultant social confusion. Vestimentary rules and regulations were more fluid than the authors (who write in the main about regulatory clothing) disclose.

   Much of what is said about female appearance in literary sources also seems to be prescriptive: what matrons wore and what prostitutes wore may not always have been completely straightforward and distinct. A woman may be described as *"stolata"* or *"togata"* not because she is *"stolate"* or *"togate,"* but rather because for many authors clothing indicated a moral system. Matron and whore were surely distinguishable from each other on the street but perhaps not as easily as our authors could have wished (and certainly they are also exaggerating the similarities between matron and prostitute for rhetorical purposes). That not every prostitute wore a brightly colored transparent toga nor every matron a modest *stola* is made abundantly clear by the passage quoted above from the *Digest of Justinian*. Ideal clothing is stressed precisely because the social and vestimentary definitions of women in Roman antiquity were not as sharply delineated as the exemplar demanded.

Notes

1. This essay is part of a larger study on women's appearance in Roman antiquity. I am grateful to K. R. Bradley, R. P. Saller, and anonymous readers for commenting on earlier drafts of this paper; all remaining mistakes are my own. This article has been abridged here due to considerations of space; a fuller version has appeared as Olson (2002). For detailed discussion and all Latin quotations I refer the reader here. Unless otherwise noted, all translations are from the Loeb Classical Library, with minor adjustments.

2. On Roman clothing see Sebesta and Bonfante (1994)—especially the essays of LaFollette and Sebesta—and Croom (2002). Also of interest: Dyck (2001); Palmer (1998); Scholz (1992); Sebesta (1997); L. M. Wilson (1924; 1938). For more references, see Olson (2002, 402–3 n.2).

3. But cf. Ovid *Tristia* 4.10.3. For a detailed discussion of male usurpation, see Olson (2002, 389–90 with notes).

4. Tacitus *Dialogus* 7 ("tunicatus . . . populus"); Suetonius *Augustus* 40; Juvenal 3.171–72; and Martial 10.47.5. The toga was a garment increasingly reserved for formal or ceremonial occasions (see Stone 1994, passim).

5. On slave clothing generally, see Bradley (1994, 95–99 with references).

6. For references on *latus clavus*, see Olson (2002, 404 n.11). On *calceos mutare*, see Cicero *Philippics* 13.13.28.

7. See Bonfante (1994), Dyck (2001), Gunderson (1998, 169–89), Heskel (1994), Scholz (1992), and Sebesta (1994a; 1997). On the subject of cosmetics as undesirable, see Richlin (1995) and Wyke (1994).

8. On *palla*, see Isidore *Origines* 19.25; Valerius Maximus 6.3.10; Seneca *Controversiae* 2.7.6; Propertius 2.23.13. On fillets, see Plautus *Miles gloriosus* 790–93; Ovid *Ars amatoria* 1.31, 3.483 and *Epistulae ex Ponto* 3.3.51–52; Isidore *Origines* 19.31.6; Valerius Maximus 5.2.1; and Tibullus 1.6.67. For fillets in the hair of young girls, see Propertius 4.11.34; Valerius Flaccus 8.6; and Nonius 353L.

9. See for instance Dench (1998, 144); Sebesta (1994a, 48–50; 1997, 535–37); L. M. Wilson (1938, 146–62); and Zanker (1988, 165–66).

10. See L. M. Wilson (1938, 161) and Tertullian *De pallio* 4.9 (discussed below). By 600 CE, Isidore of Seville could describe the *stola* as a garment of the past (*Origines* 19.25.3). For further references, see Olson (2002, 405 n.18).

11. See Scholz (1992, 33–74) for descriptions and notes; on the statues, see 8–14, 16, 19–21, 23, 25, 26, 28, 30 (Julio-Claudian) and 33–34 (Faustina Minor).

12. For a detailed discussion of veiling in Roman antiquity, see Olson (2002, 405–6 n.20).

13. I cannot locate an ancient reference indicating that Augustus also legislated the return of the *stola* and *vittae* along with the toga, contra Sebesta (1997, 531) and Zanker (1988, 165–66), although this might possibly be inferred from artistic evidence.

14. Contra Sensi (1980–81, 60). S. E. Wood (1999, 98), however, emphasizes the possibility that the *vittae* may have been painted into the braids of hair on statues—paint that has now of course disappeared. For further discussion, see Olson (2002, 406 n.22).

15. Translation is mine. See also Horace *Satires* 1.2.94–99; Tibullus 1.6.67–68; Ovid *Epistulae ex Ponto* 3.3.51; Propertius 4.11.61.

16. See also Pliny *Natural History* 33.40; ILLRP 977, on which see Palmer (1998, 30).

17. On the clothing of prostitutes, see McGinn (1998c, 156–71 and 208–11 with exhaustive references and bibliography). Navigating the subject was made considerably easier by his scholarship. Gardner (1986, 129, 251–52) gives a briefer account. See also Dyck (2001, 127) and Heskel (1994, 140–41). On prostitution in antiquity, see also J. N. Adams (1983); Flemming (1999); Herter (1957; 1960); McGinn (1998c) and Stumpp (1998).

18. For a detailed discussion of this perplexing passage, see Olson (2002, 407–8 n.30).

19. See McGinn (1998b, 165–66 with references; certain portions of this text are also found in the third-century commentator Porphyrio).

20. The toga was in fact originally worn by both sexes, and it is unclear when and why the toga went from being the normal dress of a woman to the dress of a whore or adulteress. Nonius 867–68L: "Not only men, but even women used to wear the toga. Afranius in his *Fratriae* (182): 'Indeed, she was standing there eating lunch with us dressed in a toga.' Varro in Book I of his *De Vita Populi Romani*: 'Once the toga was the common garment for both night and day, for both men and women.'" See also Servius *Ad Aenied* 1.282: "Both sexes and all social strata used to wear the toga." To confuse matters further, the toga was at some point in Rome's history a mark of status or honor for a woman; Pliny *Natural History* 34.28 tells of the equestrian statue of the Republican heroine Cloelia (510–509 BCE), which was clad in a toga. Furthermore, an article of male clothing called a *"stola"* (probably simply meaning "garment") appears in one of Ennius' plays (Ennius *Telephus* 339 and 341), but whether this was a Roman garment or a Greek one is uncertain.

21. on Coan silk, see note 40 below.

22. Prostitution was only punishable as a crime if the woman was of the upper classes: see McGinn (1998b) 156–71. For comparative evidence and detailed discussion, see Olson (2002) 409–10, n.41.

23. McGinn (1998c, 166 n.203) seems to link the dark-colored toga to the *colores meretricios* of Seneca (*Quaestiones naturales* 7.31.2); this is incorrect, I think, as *pullus* was also the color of mourning (see Livy 45.7.4, Tacitus *Histories* 3.67, and Florus *Epitome* 2.13.45). For detailed discussion of black and white in antiquity, see Olson (2002, 410 n 42).

24. See McGinn (1998c, 167): "The conclusion that not all Roman prostitutes wore the toga is supported by the wealth of evidence on the variety of garments worn by prostitutes."

25. See also *Epidicus* 214, where the harlots are *ornatae*. Seneca *Controversiae* 1.2.7; Seneca *Quaestiones naturales* 7.31.2; Tacitus *Dialogus* 26.

26. The fact that this quotation immediately follows Nonius's assertion that prostitutes wore a garment that was short may mean *"veste longa"* here merely refers to a long gown—*pace* McGinn (1998c, 158) and Daviault (1981, 180 n.12). Juvenal 8.158 notes that tavern girl Cyane is *"succincta"* (wearing a tunic that has been tucked up into her belt). Tavern girls were assumed by the Roman legal sources to be prostitutes (see *Digest of Justinian* 23.2.43 pr). For a discussion of the long dress of the Roman matron, and the terms employed for it, see Olson (2002, 410–11 n.45).

27. On sedans and litters, see Adams (1983, 329–30) and McGinn (1998b). On Hair dye/perfume, see Prudentius *Hamartia* 315.

28. On Roman underwear, including the *strophium*, see Olson (2003).

29. See Ovid *Tristia* 2.309–10. See also Tacitus *Annales* 15.37; Petronius *Satyricon* 7; Juvenal 6. 122 and 11.171–73; cf. Horace *Satires* 1.2.30 ("olenti in fornice stantem"). For further references on nudity in antiquity, see Olson (2002, 411–12, n.51).

30. My thanks go to *Fashion Theory's* anonymous reader for this point. See Cicero *Philippics* 3.12 and 13.31and Heskel (1994, 137). Matrons were supposed to be modestly well covered: see Horace *Satires* 1.2.29.

31. The wall paintings in the brothel at Pompeii (8.12, 18–20) seem to be an obvious place to look for artistic evidence concerning the appearance of prostitutes, conveniently reproduced in Clarke (1998, figs. 83–85), who correctly identifies these as "upper-class fantasies for the lower-class viewer" (202). In other words, it is unlikely that the pictures represent the doings of the brothel girls (or even prostitutes) and their clients. For detailed discussion, see Olson (2002, 412 n.53).

32. See also Servius *Ad Aenied* 7.403; Ovid *Fasti* 4.134. Unfortunately Martial gives no specific details of prostitute garments.

33. For a discussion of childish togas, see Olson (2002, 413 n.57).

34. There are too many instances in the sources of cosmetics on respectable women to enumerate here, but see, for example, Pliny *Natural History* 11.154; Cicero *Orator* 78–79; Seneca *Controversiae* 6.8; and Juvenal 6.477. For makeup on prostitutes, see Seneca *Ad Helviam matrem* 16.3. On ancient makeup, see Richlin (1995) and Wyke (1994), and Kleiner and Matheson (1996, 160–61, 165, and 175).

35. Thus, although American aristocratic women utilized cosmetics, the adjective "painted" was associated with whores (see Peiss 1990). A Roman woman did not need to be wealthy to wear perfumes or cosmetics: some inexpensive pyxides were made of wood, the blown glass used to hold unguents was cheap, and most substances used for cosmetics and scents (or substitutes for them) were widely available (see Kleiner and Matheson 1996, 164, no. 118).

36. Fashion can be influenced from below as well as from above; see Bonanno (1988).

37. On the colors of Roman fabrics, see André (1949); Forbes (1964, 99–150; "Dyes and Dyeing"); Sebesta (1994b); and L. M. Wilson (1938, 6–13). For women's clothing colors, see Plautus *Epidicus* 229–35; Ovid *Ars amatoria* 3.169–92. See also Sebesta (1994b, 65) and Olson (2002, 414–15 nn.62 and 63).

38. On Coan silk, see Seneca *Ad Helviam matrem* 16.316.4; Pliny *Natural History* 11.76; Seneca *De beneficiis* 7.9.5; Propertius 1.2.2, 2.1.5-6, 4.2.23; and Horace *Satires* 1.2.101-2. For a detailed discussion and examples, see Olson (2002, 416, nn.67-70).

39. On this passage, see McGinn (1998c, 161). On women's clothing, see Raditsa (1985).

40. The *leges* are unspecified.

41. On *cultus* as status, see D'Ambra (1996; 2000).

42. Juvenal, however, gives two instances in which women become aroused by watching an overtly sexual theatrical display (6.63-66 and 11.168-70). See also Ovid *Ars amatoria* 1.99-100; Plautus *Poenulus* 337; Aelian *Varia Historia* 7.10.

43. For a discussion of *blanditia* and the *vox obscaena*, see Olson (2002, 417-18, n.82).

Prostitution, Comedy, and Public Performance

Priestess and Courtesan

The Ambivalence of Female Leadership in Aristophanes' Lysistrata

CHRISTOPHER A. FARAONE

The *Lysistrata* has had a deeply divided reception in the last half century or so, hailed as the first feminist text in western culture and at the same time dismissed as an early example of pornography that degrades women. These reactions are each, in fact, rooted firmly in the text, for our reception of the *Lysistrata* depends entirely on which characters and themes we chose to focus on and which ones we choose to ignore. Indeed, as Henderson and others have pointed out, we find two very different images of women in the play: the foolish younger wives on the acropolis who are slaves to their desire for sex and wine, and the brave, intelligent, and pious older women in the semichorus, who prevent the men from burning down the doors to the acropolis and who serve as Lysistrata's brave allies until the very end of the play.[1] There is, however, a growing scholarly consensus that although Aristophanes alternates between these negative and positive images of women, in the end the character of Lysistrata herself swings the balance of the play toward a positive representation of women, for it is she who is portrayed as unremittingly good, self-controlled, and wise, it is she who reins in the sexual impulses of the younger women under her command, it is she who successfully co-opts the masculine modes of public performance (e.g., oratory and the interpretation of oracles), and it is she who in the end wins the day. In the last few years, I have become increasingly disenchanted with this interpretation of the character of Lysistrata. Indeed, in this essay I will argue that her characterization does not, in fact, tip the scales toward a feminist reading of the play but rather leaves unresolved the question of the source of Lysistrata's power and moral authority. As I now see it, in his portrayal of Lysistrata Aristophanes cleverly alternates between two very different images of an intelligent female leader. As scholars have recognized, in some scenes he casts her in the role of an aristocratic priestess of Athena—very like the much respected priestess of Athena at the time of the play's performance, a woman who in fact has a similar sounding name: Lysimache. Commentators have not, however, fully appreciated a second persistent image of female authority in the play: Lysistrata the courtesan, who knows how to manipulate men sexually and who controls the sexuality of a group of young and attractive women in a manner not at all unlike the way a madam runs a brothel.

My essay is divided into three parts. In the first I discuss the generally negative portrayal of the younger, sexually active wives, who appear foolish and who are easily manipulated by their bodily desires (Henderson 1987a, xxxvi–vii). This is one of the two stereotyped views that Athenian men apparently had of women: as objects of desire, who—because of their "naturally" (according to Greek males, that is) passionate and illogical nature—were always a source of danger and the object of careful surveillance. In the second section I turn to the semichorus of older women who staunchly help Lysistrata repel the attacks of the men and never waver in their resolve. Despite an occasional show of physical or verbal violence necessary for the comic slapstick, this second group is by and large depicted in a much more positive manner: they pray to the gods, boast their service in the cults of the city, and are introduced to the stage in the midst of performing a classic type of female work (carrying water from the fountain), which has numerous positive reverberations in popular myths and rituals concerned with salvation. Although in the final analysis both sets of images are designed to keep women in their "proper" places in a patriarchal society, either as "whores" or "wives," Aristophanes seems to take special care to invest the older women with an unusual kind of authority, a female heroism if you will, that stems from their repeated association with both the day-to-day household economy and with important civic rituals and cults, on which the salvation of the city depends. This authority, moreover, clearly lends credibility to their claim to know how best to save the city—one of the most important themes in the play (Faraone 1997).

In the third and final section of my talk, I turn to Lysistrata herself and begin with the positive portrayal of her character, building upon the important work of Helene Foley, Nicole Loraux, and others, who have discussed in detail how the speeches and actions of Lysistrata evoke images of the goddess Athena and the Panathenaic ritual that is central to the goddess' role as the protectress of the city (e.g., Foley 1982, 9–10 and Loraux 1980–81).[2] I close, however, with a discussion of Lysistrata as an enterprising courtesan and madam, who in some sense turns the acropolis into a whorehouse and who encourages one of her girls, Myrrhine, to titilate a man to the point of desperation—a standard feature in popular depictions of courtesans in ancient Greece. In the end, I suggest that Aristophanes has orchestrated a wonderfully rich array of images of women in classical Athens, both negative and positive, and that his Lysistrata embodies alternately—and at some points simultaneously—two very different figures of female authority, the pious priestess and the brilliant and sophisticated courtesan.

The Younger Women on the Acropolis

If we want to make sense of Aristophanes' play, it is absolutely crucial that we distinguish the younger wives, who Lysistrata summons and cajoles at the beginning of the play, from the older women who appear later as the second semichorus. These younger women, apparently neighbors in Athens, are late in arriving at the meeting called by Lysistrata, and at first they absolutely refuse to give up having sex with their husbands in order to achieve the higher goal of stopping the war with Sparta. One character, Calonice, says quite emphatically that she would rather walk through fire than give up sex (133)! But Lysistrata is able to get round this problem, because there is, in fact, only one thing that these younger women care about more than sex and that is wine. She presents them with a full wineskin but will not let them drink until they swear off sex. And even after they make their promises, the whole success of the sex strike depends on Lysistrata's ability to monitor the gate of the acropolis as these women attempt to sneak away one-by-one, compelled by their uncontrollable desire for sex. In the past, many readers—myself included—have suggested that Lysistrata seems to play the role here of a priestess of the virgin goddess Athena carefully monitoring the sexuality of her wards (the younger women), who in turn act like young college girls trying to sneak out of their dormitory for a clandestine meeting with their boyfriends. There are, however, several indications that Aristophanes' audience would have found this interpretation somewhat naive and sentimental. First and foremost is the famous encounter between Myrrhine and her husband Cinesias, which (once it gets started) clearly announces itself as a typical scene in a brothel between a teasing whore and her bewildered customer (828ff.).[3] Most telling are the names of these two characters: the man's derives from the Greek verb *"kinein,"* which in Athenian slang means "(for a man) to have sexual intercourse" (i.e., "to screw"). Thus "Cinesias" most probably means something like "The Screwer" or in the context of a brothel "The John." The name Myrrhine, on the other hand, is derived from the Greek word for "myrtle," which in slang is used to refer to a woman's vagina. Myrrhine is also an extremely common name for prostitutes and courtesans, and in this scene she repeatedly uses the oath "By Aphrodite" (an oath sworn typically by courtesans), rather than "By Demeter" or "By the Two Goddesses," oaths that are typical of chaste housewives. Scholars are also in agreement that "Myrrhine's skilful wheedling, teasing and coquettishness were surely more characteristic of *hetairai* than wives, just as Cinesias's suppliant position is that of a customer, not a husband." The scene, therefore, neatly juxtaposes the domestic and the meretricious. It begins with Cinesias's arrival, with nursemaid and child, and his attempts to play on Myrrhine's maternal affections and sense of duty in order to get her to come home, but by the end the baby and nurse are forgotten and "The Screwer" leaves the stage without having gotten what he really came for.

All of the early scenes between the younger women and Lysistrata feature the latter in her role as gatekeeper, trying desperately to keep her girls from leaving the acropolis. Here, too, Aristophanes contrives the scenes in a way that allows us to identify the younger women as *both* housewives and prostitutes. The best example is the scene in which one of them attempts to go home in order (she claims) to attend to a domestic chore (729–34):

Woman A: I want to go home, for at home I have got bunches of Milesian wool that are being cut to pieces by the moths

Lysistrata: What do you mean by "moths"? Get back inside!

Woman A: But I will return quickly, I swear by the Two Goddesses, after I have spread some apart on the bed, that's all I'll do.

Lysistrata: Don't you spread anything and don't you leave!

Woman A: But am I to allow my wool to be destroyed?
Lysistrata: Yes, if that's what's necessary![4]

At first glance, this young woman seems to invoke the right kind of domestic deities in her oath (the Two Goddesses: Demeter and Persephone) and to show real concern for a traditional wifely duty: the washing, carding, and spinning of wool—a scene of archetypal domesticity found on many a vase painting. Commentators have noted, of course, that the location of this putative work (the bed) and the verb for "spreading apart"—in both cases with a vague or unexpressed direct object—point to a much different goal: her desire to have sex with her husband (Henderson 1987a, ad loc.). Ed Cohen's discussion in this volume, however, of the Athenian wool workers who regularly "moonlighted" as whores, suggests that the audience might have also interpreted the excuse of this woman as an double entendre that once again encompasses both the domestic and the meretricious: she has a pressing need to get back to her other "wool working" job. Modern readers might, of course, be shocked that Aristophanes would equate Athenian wives with prostitutes, but as we shall see, this is a persistent theme in the play, which dovetails with a another set of allusions to them as adulteresses (for example, in the speech of the Proboulos [403–29]). It should be stressed, however, that these charges are either put in the mouths of hostile male characters who are eventually discredited, or they are framed in terms of double entendres that can be read innocently as depictions of wives longing for their lawfully wedded husbands.

The Semichorus of Older Women

Aristophanes, however, very quickly juxtaposes these pornographic images of the younger women with different and very positive images of the older women in the semichorus, who rush to the stage with full water jugs when they learn that the men are attempting to set fire to the gates of the acropolis and harm Lysistrata and her girls. In a recent article, I argued that by his very staging of their entrance, Aristophanes immediately sets up an important contrast (Faraone 1997, 38–42). On one level, the older women appear as typical Athenian housewives performing what is still a daily routine for housewives in nonindustrialized parts of the world—they have just gone to the local fountain and fetched their daily supply of water for cooking and washing. Aristophanes, however, takes this quotidian scene and invests it with important mythological and religious symbolism, thereby positioning these women as heroic saviors who will extinguish the fires that threaten to burn down the acropolis and the women on it.

Our appreciation of the heroism of their actions depends on our knowledge of Greek tragedy in which one finds many scenes, often (as here) at the very beginning of a play, where irate men threaten to immolate helpless and innocent women who have taken asylum at an alter (for example, at the beginning of Euripides' *Heracles* and his *Andromache*). In most of the plays that begin this way, the fire is averted by words not water, but we do have evidence that tragic poets also staged theatrical scenes of watery salvation like that enacted in the *Lysistrata*, for instance, in a lost play about how Alcmene was saved after she had been charged with adultery and was about to be immolated by her angry husband.[5] This kind of scene was a probable source for the staging of the chorus' entrance in the *Lysistrata*, where the women ensconced on sacred ground (Lysistrata and the younger women on the acropolis) are nearly immolated by angry torch-bearing men suspicious of their loyalty before they are saved by the older women who bring water to douse the fire. These initial scenes between the two semichoruses are often dismissed as frivolous slapstick that is not pertinent to the wider themes of the play, but in fact they introduce the older women in an extremely positive light as dynamic saviors in a play that is ultimately concerned about the salvation of the city.

Toward the end of the play Aristophanes underscores the religiously centered authority of these older women when he has them directly advise the audience and justify their advice by boasting about their special civic credentials, all of which refer to their regular participation in the religious life of the city:[6]

For I, all you citizens, begin with some useful advice for the city. And it is fitting that I do so, since it nourished me splendidly and in great comfort. When I was seven years old straightaway I served as *arrephoros* [i.e., weaver of Athena's ceremonial robe]. Next when I was ten I was a 'corn-grinder' for the Founding Goddess [i.e., Athena][7] and shedding the saffron gown I was a "bear" at the Brauronia festival. Also, once when I was a fair maiden, I was a basket carrier [i.e., in the Panathenaic procession] wearing a necklace of dried figs. Do I not then deserve a chance to give advice to the city? (638–48)

Here the description of important religious duties with their domestic-sounding titles like "corn grinder" and "basket carrier" repeats the double image of women as the caretakers of both the household economy of

Athens and its religious life, a pattern into which we can also fit the female chorus' entrance as women who carry water from the well.

The question then arises: how does Aristophanes dramatically link
these two very different groups of women, the younger sex-crazed
"whores" up above and the older citizen-wives, who stand below
guarding the gates of the acropolis? He does it, as we would expect,
with delicious irony and good humor. For example: when the older
women run onto the stage with their water jugs, they set their goal of
saving the besieged women in a larger framework of Panhellenic salvation with the following prayer to Athena: "Goddess, may I never see
these women in flames; instead let them rescue Greece and her citizens
from war and madness! O golden crested Guardian of the citadel, for
that is why they occupy your shrine. I invite thee to be our ally, Trito-
geneia, defending it with water, should any man set it afire!" (341–49,
trans. Henderson 1996, 54). This prayer represents the older women as
pious and staunch defenders of the city who see themselves as the allies
of the virgin goddess herself. Their prayer however, is quite curious, in
that it quite explicitly calls to mind another famous scene of women on
an acropolis threatened by impious men. This was the prayer that the
women of Corinth made on their own acropolis in the darkest hours
of the Persian War. It is described in a famous epigram by the poet Simonides, which was apparently set up on the Corinthian acropolis next
to a representation or list of these women:[8]

These women stood praying to Cypris [Aphrodite] for miracles on behalf of the
Greeks and the close-fighting citizens. For divine Aphrodite did not wish to
give the acropolis of the Greeks to the bow-bearing Persians.

In addition to the obvious parallels in circumstance—an acropolis
under attack—the pleonastic expression in Aristophanes ("rescuing
Greece and the citizens" at lines 342–43) recalls the first line of the Si-
monidean poem: "praying on behalf of the Greeks and the close-fighting
citizens." If this epigram was as famous as later sources suggest, Aristophanes has summoned up an image of heroic and pious women on
an acropolis praying for safety at a time of great national emergency.
And in such a comparison the fire-wielding Athenian men (later aided
by the Scythian archers) would seem to play the invidious role of the
hated Persians who once besieged and burned the Athenian citadel and
threatened the same for Corinth.

This allusion is, however, also filled with a wonderful irony, for
the women praised by Simonides were apparently wealthy *hetairai*

("courtesans"), the special devotees of Aphrodite, who like Athena in Athens was worshipped as the primary goddess of the city and the protectress of the Corinthian acropolis. If we recall how Aristophanes consistently portrays the younger women on the acropolis as sex-crazed drinkers of wine, the echo of the epigram is richly and humorously ambivalent: the women on the Athenian acropolis with Lysistrata are as heroic as the courtesans of Corinth, a town notorious in antiquity for its gold-digging prostitutes. Thus as they intone this prayer the older women in the semichorus express three different ideas simultaneously: (i) they underscore their own solidarity with Athena as the guardian of their own acropolis; (ii) they cast the besieging men in the other semichorus in the role of hostile Persians intent on burning the acropolis; and (iii) they also manage to assimilate Lysistrata and the younger women on the acropolis with a group of famous Corinthian courtesans devoted to Aphrodite.

Lysistrata Herself: Priestess or Courtesan?

To which camp of women, then, does Lysistrata herself belong: that of the citizen wife or that of the prostitute? On the one hand, she spends most of her time on the acropolis in the company of the younger women and in the opening scene she repeatedly uses the pronoun "we" to include herself among these sexually active married women who will deny their husbands sex until a peace treaty is concluded. On the other hand, Aristophanes depicts her in a manner similar to the older women in the semichorus in that she never shows any sexual desire herself and although she apparently has a husband, he never appears on stage—not even at the end of the play. She is, moreover, very smart and tough and she is willing to fight for her ideas—all characteristics that she shares with the older women. She is also linked with the semichorus by her ongoing and high-minded concern about saving Athens and Greece. Indeed, Lysistrata insists that "the salvation [sôtêria] of all Greece is in the hands of its women" (30) and that "we will save Greece by our common action" (41), a sentiment that she repeats later (525) in her famous debate with the Proboulos, a special wartime commissioner.

Scholars have shown, moreover, that the play is filled with allusions to Athena's shrines, statues, and rituals (Bodson [1973] discusses, for example, a series of jokes at lines 740–52) and that at some points in the action Aristophanes has modeled and perhaps even named his heroine after an aristocratic woman named Lysimache, who at the time of the performance of this play was most probably the priestess of Athena Polias, the chief protective deity of Athens (Lewis 1955).[9] It is thus no accident that the women choose the acropolis as their base of operations, and that Lysistrata herself seems at times to mirror the military spirit, the sound judgment, and the domestic accomplishments of the virgin goddess herself. In a similar manner, Lysistrata at the crowning moment of her wonderful speech to the Proboulos assimilates the city to raw wool that must be cleaned, spun, and then properly woven into cloth, recalling both the daily, domestic chores of Athenian housewives as well as the ritual production of the Panathenaic *peplos,* a gigantic tapestry that selected Athenian girls wove for the annual festival of Athena.[10] In this light, then, Lysistrata, like the older women in the semichorus, seems to combine housework typical of Athenian citizen-wives—who are frequently idealized in vase paintings carding and spinning their wool in the safety of their homes—with an important religious role of women in the Panatheneia, a festival of crucial importance to the safety and solidarity of the city.

Until quite recently, I strongly supported this reading of the play and I was of the firm opinion that Aristophanes recognized a real moral authority in Lysistrata and the older Athenian women and that he closed the play on a note that praised Athenian wives, who in their traditional domestic and ritual roles did much to preserve the city in times of great danger. This approach, however, seems somewhat naive to me now, because it ignores another important theme that is first hinted at by the echo of the epigram describing the Corinthian courtesans: there are several scenes in the play where Lysistrata seems far from a pious priestess of the virgin Athena and very much like a clever and conniving courtesan. In fact, just before her famous speech to the Proboulos about carding and weaving the Athenian civic body, instead of calling on Athena in her role as patron of women's handicrafts, Lysistrata invokes the help of Eros and the Aphrodite—a prayer that we would more readily expect from the mouth of a courtesan not a housewife: "But if indeed heart-delighting Eros or Aphrodite Cyprogeneia [born in Cyprus] begins to infuse desire [*himeros*] down along our breasts and thighs and thus cause a pleasurable tension and a case of 'stiff-penisitis' in our men, then I believe that one day we will be known among the Greeks as 'Lysimaches'" (551–54). Here once again, Aristophanes brings the images of chaste housewife and courtesan into comic collision, for it is quite hilarious that in the same speech Lysistrata should claim that she and her girls will be called "Lysimaches" (after the priestess of the virgin goddess Athena) if Eros and Aphrodite render them as sensual as courtesans and cause erections in their men.

This alternate role of Lysistrata as courtesan and madam is, however, most obvious in the scene of Myrrhine's encounter with her husband, which as we saw earlier seems to cast the husband Cinesias as a customer visiting a favorite prostitute (see Henderson 1987a, ad loc. for what follows here). As it turns out, it is Lysistrata herself who sets up the scene with yet another bawdy prayer to Cyprian Aphrodite when she sees Cinesias run on stage with a huge erection: "A man! I see a man coming this way, stricken, in the grip of Aphrodite's mysterious powers. May Lady Aphrodite, mistress of Cyprus and Cythera and Paphos, make thy journey straight and upright!" (831–34). Furthermore, when Cinesias asks to see Myrrhine, Lysistrata replies "What will you give me?"(860). Most commentators point out that her response mimics a madam's request for payment and they suggest quite rightly that "Lysistrata treats Cinesias as if he were a customer at a brothel" (Henderson 1987a, ad loc.)

We have seen, then, that at some points in this play Arisophanes casts Lysistrata in the role of a hard-hearted madam who controls a group of lusty young whores and who prays to Aphrodite, the patron of her trade, not to Athena. I should make it clear, however, that Lysistrata is not cast as a courtesan or a madam in every scene, for this is plainly not the case. Indeed, at some points in the play Aristophanes enjoys playing the same scene or the same lines both ways simultaneously, although we modern readers may often fail to grasp the full meaning. Lysistrata's famous speech to the Proboulos, for example, in which she reveals her plans to wash and card the citizens like wool and then spin and weave them into a new political fabric, has often been praised for the way it takes an image of respected wifely work from domestic life and the ritual sphere and projects it into the world of men (see Henderson [1987a] for discussion and bibliography). It has not been noticed, however, that for a contemporary audience the same lines probably would have evoked the same double entendre discussed earlier: the Athenian equation of wool working and prostitution. In short it is not clear in the speech whether Lysistrata, in deploying this elaborate image for political reform, is drawing from her experience as a housewife and priestess or as a "wool worker."

The poet brilliantly conflates the two images one last time in the finale of the play, when ambassadors arrive from Sparta and Athens to "sign off" on her peace plan and Lysistrata is triumphantly greeted by the chorus: "Hail, O most manly [*andreiotatê*] of all women! Now you must be harsh and soft, noble and base, stately and mild, and vastly experienced, since the most powerful of the Greeks have been seized by your *iunx* spell and have come to you en masse" (1108–11). Scholars usually interpret the adjective "most manly" figuratively and see this as the crowning moment to a series of allusions and references that connect Lysistrata with the masculine war goddess Athena. To put it in a more familiar modern context: according to this reading Lysistrata and her girls appear somewhat like the Austrian Mother Superior and her novices in the film "Sound of Music," who deal firmly but in saintly fashion with the evil Nazis and their sympathizers.

There are, however, some important details that jar with this traditional understanding of the scene. First off it ignores the fact that the assembled ambassadors all have massive and painful erections, an agitated state that is not usually associated with the worship of a virgin goddess like Athena. Secondly, Lysistrata produces at this point a naked woman named "Reconciliation," whom she promises to hand over to these erect men when and if they agree to a peace treaty. The final puzzling detail is the fact that the chorus claims that these sexually excited men have come because they have been overcome by what is referred to as Lysistrata's "*iunx*," a word whose original and primary meaning is "erotic magic spell." In this passage of the *Lysistrata*, however, commentators (including the ancient scholiasts) generally ignore this standard meaning of the word and opt instead for some vague reference to Lysistrata's "charm" or "allure" in the argument she lays out in her final speech. This approach, of course, glides over the obvious fact that *iunx* spells are designed to produce intense *sexual* desire and here it must refer to Lysistrata's successful sex strike, which has indeed had precisely the same effect as a *iunx* spell: it has produced a stage full of sexually excited men. If we press, then, for this more common meaning of the word "*iunx*," how can we connect the successful operation of Lysistrata's *iunx* spell with the triumphal designation of her as "the most manly of all women"? As it turns out, *iunx* spells and other forms of violent and invasive erotic magic are almost always used by men to drive women from the homes of their fathers or husbands, with one pervasive and consistent exception: these spells were frequently co-opted by courtesans or prostitutes to draw men out of their homes and into their own arms.[11]

I will limit myself to a single but illuminating example. At one point in Xenophon's *Memorabilia*, Socrates hears about the great beauty of an

Athenian *hetaira* named Theodote and goes to her home with some friends to watch as her portrait is being painted. Socrates marvels at the opulence of Theodote's clothes, her female servants and house, and somewhat naively asks her what her source of income is. Theodote says bluntly but graciously that she survives "on the generosity of any friend she picks up" (3.11.4), a comment that then triggers a short dialogue on friendship and the process by which one does indeed make male friends and keep them.[12] Toward the end of this conversation they discuss in a very playful manner the use of love magic in getting and keeping such friends (3.11.16–17):

> And Socrates, making light of his own laziness, said: "But it is not at all easy, Theodote, for me to get free, for much business, both private and public, keeps me busy. And I have also got my dear girls [*philai*] who neither day nor night allow me to escape from them, since they are learning both love potions [*philtra*] and incantations [*epoidai*] from me."
>
> "Indeed, do you also know how to do these things Socrates?" she said.
>
> "Why else" he said "do you think that Apollodorus here and Antisthenes never leave me? And why do you think that Cebes and Simmias come from Thebes? Know well that these things do not happen without many love potions [*philtra*], incantations [*epoidai*], and *iunx* spells [*iugges*]."
>
> "Do, then, lend me your *iunx*" she said, "so that I may draw it against you first!"
>
> "But by Zeus," he said, "I wasn't planning to be drawn to you, but rather I want you to come to me!"

This is a clever bit of dialogue in which Xenophon's Socrates—in the presence of at least four of his students—playfully compares his own knack for attracting young men and keeping them by his side with the ability of a courtesan to do the same. As in so much Socratic humor, the joke clearly depends on a good deal of ironic self-deprecation: Socrates—as in his better known allusions to himself as a midwife—assimilates himself to a class of working women famous for their cunning and their notorious manipulation of young men in many ways, including through the use of magic.[13]

In the light of this traditional image of the autonomous courtesan using a *iunx* to lead her boyfriends unerringly to herself, we should return again to the scene of Lysistrata's triumph, where she, by virtue of the manifest effect of her *iunx* spell on the erect ambassadors, is hailed as the "most masculine" of all women. As I have suggested elsewhere, this acclamation can be read in two ways: commentators usually assume that this refers to the manly courage or power that Lysistrata gains from her close association with the virgin war goddess Athena, from whose sanctuary she speaks (Faraone 1999, 158–59 and Henderson 1987a, ad loc.). This reading is undoubtedly correct, but there is another way to understand "most manly": she has in her role as courtesan or madam extraordinaire co-opted—as many courtesans apparently did—a traditionally male weapon of erotic magic and turned it on all the men of Greece, who have been drawn to her brothel (the acropolis) en masse. This second, more outrageous interpretation gains heft by what follows, for Lysistrata then procedes to dangle a naked woman before the assembled Greeks as a bribe for agreeing to a peace treaty. The scene is filled with graphic and explicit references to the naked woman's body, which is to be shared sexually by the Spartan and the Athenian men. Her speech ends with an invitation to the men: "Now then, see to it that you ratify the treaty, so that we women [*gunaikes*] may entertain you on the acropolis with the goodies we have got in our baskets [*en taisi kistaisi*]. Swear oaths there and pledge your faith to one another, and afterwards each of you grab your own woman [*gunaika*] and go away [*apeis'*]" (1184–88). The usual reading of this invitation is that each of the men will go into the sanctuary of Athena on the acropolis, swear to the peace treaty, have a feast and then grab his wife and go home. This is certainly one way to construe the Greek term *"gunaikes,"* which can mean both "women" and "wives," and there is in fact epigraphical evidence that the priestesses of Athena did host special feasts on the acropolis (Henderson 1987a, ad loc). In his commentary, however, Henderson points out that *"kistai,"* the word for "baskets" (especially as used here with the article, "in *our* baskets")would have sounded to an audience finely attuned to obscene puns much like the word *"kusthoi,"* "vaginas." He backs away from the obvious conclusion, however, on the understandable conviction that we are not to imagine the couples having sex on the acropolis, but here, too, I would argue that this is just the last of a series of scenes in which the acropolis becomes a brothel run by Lysistrata and worked by the younger wives of Athens. In her last and most triumphal scene of the play, therefore, Lysistrata continues her doubled roles: the lines above can be interpreted both as an exhortation to each man to have conjugal sex after they leave a feast in a temple compound and go back to their homes or as an invitation into the brothel to feast with his regular "woman" and then slip away from the table to a darker part of the acropolis and enjoy the goodies in her other basket. Either way the men get to have sex, now that Lysistrata has gotten her peace treaty.

Conclusion: Two Icons of Female Power in Athens

It would appear, then, that the highly polarized images of the younger and older women in Aristophanes' *Lysistrata* reappear in the somewhat contradictory treatment of the comic heroine herself, who alternately or simultaneously dons two quite different roles: the pious priestess of Athena, who in urging her peace plan draws on her knowledge and experience of running a traditional household or sanctuary, and the clever madam, who knows how to guard the entrance to her brothel, how to throw lavish a feast there, and how to manipulate men and marshal her girls to maximize her profits and influence. The brilliance of this double characterization lies, of course, in the implied similarities between the aristocratic priestess and the wealthy courtesan, between the sanctuary of a goddess and the brothel of a powerful madam. In patriarchal Athens there were, in fact, only two pathways by which intelligent and dynamic women could learn about, cultivate, and eventually occupy positions of leadership in society: citizen women of means could aspire to one of the hereditary priesthoods of the city, while foreign-born (and occasionally Athenian) women could, if they played their cards right, assume the role of a wealthy and successful courtesan and madam, much like Theodote or Aspasia, the famous paramour and (eventually) wife of Pericles.

Priestesses of certain ancestral cults, like the famous Lysimache who oversaw the cult of Athena Polias, presumably first learned how to run the domestic affairs of the aristocratic households of their parents and husbands and then how to administer the household of a goddess, with its attendant festivals, processions, slaves, and minor officials. In many ways, the sanctuary of a goddess resembled the domestic areas of a large and wealthy citizen household, which was primarily populated by female family members and slaves and was also responsible for the education of the girls and younger relatives. In the case of the cult of Athena on the acropolis and that of Artemis at Brauron, we suspect that young, probably aristocratic, girls were in fact educated in cultic traditions and trained to perform special roles, such as that of *arrephoroi* on the acropolis and that of "bears" for Artemis at Brauron, two of the roles that the semichorus of older women boast about in the famous passage quoted earlier.[14] In some ways, then, we might imagine that a senior priestess, much like an abbess in a medieval monastery, presided over a staff of other women and servants or slaves, as well as a small group of aristocratic girls placed in her hands annually for the highly sought religious duties. It is this image, I think, that rightly underpins many modern readings of Lysistrata's role as overseer of a group of unruly novices living in Athena's sanctuary on the acropolis.

There was, however, another leadership role available to the intelligent and ambitious women of ancient Athens, who were by the accident of their birth or circumstances denied access to the first: the wealthy and highly sought after courtesans, who seem to have wielded power in a similar kind of all-female household—one headed by a courtesan and madam who ruled over a group of younger women in her employ, some of whom were owned as slaves and others who were legally her own daughters by blood or adoption (see Cohen's essay in this volume and my discussion [Faraone 1999, 154]). Xenophon, for example, tells us that Theodote, lived in her richly adorned house with her "mother" and many beautiful servant girls—but strikingly no men (*Memorabilia* 3.11.4)—and we hear elsewhere of the infamous Neaira was allegedly purchased as a child by a freedwoman named Nicarete, who called her and six other bought girls her "daughters" ([Demosthenes] 59.18–19). This pattern appears in later comedy as well, for example in Plautus's *Cistellaria*, where Selenion, the putative "foster daughter" of a whore, later learns that she is really the daughter of a free citizen who exposed her at birth.[15] This older courtesan "mother," moreover, in addition to being the administrator of the "household," also apparently instructed the younger girls (like the "girlfriends" mentioned in Socrates in Xenophon's *Memorabilia*) in the tricks of the trade (see n. 69 in Cohen's essay in this volume), as is evident in a speech from a lost play of the comic writer Alexis, in which someone describes how a courtesan, once she has made enough money, can take in and teach younger women the trade (frag. 98).

I began this essay by observing that modern critics treat Aristophanes' *Lysistrata* in two contradictory ways, either praising it as the first feminist tract in history or condemning it as the first pornographic one. We can now see that this wide disparity in the recent reception of the play most probably arises from the very different kinds of dramatic interactions that involve Lysistrata. In the scenes with the younger women, she is repeatedly cast as a manipulative and gold-digging madam, a traditional figure of scorn and abuse in comedy, who in this play repeatedly treats women as mere sexual objects, to be stripped entirely (like the mute and naked character of "Reconciliation" in the end) of their clothes and their voices. On the other hand, when Aristophanes has Lysistrata interact with the men as their intellectual and political equals, he is clearly drawing on the traditional figure of the elite courtesan, not the madam, a popular comic figure who in fact appears to have been the earliest female comic protagonist in Athens and who probably influenced Aristophanes' portrayal of Lysistrata (Henderson [2002]). If we add to this the undeniably positive allusions that connect Lysistrata to Athena and her priesthood, we see that Aristophanes brilliantly plays on the commonalities between brothel and sanctuary and between the dynamic female leadership of priestesses and courtesans. For he manages to give Lysistrata a consistently intelligent character, endowed with the various rhetorical and strategic skills necessary for good leadership, while at the same time switching back and forth with great wit and humor between the morally opposed roles of madam and priestess and the very different realms of Aphrodite and the virgin Athena—all without sacrificing the dramatic unity of her character. It is no wonder that the modern reception of this play has been so fraught with paradoxes! Indeed, the poet has grandly capitalized on the similarities between the only two kinds of women who could in fact assume roles of real leadership in their communities: the wealthy courtesan and the aristocratic priestess.[16]

Notes

1. The division of female characters by generation and the generally more positive presentation of the older generation is a feature of Old Comedy; see e.g. Henderson (1987b).

2. For the duties of the priestess of Athena Polias, see Foley (1982, 9 n.20) and Loraux (1980–81, 144–45). Lines 740–52, where Lysistrata turns back the five women trying to sneak back home, are filled with detailed allusions to Athena and her cult on the acropolis; see Bodson (1973).

3. Henderson (1987a, ad loc.) provides most of the information and insights in this paragraph and the quote near the end of it.

4. All translations from *Lysistrata* are from Henderson (1987a).

5. In the literary versions of the story, Zeus simply sends a shower of rain that douses the fire, but in the painted depictions of the myth, the rain shower is imagined as two women who stand on either side of a rainbow and pour jugs of water down on to the flames; these woman are presumably rain nymphs acting on the orders of Zeus, who himself stands nearby in the upper register of the painting. See *LIMC*, s.v. "Alkmene," nos. 5–7.

6. Foley (1982, 11–12); Henderson (1987a, ad loc.); and MacDowell (1995). Loraux (1980–81, 135–36) makes the intriguing suggestion that all of these rituals were performed on or near the acropolis where the action of the play is staged.

7. I follow Henderson (1987a ad loc.) and others who argue that in an Athenian context we understand the "Founding Goddess" to mean Athena.

8. I follow (with one minor exception) the interpretation Page (1981, 207–11; "Simonides" XIV); for a more detailed version of the arguments that follow in this paragraph, see Faraone (1997, 54–57). See Keesling's essay in this volume for further discussion.

9. Although Dover (1972, 152 n.3) dismisses it, the *communis opinio* about the equation of Lysimache and Lysistrata continues to gain support; see, e.g., Foley (1982, 7), Loraux (1981–82, 148–49), and MacDowell (1995, 239–40). Henderson (1987a, xxxviii–xl) considers the identification plausible but unnecessary.

10. A duty that would have been overseen (in part) by the priestess of Athena Polias; see e.g. Foley (1992, 9 n.20) and Loraux (1981–82, 144–45).

11. See Faraone (1999, 64–69) on the *iunx*-spell, one traditionally used by males and (1999, 149–60) on the subject of courtesans co-opting the use of the *iunx.*

12. See Davidson (1997, 120–30) for an excellent analysis of this passage and a very nuanced understanding of the use of the word "friends."

13. See Faraone (1999, 1–2) where I suggest that Socrates humorously presents himself as an aging courtesan/philosopher who (as her charms fade) resorts to magic to keep her customers/students coming back to her and at the same time also begins to teach the same magic spells to younger women in her employ who will eventually take over the business. This equation of philosopher and courtesan loses some of its shock value, of course, when we remember that elsewhere Socrates claims to be the student of a similarly witty and wealthy courtesan: Aspasia, the lover of Pericles, who is alleged in Plato's *Menexenos* to have taught Socrates the funeral oration that he ends up reciting in that dialogue.

14. Until recently both of these rituals were thought to be female initiation rites, but this has recently been questioned: see Donnay (1997) for a new assessment of the *arrhephoroi* and Faraone (2003) for the Brauronian "bears."

15. See James (2003, 35–68) and in this volume for the courtesan love-object in Roman elegy, who sets up an all female house. In her essay in this volume, Glazebrook discusses the case of Neaira in detail. Ruggiero (1993, 26–29, and 42–43) collects several examples of all-female "families" of courtesans working in Renaissance Florence. In each case, the female "family" is headed by an older courtesan who has "adopted" younger women, passed them off as her own daughters, and taught them the tricks of the trade. For more discussion see Faraone (forthcoming) and the essay in this volume by Sharon James, who notes how the mother of a courtesan is often her *lena.*

16. This paper evolved from a lecture entitled "'Good Girls' and 'Bad Girls': Female Stereotypes in Aristophanes' *Lysistrata,*" that I gave in March 2000 at Willamette University and in October 2000 at "Teaching Aristophanes' Feminist Plays," a conference at Ohio University. I am extremely grateful to my hosts, respectively Mark Usher and Tom Carpenter, and to the audiences at both venues for their comments, questions and criticisms.

A Courtesan's Choreography

Female Liberty and Male Anxiety at
the Roman Dinner Party

SHARON L. JAMES

Three Latin texts, more than 150 years apart in time, comically portray Roman citizen men in a state of obsession over the minute details of the behavior of courtesans at a banquet.[1] As these works—Plautus's *Asinaria*, Ovid's *Amores* 1.4 and 2.5[2]—exaggerate this condition, to humorous effect, they demonstrate a peculiar failing of elite masculinity in the face of female freedom, subjectivity,[3] and sexuality. Hence they reveal a great deal of male anxiety and a powerful desire to control a free woman, whose very freedom, derived from her noncitizen status as a courtesan, both entices and frightens the man attracted to her. They thus both expose fault lines in elite Roman masculinity and offer insights into the lives and professions of a small, but interesting and culturally important, number of Roman women, whose livelihood depended upon maintaining competing male sexual interest. Plautus and Ovid offer us opportunity for exploring this clash of gender and status, ideology and reality, in ancient Rome.

The scene of concern is usually a banquet, though the masculine anxieties extend beyond, into the private and unknowable realm of female desires and offstage activities. The male involved is a citizen of some means, so worried about how much attention the courtesan in question attracts from other men that he tries to forbid her to engage in the very behavior that first caught his own notice, or that he himself taught her. Such anxieties defy the norms of Roman masculinity, given that Roman gender norms and social hierarchical structures posit male mastery of women[4]—historically, a wife was under the control of father, husband, or tutor; female slaves had no power against their male owners; and streetwalking prostitutes were insignificant to a male citizen's emotional life.

But these texts demonstrate a contrary and irrational concern with the minor physical gestures and postures of a woman outside the boundaries of respectable, citizen social life. Ultimately, I suggest, the male anxieties they reveal revolve around the impossibility of controlling such a woman: the woman a citizen male actually wants but cannot marry (indeed, the woman he must pay for) is the one woman he cannot control. Thus, ironically, she has more power and freedom, within the confines of their interactions, than he has. She has therefore a strikingly destabilizing effect on the young masters of the Roman universe. Such a circumstance—conceptually, if not experientially, alien to an elite Roman male—results in considerable anxiety of a sort that may produce a form of temporary identity crisis, such that a young man forgets both himself and his place in Roman society, becoming either subject to a woman's control or utterly obsessed with her.

Definitions

Some clarification of terms and paradigms is in order, regarding (1) the Roman-ness of this situation, given the Greek antecedents and settings to Roman Comedy, and (2) the status of the woman in *Amores* 1.4, who has usually been considered a wife but is in my view a courtesan. On Roman-ness: Roman Comedy presented situations that its audience understood as relevant to Rome; its social content speaks to Roman concerns, values, and structures (see James 1998a, 4–5). There were, by Plautus's time, courtesans in Rome—for example, Hispala Faecenia, contemporary of Plautus (Livy 39.9–19); notably, she was not Greek[5]—so the banquet scene from *Asinaria* (one of his early plays) would have had recognizably Roman aspects. *Asinaria* itself contains specifically Roman references: Demaenetus goes to the senate (888–89) and assists *clientes* (871). Lowe (1992, 161) notes the Roman *tresviri* in line 131, citing also *Truculentus* 761 as a Plautine addition. On the differences between comic *hetairai* and *meretrices*, Halporn (1993, 201–2) sees *meretrices* as a

particularly Plautine Romanization of Greek originals.[6] Such specific
touches amount to a Roman atmosphere laid over the Greek names;
they serve to create a Romanized context.[7] I presume here that the social and gender values at play in these banquet situations are Roman
enough that *Asinaria*'s Greek setting would not have kept Plautus's
viewers from understanding its themes as relating to life in Rome.[8] The
sexual anxieties witnessed in *Asinaria* may have seemed to Plautus especially suitable for adaptation to a Roman audience—their reappear-
ance in elegy particularly marks them as not purely Greek but Roman
as well. Regarding the scenario in *Amores* 1.4 and 2.5, Otis (1938, 206
and n.68)—speaking precisely of the mixed-company banquet scenes in
the *Ars* and citing both Brandt (1902, passim) and Friedländer (1908,
238–39)—notes of the *Ars Amatoria* that the "general background of social intercourse is primarily Roman."[9] These banquet situations are
clearly the same as those in the *Amores*. Fully developed love elegy itself is a Roman genre, its roots in Greek epigram notwithstanding; Propertius, Tibullus, and particularly Ovid mark their elegies as primarily
set in Rome itself. Finally, since elegy purports to present its speaker in
various amatory situations, its Roman-ness is taken for granted.

The *puella* of *Amores* 1.4 has usually been taken for a wife, with whom
the *amator* is having an adulterous affair. I have argued at length elsewhere (2003, 35-68) that the people in Roman love elegy cannot be actual citizen spouses, as the *puella* is generically a courtesan who requires
both payment and persuasion.[10] Here I will limit myself to a few points.
First, the lexicon of marriage does not always designate *iustum coniu-
gium*, legitimate citizen marriage; hence persons described as *"vir," "coniunx," even "uxor," "sponsus,"* and *"maritus,"* are not actually married
in the eyes of the law (see Copley 1956, 103, 165).[11] Propertius 3.20 demonstrates how elegy plays with the language of legal wedlock: it is rid-
dled with marital vocabulary, including references to technical parts of
the wedding ceremony (*"foedera ponenda," "signanda iura," "scribenda
lex"* [15-16]; *"Amor . . . suo constringit pignora signo"* [17][12]; *"pactas in foedera . . . aras, novo sacra marita toro"* [25-26]).[13] But the lover is here addressing a woman whose man has left (1-4), and he offers himself to her
not as a husband but as a boyfriend: "Your house would be fortunate, if
only you had a faithful boyfriend! / I shall be faithful: run into my bed,
girl!" (*fortunata domus, modo sit tibi fidus amicus! / fidus ero: in nostros
curre, puella, toros*) (9-10). Of course, a Roman bridegroom hardly offered himself to his bride as an *amicus*, and at the wedding he did not invite his new bride to jump into bed (indeed, that offer is displaced onto

the guests, who sing ritual songs to this effect). If elegy plays with the technical and ritual elements of a legal wedding ceremony, we may reasonably assume that it will also play fast and loose with the words for "spouse."[14]

Independent courtesans in Rome could make agreements, contracts, with individual men, by which they would enter into cohabitation without becoming owned concubines; such arrangements were supposed to be exclusive, though there was no single formula (see Zagagi 1980, 118–20, and Herter 1960, 81–82). The contracting man, known simply as the *vir*, paid an annual fee, the *merces annua*, which guaranteed him rights to the courtesan.[15] These rights had all the legal force of the *lex* at Propertius 3.20.16 (see also *leges* at *Asinaria* 234, 747, and 809), and their rights *(iura)* were a matter of custom and private agreement rather than law.[16] Since the terms of these contracts were determined *ad feminam*, the two parties could make whatever agreement they liked, but in poetry and drama, at least, the contract seems to be exclusive.[17] In fact, as comedy and elegy regularly demonstrate, the women regularly made side deals with other men (see below).[18]

Finally, *Amores* 1.4 and 2.5 themselves prove that these characters are not legally wed. Stroh (1979, 335 n.53), citing Schulz (1934), notes that at 1.4.64 the *amator* speaks of the *iura* that Corinna's[19] *vir* has over her, but at 2.5.30 speaks of his own *iura* over her.[20] There can hardly have been a secret divorce followed by a secret marriage—and the idea of the poet-lover as that most boring of persons, a legitimate husband, would be anathema to elegy, particularly to Ovidian elegy.[21] *Ars* 2.545 distinguishes between a man with rights over a woman by custom or contract and the actual husband of a legal wife *(legitima uxor)*. Such a distinction hardly needs to be made unless there are pseudomarital relationships that use the vocabulary of marriage. In addition, as McKeown (1989, 77) points out, "it seems somewhat improbable that a married couple would behave, much less be envisaged in advance as likely to behave, in the manner referred to at lines 47ff." of *Amores* 1.4. These two poems demonstrate the general rule that the word *"vir"* does not necessarily designate a husband, and that the apparently marital relationships of elegy are not citizen marriages, but what Lyne (1980, 240), citing Stroh (1979, 333–37), calls *"de facto* marriages."[22] The apparent transfer of *iura* over Corinna from the *vir* of *Amores* 1.4 to the *amator* in 2.5 demonstrates the courtesan's flexibility and independence (and note further that in 2.12 she seems to have yet another *vir*, though in 2.13 she turns up pregnant by the *amator*).[23]

Philaenium of *Asinaria* is not a marriageable woman (her mother's profession alone means that she cannot turn out to be that miraculously *intacta* courtesan-in-training who is a long-lost citizen daughter); Yardley (1987) has established *Asinaria* in particular as a source for Ovid (1987, 186 and 189 n.45), and as I will argue below, in *Amores* 1.4 and 2.5 Ovid exploits the comic possibilities offered by Plautus in this very scene of *Asinaria*. I take this source function of *Asinaria* as further evidence that the *vir* of *Amores* 1.4 is not a husband. Overall, my argument rests on the identification of the elegiac *puella* as unmarriageable, as a woman under the control of neither husband nor pimp (nor father), a woman making her living by the sexual attraction of men who have money and property, a woman of social independence if not financial security, a woman who can say both "no" and "yes" to sexual propositions without fear of legal or communal reprisal.[24] This description identifies her as an independent courtesan,[25] the one woman an elite Roman male needed to persuade.[26]

The Courtesan's Contract

Plautus's *Asinaria*, which has received little critical attention,[27] features a complex plot in which the *senex* Demaenetus helps his son Argyrippus acquire the money for exclusive rights to the courtesan Philaenium for a year; the money is wangled via a plot in which he defrauds his own wife, Artemona (perhaps the *uxor dotatissima* of extant comedy). In exchange, Demaenetus demands the first night with Philaenium. In lines 746–809 Argyrippus's rival Diabolus works out, with his parasite, the details of a contract that he plans to propose to Philaenium's mother Cleareta.[28] When Diabolus and the parasite discover that Demaenetus has used Artemona's money to beat them to the contract, they reveal the plot to her; she catches her husband with the unhappy Philaenium and drags him home for excoriation. The parasite plans to make an arrangement with Cleareta, whereby Argyrippus and Diabolus can share Philaenium for the next year, though as Slater (1985, 67) points out, we do not know if this arrangement will actually be made.

The scene detailing the specifics of the contract (*syngraphum* [238, 746, 802]) demonstrates a high degree of male suspicion and anxiety in the face of female subjectivity, sexuality, and meretricious moonlighting; it also offers a wealth of information about the kinds of behavior such women engaged in professionally. Interestingly, the nameless parasite invents all the rules, and he certainly knows his business—Diabolus simply agrees or modifies them slightly. This structure genericizes the scene, that is, it further marks these male anxieties as natural or inevitable, given the conditions, as it suggests that the parasite is experienced at drawing up contracts that pacify anxious young lovers, in every particular.[29] The details of the absurd contract, if Philaenium were to obey them, would require her to do virtually nothing but stay indoors with Diabolus: it specifies that she must not even look on, much less converse with, other young men. At a dinner party, she is to behave very modestly, though in private she is to be seductive with Diabolus. Even her speech and facial gestures come under control; she must drink wine only from Diabolus's glass, handed to her by himself.

In other words, in the company of other men, Philaenium is to behave like a stern Roman *matrona* (*"suspiciones omnes ab se segreget"* [774]), both to prevent contact with them and to avoid attracting their desirous attention. Diabolus wants, absurdly, to require her to worship only goddesses and to use him as an intermediary with male divinities. He even wants her to get rid of the erotic pictures on her wall, which are standard equipment for a courtesan's house.[30] If she takes time off for religious purification, she owes him the same amount of time back. I will discuss below how the details of the contract provide evidence of the public social behavior of courtesans who are juggling the competing sexual interest of various male parties; the point I wish to foreground here is that male anxiety, both implicit and explicit, fills this contract.[31]

Par. She may admit no other man into the house.	756
Even if she calls him a friend or a guardian,	
or the lover of her girlfriend,	
her doors must be closed to everyone but you.	
Let her post a note on the door saying she's busy.	760
If she says that a letter has been delivered from abroad,	
let there be no letter of any kind in the house,	
not even a wax tablet; and if she has any objectionable	
picture, she must sell it: if she hasn't disposed of it	
within four days of receiving your money,	765
it will become your property, and you can burn it, if you like.	
Nor let there be any wax tablets, on which she could write letters.	
She may invite nobody to dinner; you do the inviting;	
and let her cast her eyes on none of the guests.	
If she spies another man, she must immediately close her eyes.	770
She must drink only with you, and match you glass for glass.	
She must receive the glass only from you and toast you, then you	
drink; so that she will have no more or less than you have.	

Dia. That sounds good enough.
Par. Let her keep all suspicions away from herself.   775
She may not touch any man's foot with her own foot.
When she stands up, and when she sits down on the next couch,
or gets up from it, she must not give her hand to anyone.
She must not give her ring to anyone for looking at, nor ask
for his; she must pass the dice to no man but you.
When she tosses them, she must not simply say "by you!" but must
        name your name.   780
She may call on any goddess for favor,
but not on any god. If she turns out to be more religious,
let her tell you, and you can make the prayer to him on her behalf.
She must not nod at any man, nor wink, nor signal agreement.
Also, if the lamp goes out, she must not move even a   785
single limb at all in the darkness.
Dia. That's great!
For sure she has to do all that. But in the bedroom—
take out that clause—I really want her to be active there! I don't want
her to have an excuse and say the contract forbids it.
Par. I get it, you're afraid of a loophole.   790
Dia. Right.
Par. Okay, I'll take it out, just as you say.
And she must not use any confusing speech;
let her use no language but plain Greek.
If she happens to cough, she must not cough so that
she extends her tongue toward anyone.   795
And if she pretends to have a long-running cold,
she must not do this; you wipe her little lip
rather than let her pucker up her mouth openly for somebody else.
. . . .
Dia. You've fixed it up great! Excellent contract!
Par. Then if she tells her maid to take garlands,
wreaths, perfumes to either Venus or Cupid, your
servant will watch to see if she gives them to Venus or a man.   805
If by chance she says she needs to be alone for religious ritual,
she will have to give you as many unclean hours as she had pure.
Dia. These rules are perfect! Let's go!

This scene betrays an inordinate degree of both specific and free-
floating anxiety in the face of female liberty, subjectivity, and sexuality.
Other than Diabolus's two specified instructions (that Philaenium be
with no other man [754–59]) and that she be physically animated in the
bedroom (787–89), it is not possible to disentangle the contract's two

authors, Diabolus and the parasite, to determine which of them is responsible for which injunction.[32] Plautus gives no indication of whether or not the two men have discussed the details of the contract. The parasite seems to be an expert, as I have noted, but on the other hand it seems likely, to take this absurd comic scenario literally for a moment, that Diabolus would have given the parasite at least a few specifics when he asked for the contract to be drawn up. Still, its contents reveal some experience in the behavior of courtesans at dinner parties, whether that experience is Diabolus's or the parasite's.[33]

I will discuss the injunctions against specific minor activities below, in considering the evidence of *Asinaria* for how courtesans behaved at such semipublic events; here my concern is with Diabolus's fears about Philaenium's subjectivity and sexuality rather than her gestures or her consumption of food and wine. Such instructions as posting a keep-out notice on the door (a totem to ward off male visitors of rivalrous intent [760]), removing letter-writing equipment and erotic art (762–67), and locking her eyes on Diabolus alone (769–70), imply that he fears not only that she would accept the propositions of other men, but that she would welcome, even seek, them. The injunction against the generic *"te!"* in tossing the dice (780) voices not so much the fear of her communicating with another man by secret code as the fear that she might have feelings for the other man. As evidence of Diabolus's fear that her affections are elsewhere engaged, there is his interruption of the parasite's recitation, at 787–89, where he senses a loophole and adds an instruction that she is to be very active with him in the bedroom. Such an addition bespeaks his worry that she will be unresponsive with him sexually, a behavior that would indicate her lack of interest in him as well as her potential interest in another man. The absurd prohibition against worship of male divinities (781–83) may be the final proof that he is less concerned with Philaenium's actual pursuit of side engagements with other men than fearful of both rival male interest in her and her interest in his male rivals.[34] These concerns articulate Diabolus's worries about Philaenium's interiority, her subjectivity, and her sexuality—in other words, his fear that she is attracted not to him but to another man (as indeed she is, to Argyrippus).

Diabolus seems not to expect to know Philaenium's personal preferences, because he is negotiating not with her directly but with her mother, and because he anticipates her professional expertise at disguising them. In this scene, he appears both to fear and at the same time to assume, in a subterranean way, that her inner desires are contrary to

his. Hence his numerous prohibitions, even on natural and spontaneous functions like sneezing, focus on keeping her from acting on her
potential desires. Thus, absurdly, he wishes to prescribe for her a code
of inaction everywhere but in the bedroom. Her religious observation is
to be monitored by a slave. Her home will become an isolation cham-
ber, and her social life will be under constant supervision. At dinner parties, where he presumably wishes to show her off, she is to be effectively
nothing more than his shadow. He seems less to fear that Philaenium
will receive sexual advances than that she will send them, and right
under his nose. Such fear suggests anxiety about the one part of Philaenium that he cannot control with any amount of money—her interior
thoughts, feelings, and desires, as well as her readiness to act on them.
Hence, though he is arranging to become her temporary owner, he fears
proleptically that she will betray him, a betrayal that would be founded
in precisely the temporary nature of the arrangement. For, as she is neither a wife nor a slave, she ultimately controls her own life.[35] Her freedom and self-determination, then, engender in Diabolus an anxiety of
increasing proportions, which verges on panic in the face of the unknown and unknowable realm of Philaenium's personal preferences.

Elegiac Anxiety

Ovid explores, from both angles, the anxieties of the man who cannot
control a courtesan's thoughts and feelings or her behavior at a dinner
party. In *Amores* 1.4, the speaker is the rival lover to the *puella*'s *vir*; in
2.5, he actually is her *vir*. In neither case is he confident that she is not attracted to the other man, and his fears get the better of him both times,
leading to his conjuring fantasized projections of her in the other man's
bedroom. As McKeown (1989, 78) notes, the humor in both these poems
is at the expense of the Ovidian *amator*, who suffers "helpless frustration" in the face of what he can see (his beloved in the arms of another
man); what he wishes not to see (his beloved kissing another man); and
what he can't see (his beloved in bed with another man). Neither their
presumably mutual passion in 1.4 nor the lover's rights in 2.5 (*iura* [30])
can protect him from his fear of her infidelity.

 Amores 1.4 famously provides instruction to a woman in just this situation, on display at the dinner banquet. As her side lover, the Ovidian
amator, gives her detailed lessons on how to avoid her contracted *vir*
and communicate secretly with him instead, his anxieties get the better
of him far in advance of the anticipated dinner.[36] His fantasies verge on

paranoia, as he imagines the progress of the evening, at the end of which his beloved must go home with her *vir*, whom she cannot then avoid.[37] This poem, like the contract scene in *Asinaria*, develops the masculine anxieties about both male sexual rivalry and the *puella*'s own internal desires. Unlike Diabolus, the elegiac lover assumes, at least for most of the poem, that he and the *puella* share the same mutual desire, that they both equally want her to avoid contact with her *vir*. Eventually the lover-poet realizes (still proleptically, as the banquet does not actually take place in the poem) that all his instruction and supervision will ultimately fail, as the *vir* will have unimpeded access to her at home. Hence he begins by fearing his own reaction to observing the *vir* successfully cuddling with the *puella* and ends by fearing her reaction to the unavoidable sex she will have with the *vir* after the party. Thus he gives further instruction: make the sex bad, act as if he's forcing you, no pillow talk; even if the *vir* enjoys it, don't you enjoy it; and tomorrow, no matter what happened, tell me that it didn't.

The parallels to *Asinaria* are obvious—the *puella*'s secret communication with her lover, attempts to get the *vir* drunk while staying sober herself, and so forth. Again, my focus is on the speaker's escalating anxiety as he looks ahead, imagining the course of the evening and fearfully fantasizing about the unknowable regions of both the *vir*'s private bedroom and the *puella*'s private desires. He begins by envisioning his own status as a mere spectator of her physical contact with her *vir* (1–6):

So your man is coming to the same dinner party with us:
    I pray, may it be his last meal!
So must I only look at my beloved girl during
    the dinner? Will the one who enjoys being touched be another,
and will you snuggle up, cuddled nicely in another man's lap?
    Will he put his hand on your neck whenever he wants?

The substance of the poem is occupied with detailed instructions for a very specific type of public etiquette that will enable secret communication between the two of them, communication that will be undetectable by her *vir*:

Arrive before your man; I don't see what can be done, if you
    come before him, but still arrive before.
When he presses the couch, and you, his companion, go with a modest   15
    expression, to recline, secretly touch my foot.
Look at me and my nods and my expressive face:
    pick up and return secret notes.

I'll speak communicative silent words with my eyebrows;
    pick up those words with your fingers, words marked in the wine.   20
When you think of our lovemaking,
    touch your blushing cheeks with your tender thumb;
if you have any complaint, in your silent mind, about me,
    let your soft hand pull on the bottom of your ear;
when I say or do things, darling, that please you,   25
    twist your ring all about on your finger.
Touch the table with your hand, as people do in prayer,
    when you're wishing evils on your man, which he deserves.
Whatever he mixes up for you to taste, make him drink it;
    then you lightly ask the boy for what you want.   30
The goblet you give back, I'll take it first for my drinking,
    and where you drank, I'll drink from that part.
If by chance he hands you food that he's tasted,
    throw back that food tasted by his mouth.
And don't let him place his arms around your neck,   35
    nor put your soft head on his bony chest.
Nor let your dress or your touchable breasts receive his hands;
    and especially don't try to give him any kisses.
If you kiss him, I'll become an exposed lover
    and shout "those are mine" and raise my fist.   40
I can at least see those things, but the things your cloak hides,
    they'll be the cause of blind fear for me.
So don't put your thigh up to his thigh, nor cling with your knee
    nor twine your tender foot with his hard foot.
Like a wretch, I fear so many things because I've boldly done them,   45
    and I'm being tormented by fear of my own example.
Often urgent desire coming upon me and my mistress
    has conducted its sweet work under an overlying cloak.
This you must not do! But so that you not be thought to have done it,
    remove your accomplice cloak from your back.   50
Ask your man to drink (but don't kiss him while you ask),
    and while he's drinking, sneak in pure wine if you can.
If he passes out, taken over by wine and sleep,
    the place and the situation will advise us.
When you get up to go home, we'll all get up,   55
    be sure to go out in the middle of the crowd.
Find me in the crowd, or I'll find you;
    whatever part of me you can touch there, touch.

At the end of the dinner instructions, the *amator* reverts to fearing what
he can't see—the *puella* and her *vir* in the house together:

Wretched me! I've advised what can help for a few hours;
    I'll be separated from my mistress, by order of night.   60
Your man locks you up at night; miserable, with rising tears,
    I'll do what's allowed—follow you up to your cruel doors.
Then he'll take kisses, then he'll take not only kisses.
    What you give me secretly, you give him forced by rights.
For sure, give it unwillingly (you can do this!) as if you're forced: 65
    and hush your cooing, and let the sex be terrible.
If my wishes have any power, I hope he won't even enjoy it;
    if not, for sure you shouldn't enjoy it at all.
But whatever event follows the night,
    tomorrow tell me convincingly that you didn't.   70

This erotodidaxis demonstrates the lover's experience in such situations (as evidenced by 45–48, especially by the word *"saepe,"* "often" [47]): he is familiar with his own sexual anxiety. Accordingly the bulk of his instructions concern ways of alleviating it. That is, all the negative precepts (35–38, 41–44, 49–50) operate not only to keep *puella* and *vir* relatively separate but, more importantly, to keep the *amator* from experiencing jealousy and fear—a pointless task, as he admits, for he is already fearful (*"caeci causa timoris"* [41]; *"multa miser timeo"* [45]) well ahead of any actual cause for fear.

Though the *amator* seems most to fear witnessing kisses between *vir* and *puella* (38–40), the true cause of his worries is the unseen and unknowable (*"illa mihi caeci causa timoris erunt"* [42]). Thus he tells her to avoid even the appearance of impropriety with her *vir* (*"ne fecisse puteris"* [48]). But, as he admits, the worst is yet to come. The emotional climax of the poem arrives at line 59: "Wretched me! I've advised what can help for a few hours" (*"me miserum! monui, paucas quod prosit in horas"*). In the face of the *vir*'s primacy, the lover can only follow tearfully, imagining what he most fears. Lines 64–70 demonstrate that his greatest fears are about the *puella*'s unseen sexual activity and unknowable sexual desires. Thus he tells her to resist the *vir*'s advances, to be uncooperative and unresponsive, and most of all not to enjoy herself. He so fears that she might enjoy and participate in the required sex that he finally tells her to lie to him about it.[38] This denouement demonstrates that his real concern all along has been not their secret communication under the *vir*'s eyes but the *puella*'s interiority and sexuality, unknown and unknowable. As his worried projections escalate, he seems on the verge of a full-blown anxiety attack (and indeed, lines 39–40 suggest that he is aware that he may lose control of himself), as he, like Diabolus, cannot bear even to think that she might enjoy sex with another man. The liberty of the independent courtesan thus engenders obsession, irrational projection, and panic in this fictive elite Roman male.

Amores 2.5, the companion to 1.4, flips the coin, placing the lover-poet in the position of the neglected *vir*. Ovid explores here the situation feared by Diabolus in *Asinaria*: witnessing the *puella*'s infidelity. The *vir*'s position is the natural partner to the rival's,[39] and it demonstrates what Diabolus suspected—that no form of possession guarantees control of a courtesan. The speaker addresses the *puella*, charging her with the evidence to her crime: she thought he was asleep at the dinner party, but he was sober and alert, observing her performing precisely the secret communications instructed in 1.4.

> I myself saw, wretched and sober, when you thought
>   I was sleeping, your misbehavior, with the wine put away.
> I saw you both saying many things with gesticulating eyebrow;   15
>   a good part of your voice was in those nods.
> Your eyes were not silent, and there were notes drawn in the wine
>   on the table, and there was some letter writing with your finger.
> I recognized you conducting a conversation, which was not to be seen,
>   and your bidden words communicated by prearranged signs.   20
> And now everybody was getting up, once dinner was done;
>   the young men were in place, one and another.
> Then truly I saw you, exchanging wicked kisses
>   (it was clear to me that tongues were exchanged),
> such as a sister does not give to her harsh brother   25
>   but such as a soft girlfriend gives a desiring man;
> such as it is not believed that Diana gives Apollo,
>   but that Venus often gave to her lover Mars.
> "What are you doing?" I shout, "where are you now taking my delight?
>   I'll throw my hands on my mistress, according to my rights.   30
> These kisses are shared mutually back and forth between you and me;
>   why should a third party enter into those enjoyments?"

A description follows of his impulse to strike the *puella* and how her natural defenses, i.e., her beauty, disarmed him (32–48). He then reaches the worst of the matter: evidence that she has pursued her infidelity beyond mere kisses at a banquet.

> I who had just been in a rage, even begged her as a suppliant
>   that she not give me worse kisses.   50
> She laughed, and from her heart she gave the best kisses, such as could
>   have shaken the forked lightning bolt from enraged Jove:

wretched me! I am tormented, fearing that some other man felt such
    good kisses,
  and I wish they hadn't been of the same kind.
And these kisses were much better than the ones I had taught,   55
  and she seemed to add something new.
What pleases too much is bad, that your entire tongue was received
  between my lips and mine between yours.
And I'm upset not only at this, I'm complaining not only about these joined
  kisses, but that these other things were also joined: 60
you could never have learned that kissing technique except in bed;
  some other teacher has received an enormous reward.

This poem again demonstrates that the lover's greatest fear is not what he saw but what he did not; its opening lines speak of a regular wish to die whenever the speaker thinks of his *puella*'s infidelity (1–4); he regrets the strength of his case against her (5–12), and he is positively tormented (53) at the final evidence, her new kissing technique, which he immediately assumes she acquired not by random, or even prearranged, furtive meetings at parties, but in bed (59–62). The lover's envy of his rival leads him to fear that the *puella* might prefer that rival to himself. Hence he begs to be given kisses as good as those given to the rival (49–50) and contemplates the great reward *("pretium grande")* that his rival had enjoyed (61–62).

The prospect that the *puella* might prefer another man's superior technique destabilizes the lover further. Even the syntax of lines 55–60 suffers: a choppiness invades the usual smooth flow of Ovidian couplets, as if replicating a stammered, uncertain reaction to this final blow. The poem develops from the lover's tortured, legalistic approach— massing his evidence (5–23), inferring further misbehavior (24–28), making accusations (29–32)—to his inability to punish the guilty party (33–50), and to an entirely new and heightened state of anxiety based in the evidence of unwitnessed sexual activity (51–62). This is his condition at the beginning of the poem (the entire event having already occurred), where he wishes both to fall out of love and to die. In addition, the poem gives no evidence of a further confession, implied or expressed, by the *puella,* so the lover's conclusion, that she has been in bed with the rival, is his projected fantasy, his worst fear apparently come true. Without confirmation, this realized fear remains a source of unmoored anxiety, the inevitable condition of a Roman elite male who cannot divine, much less control, the activities and desires of the independent courtesan.

It Takes a Worried Man to Sing a Worried Song: Female Liberty and Male Anxiety

As we have seen, certain themes recur in each text, having to do with the woman's physical behavior: her posture, her position on the couch, her interactions with other guests, her interactions with her primary man, her consumption of food and drink, even her spontaneous bodily functions like sneezing and coughing. The worried lovers want to control every aspect of her behavior, to turn her, effectively, into a statue, in Diabolus's case. Kissing and physical contact are naturally issues of anxiety, to the point of irrationality and potential loss of control, as in *Amores* 1.4 and 2.5. The worst problems, however, really arise not from what can be observed but from what cannot be seen: what is going on when the lover is away? what is going on right before his eyes? what is going on behind the impenetrable surface of the *puella*'s face? Diabolus wishes, in essence, to place Philaenium under house arrest, even fearing, and wishing to destroy, the things she owned before she met him, and to cut her off from contact with anybody else (again, this theme recurs in Propertius 2.6, where the lover confesses being fearfully envious of everybody, even a baby). The lover who does not have *iura*, rights by custom or contract, over a courtesan, must fear what happens when she goes home with her *vir*; the *vir* must fear what goes on when he is away, or even, as in the *Amores*, what goes on before his very eyes. In all cases, the lover fears what is going on in the beloved's mind. The rights, *iura* (*Amores* 2.5.30), that a man may have over a courtesan are inadequate to alleviate his anxieties over both her physical behavior and her interiority—these men are depicted as virtually obsessed with whether or not these women are sexually interested in and involved with other men, and their obsession leads them to fear the very behavior that originally attracted them.

The social status of these women puts them beyond the control of any man. They are not, like brides or brothel prostitutes, the object of negotiation between men; they cannot, like slaves, be purchased and owned; they cannot, like streetwalkers, be rented for an hour only; and they cannot, like wives, be married and absorbed into domestic possession.[40] Thus the elite male's status, relative to these women, loses its rock-firm standing of mastery: the citizen lover must persuade this woman, and this woman only—her will and her desire become uniquely relevant, as the lover persists in trying to ascertain and secure his position, his standing, in her life.[41] The frustration engendered by this situation regularly seeks an outlet in physical, verbal, and emotional violence, as if force offers the elite male his only recourse against the woman who is proof against his position (see again *Amores* 1.4.39–40; 2.5.45–48).[42] Such violence is a source of shame to him, however, and often renders him emotionally weaker than before. Thus, I suggest, men enamored of the independent courtesans face something like a temporary identity crisis, a condition utterly foreign to the gender standards for elite Roman males.[43] Ultimately, of course, each of these men must revert to the standards for his class and abandon his courtesan-mistress, as Roman social realities do not allow long-term deviation from gender norms. The integration of the comic *adulescens'* passion into productive citizen marriage and the unraveling of the elegiac love affair into bitter disillusion (see Propertius 3.24–25 and Ovid *Amores* 3.11–14) perhaps signal a stage in developing Roman masculinity,[44] but if one generation grows up and escapes the menace of independent female sexuality,[45] the next generation is never far behind in having to confront it. The courtesan is thus established as a standing threat not only to Roman domestic property, as she is considered ruinously expensive, but to the developing masculinity of the Roman elite as well.[46] Her very self-determination and self-control both challenge Roman gender norms and prove them vulnerable at precisely the period in which the young Roman citizen male is supposed to be growing up and assuming adult responsibilities. If these young men are simply objects of literary fun, this one serious weakness—the vulnerability of young men to courtesans, which engenders many a comic plot and elegiac poem—stands out as particularly attractive to playwright and viewers. We may therefore consider it a recognized obstacle, at least in comedy and elegy, between young men and their proper development into adult men.

The Courtesan's Choreography

Comedy and elegy depict men and courtesans in situations other than banquets, but these particular scenes provide suggestive information about the lives and professions of courtesans, from which we may make limited speculation. Plautus and Ovid offer a good deal of evidence about the behavior of courtesans at dinner parties. The truth value of this evidence is of course unknowable, but it seems reasonable to assume that these women did in fact have to balance competing male sexual interest. That such interest was powerful indeed may be inferred

from the case of Volumnia Cytheris, said to be the model for Gallus's
Lycoris, the original *docta puella,* who aroused considerable male attention (see Cicero, *Ad Familiares* 9.26, on having found her present at a
dinner party).[47] In any case, such courtesans would certainly have been
under close observation at semipublic events like dinner parties.

So what are the courtesans up to? There is secret communication via
liquids (*Amores* 1.4.18, 20; 2.5.17–18; see also Tibullus 1.6.19–20), prearranged signals (*Amores* 1.4.21–28; 2.5.19–20), and facial gestures (*Asinaria* 784, 794-98; *Amores* 1.4.17, 19; 2.5.15–17; see also Tibullus 1.6.19).
There is anticipated physical contact as opportunity arises (*Asinaria*
775-77; *Amores* 1.4.16), is invented via dice and rings presented for inspection (*Asinaria* 777–78; Tibullus 1.6.25–26), and is sought in crowd
maneuvers and quick cloakroom meetings (*Asinaria* 785–86; *Amores*
1.4.53-58; 2.5.21–24). There is deceit via wine, an important component
of balancing two men, as the contracted *vir* wishes her to drink along
with himself alone (*Asinaria* 771–73), but the rival lover wants her not
only to do the opposite (*Amores* 1.4.29–34) but also to give the *vir* unmixed wine, in the hopes that he will pass out (*Amores* 1.4.51–53; 2.5.13–
14; see also Tibullus 1.6.27–28). Finally, there is much fancy choreography of physical contact. The *vir* will desire and expect the *puella* to be
available only to him (*Asinaria* 769-70 and passim; *Amores* 1.4.35–38,
43–44), but the rival will want her to converse with him instead, preferably in a flirtatious manner (*Asinaria* 774; *Amores* 1.4 passim; see also Tibullus 1.6.17–18).[48]

Such conflicting agenda require a courtesan to remain alert and in
control of herself as she negotiates the rival male sexual interest at a
party where her primary functions are companionship and entertainment.[49] Such banquets may have offered elite Roman men otherwise
rare opportunities to relax and be spontaneous, but they were professionally necessary obstacle courses for the courtesans. The shell
game of mixed and unmixed wine (or plain water, as at Tibullus 1.6.28)
alone would be a difficult maneuver to pull off, if a woman actually
came under the type of scrutiny proposed in Diabolus's exaggerated
contract, but it might have been her greatest aid, as the unconscious
condition of her *vir* would greatly assist in her opportunity to attract
and communicate with other men. Presumably there has been some
prior instruction in dinner-party business etiquette, perhaps by a *lena*[50]
(though the *praeceptor Amoris* gives such advice passim in *Ars* 3—see
esp. 349–80 and 751–68). Experience would also make a woman able to
handle these potentially explosive situations (recall the threatened

outbursts and violence at *Amores* 1.4.39–40 and 2.5.29–47) more smoothly. Regardless, these professional obligations to dine, drink, and socialize called for calculation rather than spontaneity. Indeed, the ability to keep track and control of competing interests and agents required careful attention, even if that watchfulness must often have been contrarily disguised as loss of control.[51]

Genuine loss of control is the great taboo for the courtesan, who must above all else keep her head. To maintain her lover's interest without becoming too easy, too boring, or too demanding, she must play a complex game of seduction and refusal; she must keep up her income; and she must be alert against the possibility of violence. Her job is to keep her suitors impassioned enough to keep supplying her with money and material possessions. Further, her economic condition requires her to make all her money while she is young—and her impending old age is the one threat that her lovers hold out against her, as she will attract no more lovers once her professional viability has expired. She *must* attract more than one lover at a time and she must be able to keep more than one in suspension even at the same party. Further, she knows that her relationship with any given man can neither last for very long nor support her adequately in its duration. Thus, when she goes to a dinner party she must either be on the lookout for new clients or find a way to engage with her side clients, keeping her *vir* satisfied all the while. Hence her complex choreography of communicative eating and drinking (even sneezing), of prearranged signals, of quick cloakroom rendezvous. To balance competing male anxieties on such an evening, when her every action is under observation by more than one party, whose interests are opposed, requires a cool head and a great deal of self-control (another problem for the anxious males). The women who successfully navigated their way through the Scyllas and Charybdises of male anxiety and sexual jealousy must have been formidable characters indeed, and posed a significant, if short-lived, threat to elite Roman masculinity.

Conclusion: Female Sexuality and Roman Masculinity

Though they contain a high degree of comic exaggeration, *Asinaria* and *Amores* 1.4 and 2.5 present citizen males in a near-obsessive state of worry over the physical behavior and the interior desires and thoughts of women whose social status was far below their own. They thus open up a space for considering both the constructions of masculinity in ancient Rome and its vulnerabilities within the very structure of social hierarchy that favors it, as well as a space for speculating about the complex social (and dining) choreography practiced by the courtesan. Both comedy and elegy demonstrate the powerful influence of the courtesan on Romen men as well as their household bank accounts; the male anxieties she engenders are everywhere to be seen on the Roman comic stage and in the texts of love elegy. The dinner party, a courtesan's standing professional obligation, presents her with both opportunity and risk and exposes the weakness of Roman masculinity in the face of her independence and her sexuality. The male anxiety engendered by such female liberty perhaps only underscores some of the standard gender ideologies of the ancient Romans—who, after all feared, female sexuality enough to establish religious cults to female chastity—but it also testifies to the intelligence, charm, and self-determination of the independent courtesan.

Notes

1. This paper was originally written in honor of W. S. Anderson, to whom it is dedicated with gratitude and by whose kind agreement it appears here. A longer version (with full Latin texts) appears in Batstone and Tissol (2005).

2. In these two poems Ovid draws on Tibullus 1.6.9–37, which likewise focuses on female liberty at a dinner party.

3. It has been suggested that I use the words "agency" or "independence" in this paper, rather than "subjectivity." I include agency and self-consciousness under this term, which I prefer: though subjectivity can be passive, in the case of the courtesans of elegy and comedy, it clearly is not. These women look out for themselves and their interests very actively. In addition, as I will argue here, while the men acknowledge the *puella*'s independence and can often perceive her agency, they never know for certain what the *puella* is thinking or desiring, and their inability to know is what destabilizes them. Hence I have chosen to speak of her subjectivity rather than her agency.

4. Whether or not such norms were valid for any given man is both indeterminable and irrelevant to my argument, as they govern social behavior and expectations. Thus when Cicero refers to Volumnia Cytheris as the *mima uxor* of Antony (*Philippics* 2.20) or to their subsequent "divorce" (2.69), he is ridiculing Antony for violating these norms by having raised Cytheris above her normal status. The figure of *servitium amoris* marks the elegiac speaker as guilty of the same social deviation. *Asinaria* provides ample evidence of the young lover's violation of social norms: Argyrippus embraces the knees of one slave (670–73) and carries another on his back (704–10), after calling himself *libertus* to this *patronus* slave (689–90). Such saturnalian behavior, assumed in pursuit of his love for the courtesan Philaenium, marks Argyrippus as not exhibiting proper masculine mastery over his slaves; this inadequate masculinity extends to his relationship with Philaenium as well. Konstan (1983, 55) remarks that "the only motive for this groveling is cash," but the cash is merely a means to

Argyrippus's true end, which is access to Philaenium. I would say, rather, that Argyrippus debases himself not for money, as his father does (particularly at the end of the play), but for love of a courtesan.

5. By the time of the second edition of the *Amores,* courtesans were among the few women not forbidden to elite men by the *lex Iulia de adulteriis coercendis.* As della Corte (1982, 547) points out, with courtesans the formula *stuprum non committitur* applies, making them particularly appropriate love objects for elegy. In addition, Volumnia Cytheris, the original elegiac *puella* and model for Gallus's Lycoris, marks the courtesan as a recognized figure in Rome.

6. Halporn (1993) distinguishes Greek *hetairai* from Roman *meretrices.* He also notes that the specific settings of several of Plautus's plays move the action "from Greek city street to Plautine red-light district and brothel" (201). Treggiari (1971, 197) comments that Plautus's *Cistellaria* 36–37, about *lenae* who brought up their daughters to be *meretrices,* are "surely a Roman allusion." Thus the courtesan, in Plautus at least, may well be an especially Romanized character.

7. Lowe (1992, 175) notes that "the unashamed insertion of Roman allusions into plays with a Greek setting, together with Plautus' penchant for grotesque exaggeration, creates a Saturnalian fantasy world, an anti-Rome, which to a considerable extent turns the real world upside down." He cites a variety of authorities in n.131. I have previously discussed (James 1998a, 4) Segal's (1987, 141) similar view of Plautus, that even overturned aspects of Roman life ("topsy-turvy," in his phrase) remain both recognizable and Roman. On women and dining in Rome, see Roller (2003).

8. Thus although the language specified for Philaenium to speak in Diabolus's contract (*Asinaria* 792–93) is plain Greek (a language all educated Romans knew), her worship of divinities is described in Roman terms, as Venus and Cupid rather than Aphrodite and Eros.

9. See Yardley (1991) on the frequent appearances of the symposium or banquet scene in Roman elegy. See also Roller (2003, 395).

10. Although Clodia and Sallust's Sempronia, for example, are described as acting in meretricious fashion, it is appropriate to take those descriptions with a few grains of salt as already influenced by prior and perhaps contemporary depictions of courtesans. In addition, they are never represented as potentially obedient to a man's wishes, whether or not those wishes are enforced by contract. For Cicero's representation of Clodia as a *meretrix,* see McCoy's essay in this volume. On elegy as designed to persuade, see Stroh (1971); see also James (2003, passim).

11. Della Corte (1982, 550) points out that the word *"coniunx"* "does not imply legal matrimony but simply cohabitation *more uxorio"* ("in the manner of a wife"), the very relationship previously engaged in by Phronesium and Stratophanes: "quasi uxorem sibi / me habebat anno" (*Truculentus* 392–93). Likewise at *Andria* 145–46, Pamphilus is thought to have taken Glycerium *more uxorio:* "Pamphilum / pro uxore habere hanc peregrinam" (a word used, as Ashmore [1910, ad loc.] notes, citing Donatus, "euphemistically for *meretricem"*); the formula *"habere pro uxore"* is used also at *Heauton Timoroumenos* 98. Tibullus 1.6.15 addresses Delia's *vir* as *"coniunx,"* but makes clear at 67–68 that

she is not a respectable *matrona*, as she does not wear the *stola* and the *vitta*. As Treggiari (1971, 197) points out, when Cicero calls Volumnia the *"mima uxor"* of Antony, and their final breakup a divorce, he is speaking ironically; such lexical play in oratory makes its presence in elegy less surprising.

12. Butler and Barber (1964, ad loc.) suggest that Propertius is here referring to the *tabulae nuptiales* (marriage settlement agreements) that were sealed and placed on deposit.

13. See Camps (1966), Richardson (1977), and Butler and Barber (1964), on the wedding language in this poem; see also James (2003, 35–68). The *foedera* (Propertius 3.20.15 and 25) also arise at Tibullus 1.5.7.

14. Even given Ovid's famously impudent wit, there is no other explanation for such absurdities as the heifer *coniunx* of *Amores* 2.12.25, over whom two bulls are fighting. See also the sneering remark at 2.7.21–22 ("quis Veneris famulae conubia liber inire / . . . velit?"). Unless otherwise indicated, all translations are mine.

15. In *Asinaria*, the contract is called a *syngraphum* (238, 746, and 802) containing *leges* (749 and 809). Despite this Greek name, the custom of the contract is recognizably Roman as well. See also *Truculentus* 31, where Diniarchus complains that the *merces annua* buys only three nights, and *Hecyra* 85–95, where the young *meretrix* Philotis has just returned from two years on tour in Corinth with a soldier to whom she was under contract. See also Cohen in this volume regarding the Greek *sungraphê* and the active agency of the Greek courtesans who entered into them.

16. See Davis (1993, 67) on *iure* at *Amores* 1.4.64 as meaning "by right" rather than by law. In *Amores* 1.4, as we shall see, this "right" is imaginary, residing in the lover's head rather than in either law or civil contract. Davis argues (69) that "Ovid uses the language of the law to mock it." Propertius 3.20 establishes this play with legal vocabulary as elegiac rather than purely Ovidian.

17. Hence the *adulescens* needs money to keep his beloved from being leased out to another man. The agreement of Phaedria and Gnatho at the end of *Eunuchus*, for the division of Thais's services, thus stands out as abnormal. A similar deal is suggested but not arranged at the end of *Asinaria*. Notably both these arrangements to share a *puella* are suggested not by an enamored *adulescens* but by a practical parasite.

18. The *puella* of *Amores* 3.8, for instance, like Delia in Tibullus 1.6, must be both clever and careful: she is cheating on both her *vir* and her poet-lover with a third man. Treggiari (1971, 197) notes of Volumnia Cytheris that nothing would have stopped her "having several lovers concurrently—though we may assume that Antony for a time had exclusive rights." See Rosivach (1998, 136–37) on various types of contracted relationships in comedy.

19. This is presuming that the *puella* in both 1.4 and 2.5 is Corinna, which seems likely, as she is the primary *puella* of book 1 and figures centrally in 2.6–14. The lover-poet likewise mentions his *iura* at 3.11.45; I take this *puella* not to be Corinna, but the same objection stands—he cannot have forgotten to mention a marriage. In addition, the *puella* of 3.11 seems to have her own home, in which the *amator* does not reside.

20. Even the nature of these rights *(iura)* is dubious. Elsewhere in elegy, they are clearly identified as part of extramarital sexual relationships: *Amores* 3.11.45 *("lecti socialia iura")*; Tibullus 1.5.7 *("furtivi foedera lecti")*; see also Propertius 3.20.21 *("non certo foedere . . . lectus")*. *Amores* 2.17.23–24 likewise plays with the language of law and the bed. See below, on the similar use of the word *"lex"* to describe a contract with a courtesan at *Asinaria* 747.

21. I have previously argued that marriage would be the end of elegy (James 1998a, 12; 2003, 41–52). Nowhere in elegy does a lover propose legitimate marriage by asking a *puella* to divorce her husband and marry him or by threatening to divorce an unfaithful *puella,* etc. Since marriage and elegiac love are polar opposites (see *Amores* 3.585–86), marriage is the last thing an elegiac lover wants. Thus, as Veyne (1988, 2) puts it, the elegiac lovers "are ready to do anything for their beloved except marry her." Elegy would, as it were, say of a married woman, "'tis pity she's a wife," as wives are generically of no interest to a lover.

22. Concubinage is generically impossible here, as elegy requires persuasion, which ownership does not. The elegiac *puella* must be an independent courtesan, if elegy's arguments are to make any sense.

23. See also the comment of McKeown (1998, at 2.5.36) about the girl seen by her new fiancé/husband, which he rightly calls "a deliberately incongruous comparison in this context." The *amator* speaks at *Amores* 2.5.10 not of a wife but of a girlfriend *(amica).*

24. She does risk violence: Herodas 2, Terence *Eunuchus,* Horace *Ode* 3.26, and *Amores* 1.9 all advert to, or feature, violent assault on the courtesan's house, usually by an angry lover or disgruntled customer. Horace *Ode* 3.26 lists some of the lover's arsenal, designed for breaking open doors. Copley (1956, 57–58 and 160 n.38) discusses this armature. Such assaults are usually intended to gain a young man entry into the house and sexual access to the woman inside.

25. Halporn (1993, 201–2) rightly criticizes the inadequate terms usually employed to denote the Greek *hetaira* or Roman *meretrix;* he particularly singles out the term "courtesan" as euphemistic. I am not convinced that his description of Plautus's *meretrices* as "working girls" is accurate, as I see a range of courtesan-types operating in Plautus (nor does it adequately describe some of Terence's *meretrices,* specifically Bacchis of *Hecyra* and Thais of *Eunuchus*). *Asinaria* particularly offers evidence that not all *meretrices* are the same: Philaenium, who seems relatively new to her profession (unlike, say, Phronesium of *Truculentus,* perhaps the textbook example of the grasping comic *meretrix*), actually loves Argyrippus and obeys her mother's instructions to disregard him with sadness and some bitterness. Konstan (1993) identifies a type of *hetaira* in Menander whose character merits a marital-type relationship with a citizen; her presence further extends the range of *meretrices* in comedy; see also Wiles (1989) and Luck (1974, 19–20) on the different types of courtesans in comedy. Davidson (1997) distinguishes between elegant, high-class courtesans and other women who lived by their bodies; see particularly his chapter 4 on the *hetaira.* Though he discusses Athenian *hetairai,* much of his analysis applies to Roman *meretrices* as well. Bearing Halporn's objections in mind, I have chosen to keep using the outmoded and inadequate word "courtesan" here for the sake

of convenience, as an accurate designation (such as "young woman of no social standing or protection, relying on male sexual attraction to her youth and beauty to support herself and her household") would be both awkward and verbose. The word *lena* is similarly difficult to render into English, so I have chosen to leave it in Latin rather than translate it.

26. As P. A. Miller (2004, 170) points out, this identification, argued most strongly first in Stroh (1979), in opposition to G. Williams (1968), who considered the elegiac *puella* an elite woman, is a minority view. I have argued this position in detail (James 2003, 35–68). Ovid's play with the lexicon of marriage has misled scholars into considering the *puella* a citizen wife. As I have remarked here, Propertius too (3.20) plays with this lexicon; see also Tibullus 1.5.7, as noted above.

27. Other than standard analysis studies, on which see Slater (1985, 55), Konstan (1983, 52–53), and especially Lowe (1992), scholarly attention to *Asinaria* has tended to focus on the father-son plot (Konstan 1983), with secondary focus on the father-mother dynamics (Konstan 1983) and the antics of the slaves (for instance, Segal 1987, 104–9). Slater's metatheatrical approach encompasses all three.

28. Although as Cohen demonstrates in his essay in this volume, Greek *hetairai* and, presumably, Roman *meretrices* could stipulate the terms of their own contracts, thus acting as their own agents, Philaenium is the object, rather than the agent or subject of this contract—her mother is in charge of her, though she clearly resists some of her mother's instructions.

29. Diabolus calls him "poeta . . . prosus ad eam rem unicus" (748), an indication that he may be an expert at such contracts. He knows what to specify in the contract, and he remarks at 918–19 that if he cannot work out a solution in which Diabolus and Argyrippus share Philaenium, he will lose Diabolus's support: "nam ni impetro, / regem perdidi." (This proposal anticipates the arrangement suggested by Gnatho at the end of Terence's *Eunuchus*.) Further genericizing the notion of an exclusive contract is Argyrippus's desire for one (234–36).

30. Propertius (2.6.27–34) complains about these same pictures.

31. The Latin texts are those of Lindsay (1904) and McKeown (1987); translations are mine.

32. Slater (1985) sees the characters in this play as authors of dramas they wish to see performed. He rightly points out that the parasite's script is marked as impossible to perform because of its many stage directions and calls Diabolus a moral reformer fearful of "the power of art to shape the life of the viewer" (64). I would say, rather, that Diabolus and the parasite are composing and choreographing a male fantasy, whose details reveal that they already know it is impossible. Why else would Diabolus fear that Philaenium will consider the instructions at 783–84 a loophole preventing her from engaging in a full range of private sexual activity? He already fears in advance that she is not attracted to him. In addition, the numerous second-person singular forms used of Diabolus (760, 768, 771–73, 783, 797, 805), which clash with the formal use of third-person forms in its opening (751–54), further mark this contract as identifying Diabolus's anxieties rather than laying down the law to Philaenium.

33. Konstan (1983, 55 n.7) accepts the arguments of Havet (1905) that the

young man arguing with Cleareta in act 1.2–3, is Diabolus rather than Argyrippus (as in the manuscripts). If so, his experience might have come from observing Philaenium herself (though his anxieties suggest otherwise), as the *adulescens* in this scene argues to Cleareta that he has already paid (she effectively claims that his fee has expired). See Lowe (1992, 159–63) for a convincing refutation of Havet's thesis. I would add to his arguments only this: if Diabolus were the original *adulescens*, we would expect at least a single further reference, in just this scene, to his belief that he has already paid for this contract and is thus being double-charged, or to his observation of her prior behavior (the contract scene gives no indication that Diabolus has seen Philaenium perform any of the forbidden activities). In any case, it is more than likely that he has attended a few dinner parties in either the company or the presence of a courtesan like Philaenium and is thus fully aware that she has the ability and opportunity to attract male sexual attention.

34. It is worth noting here that when Argyrippus seeks an exclusive contract with Philaenium for a year, he too specifically plans to forbid her any contact with other men. Her mother responds with an ironic offer to transform her male slaves into women by castration (234–37).

35. Though Philaenium's mother, the *lena* Cleareta, seems to control her, she will eventually develop into her own mistress. The major courtesans of comedy are independent of a *leno* or *lena* (see, for example, Phronesium of *Truculentus*, Bacchis of *Hecyra* and *Heauton Timoroumenos*, Thais of *Eunuchus*, and the sisters of *Bacchides*), and an elegiac *puella* must also be independent—it would be patently absurd, even for elegy, to write poetic persuasion for a slave. Hence there is no *leno* in elegy (see *Amores* 1.10.23–24) and the elegiac *lena* is merely an advisor (Tibullus 1.5, 1.6, 2.6, Propertius 4.5, and *Amores* 1.8). In general, the comic courtesans who belong to someone else, usually a *leno*, are underdeveloped characters (unless, like Palaestra of *Rudens*, they turn out to be citizen daughters). Philaenium occupies a middle ground between such generic property as flute-girls and the full-blown personalities like Phronesium. She shows a certain individuality: she loves Argyrippus and detests Demaenetus but knows how to flirt on demand and handle herself when Artemona discovers Demaenetus with her. It may be that her semideveloped personality and independence are the signs of both her maturing into an independent courtesan and her status as daughter to a *lena* rather than property of a *leno* (and in any case, a prostitute belonging to a *leno* seems less likely to become an independent courtesan). It is worth noting here that Thais of *Eunuchus*, certainly a free woman, likewise had a mother (and even an uncle as well). Words pertaining to family relationships are used lightly in irregular sexual associations—*mater* in these contexts need not denote biological maternity. At *Satyricon* 7.1 it turns out to mean "*lena*," just as "*frater*" means "lover," not "brother" (likewise at [Tibullus] 3.1.23). Familial nomenclature for the relationships between members of the fully populated *familiae* in the household of the comic and elegiac courtesan should not be surprising, particularly given the relatively high incidence of young courtesans and adopted sisters who turn out to be citizen daughters (*Andria, Eunuchus, Cistellaria, Heauton Timoroumenos);* see the conclusion of Faraone's essay in this volume.

36. On this poem, see Miller (2004) and the sources he cites; see also G. B Ford Jr. (1966) for a good general analysis.

37. Tibullus 1.6 provides an intermediary stage in the transition from Plautus to Ovid, and an immediate elegiac background to the *Amores*. In this elegy, Delia is cheating on both the speaker and her contracted *vir*—most shocking of all, she is using techniques taught her by the speaker himself. He warns the *vir* to keep a close eye on her, especially at dinner parties. This text shows a few of the techniques a courtesan used for communicating secretly with a lover, right in front of her *vir*, and it gives Ovid a chance to expand in detail, in *Amores* 1.4. She chats with young men (18); leans back with her garment open to her waist (19); sends messages by nodding and writing notes on the table with her wine (19–20); puts out her hand, as if to show off her ring to another man (25–26); she and the lover prepare pure wine *(merum)* for the *vir*, to get him to pass out (27–28). The Tibullan speaker absurdly accuses the *vir* of being inadequately anxious *(incaute)* at the banquet (15).

38. This is a typically Ovidian touch, and this coda (D. Parker's [1969] term), lays out the instability of the entire situation, which must (especially in Ovidian elegy) ultimately become untenable, as the *amator* is already known to be fickle and untrustworthy (45–48, not to mention all of 2.4) and the *puella* will be also known to him as untruthful.

39. Thus, as Miller (2004, 172) notes, there is no need to believe with Maleuvre (1998, 195–96) that the speaker of *Amores* 2.5 constitutes an entirely new poetic character. It was inevitable that the Ovidian *amator* should witness the *puella's* deception at a dinner party, particularly given the immediate roots of this situation in Tibullus 1.6. See Miller (2004, 169–82) on the structural relationship of the *vir* and the lover.

40. Though note that the *uxor dotata*, the most frightening figure in Roman Comedy, reverses the normal polarities of marriage by exerting control over her husband. Indeed, the lecherous and sneaky Demaenetus says that his wife Artemona plays the role of the normal cautious father to their son (77–78) and that he sold his power *(imperium)* for her dowry (97). Their behavior toward each other in the play's final scene suggests that money may interfere with normal gender roles in the Roman household, though Demaenetus demonstrates throughout that he finds this reversal both loathsome and abnormal. See also Megadorus's diatribe against the dowered wife *(Aulularia* 478–535).

41. Davidson (1997, 124–25) notes similarly of the Athenian *hetaira* that she needs to exert careful control over her sexual partners; they, consequently, must use persuasion on her.

42. Such violence occurs elsewhere in elegy and comedy, as noted above; see McKeown (1989) on *Amores* 1.7 for citations. See also James (2003, 184–97) and Fredrick (1997). The motivating factor for male violence toward a courtesan is her infidelity, whether presumed or proven. Since infidelity is a necessity for the courtesan, violence is a predictable element in the irregular love relationship.

43. That this superior male identity rests on property and social status, thwarted by the courtesan's independence, is no accident. Comedy's terror of the *uxor dotata*, who takes control of the Roman household, suggests a

permanent vulnerability of Roman elite masculinity—the lack of money can undermine it as surely as sexual anxiety can destabilize it, and for considerably longer (see, as noted above, the relationship of Demaenetus and Artemona in *Asinaria*).

44. At the end of *Heauton Timoroumenos*, Clitipho's guilty conscience, engendered precisely by his relationship with Bacchis, suggests that he is developing a greater sense of adult responsibility and obligation toward his father—he even agrees to take a wife, as a means of appeasing his father, though he haggles over which woman he must marry. I have argued elsewhere (James 1998b) that rape in Roman Comedy signifies a more advanced stage in the development of adult male sexuality.

45. A big if—the persistence of male sexual attraction to the courtesan, as enacted onstage by the *senex amator*, suggests otherwise. Interestingly, the banquet proves especially dangerous to the older man: see the end of *Bacchides*, in which the banquet invitation of the two courtesan sisters proves fatal to the resolve of Philoxenus and Nicobulus. It seems no accident that *Asinaria* ends in a banquet scene, in which Argyrippus resentfully watches his father pawing the reluctant Philaenium, and that the agent of his immediate revenge is his irate mother, who breaks up the dinner party and drags her fearful, dawdling husband home.

46. Here it is relevant that Phaedria of *Eunuchus* was famously sober and well-behaved before he met Thais (225–27) and that Pistoclerus of *Bacchides*, sent to liberate his friend Mnesilochus's girlfriend, falls in love with her twin sister, to the horror of his tutor Lydus. Chaerea of *Eunuchus* loses all his inhibitions when he sees the beautiful young Pamphila—he goes AWOL to chase her. Comedy presents infatuation and loss of self-control as inevitable whenever a young man meets a courtesan; the capitulation of the surly title character in *Truculentus* to Astaphium demonstrates this phenomenon even among slaves. Finally, elegy too presents love as virtually inevitable, particularly for poets, but for other men as well. In Propertius's Monobiblos, even the playboy Gallus falls in love (1.10); so do Ponticus (1.9) and Lynceus (2.34). In Tibullus everybody falls in love: the eponymous speaker, the *puer* Marathus, the old men who buy youth and beauty, and those who scoff at foolish lovers (1.2.87–96). The *Ars amatoria* presupposes, at least for literary purposes, an entire class of young men who wish to pursue precisely the kinds of nonmarital, nonreproductive sexual relationships that will lead them into states of anxiety at a dinner banquet. In elegy, notably, the young lover (like the comic *miles*) is free of parental control, a condition that extends the lure of the courtesan past the dangerous stage of foolish adolescence into independent adulthood.

47. Comedy's plots often revolve around just this male competition and anxiety, particularly whenever a soldier is in town; but see especially the complex strategies of Phronesium in *Truculentus*, who juggles three different men. This anxiety and competition are treated as predictable reactions, as in physics or astronomy, whenever a young man comes into the orbit of that irresistible object, the beautiful independent courtesan. I presume that such reactions are being presented, then, not as fantastic but as plausible, if comically exaggerated on stage.

48. As W. S. Anderson has reminded me, *per litteras,* other comic courtesans cause male anxiety and trouble at dinner parties. See, for instance, Bacchis in *Heauton Timoroumenos,* when she is pretending to be Clinia's *amica* rather than Clitipho's; her demanding behavior and expensive tastes are supposed to frighten Clitipho's father. She demonstrates impressive liberty at this particular dinner party. Likewise, Thais of *Eunuchus* performs a delicate balancing act between two men who aren't actually rivals, because one of them, the soldier Thraso, believes they are (612–28). She employs subtle signals of communication: she hands her jewelry to her slave Dorias, which means, as the slave says (628), that she will leave as soon as she can. She signals to the other man, Chremes, whose long-lost sister Pamphila (brought to her by Thraso) she is sheltering, that he should follow her. He does not catch her signal (a nod of the head, which Dorias considers sufficient, 735–36) but Thraso does—he turns violent, believing that Chremes is his rival. He exemplifies the danger posed to the courtesan by jealous men, as he plans a violent assault on Thais' house (771–816).

49. Similar multiple simultaneous acts of flirtation occur in Naevius's *Tarentilla* (Naevius frag. 2), in which the title character, a dancing girl from Tarentum, entices several men at once, handing a ring to one while pouting suggestively at another, and so forth. This dancing girl may well be a literary ancestor for the comic courtesan and elegiac *puella.* She certainly establishes a preexisting recognition that "working girls" are able to multitask in public and that they are expert at exploiting the simultaneous competing sexual attraction of different men.

50. Although Philaenium in *Asinaria* is still young enough to have fallen in love with Argyrippus and can thus be designated a relative novice at her profession, Diabolus and the parasite expect her to be already expert at such tactics. And indeed her behavior in the play's final scene shows that she knows how to flirt even with a man she dislikes, in front of the man she loves. Lowe (1992, 171) sees Philaenium's behavior in this scene as "pertness ... inconsistent with her [prior] characterization," citing other scholars in n.113; he therefore thinks it likely that Plautus is here depicting her "as a typical *meretrix* ... for momentary comic effect." Perhaps, but on a generic level the comic *meretrix* knows how to handle lascivious old men, and her distaste for Demaenetus certainly motivates her to get him into more trouble with his already angry wife. See Anne Duncan, in this volume, for a view that comic courtesans divide into "good faith" or "bad faith." I have taken the view here that comedy (and, later, elegy as well) demonstrates a spectrum of courtesan-types, showing stages in a predictable trajectory over a courtesan's career, from the naive and idealistic (Philotis in *Hecyra*) to a more realistic but still emotionally open condition (Thais in *Eunuchus,* Philaenium in *Asinaria*) to a fully experienced model (Phronesium in *Truculentus,* among others), who knows but does not articulate what the retired courtesan (i.e., the *lena*) talks of—that courtesans must look out for their own interests. See James (2003, 37–41). These stages of courtesanry correspond with Duncan's "good faith/bad faith" designations.

51. At Propertius 4.5.43–46, Acanthis tells the *puella* to act drunk if her current boyfriend is drunk and to mirror his behavior, in the manner of a Menandrian courtesan. Tibullus 1.6.17–18 suggests an excessively relaxed posture and

lapsed garment as signs of a woman's interaction with a man other than her *vir*. Loss of control, especially to drink, presents considerable present danger—as the *praeceptor Amoris* says, a *puella* who passes out at a party risks rape (*Ars amatoria* 3.765–68). Propertius 2.33 warns of lesser, but still real, risks of drinking— a risk both to the lover, as the *puella* may forget her man when she's drinking (34), and to the woman who drinks too much, whose youth and beauty will be ruined (33). See Phronesium at *Truculentus* 854–55, about how a *meretrix* must be able to drink and think at the same time. Rosivach (1998, 192 n.35) notes, citing Reinsberg (1989, 153), that many courtesans and prostitutes in antiquity may have developed alcohol-related illnesses, as they were professionally required to drink a fair amount. Rosivach and Reinsberg are discussing Greek *hetairai*, but the risk to the Roman *meretrix* is similar, as seen in the anxiety of Diabolus about Philaenium's future drinking. In addition the retired courtesan (i.e., the *lena*) is always considered an alcoholic; hence Diabolus threatens Cleareta's wine supply at *Asinaria* 799–802. Note also that the name of the *lena* in *Amores* 1.8 is Dipsas, which the *amator* calls an appropriate name for her, as she gets drunk every night (lines 3–4). The occupational hazard of alcoholism significantly reduces the glamor quotient, so to speak, of the courtesan's life. That glamorous appearance may be a pretense in any case: as Rosivach (1998, 117) notes, comedy adverts to the facade of expensive elegance in such women's lives, citing *Eunuchus* 934–40 on the cheap and meager food they eat in private; see also *Asinaria* 138–43.

Infamous Performers
Comic Actors and Female Prostitutes in Rome

ANNE DUNCAN

The Romans made frequent connections between prostitutes and actors in law, in literature, and in clothing conventions.[1] These connections suggest an association in the Roman cultural imagination between sexuality, public life, and performance. Essentially, both prostitutes and actors were thought to be people who "faked it" for a living. The stigmatization of both groups by the upper classes as "low-Other" worked to construct both prostitutes and actors as objects of desire. In Roman law, both professions were decreed *infamis*. In Roman Comedy, the association between the two was represented by the stock character of the duplicitous, self-serving *meretrix* and in Roman clothing conventions, by the customary cross-dressing of both female prostitutes and male actors. In each of these three arenas, we will see that the very traits that were used to marginalize prostitutes and actors in terms of their social status also worked to establish them as symbolically central to the construction of the ideal Roman subject, and that the qualities imputed to them that were used to justify viewing them as objects of suspicion also served, not coincidentally, to make them objects of desire.

Preliminaries: Stallybrass and White and
Roman Subject Formation

In their influential 1986 study, *The Politics and Poetics of Transgression*, Peter Stallybrass and Allon White describe the ways in which English subject formation from the seventeenth to nineteenth centuries was developed by constructing a series of "low-Others" who were contrasted with the normative bourgeois subject. These low-Others were always changing, as the discourses of medicine, science, technology, and the law informed emerging bourgeois notions of respectability, but they were always tied to carnival, to the grotesque body, to the "lower bodily stratum," and to sites seen as analogous to the lower bodily stratum: the working classes, the sewer, the slum, the Unconscious. Over and over again, Stallybrass and White find that "what is socially peripheral is symbolically central"; the more certain areas of human experience are marked off as beyond the bounds of bourgeois taste and respectability, the more those areas loom large in the images, thoughts, and writings of the bourgeois. Transgression, in Stallybrass and White's reading, is a way of designating boundaries; even as the transgressive agent cuts across boundaries of class, geography, gender, or taste, the horror that the transgressive agent arouses reassures the bourgeois subject that he is on the "right" side of the boundary, and that the agent is on the "wrong" side.

Paradoxically, this very horror works not only to arouse disgust and thus reassurance, but also to arouse desire; as the bourgeois subject increasingly cordons himself off from the various low-Others who help define him, he finds them increasingly, and disturbingly, desirable. "A fundamental rule seems to be that what is excluded at the overt level of identity-formation is productive of new objects of desire" (25; see also 77). This mechanism, in which rejection of identification leads to desire for the Other, means that politics and *erôs* are at odds with each other: "Repugnance and fascination are the twin poles of the process in which a *political* imperative to reject and eliminate the debasing 'low' conflicts powerfully and unpredictably with a desire for this Other" (4–5; emphasis in original). Stallybrass and White present several accounts of the desire of a higher-class man for a woman of low social status, including Freud's boyhood fascination with his governess (152–70). As society, and the city in which society is based, becomes more stratified, the bourgeois subject experiences a greater desire to transgress the boundaries of his station, culminating in the extreme polarities of nineteenth-century London, with its prostitutes' quarter, slums, and sewers, extensively visited and analyzed by bourgeois journalists, doctors, government commissions, and—in the case of the prostitutes—customers (ch.3, esp. 126).

Like London, Rome was a city of extreme disparities in wealth, a city intersected and divided by aqueducts and sewers (Gowers 1995), a city with its own market center, slums, graveyards, mansions, theater, and prostitutes' quarter.[2] And like London, Rome was the center of a number of discourses—legal, scientific, literary, rhetorical, philosophical—that worked to establish a normative Roman subject by contrasting him with undesirable alternatives: women, foreigners (especially Greeks), slaves, and all those who were seen as not masters of themselves. Obviously, republican Rome and early modern or Victorian England are literally and figuratively worlds apart, and I do not mean to suggest that Stallybrass and White's theories of English subject formation are simply and unproblematically applicable to Roman subject formation. But there are significant correspondences between the two urban cultures, and what Stallybrass and White claim for the bourgeois subject in early modern and later England is applicable to the Roman elite—and its construction of an ideal Roman male subject—in the last two centuries BCE.

The ideal Roman subject was created through a number of discourses and practices: through the emergence of a popular Roman theater culture, financed by the elite, in the second century BCE (see, e.g., Gruen 1992, ch.5); through the sumptuary legislation enacted to regulate ostentation based on strict class demarcations, such as the *lex Oppia*, which passed in 215 BCE and was repealed 195 BCE (see Culham 1982; see also Plautus *Aulularia* 474–536);[3] through the expansion of the Roman empire, especially with regard to Greece and the self-conscious appropriation of Greek culture (see Gruen 1992, ch.2 and ch.6).; through the development of the patronage system (see Wallace-Hadrill 1989); through the publication of (supposedly) nonfictional, autobiographical prose narratives (see Cicero's letters and Caesar's commentaries on the Gallic War); and through the proliferation of didactic handbooks, whether rhetorical (*Rhetorica ad Haerennium*, Cicero *De oratore, Brutus,* and *Orator*), agricultural (Cato *De agricultura* and Varro *De re rustica*), philosophical (Varro *Disciplinae* [lost] and Cicero *De republica* and *Consolatio*), or literary (Horace *Ars Poetica*), all of which claimed to teach the elite man what to think, how to live, and just as importantly, how to present himself. All these discourses and practices combined in the last two centuries BCE to produce the image of an ideal Roman subject, who was wealthy, an effective manager of his estates, cultured but not too effete, politically engaged but not "a slave to the mob," an excellent public speaker (without seeming too histrionic), virtuous, brave, and self-controlled. (This image, it must be said, was informed by a great deal of nostalgia; it seems to be a distinguishing feature of Roman ideology that it constantly located its ideals in the past, as if gloomily acknowledging that they could never be fulfilled.)

The construction of this ideal was aided by the positing of a number of low-Others as well. The list of ideal qualities above implies a list of counterexamples: among the low-Others were slaves, the poor, women, eunuchs (Catullus 63), foreigners (Plautus *Poenulus*), gladiators (see Barton 1993, ch.1), pimps, actors, and prostitutes. Yet, as Stallybrass and White note about the low-Others of English bourgeois sensibility, "difference is productive of desire"; what is despised can also come to be intensely desired, as the maid and the prostitute were in Victorian London. It is the connections between the last two groups of Roman low-others listed above, actors and prostitutes, and their place in the "desiring economy" of Roman thought, that the rest of this paper will take up and explore.

Infamis Performers: Prostitutes, Actors, and the Law

The Romans consistently placed actors and prostitutes at the bottom of the ladder in terms of their legal status. Numerous republican-era statutes ascribe to both professions *infamis* status (as well as to a number of other despised occupations, such as gladiator, gladiator-trainer, and pimp).[4] During the republican period, prostitutes could marry freeborn men, although the man would then share his wife's *infamia*; after Augustus's marriage legislation, even retired prostitutes were forbidden to marry freeborn citizen men (J. F. Gardner 1986, 133). One leading sign of actors' *infamis* status was a law that existed during the republic that empowered magistrates to beat actors at any time, onstage or off, for any reason; it was restricted by Augustus around 10 BCE to allow beatings only at the time and place of performances (Suetonius, *Augustus* 45.3). Cicero reports that his fellow citizens felt actors should even be removed from their tribes by the censors (*De republica* 4.10).

Yet the legal infamy in which actors and prostitutes lived and worked did not function entirely unproblematically as a social stigma.

A number of statutes were passed (suggesting their ineffectiveness) by the time of Augustus's marriage legislation, the *lex Julia et Papia*, in 18 BCE, prohibiting marriage between members of the higher social ranks (equestrian and up) and actors (D. R. French 1998, 298–99; J. F. Gardner 1986, 32, 129; McGinn 1998b, 72, 103). Conversely, under the *lex Julia*, the daughter of a senator who had been a prostitute or an actress could legally marry a freedman, because she gave up her honor when she pursued those professions (D. R. French 1998, 295 n.9). A law was also passed prohibiting women of the senatorial classes from registering themselves as prostitutes in order to evade prosecution for adultery (J. F. Gardner 1986, 130; see also Flemming 1999, 53–54), and statutes were passed repeatedly (suggesting their ineffectiveness) prohibiting men and women of senatorial rank from degrading themselves by appearing onstage or in the arena (J. F. Gardner 1986, 247–48; D. R. French 1998, 297; Bradley 1989, 85). All of these laws suggest the paradoxical allure of social stigma and cross-class desire. That laws were repeatedly passed in an attempt to prohibit the aristocracy from marrying *infames* or adopting *infamis* occupations is powerful testimony to the illicit appeal of the low-other in this time period.[5]

Catharine Edwards (1997) has discussed the ways in which the Romans in the early imperial era viewed actors, prostitutes, and gladiators as low, shameful, yet desirable performers; she argues that the Romans associated public performance of any kind with immorality, especially if women were involved. Her findings are supported by Dorothea French's study of the status of mime actresses in the Christian era of the Roman Empire (1998). Both scholars make the case for a Roman tendency to view women who "performed" in public as whores, both figuratively and literally (French 1998, 296).[6] The Romans punished public performers (male and female) for their occupations, but their repeated attempts to isolate and stigmatize these groups of people also worked to construct them as objects of desire.

Some elite Roman men kept actors as boyfriends, and a few elite women took the bold step of registering as prostitutes in order to avoid the financial penalties of adultery (and, perhaps, to increase their sex appeal).[7] Actors and prostitutes were both *infamis;* they were both versions of the Roman masculine subject's low-other. But a crucial difference separated them from citizen women, eunuchs, foreigners, slaves, or even gladiators: actors and prostitutes operated under the sign of the fictional, the feigned, the fake.[8] Actors and prostitutes could thus be seen as equivalent: the actor is a prostitute, the prostitute is an actor.

The fact that the *meretrix* in Roman Comedy is so often accused of lying is another sign of the interrelatedness of prostitutes and actors; the sincerity of her affections is never above question.

Prostitutes in Roman Comedy

Much productive work has been done on metatheater in Roman Comedy, especially in terms of the *servus callidus* as playwright/director/lead actor in the plays of Plautus (Slater 1985, 16, 28, 32–33, 47–53, and passim; Anderson 1996, ch.4). Like the tricky slave, the *meretrix* has a methatheatrical dimension. By examining this stock character as a figure for the actor onstage, we can gain insight into how the Romans connected prostitution and acting through the mechanisms of deception and desire.

Meretrices in Roman Comedy sort themselves into two basic types: the "sincere" one, who acts in "good faith" and truly loves the *adulescens,* and the one who acts in "bad faith," who does not truly love anyone but plays everyone for money. The "bad faith" *meretrix* lies about her feelings and intentions to everyone in order to get what she wants; she occasionally even impersonates someone else. But even the "good," "sincere" *meretrix* feigns affection for her less appealing clients in order to wring more money and gifts out of them. Sometimes the "good faith" *meretrix* is really a *pseudo-hetaira,* a freeborn girl who has been brought up as a *meretrix* but is revealed to be of citizen birth and therefore eligible to marry the *adulescens* (which then "explains" her nicer-than-usual character while she was living as a *meretrix*) (Gilula 1980, 147; Fantham 1975, 57–58). Significantly, the "bad faith" *meretrices* are always real prostitutes.

But whether they are "good," sincere courtesans who are truly in love with their young men—the proverbial hookers with hearts of gold—or "bad," self-serving, conniving whores, all *meretrices* in Roman Comedy display a metatheatrical ability to seduce, charm, and deceive, and all of them display an awareness that they have to take certain measures to ensure their own financial security. And regardless of whether a given *meretrix* is "really" good or bad, most *meretrices* are accused of being bad (that is, faithless, self-interested, and mercenary) at some point during a given play, whether by the *adulescens,* his slave, or both.[9]

The *adulescens* typically complains about the two-facedness of the *meretrix:* when he has money, she is sweet and welcoming, but when his money runs out, she shuts him out of the house. This complaint reveals the two-facedness of the *meretrix*'s client: he values the *meretrix* because she will love him because of his money—that is, he values her availability—but he wants her to love only him—that is, he devalues her availability. He wants to be able to buy an exclusive relationship, but he does not want to have to keep paying for it, and he does not want anyone else to be able to buy it.[10] He loves the appearance that the *meretrix* presents when all is going well: that they are in love, that she loves only him, that her beauty and her hospitality and her costly up-keep and her attentions are all for his sake (and not for his money). But he hates the moments when he feels he has glimpsed the truth behind the appearance: that the *meretrix* loves only money, that she has been putting on a show for him, in order to get his money, and that she will put on that show for anyone who has money—and won't for anyone who doesn't.

In this way, the *meretrix* in Roman Comedy functions as a figure for the actor; she feigns for a living, enchanting the spectator. And there-fore, the *adulescens*, who oscillates between rapturous delight and desire for his beloved girl, and bitter, disillusioned contempt for his mercenary whore, functions as a figure for the Roman theatrical audience, oscillat-ing between delight in theatrical pretense and suspicion of the perform-ance and the performers that they are watching. Neither view is "the" Roman view of prostitutes or actors—both were available in Roman culture, and audiences could tap into either one at any given moment. But the more the *adulescens* desires the *meretrix*, the more bitterly he feels he has been duped when she shuts him out of the house—and the more the audience enjoys the actor, the more anxious they feel about their desire for empty spectacle and literally infamous performers.

PLAUTUS'S PROSTITUTES

The *meretrix* appears in a number of Plautine plays, and whenever she has a significant speaking role, she functions as a figure for the actor.[11] The Plautine *meretrix* is an expert dissembler, sometimes compared ex-plicitly to an actor, who typically tells her "director" that she needs no coaching in deception.

Asinaria contains a "good faith" *meretrix* named Philaenium. The *adulescens*, Argyrippus, has run out of money to continue paying her mother/*lena* for her company. The *lena* shuts him out of their house, and he bitterly chastises her for her unfairness and hard-heartedness; she responds that this is business, and that he is welcome back when he gets more money. Argyrippus then proposes to raise enough money to pay to have Philaenium exclusively for himself for one whole year—the first appearance of the motif of the desire for exclusivity, which we will see over and over again.[12] With his father's blessing, Argyrippus's tricky slave steals money to continue paying for the young man's good time. In return, the father asks for a night with the girl, which the son grudgingly grants, but the threatened paternal intrusion is thwarted by the intervention of the shrewish *matrona*.

As a "good faith" *meretrix* who truly loves the *adulescens*, Philaenium meekly protests against her *lena*'s advice to string multiple men along at once. But she also plays along when the tricky slave demands that she sweet-talk them to get the money they have obtained for the lovers (664–92), quoting a proverb, "Whatever poverty demands" (671), and making what sounds like a "bad faith" statement: "Please, I'll do what you want, just give us that money" (692).[13] She plays the attentive companion at the banquet with Argyrippus's father—until his wife arrives and Philaenium, relieved of her duty, can confess that she was bored by him (920–21). Even the "good faith" *meretrix* has to make nice to anyone who has any kind of hold over her; even the sincerest prostitute has to playact in some situations (see W. S. Anderson 1996, 83).

Bacchides features identical twin sister *meretrices* with the same name, Bacchis. They are "bad faith" prostitutes who ensnare two *adulescentes* with their charms, and then, when the young men's fathers object, they ensnare them as well. Although the *meretrices* are onstage only at the beginning and end of the play, in both scenes they showcase their seductive techniques, complete with asides to each other about their performances. Bacchis I, in the earliest preserved scene in the play, urges her *adulescens* to "pretend you love me" (*simulato me amare* [75]) in order to make the *miles* jealous (this exhortation combines her interest in prostitution and acting concisely and elegantly). Despite his fears of her wiles, he capitulates. In the last scene in the play, Bacchis II confesses in an aside to her sister that she will do her part in seducing one of the *senes*, even though it will be like embracing a death's head (1152); she then proceeds to wheedle and flatter him. The audience is treated to seeing two consummate professionals at work.

Cistellaria contains two *meretrices*, Selenium and Gymnasium. Selenium is a "good faith" prostitute who truly loves the *adulescens*; in fact, she has never had sex with any other man but him. It is thus unsurprising that she is a *pseudo-hetaira* who will be revealed to be of legitimate citizen birth at the end of the play, when she and her lover can get married.

She is accordingly the least deceptive or theatrical of Plautus's *me-retrices*; significantly, her one deception consists in pretending not to be a prostitute (83–85). The other prostitute, Gymnasium, has a much smaller role; she is a weak advocate of the stereotypical "bad faith" prostitute's lifestyle, agreeing to do whatever her mother/*lena* wishes, and counseling Selenium against having any genuine feelings for any customer (46–75).

Menaechmi concerns long-lost identical (and identically named) twin brothers, one of whom keeps getting mistaken for the other through the course of the play. Menaechmus in Epidamnus, who is married, has been carrying on a relationship with a *meretrix*, Erotium; the arrival of Menaechmus II throws Menaechmus I's lifestyle into chaos, as wife and mistress both become enraged at real and perceived deceptions and thefts by "Menaechmus." Erotium is initially flattering to Menaechmus I, telling him that her house is always open to him (351–68), but when she believes she has been swindled by him, she turns nasty and shuts him out (688–95), saying, "Unless you bring money, you won't be able to take me home for nothing" (694). As the parasite remarks, "A prostitute is always flattering, while she sees something she can take" (193). While not very developed, her character is the stereotypical "bad faith" prostitute: mercenary, greedy, and two-faced. It is perhaps significant that at the end of this play, Menaechmus I takes leave of both wife and *meretrix* to sail away with his long-lost twin; both women have become unappealing (see McCarthy 2000, 40 and 63–66).

Miles Gloriosus contains two *meretrices*, the love object Philocomasium, and Acroteleutium, a client of the helpful *senex* Periplectomenus. Both prostitutes are consummate actresses, but Philocomasium is a "good faith" *meretrix* in that she truly loves the *adulescens* and uses her deceptive abilities on the *miles* in order to escape his clutches, while Acroteleutium is a "bad faith" *meretrix* in that she seems simply to enjoy lying. The plot of the play hinges on two scenes in which the *me-retrices* must play other characters in order to fool the *Miles Gloriosus* or his slaves. Philocomasium has to play identical twins in order to fool the slave who is set as a guard over her; by convincing him that he glimpsed her twin sister kissing a strange young man, she prevents the slave from reporting her infidelity with the *adulescens*. Acroteleutium is costumed as a *matrona* by the tricky slave Palaestrio and set to play the role of the *senex*'s estranged wife who supposedly lusts after the *miles*; her acting ability is essential to the final deception of the *miles*:

Peri. See, I have my client right here, a young little prostitute.
But what use is she? *Pal.* See to it that you lead her away to your home at once
And then lead her back here costumed like a married woman,
With her head arranged, let her have plaits and headbands
And let her pretend that she is your wife: she has to be instructed thus. (789–93)

Note the use of the term *ornata* in line 791, "adorned" (but more precisely "costumed"), and note the attention paid to the markers of identity for a *matrona*: hairstyle and hair ribbons. The verb *adsimulare* completes the theatrical context. We could say that she is dressing as the stock *matrona* character, since she adopts all the simple markers of the *matrona*'s identity onstage: hairstyle (mask) and deportment (walk). "How appropriately she walks in costume, not like a prostitute at all!" (*quam digne ornata incedit, hau meretricie!* [872]) exclaims Palaestrio as Acroteleutium approaches him in her *matrona* costume.[14]

The tricky slave coaches the *senex* and the *adulescens* about their roles in this fake marriage, both of whom express nervousness about playing their parts. But when any character attempts to coach either of the *meretrices*, both women reply that they need no coaching; they are expert actors. To Philocomasium as she prepares to play her "twin sister," Palaestrio says:

Pal. See to it that you remember what you've been taught.
     Phil. It's a wonder you warn me so often.
Pal. But I'm afraid that you won't be deceitful enough.
     Phil. If you like, give me ten girls; I'll teach the least bad ones
To be bad with what I alone have left over. (354–56)

When the *senex* tries to coach Acroteleutium in playing her role as the *matrona*, she responds:

Acro. I'd be stupid or foolish, my dear patron,
To undertake someone else's work or promise to help him there,
If I didn't know how to be bad or deceitful in the workshop.
Peri. But it's better to warn you.
     Acro. Of *course*, it's no secret that it's *very* important
To warn a prostitute. In fact, moreover, after my ears
Drank in just the coastline of your ocean of oratory,
I personally described to you how the soldier could best be cheated. (878–84)

Acroteleutim goes on to say that women are naturally good at being bad. Despite the standard comic misogyny of this sort of line in Plautus, not all women are good at being bad, but just *meretrices*; their actor-like occupation brings out the liar in them. Even Acroteleutium's maid, Milphidippa, is a skilled actress, feigning admiration for the *miles* in her role as go-between while exchanging asides with the tricky slave. In fact, Palaestrio is so impressed with Milphidippa's acting abilities that when she later salutes him as "architectus" of the plot, he replies that compared to her, he is nothing (1140). *Miles Gloriosus* reveals two prostitutes enthusiastically and skillfully playing roles and engaging in theatrical deception; the "good faith" one out of a desire to escape with her true love, the "bad faith" one out of a simple love of deceit and mockery.

The *Mostellaria* contains one significant *meretrix*, Philematium. Philematium is the ideal of the "good faith" *meretrix*—and the antitype of the "bad faith," scheming prostitute, who is represented by Scapha, Philematium's slave and a retired prostitute herself. Scapha and Philematium engage in an argument over Philematium's unprofessional and surprisingly selfless devotion to the *adulescens* Philolaches, which Scapha warns her is imprudent (157-290). This is a stock scene in plays with a "good faith" *meretrix*.[15] The "good faith" *meretrix* presents the surprising (and, to the eavesdropping *adulescens*, pleasing) news that she sincerely loves Philolaches, even against her own professional interests; Scapha presents the stereotypical, "bad faith" side of the argument, urging her to think of her retirement. This scene typically occurs either with the *adulescens* or his slave eavesdropping unobserved, as here in *Mostellaria*, or with only the audience as "eavesdroppers"—in other words, its function is to establish the "good faith" *meretrix*'s sincerity by having her make a speech for which she believes she has no audience, other than her slave (see Moore 1998, ch.2). We could say it makes her less metatheatrical, that it increases her sincerity by deliberately dethreatricalizing her character. If the *adulescens* is eavesdropping, as in the *Mostellaria*, he exhibits both reactions to the prostitutes that have been outlined above, only split into responses to the two characters: in reaction to the "good faith" *meretrix*'s statements, he swoons and swears that losing his fortune to buy her is worth it; in reaction to the "bad faith" prostitute Scapha, he threatens violence and expresses outrage at her callous manipulation of lovers.[16] Philematium repeatedly asserts her sense of obligation and fidelity to Philolaches and disavows any stereotypical prostitute's ploys, saying, "I love truth, I want truth to be spoken to me; I hate a liar" (181). It is no coincidence that this conversation takes place during the *meretrix*'s "toilet scene"—that is, she and her slave have a conversation over whether sincerity or manipulation is the best policy with the *adulescens* while she applies makeup and adorns herself. It is one degree removed from a costuming scene, such as we have examined in *Miles Gloriosus*—and it may add an ominous note to Philematium's repeated protestations of sincerity that she keeps putting on more makeup, while Scapha, the cynical old slave, assures her that her real, unadorned self is pretty enough.

By far the baddest of the "bad faith" *meretrices* in Plautus's extant corpus is the aptly named Phronesium in *Truculentus*. *Truculentus* is an experiment with combining stock characters: the *meretrix* Phronesium is the *servus callidus*, the "tricky slave" (Dessen 1977, 160). She proves to be a master of clever intrigue as she plays three lovers off against each other, using each one in turn to leverage gifts and cash out of the other two.

Of Phronesium's three lovers—an *adulescens* from the city, a rustic youth, and a *miles*—the *adulescens*, Diniarchus, is clearly supposed to be the most sympathetic.[17] He is bitter over his fall from favor, the result of his money having run out. In his monologue opening the play (21–94), he reiterates many of the standard complaints about the mercenary nature of *meretrices* and simultaneously reveals the effectiveness of their wiles—for he, and the rest of Rome's youth, cannot resist throwing away their inheritances on them. Thus the peculiar tone of the Roman discourse on prostitutes is set early on in this play: the *adulescens* knows he is being gulled out of his money, but he can't resist her charms— even though he knows her "charms" are all an act.

In this opening monologue, Diniarchus also reveals Phronesium's most outrageous plot to date, which involves passing off a "borrowed" baby as her own by another one of her lovers, the *miles*, in order to extort "child support" out of him (this baby turns out to be Diniarchus's with the respectable girl to whom he is engaged—and whom, it turns out, he raped nine months ago while drunk at a festival). Phronesium is deliberately and self-consciously impersonating a mother, as the *adulescens* bitterly complains: "She pretends [*simulat*] to have given birth, so that she can force me out of doors; she pretends [*simulat*] that this soldier is the father of the baby, so that she can 'Greek it up' with only the soldier" (86–88). The use of the verb *simulat* twice in three lines suggests the feigning, theatrical quality of this deception.[18] Phronesium herself discusses her scam in some detail with the audience (450–80), complete with a reference to her maternity clothes, which is to say, her costume as a new mother: "You see me now, how I'm going out in costume [*ornata*]; I'm feigning [*adsimulo*] that I'm sick from childbirth just now" (463–64). She, too, uses a compound of *simulare* to describe her act. Plautus uses the word *ornata*, "costumed," when a character disguises him- or herself; by using this word here to describe herself dressed in maternity clothes, Phronesium is calling attention to her outfit as a theatrical costume (Muecke 1986, 219–20 and n.14; Duckworth 1994, 74). She presents herself to the audience as an actor playing a role (see Williams 1999, 40–42; Slater 1985, 24 and n.8, 27 n.10, 162, and ch.8).

If Phronesium is likened to an actor, then the *adulescens* especially, but all her lovers in general, are stand-ins for the spectators. All are captivated by her charming performance. And yet they fret about their expenditures on something so essentially wasteful (21–94, 341–49, 645–62, 893–95). This oscillation between enchantment and unease, especially unease about a leisure activity, is the same dynamic at work in Roman culture at large in terms of theater. We see it in this play in Diniarchus's oscillation between suspicion of Phronesium and the rapturous belief that he is the only man to whom she has revealed her plot.[19]

But the split is perhaps most vividly illuminated in the character of Truculentus himself, who at first upbraids Phronesium's maid Astaphium for helping her mistress send Truculentus's rustic young master Strabax on the road to ruin, and then slowly comes to find himself irresistibly captivated by Astaphium's charms. The slave of the prostitute and the slave of the rustic youth duplicate the relationship of their social superiors, and Truculentus eventually hands over his wallet to Astaphium—though not without some grumbling: "I'm being put up in an inn where I'll be entertained badly for my money" (697–98). Truculentus is the living embodiment of Roman nostalgia: he is the rustic Roman yeoman of yore, who is satisfied with the simple country life and distrusts "painted" and loose women and would never, ever, give them his hard-earned cash. But Truculentus is really more of a caricature than a character, a stereotype of a certain idea about the good old days, and thus he serves, not exactly as a character who the audience identifies with (he is a slave, after all), but as a foil to the audience; they can feel superior but akin to him, as he falls prey to Astaphium's charms and hands her his wallet (see Dessen 1977, 152–53; Moore 1998, 150). In Truculentus's succumbing to the charms of the *meretrices*, we see the succumbing of Rome (or Roman men) to luxuries in general: wine, prostitutes, loose living, wasteful extravagance—and theater.

The *adulescens* Diniarchus sums up this fear of Rome's decline when he says: "In short, this is what a great and populous people does when the state is peaceful and leisure-full, after the enemies have been defeated: everyone who has some cash to give must have love" (74–76). Here we see the standard accusation of the old against the young in

Roman Comedy: that the young squander their money (that is, their fathers' money) on high living, instead of practicing traditional Roman thrift (see Dessen 1977, 152; Moore 1998, 142, 144). But this statement, in the context of this play, makes particularly clear what is at stake: instead of conserving their paternal estates, young men are squandering their patrimony on *meretrices—meretrices* who are, essentially, actors. Young men pay lavish sums to be entertained by a *meretrix* for a very brief time, or, put more negatively, they waste money on an actor who temporarily flatters them. And Phronesium confirms this association between going to the theater and going to a prostitute when Stratophanes the *miles* asks her incredulously:

Stra. How, dammit, can you be pretty or clever, if you love a man of that sort?
Phro. Don't you remember what the actor said in the theater?
"All men are eager or squeamish, as their own profit calls for." (930–32)

How can you love that other man, asks the *miles*, when he is a poor rustic, and I, a fine soldier, am a much better match for you? The soldier's question implies that Phronesium is wasting her charms on an unworthy customer. Phronesium replies that there is no such thing as an unworthy customer: she "loves" the other man, the rustic Strabax, because it profits her to do so. The quotation from the actor claims that all men act as they need to in order to protect their own interests, but it takes an actor to articulate the prostitute's principle of conduct.

Phronesium is no "hooker with a heart of gold"—she is a hooker whose heart is set on gold, and she is a consummate actress. At the end of the play, she has lost Diniarchus to marriage (perhaps), but she is still successfully stringing along the other two men; in fact, she compels them to compete with each other in giving her cash. In the last lines of the play, Phronesium ties together the themes of prostitution and acting by making a direct appeal to the audience—not only for the usual applause, but for business: "By Castor, how cleverly I've gone bird-catching to my satisfaction, And since I see my own affairs well arranged, I'll arrange yours too: If anyone has a mind to make his affairs pleasant, please let me know. For Venus's sake applaud: this play is in her care. Spectators, fare well; applaud, and arise" (964–68). Usually, the character speaking the last words to the audience steps at least somewhat out of character and asks for applause; here, Phronesium is both out of character (in that she addresses the audience directly) and fully in character (in that she solicits new customers boldly). As the star of *Truculentus*, she seduces the entire Roman audience with her enchanting performances (see Dessen 1977, 147 and 164; Moore 1998, 157). Even though everyone knows her character, they find her irresistible.

TERENCE'S PROSTITUTES

Meretrices in Terence's comedies are often seen as the exception to the rule. In the prologue to the *Eunuchus,* Terence himself implies that the audience will find no "bad prostitutes" (*meretrices malas* [37]) in this play, the implied contrast being to the plays of his rivals. And in general, Terence shows a great deal of interest in unsettling audience expectations, whether through rewriting stock characters to play opposite to type or through stretching generic conventions to the breaking point (Goldberg 1986, 16, 152–58, and 211). Yet Terence's *meretrices,* on close examination, fall into the same dichotomy of "good faith" and "bad faith" that we have seen in Plautus, and they are just as bound up in issues of theatricality and sincerity.

The *Eunuchus* presents us with a *meretrix,* Thais, who appears to be the standard mercenary prostitute, but in fact is sincere and "good faith" (Goldberg 1986, 22 and 117–19; see also Gilula 1980, 149). In the opening scene of the play, the *adulescens,* Phaedria, laments that she has shut him out of the house and attempts to berate her for it, but he is thwarted by her protestations of sincere affection and her revelation that her behavior is part of a plan to save her foster sister from the clutches of a *miles.* The prostitute's sincerity is proven by her addresses to the audience when she is alone (or believes herself to be alone) (81–83 and 197–206; see W. S. Anderson 1984, 131, Knorr 1995, 226–27). Despite her sincerity, she engages in quite a bit of theatrical manipulation and playacting in order to achieve her laudable objective; in other words, even this sincere *meretrix* acts very much like a "bad faith" *meretrix.*[20] The line is hard to draw, and the *adulescens'* anxiety over whether he is being duped is understandable: "If only you were speaking that word from the heart and truthfully, 'Rather than have you as an enemy'! If I could believe you said that sincerely, I could endure anything" (175–77). He grudgingly agrees to leave town for a few days while she plays up to the soldier, even though he fears that Thais is simply shutting him out and leaving him for a wealthier customer. His final request to her before leaving sums up every comic *adulescens'* wish of his *meretrix,* in fact the wish of every customer who hires a prostitute in Roman Comedy, and thus it sums up the problem with all comic prostitutes: "Is there something I'd like? When you're with that soldier, be absent; night and day love me, desire me, dream of me, wait for me, think of me, hope for me, enjoy yourself with me, be with me wholly: please make your heart mine, in short, since I am yours" (191–96). He desires her to desire only him, to think only of him, to be faithful (in spirit, if not in body) to him. Act with *him*, Phaedria is urging, because you're being sincere with *me*. But that, of course, is the one thing that a customer cannot ask of a prostitute—that is, unless he pays her for the privilege of exclusivity, and that is no reassurance of sincerity at all.

The *Heauton Timoroumenos* features a *meretrix*, Bacchis, the girlfriend of one *adulescens* who impersonates the girlfriend of another *adulescens* in order to fool both men's fathers. She is described by the *senex* Chremes who hosts her as ruinously costly to provide for; he makes all the standard accusations of excessively luxurious living and demanding behavior we have come to expect of prostitutes in comedy by now (see Knorr 1995, 229). In a twist on the usual *meretrix-lena* conversation, Bacchis has a conversation with the other love interest in the play, a poor *virgo* who truly loves her *adulescens* (381–95). Bacchis compliments the other girl, the significantly named Antiphila, on having her character match her beauty. This is exactly what does not happen in the case of *meretrices*, whose surface beauty does not match their mercenary natures, and it is the job description of actors; this is another instance in which the *meretrix* figures the actor onstage. Bacchis offers the standard defense that she does not enjoy fleecing men of their wealth, but her customers value only her beauty, and she has to think about her retirement. Not surprisingly, Bacchis is also adept at pretending to be somebody else's girlfriend; she is a competent actor. In fact, when she believes that her *adulescens* is going to abandon her, she pretends to prepare to seek the affection of a *miles* nearby (Knorr 1995, 229–30). The tricky slave makes the usual reassurances about her acting abilities: "she's been thoroughly taught" (361). Bacchis, then, is a typical "bad faith" *meretrix* who has chosen her duplicitous profession with open eyes, yet looks with momentary longing at the life of the *virgo* (see Duckworth 1994, 259; Gilula 1980, 152–53).

The *Hecyra* contains three *meretrices*, Philotis, Syra, and Bacchis. Syra is an old retired prostitute, Philotis is a minor "good faith" *meretrix* character, and together they have the standard conversation about taking care of one's retirement (58–75) (see Gilula 1980, 150–51; McGarrity 1980–81, 150–51). Although she only appears onstage at the end of the play, Bacchis is a more major character, for she is the hinge on which the plot turns. She is the former lover of the *adulescens*, Pamphilus, who grudgingly gave her up at his father's insistence to marry his wife. As Pamphilus's slave Parmeno tells it, after initially refusing all conjugal duties with his new wife, the *adulescens* found himself gradually coming to love her, because of her meek, submissive, properly wifely behavior, and coming to despise Bacchis, because she became more mercenary. Pamphilus left on a business trip and when he returned, found that his wife had given birth to a child in his absence. Furious at his apparent betrayal, he prepares to divorce her. It is Bacchis who figures out that the child is his—he raped his future wife at a festival in the dark—and selflessly effects the reunion of husband and wife, at the expense of a good customer for herself.

Yet even this remarkably selfless *meretrix* engages in deceit; she lies to the *senex* about having been the one to end the relationship with the *adulescens* as soon as he got married (750–52), when in fact, as the slave earlier revealed to the audience, he was the one who gradually ended relations with her after his marriage (167–70).[21] Bacchis is perhaps the most ambivalent prostitute we have encountered in this survey: she is reported to exhibit all of the typical mercenary behaviors of "bad faith" prostitutes in the first four acts of the play, yet she resolves the problem of the plot at her own expense; she seems to conduct herself in "good faith," yet she lies.

SUMMARY

Plautus's prostitutes tend to be rather clear-cut, with the major *meretrix* characters fairly evenly distributed between "good faith" and "bad faith" types. Terence's prostitutes are slightly more ambiguous, in keeping with Terence's general interest in unsettling audience expectations of stock characters. But every major *meretrix* character displays an ability to lie, flatter, and feign when it suits her purposes, and no *adulescens* rests completely secure in his relationship.

The prostitute's dangerous allure for the *adulescens* in Roman Comedy demonstrates the mechanism by which a society's low-Other becomes the object of desire. Prostitutes in Plautus and Terence all display a knack for acting, and all are accused, to some extent rightly, of being insincere performers. What seems especially marked is the *adulescens'* use of the language of love and trust, rather than that of commercial sex; the ideology of Roman Comedy makes the *meretrix emotionally* important. The *adulescens'* desire for the "good faith" *meretrix* is based on the idea of mutual devotion, but he expects her to help him in his money-swindling schemes; while the *adulescens'* desire for the "bad faith" *meretrix* is whipped to a froth by her teasing and flirting, her inconstancy, her elaborate adornment, her demands for money. In both cases, what ultimately arouses the *adulescens* and, at the same time, makes him anxious, are the markers of her despised status. The prostitute is *infamis;* the prostitute is a hired actor.[22] And the *adulescens* frets about the prostitute's trustworthiness in the same way that Roman intellectuals fret about theater's value.[23]

The insistent connections between prostitutes and actors made by the prostitute characters themselves, by the other characters onstage, and by structural features in the comedies, reveal that the *meretrix* is as much a metatheatrical figure for the actor as the *servus callidus.* The split of the stock character into "good faith" and "bad faith" *meretrices,* moreover, suggests a desire to clarify the character's essential duplicity, to maintain some control, through audience expectation, over the *meretrix's* mendaciousness. In a culture that both denigrated and desired theatrical entertainment, such a reaction is not surprising (see Barish 1981, ch.2; Beacham 1991, 65–67). But it is the "bad" qualities of prostitutes—their accessibility to anyone who can pay, their lack of commitment or loyalty, their very *infamia*—that make them, as low-Others, so useful and so desirable to the Roman cultural imagination.

Transvestite Trades

The third component of the correspondence between the actor and the prostitute at Rome is their shared custom of cross-dressing. Both female prostitutes and male actors (which is to say, all actors, except for mime actresses—who were commonly assumed to be whores) cross-dressed as part of their professional presentation: female prostitutes wore the toga, and male actors regularly costumed themselves as women to play female roles.[24]

The assumption of the toga is a complex cultural signifier. To contemporary Westerners, cross-dressing signifies gender deviance, perhaps gender defiance (thus, e.g., Butler 1990). But a woman dressing as a man can also signify within a culture what Marjorie Garber calls the "progress narrative"—that is, she "has" to cross-dress because it allows her access to opportunities or resources that she could not gain access to as a woman.[25] To the Romans, the woman wearing a toga signified that her sexual appetites exceeded the womanly ideal; she had "masculine" levels of lust (see Parker 1997, 58–59). We must be careful to "read" the cross-dressed female prostitute as the Romans did, not as we are tempted to by our own cultural predilections. It is instructive to note that female prostitutes in Elizabethan England and sixteenth-century Venice cross-dressed as well; they wore men's breeches (Garber 1992, 86). And they were similarly regarded as having unwomanly sexual appetites, lust beyond what a good woman should feel—lust more like that of a man. So to the Romans, the cross-dressed female prostitute makes a statement about sexuality, whereas to us, she makes a statement about gender.[26]

But why the toga, of all garments? It was not only because it signified that the prostitute had lusts more appropriate to a man. Wearing the toga, the ultimate signifier of Roman citizen manhood, marked out the female prostitute as a public figure, while working both to naturalize and to privilege the customary garment of respectable Roman women, the *palla*. Respectable citizen women wore the *palla*; citizen men, would-be ideal Roman masculine subjects, wore the toga; prostitutes (and convicted adulteresses), those women of insatiable appetite and no honor, wore the toga too (see Vout 1996, 215–16). Respectable Roman women, while apparently not as secluded as women were (at least ideally) in classical Athens, did not go out in public unattended, and they did not conduct business in the public eye alone. The female prostitute, on the other hand, made her living in the streets, or sitting in front of a brothel, or, if she was very unfortunate, in places like graveyards; she worked in the public eye, and she worked alone.[27] She acted, in this way, more like a citizen man, out on business in the Forum, than like a woman, tending to stay at home, or to go out accompanied by servants and/or male guardians.

This brings us to the final significance of the toga for the Roman prostitute: it signified that she acted. It was her costume. The prostitute's toga worked like any actor's costume: it called attention to the appearance-reality gap (that is, to the fact that she was a woman, but not one wearing a *palla*, not a good woman), even as it worked to assimilate the woman wearing it to her known role. It both revealed and concealed.

Conclusion

Prostitutes and actors were seen as analogous or equivalent low-Others from the point of view of the ideal Roman subject. The *meretrix* in Roman Comedy could be seen as a figure for the actor in society—and conversely, the actor could be seen as just another kind of prostitute:

they both displayed themselves in costume for the enjoyment of an audience, and they were both legally *infamis*. It was *because* the prostitute's appearance did not match her reality in many ways (in her cross-dressing, in her feigned affection, in her affluent appearance yet constant demands for more money) that she was low-Other, like the actor. Neither the prostitute nor the actor had any place in the high-stakes elite Roman game of politics and power, where it was of the utmost concern that a man's appearance as a public speaker should match his gestures, his words, and his conduct. It was the rhetoric of sincerity, ultimately, that defined the prostitute and the actor as *infamis*, and therefore as useful ideological opposites of the ideal Roman subject. And it was because prostitutes and actors flaunted their insincerity that they were terribly appealing to the upper orders as objects of desire. Their status as low-Other and their work as performers eroticized a status boundary, and in the process, revealed the dynamics of Roman subject formation.

Notes

1. I would like to thank the Women's Studies Program at Arizona State University for a summer research grant and the Department of Classics at Columbia University for allowing me access to Columbia's libraries, both of which aided in the completion of this paper.

2. On prostitutes' quarters in the Subura, see Juvenal 11.51, 141; Martial 2.17, 5.22.5–9, 6.66.1–3, 7.31, 10.94.5–6, 12.18.2; and Persius 5.32. For prostitutes in other sections of Rome, see Plautus *Curculio* 465–83, *Truculentus* 64–73, and *Cistellaria* 562; see also Williams (1999, 39).

3. Although the *lex Oppia* targeted women, Culham (1982, 792) makes the point that the true object of female ostentation is to reflect the man's status.

4. McGinn (1998c, 33, 41–42, 59, 65–69); Edwards (1997, passim, esp. 70, 72–73); Flemming (1999, 50–51); see also Dupont (1985, 95–102).

5. For connections between prostitutes and actors continuing into the imperial period, see Dupont (1985, 95), Edwards (1997), Flemming (1999), and D. R. French (1998).

6. See also Dupont (1985, 98–99). On the connections between actresses and prostitutes in Roman law, see D. R. French (1998, 296–97) and J. F. Gardner (1986, 246–47).

7. On Sulla and Metrobius (Plutarch *Sulla* 3.3), see Garton (1972, 148). On Catulus and Roscius (Cicero *De natura deorum* 1.79), see Weber (1996). See also Maecenas and Bathyllus in Tacitus *Annales* 1.54.

8. Edwards (1997, 79): "actors were explicitly in the business of trickery and illusion." I would argue that prostitutes were seen to be as well, but that gladiators, Edwards's other subject, were emphatically not.

9. The "good"/"bad" distinction among comic prostitutes goes back to remarks by Donatus *Ad Hecyra* 774 and Plutarch *Moralia* 712c. Some scholars use

these terms without reservation, such as W. S. Anderson (1984) and Gilula (1980). Other scholars, such as Brown (1990), Goldberg (1986), and Knorr (1995), question the utility of these categories, noting that they are ideologically loaded. For this reason, I use the terms "good faith" and "bad faith" (from the customer's point of view) to describe Roman comic *meretrices*.

10. See, e.g., *Heauton Timoroumenos* 322–25; J. N. Adams (1983, 325–26).

11. I therefore exclude Delphium in *Mostellaria* and Lemniselenis in *Persa*, although even these small roles may contain hints of deception (see *Persa* 798–801).

12. For an extended treatment of elite male anxiety about trying to have an exclusive relationship with a wily courtesan, see Sharon James's article in this volume.

13. All translations are my own; I follow Lindsay's (1980) edition of Plautus and Kauer, Lindsay, and Skutsch's (1961) edition of Terence, with occasional slight changes.

14. On *ornata*, see the discussion of *Truculentus*. That the prostitute could "pass" as a *matrona* is obviously a subject of some anxiety as well as of much comedy in a society as class conscious as Rome. After all, if clothing is used to indicate status (on which see "Transvestite Trades"), then a simple change of costume could potentially undermine the social order. See also D. R. French (1998, 296).

15. Cf. *Asinaria* 504–44, *Cistellaria* 78–81, *Mostellaria* 184–247, and *Hecyra* 58–75. Scapha here is the mother/*lena* figure.

16. Asides praising the "good faith" *meretrix*: 206–7, 222–23, 227–28, 233–34, 241–44. Asides threatening the "bad faith" *meretrix*: 191–93, 203, 212–13, 218–19, 237–38.

17. On the audience's sympathy for Diniarchus, see Moore (1998, 144–47). W. S. Anderson (1996) 85 finds him to be a "scoundrel," however.

18. See Muecke (1986, 224 n.44); cf. *Amphitruo* 200, *Bacchides* 75, *Curculio* 391, *Epidicus* 373, *Miles Gloriosus* 909, *Persa* 677, *Rudens* 1399, *Truculentus* 86, *Adelphoe* 734, *Heauton Timoroumenos* 782–83, 888, and 901, and *Hecyra* 188.

19. On Diniarchus's unusual position as both customer and confidante in this play, see Dessen (1977, 152–56).

20. Gilula (1980, 161–64) argues that Thais is as "bad" as any of Terence's other prostitutes, even though she admits that Thais's soliloquy proves the sincerity of her affections.

21. See Gilula (1980, 157–61); Goldberg (1986, 157–5); Knorr (1995, 224 n.11); McGarrity (1980–81, 154–55).

22. See Richlin (1993, 568) on the Roman actor as a sex object.

23. As is well known, a permanent stone amphitheater was not built at Rome until 55 BCE. See also Cicero *De republica* 4.9–10; Cornelius Nepos *De excellentibus ducibus exterarum gentium, prologus*.

24. On mime actresses, see D. R. French (1998) and J. F. Gardner (1986, 246–47. On *togate* prostitutes, see Cicero *Philippics* 2.44–5, [Tibullus] 3.16.3–5, Nonius 635L, possibly Martial 6.64.4, and possibly Horace *Satires* 1.2.63; see also Adams (1983, 340), Edwards (1997, 81), J. F. Gardner (1986, 251–52), and Richlin (1993b, 545). Kelly Olson's essay in this volume argues that the toga was not always worn by prostitutes, regardless of whether it was legally required and

even if it was a rhetorical commonplace. My thesis complements Olson's, since I am analyzing the discourse, the ideology, about prostitutes, as well as what we can glean of their social reality—and the discourse proscriptively insists that they wore the toga, as *the* sign of their status, even if in practice they did not always do so.

25. Garber (1992, 67–92) argues that the "progress narrative" often serves as a "cover story," that it often is not a sufficient explanation for a person's (or character's) cross-dressing.

26. McGinn (1998c,) 159, 164, 202 and n.499) discusses the prostitute's toga as "symbolic transvestism."

27. Even the high-class courtesans of Roman Comedy do much of their "work" in the public setting of the dinner party.

The Phallic Lesbian

Philosophy, Comedy, and Social Inversion in Lucian's Dialogues of the Courtesans

KATE GILHULY

Contrary to expectations that may be roused by the title, Lucian's *Dialogues of the Courtesans* have little to say about sex. The fifth dialogue is the only one that approaches an overt description of a courtesan's sexual exploits: one *hetaira*, Klonarion, interrogates her colleague, Leaina, about curious rumors that she has taken up with a rich woman from Lesbos. Leaina provides some details, but in the end shies away from providing the information crucial to satisfying her friend's curiosity. Although Lucian never answers the question that drives the dialogue— how do women do it?—he presents a fuller depiction of love between women than any of his literary predecessors. This paper seeks to understand what is at stake in this representation. Why does Lucian choose a female homosexual relationship, a topic which Greek literature seems largely to have passed over in silence, as the frame of the most explicit discussion of sex in the *Dialogues of the Courtesans?* In what follows, I will suggest that the way that Lucian conjures the lesbian out of archaic Greek and classical Athenian literature is designed to evoke the Greek literary tradition in an alienated way and thus problematizes the Athenian past of the Second Sophistic.[1]

Lucian constructs the marginal character of the Greek homosexual woman out of images of sexual and geographical alterity drawn from the center of the classical tradition. The ways that Lucian evokes classical notions of sexual difference are varied, and some allusions are more nebulous than others. There is one allusion, however, that seems overwhelmingly deliberate and clear: after some groping in the dark, Klonarion identifies Leaina's new friend as a *hetairistria*, a noun that identifies her as a woman who has sexual relations with other women. It is found elsewhere in classical Greek literature only in Plato's *Symposium*, in Aristophanes' speech about Eros (189c2–d6). David Halperin has suggested that Lucian's use of the term is a deliberate gloss on this passage.[2] Sir Kenneth Dover notes that Aristophanes' discussion of Eros is "the only surviving passage from classical literature which acknowledges the existence of female homosexuality" (1980, 118). It is doubtless that Lucian's resuscitation of this anomaly is an explicit reference to Plato. Lucian's evocation of a spectrum of alternative sexualities in this dialogue only makes sense in the context of the reference to Plato's *Symposium*.

The possibility that these dialogues were performed by Lucian himself, which the *prolaliai*, or introductory pieces, generally suggest, makes the unprecedented portrayal of a female homosexual even more extraordinary.[3] While the character in question, Megilla, has no actual role in the dialogue—she speaks only through quotation—the idea that Lucian would inhabit this subject position even from two removes seems to further flaunt the conventional silence accorded this sexual subject. I think the assumption of a performance context draws Lucian's own subjectivity into the interpretive arena, and for this reason I read this dialogue with reference to the persona that Lucian constructs for himself elsewhere in his writings.

Lucian lived approximately between 115–180 CE, during the period named by Philostratus as the Second Sophistic. While Lucian is not included among the sophists Philostratus remembers, it seems clear that he participated in this intellectual culture, traveling and performing before highly educated Greek-speaking audiences. In his extensive corpus, he presents himself as a native Syrian who has become culturally Greek in order to make a life for himself in the economy of the Roman empire. Simon Swain describes Lucian as having a Semitic "cultural-religious identity," while being cognitively Hellenic and politically Roman (1996, 314). Lucian frequently depicts an author figure

defending his literary innovations: in the *Double Accusation* this character is identified as the Syrian, while in *Fisherman* the defensive creator
speaks as *Parrhesiades*—son of the embodiment of the Athenian democratic ideal, free speech. Tim Whitmarsh cautions against searching for
a unified subject behind the masks Lucian wears, noting that, "for Lucian (always exploiting his marginal position vis-à-vis the Graeco-
Roman mainstream), identity is, as we shall see, not the motivating
force for composing, but part of the literary game that he plays: it is a
ludic construct, not an inspirational force" (2001, 250). His writing reveals that he is an astute reader of the classical tradition. Even R. Helm,
who derided Lucian as a sensation-mongering journalist and described
him as unprincipled and unoriginal, had to admit the purity of Lucian's
Attic style (1906, 6-7; see also Wilamowitz-Moellendorff 1912, 248-49).[4]

Throughout his writing, Lucian seems to play with the tension between self and other created by his status as a foreigner who traffics in
the Greek cultural past. His variegated identity is perhaps captured in
an intriguing remark he makes in the *Double Accusation,* in which he describes himself as *barbaros*—paradoxically designating himself as other.[5]
This self-description reveals a "double-consciousness" (Winkler 1990,
162-88): from his position within the Greek cultural tradition he identifies himself as an ethnic outsider. The dissonant juncture of self and
other, I think, is a thematic program that permeates Lucian's writing.
Here I argue that Lucian's depiction of the phallic lesbian in the fifth dialogue is an emblem of the discordant union of self and other; a strident
juxtaposition of identity and alienation operates in this text on the levels
of genre, gender, and cultural identity.

Genre

The *Dialogues of the Courtesans* belong to a literary form that Lucian
claims to have invented—the comic dialogue—in which he combines
elements of comedy and philosophy, noting that the two make an uncomfortable fit. In the *You Are a Prometheus in Words* (hereafter referred
to as *Prometheus Es*), Dialogue and Comedy are personified. Dialogue is
portrayed as a serious person who spends his time philosophizing,
while Comedy is given over to Dionysus and is in the habit of mocking
Dialogue and his cohorts. The speaker takes credit for bringing these
disparate types together: "And in fact we dared to bring these elements
thus disposed toward each other together and to harmonize them, even
though they were not entirely ready to be persuaded, nor did they

readily put up with the union" (6).[6] Scholars have disputed which of his dialogues Lucian is referring to in these remarks, since the chronology of his works is uncertain. R. Helm (1906, 280–82) and J. Schwartz (1965, 144) both believe that the remarks in *Zeuxis* and *Prometheus Es* refer to the *Dialogues of the Courtesans* and other works that they argue precede Lucian's "Menippean" phase. J Hall (1981, 31) and P. McCarthy (1934) disagree with this claim, arguing that the comedy Lucian refers to in *Prometheus Es* is Old as opposed to New Comedy because Dialogue's companions seem modeled on one of the inhabitants of the think tank in Aristophanes' *Clouds* (Hall 1981, 29). Therefore, they reason, these remarks could not apply to the *Dialogues of the Courtesans,* which are obviously inspired by New Comedy.[7] I find the argument that Lucian implies that he yoked Dialogue to Old Comedy *exclusively* to be specious. The specific allusion to Aristophanes gives authority to Lucian's comic roots, but does not in any way exclude Middle or New Comedy from the reference. "*Komoidia*" means comedy as a whole, and as I argue here this dialogue evokes both New and Old Comedy. Lucian's description of his works as an uneasy combination of comedy and philosophy provides a useful generic characterization of these dialogues, and informs my approach to them.[8]

The courtesan, at home on the comic stage and frequently associated with philosophers and statesmen, makes a perfect mouthpiece for this new genre that joins the characters of comedy with the form of philosophical dialogue.[9] A scholiast remarks on the debt Lucian's courtesans owe to New Comedy: "One must know that all these *hetairai* have been the subjects of comedy for all the comic poets, but especially for Menander, from whom, in fact, all the material for the Lucian in the present work is provided in abundance" (Rabe 1906, 275). Karl Mras's study on the personal names in the *Dialogues of the Courtesans* provides interesting statistics about literary origins of the characters who people these dialogues. Almost one half of the names of the lovers, their fathers, and other Athenian personalities (sixteen out of thirty-six) are at least mentioned in other works by Lucian, whereas the majority of the courtesan names (twenty-two out of thirty-seven) are not, but are rather drawn from New Comedy (1916).[10] By thus mingling the courtesans of New Comedy with his own characters, Lucian has, in a sense, disembedded courtesans from New Comedy and relocated them in the midst of a world of his own making.

In one of the few studies exclusively devoted to this text, Philippe LeGrand methodically elucidates the character types, themes, plots and even physiognomical traits that Lucian drew *("a tiré")* from Menander. Indeed Leaina is a common name for a *hetaira*. The oldest attested courtesan with this name was the associate of Harmodius and Aristogeiton whom Hippias tortured to death in 514 BCE, trying to compel her to betray the tyrannicides' plot. To honor her, the Athenians erected a statue of a lioness with no tongue.[11] The second Leaina was the lover of Demetrios Poliorcetes (Kurke 2002).

LeGrand is forced to admit, however, that Megilla and Demonassa, the lesbian couple in the fifth dialogue, whom he refers to as *"vicieuses personnes,"* have no comic precedent.[12] We must then turn to philosophy for the forerunners of Lucian's lesbian lovers.[13] Casting courtesans in this hybrid genre, Lucian depicts the prostitute by drawing on various representational strategies present in her literary heritage, at the same time that he destabilizes the generic strictures that contain these depictions, and to some extent determine them.

Gender

When we consider these dialogues in terms of our expectations of philosophy, they present other problems. In the classical context, the dialogue form is the province of men, who are at leisure to pursue philosophical abstractions. It could be argued that the form itself constitutes its subjects as elite. Lucian's dialogues, in contrast, depict discussions by socially marginalized women that concern the issues of plying a bodily trade. Since the classical period, *hetairai*, in Athens at least, usually had been members of politically excluded groups. During the Second Sophistic, there is evidence of a growing negative moral tinge to this profession.[14] This transposition of the dialogue form from the masculine, abstract domain of philosophy to the volatile and feminized realm of the body,[15] erotics, and economics constitutes a social inversion, in which outsiders inhabit the position of the social elite.[16]

Before I begin to elaborate the effects that gender inversion (and the other overturned social hierarchies such as class, status, and ethnic identity that follow from this transposition) has on (what Lucian read as) the philosophical construction of sex, I will begin with a brief summary of Lucian's text. In response to her friend's questioning about the strange *(kaina)* rumors circulating about her intimate relationship with another woman, Leaina admits that the gossip is true. This piques Klonarion's curiosity about the mechanics of lesbian sex. She probes for practical details. Leaina reluctantly narrates to Klonarion her experience of a postsympotic night of three-way sex with the Lesbian Megilla and her wealthy Corinthian friend Demonassa. Megilla, aroused by foreplay, removes her close-fitting wig to reveal a close shaven head, after the manner of a male athlete. Megilla asks Leaina if she has ever seen such a handsome young man. Leaina denies that Megilla is a man, and Megilla retorts: "Don't make a woman out of me" (5.3).

Then Megilla calls herself Megillos, the husband of Demonassa (5.3). Leaina asks her if she is a transvestite, hiding among women like Achilles? Equipped with a penis and therefore able to mimic a man sexually? "Do you even have a penis *(to andreion)* and do you do to Demonassa what men do?" (5.3). Megilla/Megillos replies that she doesn't have a penis but something far more pleasant. When Leaina asks if she is a hermaphrodite, Megilla responds that she is "all man" *(pan anêr)*. In her incomprehension, Leaina conjectures that perhaps Megilla is a transsexual, like Tiresias. Megilla explains to Leaina that she was born similar to women but with the mind *(gnômê)* and the desire *(epithumia)* of a man. In the course of attempting to coax Leaina into trying her, Megilla says that she has a penis substitute *(exô gar ti anti tou andreiou* [5.4]). At last Leaina, persuaded by entreaties and gifts, has sex with Megilla, which, she says, Megilla enjoyed very much. Klonarion, persisting in her efforts to understand the mechanics of this encounter, presses Leaina further, who refuses the information so eagerly sought: "Don't question me too closely about these things, they're shameful; so, by heavenly Aphrodite, I won't tell you!" (5.4).

When Megilla takes on the masculine form of her name, Megillos, she calls to mind the Spartan interlocutor in Plato's *Laws*. The passages relevant to our discussion here are those in which the legislation of sexuality is discussed. On two occasions, the Athenian employs the Socratic method against Megillos on the subject of Spartan sexual practices as a means of justifying his exclusion of pederasty from the constitution he is suggesting for the incipient Cretan city. First the lawgiver finds fault with the Spartan (and Cretan) gymnasia and common meals *(sussitia)*, characterizing them as institutions responsible for the corruption of pleasure:

So for example these gymnasia and these common meals, while for the time being they are useful for the states in many other respects, in times of civil strife they are a liability. The young men of Milesia and Boeotia and Thurii show this. Moreover, this ancient custom seems to have corrupted the pleasures of love, which are natural not only to men but also to beasts. Your states are primarily blamed for this, along with as many others that are especially supportive of gymnasia; whether considering these things either in fun or in earnest, one must consider that when the female goes into a shared state of generation with the nature of males, the pleasure under these circumstances seems to be given in return according to nature, but when male mates male or female mates female it is held to be against nature and this brazen act exists because of the powerlessness of the first practitioners against pleasure. (636B)

For Plato here, heterosexuality is a natural timeless state of affairs, in which there is an equilibrium between pleasure and product. Homosexuality, on the other hand, is an historical development, invented by early practitioners of pleasure and developed within the institution of the gymnasium. In the second passage, Plato opposes Spartan practice to nature and argues that pederasty does not encourage virtue because it necessitates that a male play the woman's part:

For whereas in regard to other matters not a few, Crete generally and Lacedaemon furnish us (and rightly) with no little assistance in the framing of laws which differ from those in common use,—in regard to the passions of sex (for we are alone by ourselves) they contradict us absolutely. For if we were to follow in nature's steps and enact that law which held good before the days of Laius, declaring that it is right to refrain from indulging in the same kind of intercourse with men and boys as with women, and adducing as evidence thereof the nature of wild beasts, and pointing out how male does not touch male for this purpose, since it is unnatural,—in all this we would probably be using an argument neither convincing nor in any way consonant with your States. Moreover, that object which, as we affirm, the lawgiver ought always to have in view does not agree with these practices. For the enquiry we always make is this—which of the proposed law tends toward virtue and which not. Come then, suppose we grant that this practice is now legalized, and that it is noble and in no way ignoble, how far would it promote virtue? Will it engender in the soul of him who is seduced a courageous character, or in the soul of the seducer the quality of temperance? Nobody would ever believe this; on the contrary, as all men will blame the cowardice of the man who always yields to pleasures and is never able to hold out against them, will they not likewise reproach that man who plays the woman's part with the resemblance he bears to his model? Is there any man who will ordain by law a practice like that? Not one I should say, if he has a notion of what true law is. (836B; tr. Bury [1926] 1984, 151–52)

In this passage, the historical specificity of the development of pederasty is elaborated and given temporal and spatial dimensions: Laius is identified as the first to have discovered homosexual sex, and Sparta and Crete are identified as the primary locations that support homosexuality. Because he is Spartan, Megillos represents a pro-pederasty perspective and it is for this reason that he assumes the position of interlocutor when extramarital love is at issue.[17] Dover argues that the passages from the *Laws* spawned long-held generalizations that see Doric culture as the breeding ground of Greek homosexuality and classical Sparta and Crete as permissive hotbeds of homosexual behavior (1978, 196).

Lucian's characterization of Megilla relies not only on the image of Spartan sexual practice evoked in the *Laws*, but also on the subsequent tradition it inaugurated. In the Athenian imagination at least, Spartan sexual mores were divergent on a number of counts. Numerous Greek historians comment on the Spartan practice of having more than one sexual or marriage partner (for a discussion of these practices see Cartledge [2001, 124]). Perhaps related to these variant marriage practices is the perception that Spartan women were loose and licentious. This sentiment was famously expressed in Aristotle's *Politics*. In a discussion introduced by an explicit reference to Plato's *Laws*, he faults Lycurgus for failing to create laws capable of controlling women: "For the lawgiver, wishing the whole city to be of strong character, displays his intention clearly in relation to the men, but in the case of the women has entirely neglected the matter; for they live dissolutely in respect of every sort of dissoluteness, and luxuriously. So that the inevitable result is that in a state thus constituted wealth is held in honor, especially if it is the case that the people are ruled by their women" (1269b20–25; tr. Rackham [1932] 1990, 135). That a lesbian who hosts a symposium that runs late into the night and that culminates in a ménage à trois would be thought of as intemperate and abandoned to luxury hardly needs saying. Megilla has more than one sexual partner, inviting Leaina into her marriage with Demonassa. She is obviously wealthy, suggested not only by her ability to host a symposium with hired entertainment but also by the fact that she can overcome Leaina's reluctance with jewelry and fine clothes.

Megilla's masculine-looking features, and the detail that her head has been shaved like that of an athlete, combine to provide an image of a physically fit figure, an image perhaps intended to elicit the Spartan practice of incorporating exercise in the education of women. The image of the buff Spartan woman is also evoked by Aristophanes in *Lysistrata*, when the heroine marvels at Lampito's well-conditioned physique (78–84). Megilla's shaved head recalls the Spartan marriage ritual, as recorded by Plutarch (*Life of Lycurgus* 15.5) in which the bride's hair was cut very short and she was dressed in men's clothing and then laid in the dark on a bed waiting to be "captured" by her husband.[18] Plutarch also notes that the practice of female pederasty was not unusual in Spartan culture: "So distinguished are erotics among them that even noble women love maidens" (18.4).

There is one way in which the dialogue conforms to normative Athenian sexuality. It is relentlessly focused on phallic sexuality: Leaina cannot imagine sex without a phallus, and Megilla indeed admits that she has a substitute penis. According to Halperin, Greek sexual discourse is phallic, "because (1) sexual contacts are polarized around phallic action—i.e., they are defined by who has the phallus and what is done with it; (2) sexual pleasures other than phallic pleasures do not count in categorizing sexual contacts; (3) in order for a contact to qualify as sexual, one—and no more than one—of the two partners is required to have a phallus. . . . [I]n the case of sex between women, one partner—the 'tribad'—is assumed to possess a phallus equivalent [an overdeveloped clitoris] and to penetrate the other" (1990a, 166 n.83). The substitute that Megilla has could be an overdeveloped clitoris (see Halperin 1993, 429 n.29), or maybe even an *olisbos*, although these implements are associated with masturbation rather than intercourse (see Henderson 1991, 115 n.40 and 133). It is significant that Megilla's substitute is articulated only by hints and oblique reference. Its exact form is never named. This reticence to define the substitute penis deprives it of concrete form and forces us to interpret it on the symbolic level. It is, to borrow the formulation of Judith Butler, a lesbian phallus (1993, 57–92).

Although Lucian does not make explicit the cultural signification of a woman's possession of the phallus, one of his contemporaries does address the symbolism of body parts, and their transference. Artemidorus provides an explication of the penis as symbol, which I quote here at length:

The penis corresponds to one's parents, on the one hand, because it has a relationship with the seed. It resembles children, on the other hand, in that it is itself the cause of children. It signifies a wife or a mistress, since it is made for sexual intercourse. It indicates brothers and all blood relatives, since the interrelation of the entire house depends upon the penis. It is a symbol of strength and physical vigor, because it is itself the cause of these qualities. That is why some people call the penis "one's manhood" ["*andreia*"]. It corresponds to speech and education because the penis [like speech] is very fertile. . . .

Furthermore, the penis is also a sign of wealth and possessions because it alternately expands and contracts and because it is able to produce and eliminate.

It signifies secret plans in that the word [*mêdea*] is used to designate both plans and a penis. It indicates poverty, servitude, and bonds, because it is also called "the essential thing" [*"anagkaion"*]) and is a symbol of necessity [*anagkê*].

The penis signifies, moreover, the enjoyment of dignity and respect. For the enjoyment of all of one's civil rights [*epitimia*] is also called "respect" [*"aidôs"*]. Therefore if the penis is present and it stays in its proper place, it signifies that whatever is represented by the penis will remain in its present state. If the penis grows larger, what it represents will increase; if the penis is taken away, what it represents will be lost. If the penis is doubled, everything will be doubled, with the exception of a wife or mistress; these will be lost. For it is impossible to use two penises at one time. (*Interpretation of Dreams* 1.45; tr. R. White 1975, 38–39)

Clearly the penis had a broad range of signification: the extended family, power, language facility, wealth, property, poverty, servitude and civil rights. Artemidorus describes a cultural symbolism in which one's sexual disposition toward the phallus is linked to one's social, political, and economic position. A person's dream image of a penis reveals the power dynamic between the person and what the phallus represents. For Foucault, the penis, as it is described in this passage, is a symbol of mastery: "Self-mastery, since its demands are likely to enslave us if we allow ourselves to be coerced by it; superiority over sexual partners since it is by means of the penis that penetration is carried out; status and privileges, since it signifies the whole field of kinship and social activity" (1986, 34). Megilla refers to the penis for which she has a substitute as *"to andreion"* ("the man thing"), a term that Artemidorus associates particularly with a connotation of masculine power and strength. The phallus that is represented in negative relief in this dialogue attributes to Megilla the qualities of power and dominance that the Greeks associated with male sexuality. Her masculinity is emphasized in the dialogue, she is "manfaced," "terribly manly"; she doesn't have "the man thing" (*"to andreion"*), but she does have a substitute. Like so many other men in the dialogues, she is able to buy Leaina and enjoys herself while the unimpassioned flute girl looks on.

What does the phallus mean in a feminine context? Again, Artemidorus provides information regarding the cultural conception of women having sex with each other: this act, along with sex with gods, animals, corpses and oneself is classified under the rubric of unnatural sexual intercourse (1.80). Within his interpretation of dreams of "unnatural acts," Artemidorus deems those dreams propitious in which a woman is the actor and ominous if she is acted on. Though it is unnatural for a woman to master anyone, in the code of dreams, it is better than being mastered. Foucault attributes the inclusion of lesbian sex in the category of "unnatural intercourse" to the implication of penetration in this relationship: "By some artificial means or other, a woman contrives to usurp the role of the man, wrongfully takes his position and possesses another woman. Between two men, penetration, the manly act, par excellence, is not a transgression of nature. . . . By contrast, between two women a similar act, which is performed in defiance of what they both are and by resorting to subterfuge, is every bit as unnatural as human intercourse with a god or an animal" (1986, 24). If we accept Foucault's reading and use Artemidorus's text as some kind of barometer of the social signification of female penetration of the female, the fifth dialogue seems all the more strange. In fact, even Lucian's text suggests that the subject is taboo: Leaina and Klonarion are both a little uncomfortable with the topic. Klonarion's curiosity reveals her inexperience in such matters and Leaina makes it perfectly clear that she was persuaded to participate only because of the gifts offered in return (Cantarella 1992, 93).

When Leaina describes Megilla as "terribly manly" (5.1), Klonarion construes this as a reference to a *hetairistria*,[19] which she goes on to describe as a man-faced woman who doesn't like to associate with men but only with women. As I mentioned above, this calls to mind Plato's use of the word "*hetairistria.*" This occurs when it is Aristophanes' turn to hymn Eros. He describes an earlier incarnation of humanity made up of spherical beings belonging to three genders, male, female, and androgyne. Confident in their size and strength, they make an attack on Olympus. In punishment for their insolent and incorrigible behavior, Zeus orders these round beings cut in half and thus it is that we spend our lives longing for the other cutlet of our former selves. From the androgynous ball come men and women who love each other, the divided male produced boys who love men and men who love boys, and the female sphere produced women who love women:

So then, as many men as are cut from the combined (sphere), which at the time was called androgyne, they are lovers of women and many adulterers have been born from this breed, also as many women who love men and are adulteresses come from this group. As many women as have been cut from the female (sphere), these pay no attention to men, but rather are attracted to women and *hetairistriai* come from this breed. As many as are cut from the male sphere, they pursue the male. While they are boys, since they are slices of the male, they love men and they enjoy lying down together with and embracing men, and these are the best of boys and young men, because they are the bravest by nature. (*Symposium* 191e–92a)

Both the androgyne and the pure male spheres produce complementary individuals—men and women, or *erastai* and *eromenoi*. Plato's Aristophanes doesn't acknowledge any power differential or identify distinct roles for the female slices. If we consider Lucian's text a gloss in our understanding of the word *"hetairistria,"* then Aristophanes has perhaps identified one part of a complementary pair. *"Hetairistria"* is an agent noun that is a secondary formation verbally derived from *"hetairizein,"* which means to be *"hetairos"* with an emphasis on habituality. *"Hetairistria"* denotes the female analog to the male relationship of *"hetairesis"*—the abstract noun, used of a man who played the homosexual role analogous to that of a *hetaira* (Dover 1978, 20 and 172).[20] Dover suggests that the word is so infrequently used because it was taboo: "The complete silence of comedy on the subject of female homosexuality is a reflex of male anxiety. There are such things as 'taboo' subjects which the comic poets did not try to exploit for humorous purposes; the plague of 430 BC is one and menstruation is another" (1978, 173). If the topic of female homosexuality was considered inappropriate for the comic stage, then we must consider Plato's depiction of Aristophanes with this in mind. It has been noted that Plato's *Symposium* takes many opportunities to portray Aristophanes in an unflattering light. In the original grouping of speakers, Aristophanes was relegated to the less exalted group, together with Pausanius and Phaedrus; he only obtained a better position in the lineup through the undignified bodily eruption of hiccups. Later, Alcibiades' drunken interruption contrives to deny Aristophanes the opportunity of responding to Diotima's refutation of his version of *erôs*. When Alcibiades enters as "Dionysus," he crowns Agathon for his victory in the tragic competition, after noting that Socrates has not chosen to sit next to a joker like Aristophanes (213c4) but instead the beautiful Agathon (213c4–5). He also crowns Socrates "for he is the conqueror of all in conversation" (213e3). Even the authors' sympotic endurance is agonistic: at the end of the evening as Socrates compels his listeners to agree that the genius behind comedy and tragedy are the same, Aristophanes drops off to sleep, and is followed by Agathon (223d6–8). The text poses a myriad of suppressed contests in which Aristophanes comes up the loser. It has been suggested that Plato's unflattering portrayal of Aristophanes was meant as a retaliation for his depiction of Socrates in *Clouds* (Brochard 1926, 89–90; Clay 1975; Nightingale 1995, 172–73). We should add to this characterization the extreme coarseness Plato's audience would have understood when Aristophanes mentions the *hetiaristria*, uttering a word in the sanctity of a symposium that is not even fit for the comic stage.[21]

Lucian is entering into a moment in the classical past when comedy and philosophy, as embodied by Aristophanes and Socrates, struggled with one another in dialogue. In the fifth of the *Dialogues of the Courtesans* he revives the competition, but the tables are turned. In this instance, philosophy is brought to task through the filter of comic subjects, to be exposed for the inconsistencies and incompleteness of its construction of sexuality.

Lucian's dialogue makes one other reference to Plato's *Symposium:* when Leaina becomes reticent about the specific details of her sexual encounter at the end of the dialogue, she pointedly swears her silence by Ouranian Aphrodite, thus ending the conversation between the two *hetairai.* Here we might remember the stalwart Leaina who withstood torture and was memorialized by the tongueless lion, and we will certainly think of the distinction Pausanias made early on in Plato's *Symposium* between Pandemian ("Common") Eros and Ouranian ("Heavenly") Eros (180c1–82a6). Pandemian Eros is the child of the Aphrodite born from a female (Dione) and describes indiscriminate love of the flesh, including the flesh of women. Ouranian Love describes the noble Eros that motivates *paiderasts* (180c1–85c5). The symposiasts devote themselves mainly to descriptions of the less bodily, nobler aspects of desire; Lucian's dialogue, on the other hand, describes an erotic pursuit that would have to be classified as *pandemian:* the subjects are exclusively female and their relationship is devoted strictly to pleasure. The telos of the dialogue is the expression of a body part. For a prostitute homosexual lover to restrain her communication about the phallus in the name of Ouranian Aphrodite enacts a complete inversion of Plato's erotic hierarchy.

In *The Symposium,* the distinction between Ouranian and Pandemian Aphrodite is raised again by Diotima when she discredits Pausanias's interpretation of *erôs.* Since Socrates is purportedly recalling an interaction he had in the past with Diotima, and she is not present at the symposium, this reference to Pausanias's speech has been interpreted as Socrates' covert acknowledgement that Diotima was merely a persona he donned, in the spirit of sympotic play (Halperin 1990a, 289).

The verbal echoes of the *Symposium* invite connections between it and the dialogue: both the figure of Diotima and phallus of Megilla are absent presences. Diotima is a disembodied female voice appropriated by a male. Similarly, we never actually confront Megilla's phallus in Lucian's dialogue. It is a disembodied male part possessed by a woman. Halperin argues that Diotima's gender is a mask that Socrates wears in order to appropriate positive aspects of Greek notions of female sexuality for his (male) philosophical project. By speaking through Diotima, Socrates incorporates reciprocity and procreation, elements associated with feminine sexuality, into a system of emphatically masculine erotics (1990a, 288). The fifth *Dialogue of the Courtesans* systematically inverts Plato's gender play: here, a woman appropriates masculine attributes for an exclusively feminine erotics that is neither reciprocal nor reproductive.

While the notion of a lesbian phallus is anomalous in literature from the classical period, through various means of allusion, Lucian has nonetheless succeeded in situating his gender play in the classical Greek literary and philosophical tradition. Indeed literary allusion is itself all about absent presences. Lucian's narrative makes direct mention of Achilles and Tiresias to remind his audience of the role of crossdressing and transsexuality in the mythic record. The name of the character Megilla/Megillos, as well as her actions and looks evoke a myriad of images of Sparta as a site of alterity. The verbal references to the *Symposium* recall Plato's manipulation of gender through the figure of Diotima. Even the native cities of Demonassa and Megilla encode sexual stereotypes. But while Lucian's dialogue may recycle classical representations of sexuality, the resulting image resists being integrated with that tradition.

Instead, Lucian's dialogue focuses on the feminine penetration of the feminine, precisely the sexual power relation that is all but unnamed and excluded from the sexual-social hierarchy of the ancient Greeks. Numerous modern theorists of ancient sexuality have described an almost seamless cathexis of gender and sexual role in which "male" means "actor/penetrator" and female means "submissive receptor."[22] Judith Butler reads this sexual system of male as penetrator and female as penetrated as a heterosexual matrix that assures the stability of gendered positions. This matrix is constituted through exclusions and prohibitions. "He is the impenetrable penetrator, and she, the invariably penetrated" (1993, 50.) While James Davidson has recently questioned the stability of the equation of male and penetrator, the designation of female as receptive remains uncontested (2001). Perhaps it would be enough to say that it was the exclusion of the penetrating female alone that grounded the matrix of Athenian gender and power.

On the level of culture, perhaps we might understand the Roman literary tradition as the absent presence that underwrites the construction of sexuality in this dialogue. Judith Hallett has shown that a pattern of denial of the reality of Roman female homosexuality can be detected in the work of authors in the republican and early imperial periods. In an analysis of depictions of female homosexuality in a spectrum of Latin writers including Plautus, Ovid, Seneca the younger and Seneca the elder, Phaedrus, and Martial, she identifies a practice of representing female homosexuals as masculine women associated with the Greek past. Her assessment of Roman literary practice precisely conforms to Lucian's strategy in the fifth dialogue, except that he imports this Latin literary practice into the sphere of Greek literature (1989a).

Lucian's dialogue uses the spectrum of gendered representations in the classical tradition in order to extend the limit of that spectrum. In the representational economy of classical Athens, it is not merely the case that the phallic lesbian did not exist, but more than that, she could not exist. Megilla's possession of the phallus serves as an overbearing advertisement that the system that created all her parts is no longer live. The inversion of the Greek cultural legacy as represented by the lesbian phallus can be read as suggesting the possibility of the transference of power on a broad scale to the one excluded. Lucian's play with the past problematizes the authority and prestige inherent in the Greek cultural tradition. In his hands, it has become a malleable material that can be shaped by anyone, to appropriate authority even for a foreign feminine sexual subaltern.

Cultural Identity

If Lucian's characterization of Megilla is meant to refer to Plato's Megillos and elicit an association with Sparta, then we must consider why it is that Leaina explicitly mentions that Megilla is from Lesbos and Demonassa is Corinthian. Dover suggests that the significance lies in the fact that these cities were famed for their "sexual enterprise." Corinth was known for its prostitutes, while Lesbos gave its name to the verb "lesbiazein," the meaning of which ranges from "flirtation" to "prostitution" to "fellatio" (Dover [1978] 1989, 183, and 135). In fact this dialogue is the oldest preserved text in which an explicit association between female homosexuality and the island of Lesbos is made. When Klonarion is asking Leaina about her new client, she says: "I don't understand what you are talking about, unless she happens to be a *hetairistria;* for they say there are such man-faced women on Lesbos who do not like to endure it from men, but like to get close to women as though they were men" (5.2) Lucian is able to leverage the sex reputations of three cities for his two characters.

When Leaina was seeking to understand the nature of Megilla's sexuality, she tried to draw a comparison to Tiresias, whom she naively says she had heard about from her Boeotian courtesan colleague, Ismenadora, when she repeated her hearth stories (5.4). The specific regional identification draws attention to notions of Theban nonnormative sexuality of which Tiresias is an example.[23] Lucian expands on an Athenian tradition of associating peculiar sexual cultures with various non-Athenian locations. He maps out a sexual geography of Greece eliciting the sexual reputations of Lesbos, Corinth, Sparta, and Thebes in the process of defining Megilla.[24] The result is that she doesn't bear the stereotype of any particular place but is explicitly constructed as a mélange of images of sexual alterity.

In his creation of the phallic lesbian, Lucian adds a new position to the constellation of sex and gender positions in Greek literature—one that undermines the stability of the system that created them. This impossible position, I think, is a local manifestation of Lucian's invented genre—the uncomfortable mingling of philosophy and comedy. When a courtesan occupies the place of a philosopher, a world of other impossibilities follows. Lucian's motivation for creating this jarring genre might be found in "the Syrian's" defense of his pairing of philosophical dialogue with comedy. In the *Double Accusation*, he says that although he has brought dialogue down from its lofty heights, making it accessible and funny, it's not the worse thing he could have done (34):[25] "I don't think Dialogue could charge that I stripped him of his Hellenic cloak, exchanging it for a foreign one, even though I myself appear to be a barbarian [*barbaros*]." This statement seems to indicate that Lucian's desire to alter conventions of the Greek literary tradition is a manifestation of his relationship to this tradition as an outsider. The new and strange possibilities opened up by the Greek comic dialogue were necessary to make room for the barbarian self.

Notes

I would like to thank Leslie Kurke, Mark Griffith, Greg Thalmann, and Amy Richlin for reading earlier drafts. Parts of this paper were presented at the 2002 annual meeting of the American Philological Association for the Lambda Classical Caucus panel "Beyond Marriage: Configurations of Same-Sex Bonding in the Ancient Mediterranean" and at the conference "Prostitution in the Ancient World" in Madison, Wisconsin. Thanks are due to the helpful comments of participants at both conferences.

1. Some scholars avoid using the term "lesbian" to refer to female homosexuals because it does not correlate with ancient sexual associations with the

island of Lesbos (e.g., Dover [1978] 1989, 182). For a discussion of terminology see Brooten (1996, 4–26). Since this dialogue does make the association explicit, the issue is moot here.

2. This usage is the only surviving record of this word in a nongrammatical context (Halperin 1990a, 180 n.2).

3. Branham (1989, 237) notes that "the *prolaliai* mediate between Lucian the performing artist and his audience." For a study of *prolaliai* that has interesting implications for the context of Lucian's performances as well as his artistic development see Nesselrath (1990, 111–40).

4. For a fascinating discussion of Lucian's reception in Germany with interesting implications about racial politics see Holzberg (1988).

5. Lucian refers to himself as barbarian in numerous places, e.g., *Scythian* 9, *The Uneducated Book Collector* 19; *The False Critic* 1 and 11. See Swain (1996, 299).

6. Greek translations are my own unless otherwise indicated.

7. Hall (1981, 32–33) does not accept these dialogues and others in their category (i.e., *Dialogues of the Gods, Dialogues of the Sea Gods*) as generically original; rather she classifies them as "transpositions," borrowing the term from Bompaire (1958), by which she means a paraphrase of poetry into prose. She cites Dio Chrysostom 58 and 59 as earlier examples of this genre.

8. Swain (1996, 311) notes that commentators are obsessed with this question and also interprets Lucian to be referring to a broad range of works, including the comic dialogues.

9. For a discussion of prostitution in Roman Comedy, see Anne Duncan's essay in this volume.

10. It should also be noted that seven of the courtesan names appear elsewhere in Lucian's work.

11. For further discussion see Catherine Keesling's essay in this volume.

12. "Rien, absolument rien n'autorise à penser que ses vicieuses personnes aient jamais eu leurs pareilles dans une aucune oeuvre comique" (LeGrand 1907, 230–31). This approach fits neatly into a debate about Lucian's literary methods that has polarized recent contributions to Lucianic studies. One side of the issue is represented by Bompaire (1958), who argues that Lucian's corpus is characterized by mimesis of pre-Roman Greek literature and can be understood almost exclusively in terms of that tradition. On the other side of the issue, Jones (1986) suggests that we understand Lucian as a contemporary satirist whose work can only be fully appreciated when interpreted in light of its second-century context. See also Baldwin (1973). As Branham (1989, 1) notes, this opposition of terms is a false dichotomy: using traditional models and making a contemporary comment are not mutually exclusive.

13. We might also see the genre of mime as influencing Lucian's *Dialogues* in their conception, but I don't think he engages with that genre in the same sort of dialogic way that he does with philosophy.

14. Artemidorus says that there is a "little disgrace" in visiting *hetairai* in brothels (*Interpretation of Dreams* 1.78). Foucault (1986, 165–75) suggests that this association may be due to the growing emphasis on companionship marriage.

15. I don't mean to imply that these topics don't figure heavily into philosophical discussion, merely that its speaking subjects do not inhabit this realm in the same immediate way that Lucian's courtesans do.

16. Prostitutes are generally presumed to be non-Athenians; see Fantham (1975, 51). However, [Demosthenes] 59.41 suggests that there was a market for Athenian citizens' wives (Neaira is able to charge higher prices because she appears to be Stephanus's wife).

17. That there was an emphasis on homosexuality at Sparta is attested in a variety of sources. For a discussion of Spartan sexuality see Cartledge (2001, 91–126).

18. Cartledge (2001, 122) suggests that perhaps this practice was designed to "ease the transition for the groom from his all-male and actively homosexual *agôgê* and common mess to full heterosexual intercourse."

19. The historian Timaeus in a gloss on this passage defines *"hetairistriai"* as those women called "tribads"; see Rabe (1906, 277). For a fascinating discussion of the scholia on this passage and its validity as evidence for female same-sex marriage see Cameron (1998, 137–56).

20. *"Hetairistria"* may have absorbed a pejorative tenor by association with *"laikastria."* See Jocelyn (1980), Dover ([1978] 1989, 172).

21. A fragment of Xenophanes emphasizes the importance of appropriate speech at the symposium; see Bergk (1915, frag. 94).

22. Halperin (1990a, 130) argues further that Athenian political ideology was bound up with this system of sex and gender. Gender was idealized and carried with it not only sexual but also political ramifications: "Sex, as it is represented in classical Athenian documents, is a deeply polarizing experience: constructed according to a model of penetration that interprets 'penetration' as an intrinsically unidirectional act, sex divides its participants into asymmetrical and, ultimately, into hierarchical positions, defining one partner as 'active' and 'dominant' and the other partner as 'passive' and 'submissive.' Sexual roles, moreover, are isomorphic with status and gender roles; 'masculinity' is an aggregate combining the congruent functions of penetration, activity, dominance and social precedence whereas 'femininity' signifies penetrability, passivity, submission and social subordination."

23. For analysis of the way Thebes functions as a site of alterity in general in Athenian tragedy see Zeitlin (1990, 21–63).

24. Perhaps the emphasis on sexual geography is meant to have some interplay with the spectacle of an orator from the east playing the role of a courtesan, thus evoking the same stereotype that, for example, Dionysius of Halicarnasus uses in *Ancient Orators* 1. On the persistent association between orators and courtesans see Gunderson (2000) and Gleason (1995).

25. I thank Siobhan McElduff for bringing this passage to my attention.

Bibliography
Contributors
Indices

Bibliography

Adams, C. D., trans. 1919. *The Speeches of Aeschines*. Loeb Classical Library. Cambridge, MA.

Adams, J. N. 1983. "Words for 'Prostitute' in Latin." *Rheinisches Museum* 126: 321–58.

Adler, E. 1989. "The Backgound for the Metaphor of Covenant as Marriage in the Hebrew Bible." PhD dissertation, University of California at Berkeley.

Ajootian, A. 1996. "Praxiteles." In *Personal Styles in Greek Sculpture*, ed. O. Palagia and J. J. Pollitt, 91–129. Yale Classical Studies 30. Cambridge, UK.

Albert, A. 2001. *Brothel: Mustang Ranch and Its Women*. New York.

Aleshire, S. B. 1992. "The Economics of Dedication at the Athenian Asklepieion." In *Economics of Cult in the Ancient Greek World*, ed. T. Linders and B. Alroth, 85–99. Boreas 21. Uppsala.

Alessandri, S. 1984. "Il significato storico della legge di Nicofonte sul dokimastes monetario." *Annali della Scuola Normale Superiore di Pisa* 14:369–93.

Alexander, M. 1990. *Trials in the Late Roman Republic, 149 BC to 50 BC*. Toronto.

Allen, D. 2000a. "Changing the Authoritative Voice: Lycurgus' *Against Leocrates*." *Classical Antiquity* 19.1:5–33.

———. 2000b. *The World of Prometheus: The Politics of Punishing in Democratic Athens*. Princeton, NJ.

Alster, B., ed and trans. 1974. *The Instructions of Suruppak: A Sumerian Proverb Collection*. Mesopotamia 2. Copenhagen.

———. 1993. "Marriage and Love in the Sumerian Love Songs, with Some Notes on the Manchester Tammuz." In *The Tablet and the Scroll: Near Eastern Studies in Honor of William H. Hallo*, ed. M. Cohen et al., 15–27. Bethesda, MD.

———. 1997. "Instructions." In vol. 1 of *Context of Scripture*, ed. W. W. Hallo, 569–70. Leiden.

Alston, R. 2002. *The City in Roman and Byzantine Egypt*. London.

Alston, R., and R. D. Alston. 1997. "Urbanism and the Urban Community in Roman Egypt." *Journal of Egyptian Archaeology* 83:199–216.

Anbar-Bernstein, M. 1975. "Textes de l'époque babylonienne ancienne." *Revue d'Assyriologie* 69:109–36.

Anderson, B. W. 1957. *Understanding the Old Testament*. Englewood Cliffs, NJ.

Anderson, W. S. 1984. "Love Plots in Menander and His Roman Adapters." *Ramus* 13:124–34.

———. 1996. *Barbarian Play: Plautus' Roman Comedy.* Toronto and London.

André, J. 1949. *Étude sur les termes de couleur dans la langue latine.* Paris.

Arafat, K. 2000. "The Recalcitrant Mass: Athenaeus and Pausanias." In *Athenaeus and His World: Reading Greek Culture in the Roman Empire,* ed. D. Braund and J. Wilkins, 191–202. Exeter, UK.

Arnaud, D. 1986. *Recherches du pays d'Aātata, Emar 6/3: Textes sumériens et accadiens.* Paris.

Ashmore, S. G., ed. 1910. *The Comedies of Terence.* 2nd ed. New York.

Assante, J. 1998. "The *kar.kid / harīmtu:* Prostitute or Single Woman? A Reconsideration of the Evidence." *Ugarit-Forschung* 30:5–96.

Astour, M. C. 1966. "Tamar the Hierodule: An Essay in the Method of Vestigial Motifs." *Journal of Biblical Literature* 85:185–96.

Attinger, P. 1998. "Un sicle la passee." *Nouvelles Assyriologiques Brèves et Utilitaires* 40.

Austin, R. G., ed. 1960. *Pro caelio.* 3rd ed. Oxford, UK.

Azize, Y., K. Kempadoo, and T. Cordero. 1996. *Trafficking in Women: Latin American and Caribbean Region.* Utrecht.

Bakhtin, M. 1984. *Rabelais and His World.* Trans. H. Iswolsky. Bloomington, IN.

Baldwin, B. 1973. *Studies in Lucian.* Toronto.

Balot, R. 2001. *Greed and Injustice in Classical Athens.* Princeton, NJ.

Balsdon, J. P. V. D. 1962. *Roman Women: Their History and Habits.* London.

Barber, E. 1992. "The Peplos of Athena." In *Goddess and Polis: The Panathenaic Festival in Ancient Athens,* ed. J. Neils, 112–17. Princeton, NJ.

Barish, J. 1981. *The Antitheatrical Prejudice.* Berkeley, CA.

Barton, C. A. 1993. *The Sorrows of the Ancient Romans: The Gladiator and the Monster.* Princeton, NJ.

Batstone, W. W., and G. Tissol, eds. 2005. *Defining Genre and Gender in Roman Literature: Essays Presented to William S. Anderson on His Seventy-fifth Birthday.* New York.

Beacham, R. C. 1992. *The Roman Theatre and Its Audience.* Cambridge, MA.

Beagon, M. 1992. *Roman Nature: The Thought of Pliny the Elder.* Oxford, UK.

Beard, M., and M. Crawford. 1985. *Rome in the Late Republic.* Ithaca, NY.

Beard, M., and J. Henderson. 1998. "With this Body I Thee Worship: Sacred Prostitution in Antiquity." In *Gender and the Body in the Ancient Mediterranean,* ed. M. Wyke, 56–79. Oxford, UK.

Beauvoir, S. de. 1974. *The Second Sex.* Trans. H. Parshley. New York.

Benveniste, E. 1973. *Indo-European Language and Society.* Trans. E. Palmer. London.

Bergk, T., ed. 1915. *Poetae lyrici graeci.* 4th ed. Leipzig.

Berlinerblau, J. 1996. *The Vow and the 'Popular Religious Groups' of Ancient Israel: A Philological and Sociological Inquiry.* Sheffield, UK.

Bernheimer, C. 1989. *Figures of Ill Repute: Representing Prostitution in Nineteenth-Century France.* Cambridge, MA.

Bertini, F., ed. 1968. *Plauti asinaria.* Genoa.

Beschi, L. 1967–68. "Contributi di topografia ateniese." *Annuario della Scuola archeologica di Atene* 45/46:520–26.

Bettalli, M. 1982. "Note sulla produzione tessile ad Atene in età classica." *Opus* 1:261–78.

———. 1985. "Case, Botteghe, Ergasteria: Note sui luoghi di produzione et di vendita nell' Atgene classica." *Opus* 4:29–41.

Bird, P. A. 1993. "Prostitution." In *The Oxford Companion to the Bible*, ed. B. Metzger and M. Coogan, 623–24. Oxford, UK.

———. 1996. "The End of the Male Cult Prostitute: A Literary-Historical and Sociological Analysis of Hebrew *qadesh-qedeshim*." In *Congress Volume: Cambridge, 1995*, ed. J. A. Emerton, 33–80. Supplements to Vetus Testamentum 66. Leiden.

———. 1997. *Missing Persons and Mistaken Identities: Women and Gender in Ancient Israel*. Minneapolis.

———. 2000. "The Bible in Christian Ethical Deliberation concerning Homosexuality: Old Testament Contributions." In *Homosexuality, Science, and the "Plain Sense" of Scripture*, ed. D. Balch, 142–76. Grand Rapids, MI.

Black, J., A. George, and N. Postgate, eds. 2000. *A Concise Dictionary of Akkadian*. Wiesbaden.

Bloch, I. 1912. *Die Prostitution*. Berlin.

Blümner, H. 1912. *Technologie und Terminologie der Gewerbe und Künste bei Griechen und Römern*. 2nd ed. Leipzig.

Blundell, S. 1995. *Women in Ancient Greece*. Cambridge, MA.

Boadt, L. 1984. *Reading the Old Testament: An Introduction*. New York.

Boardman, J. 1986. "Leaina." In *Enthousiasmos: Essays on Greek and Related Pottery Presented to J. M. Hemelrijk*, ed. H. A. G. Brijder, A. A. Drukker, and C. W. Neeft, 93–96. Amsterdam.

Bodson, L. 1973. "Gai, gai! Sauvons-nous!: Procédés et effets du comique dans *Lysistrata* 740–52." *l'Antiquité classique* 42:5–27.

Boegehold, A. L. 1994. "Perikles' Citizenship Law of 451/0 BC." In *Athenian Identity and Civic Ideology*, ed. Alan L. Boegehold and Adele C. Scafuro, 57–66. Baltimore.

Bogaert, R. 1968. *Banques et banquiers dans les cités grecques*. Leiden.

Bolkestein, H. 1958. *Economic Life in Greece's Golden Age*. 2nd ed. Leiden.

Bolles, L. 1992. "Sand, Sea and the Forbidden." *Transforming Anthropology* 3: 30–34.

Bompaire, J. 1958. *Lucien ecrivain: Imitation et création*. Paris.

Bonanno, A. 1988. "Imperial and Private Portraiture: A Case of Non-Dependence." In *Ritratto ufficiale e ritratto privato: Atti della II Conferenza Internazionale sul ritratto romano*, ed. N. Binacasa and G. Rizza, 157–64. Rome.

Bonfante, L. 1994. "Introduction." In *The World of Roman Costume*, ed. J. L. Sebesta and L. Bonfante, 3–10. Madison, WI.

Bongenaar, J. 1933. *Isocrates' trapeziticus vertaald en toegelicht*. Utrecht.

Boston Women's Health Book Collective. 1992. *The New Our Bodies, Ourselves: A Book by and for Women*. New York.

Boswell, J. 1990. *The Kindness of Strangers*. New York.

Bourdieu, P. 1977. *Outline of a Theory of Practice*. Trans. R. Nice. Cambridge, UK.

Bourriot, F. 1995. *Kalos kagathos, kalokagathia: D'un terme de propagande de sophistes à une notion sociale et philosophique: Etude d'histoire athénienne.* Hildescheim, Ger.

Boyarin, D. 1993. *Carnal Israel: Reading Sex in Talmudic Culture.* Berkeley, CA.

Bradley, K. R. 1989. *Slavery and Rebellion in the Roman World, 140 B.C.–70 B.C.* Bloomington, IN.

———. 1994. *Slavery and Society at Rome.* Cambridge, UK.

Brandt, P. 1902, ed. Bk. 3 of *De arte amatoria.* Leipzig.

———. 1932. *Sexual Life in Ancient Greece.* Trans. J. Freese. New York.

Branham, R. B. 1989. *Unruly Eloquence: Lucian and the Comedy of Traditions.* Cambridge, MA.

Braund, S. M. 2002. *Latin Literature.* London.

Brendel, O. 1970. "The Scope and Temperament of Erotic Art in the Graeco-Roman World." In *Studies in Erotic Art,* ed. T. Bowie et al., 3–107. New York.

Brochard, V. 1926. "Sur le Banquet Platon." In *Études de philosophie ancienne et de philosophie moderne,* 72–94. New ed. Paris.

Brock, R. 1994. "The Labour of Women in Classical Athens." *Classical Quarterly* 44:336–46.

Brooten, B. 1996. *Love between Women.* Chicago.

Broughton, T. R. S. 1952. Vol. 2 of *Magistrates of the Roman Republic.* New York.

Brown, F., S. R. Driver, and C. A. Briggs. 1907. *A Hebrew and English Lexicon of the Old Testament.* Oxford, UK.

Brown, P. 1988. *The Body and Society: Men, Women, and Sexual Renunciation in Early Christianity.* New York.

———. [1967] 2000. *Augustine of Hippo: A Biography.* Berkeley, CA.

Brown, P. G. McC. 1990. "Plots and Prostitutes in Greek New Comedy." *Papers of the Leeds International Latin Seminar* 6:241–66.

Brulé, P. 2001. *Les femmes grecques à l'époque classique.* Paris.

Brundage, J. A. 1987. *Law, Sex, and Christian Society in Medieval Europe.* Chicago.

Brunt, P. A. 1988. *The Fall of the Roman Republic and Related Essays.* Oxford, UK.

Bruschweiler, F. 1989. *Inanna: La deese triomphante et vaincue dans la cosmologie sumerienne.* Leuven, Neth.

Buckler, J. 2000. "Demosthenes and Aeschines." In *Demosthenes: Orator and Statesman,* ed. I. Worthington, 90–114. London.

Buckley, T., and A. Gottlieb. 1988. "A Critical Appraisal of Theories of Menstrual Symbolism." In *Blood and Magic,* ed. T. Buckley and A. Gottlieb, 3–50. Berkeley, CA.

Budin, S. L. 2002. *The Origins of Aphrodite.* Bethesda, MD.

———. 2003. "*Pallakai,* Prostitutes, and Prophetesses." *Classical Philology* 98: 148–59.

Burford, A. 1963. "The Builders of the Parthenon." In *Parthenos and Parthenon,* ed. G. T. W. Hooker, 23–35. Oxford, UK.

———. 1972. *Craftsmen in Greek and Roman Society.* London.

Burke, E. 1992. "The Economy of Athens in the Classical Era." *Transactions of the American Philological Association* 122:199–226.

Butler, H. E., and E. A. Barber, eds. [1933] 1964. *The Elegies of Propertius.* Hildesheim, Ger.

Butler, J. 1990. *Gender Trouble: Feminism and the Subversion of Identity.* New York.

———. 1993. *Bodies That Matter*. New York.

Bury, R. G., ed. and trans. [1926] 1984. *Laws*. 2 vols. Loeb Classical Library. Cambridge, MA.

Bynum, C. W. 1987. *Holy Feast and Holy Fast*. Berkeley, CA.

Cagni, L., ed. 1969. *l'epopea di Erra*. Rome.

Cairns, D. L. 1996. "*Hybris*, Dishonour, and Thinking Big." *Journal of Hellenic Studies* 116:1–32.

Calame, C. 1989. "Entre rapports de parenté et relations civiques: Aphrodite l'hétaïre au banquet politique des *hétaîroi*." In *Aux Sources de la Puissance: Sociabilité et Parenté*, ed. F. Thélamon, 101–11. Rouen.

———. 1996. *l'Éros dans la Grèce antique*. Paris.

Calderini, A. [1908] 1965. *La manomissione e la condizione dei liberti in Grecia*. Rome.

Cameron A. 1998. "Love (and Marriage) between Women." *Greek, Roman and Byzantine Studies* 39:137–56.

Camps, W. A., ed. 1966. Bk. 3 of *Elegies*. Loeb Classical Library. Cambridge, MA.

Cantarella, E. 1987. *Pandora's Daughters: The Role and Status of Women in Greek and Roman Antiquity*. Baltimore.

———. 1992. *Greek Bisexuality*. New Haven, CT.

Carey, C., ed. and trans. 1992. *Against Neaira: [Demosthenes] 59*. Warminster, UK.

———. 1994. "Rhetorical Means of Persuasion." In *Persuasion: Greek Rhetoric in Action*, ed. Ian Worthington, 26–45. London.

———, trans. 2000. *Aeschines*. Austin, TX.

Carnes, J. 1998. "This Myth Which Is Not One: Construction of Discourse in Plato's *Symposium*." In *Rethinking Sexuality: Foucault and Classical Antiquity*, ed. D. Larmour, P. A. Miller, and C. Platter, 104–21. Princeton, NJ.

Carrière-Hervagault, M.-P. 1973. "Esclaves et affranchis chez les orateurs attiques: Documents et étude." In *Actes du colloque 1971 sur l'esclavage*, 45–79. Annales Littéraires de l'Université de Besançon 140. Paris.

Carson, A. 1990. "Putting Her in Her Place: Woman, Dirt, and Desire." In *Before Sexuality: The Construction of Erotic Experience in the Ancient Greek World*, ed. D. M. Halperin, J. J. Winkler, and F. I. Zeitlin, 309–38. Princeton, NJ.

Carson, D. A. 1987. *Showing the Spirit: A Theological Exposition of 1 Corinthians 12–14*. Grand Rapids, MI.

Carter, J. C. 1983. *The Sculpture of the Sanctuary of Athena Polias at Priene*. London.

Cartledge, P. 1993. *The Greeks: A Portrait of Self and Others*. Oxford, UK.

———. 2001. *Spartan Reflections*. Berkeley, CA.

———. 2002. "The Political Economy of Greek Slavery." In *Money, Labor and Land: Approaches to the Economies of Ancient Greece*, ed. P. Cartledge, E. Cohen, and L. Foxhall, 156–66. London.

Chantraine, P. [1968–70] 1999. *Dictionnaire étymologique de la Langue grecque*. 2 vols. Paris.

Chauvin, C. 1983. *Les chrétiens et la prostitution*. Paris.

Chibnall, M. 1975. "Pliny's Natural History and the Middle Ages." In *Empire and Aftermath: Silver Latin II*, ed. T. A. Dorey, 57–78. London.

Citti, V. 1997. "Una coppia nominale in Lisia." In *Schiavi e dipendenti nell'ambito dell' "oikos" e della "familia*," ed. M. Moggi and G. Cordiano, 91–96. Pisa.

Clarke, J. 1998. *Looking at Lovemaking: Constructions of Sexuality in Roman Art 100 B.C.–A.D. 250*. Berkeley, CA.

Clarke, S. 1993. "The Pre-Industrial City in Roman Britain." In *Theoretical Roman Archaeology: First Conference Proceedings*, ed. E. Scott, 49–66. Aldershot, UK.

Classen, C. J. 1973. "Ciceros Rede für Caelius." *Aufstieg und Niedergang der römischen Welt* 1.3:60–94.

Clay, D. 1975. "The Tragic and Comic Poet of the Symposium." *Arion* 2:238–61.

Clayson, H. 1991. *Painted Love: Prostitution in French Art of the Impressionist Era*. New Haven, CT.

Cohen, D. 1991a. *Law, Sexuality and Society: The Enforcement of Morals in Classical Athens*. Cambridge, UK.

———. 1991b. "Sexuality, Violence, and the Athenian Law of *Hubris*." *Greece & Rome* 38:171–88.

———. 1995. *Law, Violence, and Community in Classical Athens*. Cambridge, UK.

Cohen, E. E. 1990. "A Study in Contrast: 'Maritime Loans' and 'Landed Loans' at Athens." In *Symposion 1988*, ed. A. Biscardi, J. Mélèze-Modrzejewski, and G. Thür, 57–79. Cologne.

———. 1992. *Athenian Economy and Society: A Banking Perspective*. Princeton, NJ.

———. 2000a. *The Athenian Nation*. Princeton, NJ.

———. 2000b. "'Whoring Under Contract': The Legal Context of Prostitution in Fourth-Century Athens." In *Law and Social Status in Classical Athens*, ed. Virginia Hunter and Jonathan Edmondson, 113–48. Oxford, UK.

———. Forthcoming. *Athenian Prostitution: The Business of Sex*.

Cohen, E. S. 1991. "'Courtesans' and 'Whores': Words and Behavior in Roman Streets." *Women's Studies* 19:201–8.

Cohen, M. 1993. *The Cultic Calendars of the Ancient Near East*. Bethesda, MD.

Cohen, S. J. D. 1991. "Menstruants and the Sacred in Judaism and Christianity." In *Women's History and Ancient History*, ed. S. B. Pomeroy, 273–99. Chapel Hill, NC.

Cole, S. G. 1984. "The Social Function of Rituals of Maturation: The Koureion and Arkteia." *Zeitschrift für Papyrologieund Epigraphik* 55:233–44.

———. 1992. "*Gunaiki ou Themis*: Gender Difference in the Greek *Leges sacrae*." *Helios* 19.1/2:104–22.

Collins, R. F. 1999. *First Corinthians*. Sacra Pagina Series 7. Collegeville, MN.

Connelly, M. T. 1980. *The Response to Prostitution in the Progressive Era*. Chapel Hill, NC.

Connor, W. R. [1971] 1992. *The New Politicians of Fifth-Century Athens*. Indianapolis, IN.

Cook, A. B. 1914–40. *Zeus: A Study in Ancient Religion*. 3 vols. Cambridge, UK.

Cooper, G. 1993. "Sacred Marriage and Popular Cult in Early Mesopotamia." In *Official Cult and Popular Religion in the Ancient Near East*, ed. E. Matsushima, 81–96. Heidelberg.

Copley, F. 1956. *Exclusus Amator: A Study in Latin Love Poetry*. APA Monograph Series 17. Baltimore.

Corbeill, A. 1996. *Controlling Laughter: Political Humor in the Late Roman Republic*. Princeton, NJ.

Corbin, A. 1990. *Women for Hire: Prostitution and Sexuality in France after 1850.* Trans. A. Sheridan. Cambridge, MA.

Costecalde, C. 1985. "Sacré (et sainteté): I. La racine 'qdsh' et ses dérivés en milieu ouest-sémitique et dans les cunéiformes; II. Sacré et sainteté dans l'Ancien Testament, A. and B." In *Dictionaire de la Bible: Supplément,* ed. L. Pirot and A. Robert, 1346–414. Paris.

Courbin, P. 1983. "*Obeloi* d'Argolide et d'ailleurs." In *The Greek Renaissance of the Eighth Century B.C.,* ed. R. Hägg, 149–56. Stockholm.

Courtney, E. 1980. *A Commentary on the Satires of Juvenal.* London.

Cox, C. A. 1998. *Household Interests: Property, Marriage Strategies and Family Dynamics in Ancient Athens.* Princeton, NJ.

Croom, A. 2002. *Roman Clothing and Fashion.* Gloucestershire, UK.

Culham, P. 1982. "The *Lex Oppia.*" *Latomus* 41:769–83.

Cumont, F. V. M. 1909. *Les religions orientales dans le paganisme Romain.* 2nd ed. Paris.

Cunningham, I. C., ed. 1971. *Herodas mimiambi.* Oxford.

Dahlburg, J.-T. 1994. "The Fight to Save India's Baby Girls." *Los Angeles Times.* February 22: A1 and A14.

Dalby, A. 2000. *Empire of Pleasures: Luxury and Indulgence in the Roman World.* New York.

D'Ambra, E. 1996. "The Calculus of Venus: Nude Portraits of Roman Matrons." In *Sexuality in Ancient Art: Near East, Egypt, Greece, and Italy,* ed. N. Kampen, 219–32. Cambridge, UK.

———. 2000. "Nudity and Adornment in Female Portrait Sculpture of the Second Century A.D." In *I, Claudia II: Women in Roman Art and Society,* ed. D. E. E. Kleiner and S. B. Matheson, 101–14. Austin, TX.

Dandamaev, M. A. 1984. *Slavery in Babylonia: From Nabopolassar to Alexander the Great* (626–331 BC). Ed. M. A. Powell. Trans. V. A. Powell. Rev. ed. DeKalb, IL.

Daviault, A., ed. and trans. 1981. *Comoedia togata: Fragments.* Paris.

Davidson, J. N. 1994. "Consuming Passions: Appetite, Addiction and Spending in Classical Athens." PhD dissertation, Trinity College, Oxford University.

———. 1997. *Courtesans and Fishcakes: The Consuming Passions of Classical Athens.* London.

———. 2001. "Dover, Foucault and Greek Homosexuality: Penetration and the Truth of Sex." *Past and Present* 170:3–51.

Davies, J. K. 1971. *Athenian Propertied Families 600–300 BC.* Oxford, UK.

Davis, J. T. 1993. "Thou Shalt Not Cuddle: *Amores* 1.4 and the Law." *Syllecta Classica* 4:65–69.

Day, P. 2000. "Adulterous Jerusalem's Imagined Demise: Death of a Metaphor in Ezekiel xvi." *Vetus Testamentum* 50:285–309.

Dean-Jones, L. 1992. "The Politics of Pleasure: Female Sexual Appetite in the Hippocratic Corpus." *Helios* 19.1/2:72–91.

———. 1994. *Women's Bodies in Classical Greek Science.* Oxford, UK.

De Brauw, M. 2001–02. "Listen to the Laws Themselves: Citations of Laws and Portrayal of Character in Attic Oratory." *Classical Journal* 97.2:161–76.

De Brauw, M., and J. Miner. 2004. "Androtion's Alleged Prostitution Contract: Aes. 1.165 and Dem. 22.23 in Light of *P. Oxy.* VII 1012." *Zeitschrift der Savigny-Stiftung*, Rom. ab. 121:301–13.

DeFelice, J. 2001. *Roman Hospitality: The Professional Women of Pompeii.* Warren Center, PA.

Delaney, C. 1988. "Mortal Flow: Menstruation in Turkish Village Society." In *Blood Magic*, ed. T. Buckley and A. Gottlieb, 75–93. Berkeley, CA.

della Corte, F. 1982. "Le *leges Iuliae* e l'elegia romana." *Aufstieg und Niedergang der römischen Welt* 2.30.1:539–58.

Dench, E. 1998. "Austerity, Excess, Success, and Failure in Hellenistic and Early Imperial Italy." In *Parchments of Gender: Deciphering the Bodies of Antiquity*, ed. M. Wyke, 121–46. Oxford, UK.

Dessen, C. S. 1977. "Plautus' Satiric Comedy: The *Truculentus.*" *PQ* 56:145–68.

Dilts, M. R., ed. 1986. Vol. 2 of *Scholia Demosthenica*. Leipzig.

———. ed. 1992. *Scholia in Aeschinem*. Leipzig.

Dimakis, P. 1988. "Orateurs et hetaïres dans l'Athènes classique." In *Éros et droit en Grèce classique*, ed. P. Dimakis, 43–54. Paris.

Dixon, S. 1988. *The Roman Mother*. Norman, OK.

Doignon, J. 1997. *Oeuvres de Saint Augustin 4.2: Dialogues philosophiques, De Ordine—l'ordre*. Paris.

Donnay, G. 1997. "l'arrhéphorie: initiation ou rite civique? Un cas d'école." *Kernos* 10:177–205.

Dorey, T. A. 1958. "Cicero, Clodia and the *Pro Caelio.*" *Greece & Rome* 5:175–96.

Dougherty, C. 1996. "Democratic Contradictions and the Synoptic Illusion of Euripides' *Ion.*" In *Dêmokratia: A Conversation on Democracies, Ancient and Modern*, ed. J. Ober and C. Hedrick, 249–70. Princeton, NJ.

Dover, K. J. 1964. "Eros and Nomos in Plato, *Symposium* 182a–85c." *Bulletin of the Institute of Classical Studies of the University of London* 11:31–42.

———. 1972. *Aristophanic Comedy*. London.

———. 1974. *Greek Popular Morality in the Time of Plato and Aristotle*. Oxford, UK.

———. 1984. "Classical Greek Attitudes to Sexual Behaviour." In *Women in the Ancient World: The Arethusa Papers*, ed. J. Peradotto and J. P. Sullivan, 143–57. Albany, NY.

———. [1978] 1989. *Greek Homosexuality*. 2nd ed. Cambridge, MA.

———, ed. [1980] 2001. *Symposium*. New York.

Driver, G. R., and J. C. Miles, eds. and trans. 1952. *The Babylonian Laws*. Vol. 1 of *Legal Commentary*. Oxford, UK.

Duckworth, G. E. 1994. *The Nature of Roman Comedy: A Study in Popular Entertainment*. 2nd ed. Norman, OK.

Dupont, F. 1985. *l'acteur-roi ou le théâtre dans la Rome antique*. Paris.

Dyck, A. R. 2001. "Dressing to Kill: Attire as a Proof and Means of Characterization in Cicero's Speeches." *Arethusa* 34:119–30.

Easterling, P. E. 1999. "Actors and Voices: Reading between the Lines in Aeschines and Demosthenes." In *Performance Culture and Athenian Democracy*, ed. S. Goldhill and R. Osborne, 154–65. Cambridge, UK.

Eck, W. 1997. "Cum dignitate otium: Senatorial Domus in Imperial Rome." *Scripta Classica Israelica* 16:162–90.

Edwards, C. 1993. *The Politics of Immorality in Ancient Rome.* Cambridge, UK.
———. 1997. "Unspeakable Professions: Public Performance and Prostitution in Ancient Rome." In *Roman Sexualities,* ed. J. P. Hallet and M. Skinner, 66–95. Princeton, NJ.
Ehrenberg, V. 1962. *The People of Aristophanes: A Sociology of Old Attic Comedy.* New York.
Ehrenreich, B., and D. English. 1973. *Witches, Midwives, and Nurses: A History of Women Healers.* New York.
Elderkin, G. W. 1940. "Aphrodite and Athena in the *Lysistrata* of Aristophanes." *Classical Philology* 35:387–96
Ellis, J. R. 1976. *Philip II and Macedonian Imperialism.* London.
Ericcson, L. 1980. "Charges against Prostitution: An Attempt at a Philosophical Assessment." *Ethics* 90:335–66.
ETCSL. "A Balbale to Inana as Nanaya." http://www-etcsl.orient.ox.ac.uk/section4/c4078.htm.
———. "Instructions of Shuruppak." http://www-etcsl.orient.ox.ac.uk/section5/c561.htm.
Evans, J. K. 1991. *War, Women and Children in Ancient Rome.* London.
Fantham, E. 1975. "Sex, Status, and Survival in Hellenistic Athens: A Study of Women in New Comedy." *Phoenix* 29:44–74.
Faraguna, M. 1999. "Aspetti della schiavitù domestica femminile in Attica tra oratoria ed epigrafia." In *Femmes-esclaves: Modèles d'interprétation anthropologique, économique, juridique,* ed. F. Merola and A. Storchi Marino, 57–79. Diáphora 9. Naples.
Faraone, C. A. 1992. "Sex and Power: Male-Targetting Aphrodisiacs in the Greek Magical Tradition." *Helios* 19.1/2:92–103.
———. 1997. "Salvation and Female Heroics in the Parodos of Aristophanes' *Lysistrata.*" *Journal of Hellenic Studies* 117:38–59.
———. 1999. *Ancient Greek Love Magic.* Cambridge, MA.
———. 2003. "Playing the Bear and Fawn for Artemis: Female Initiation or Substitute Sacrifice?" In *Initiation in Ancient Greek Rituals and Narratives: New Critical Perspectives,* ed. D. Dodd and C. A. Faraone, 43–68. London.
———. 2006. "The Masculine Arts of Ancient Greek Courtesans: Male Fantasy or Female Self-Representation?" In *The Courtesan's Arts,* ed. M. Feldman and B. Gordon. New York.
Farnell, L. 1904. "Sociological Hypotheses concerning the Position of Women in Ancient Religion." *Archiv für Religionswissenschaft* 7:70–94.
Fezzi, L. 1999. "La legislazione tribunizia di Publio Clodio Pulchro." *Studi Classici e Orientali* 47.1:245–341.
Figueira, T. 1998. *The Power of Money: Coinage and Politics in the Athenian Empire.* Philadelphia.
Finkelstein, J. J. 1966. "Sex Offenses in Sumerian Laws." *Journal of the American Oriental Society* 86:355–72.
Finley, M. 1981. *Economy and Society in Ancient Greece.* Ed. B. Shaw and R. Saller. London.
———. 1985. *Studies in Land and Credit in Ancient Athens.* New introduc. by P. Millett. New Brunswick, NJ.

Fisher, N. R. E. 1992. *Hybris: A Study in the Values of Honour and Shame in Ancient Greece*. Warminster, UK.

———. 1993. *Slavery in Classical Greece*. London.

———. 1995. "*Hybris,* Status and Slavery." In *The Greek World,* ed. A. Powell, 44–84. London.

———. 1998a. "Gymnasia and the Democratic Values of Leisure." In *Kosmos: Essays in Order, Conflict and Community in Classical Athens,* ed. P. Cartledge, P. Millett, and S. von Reden, 84–104. Cambridge, UK.

———. 1998b. "Violence, Masculinity and the Law in Athens." In *When Men Were Men: Masculinity, Power and Identity in Classical Antiquity,* ed. L. Foxhall and J. Salmon, 68–97. London.

———, trans. 2001. *Against Timarchos*. Oxford, UK.

Flemming, R. 1999. "*Quae corpore quaestum fecit:* The Sexual Economy of Female Prostitution in the Roman Empire." *Journal of Roman Studies* 89:38–61.

Foerster, R., ed. 1903–27. *Libanii opera*. Leipzig.

Fohrer, G. 1972. *History of Israelite Religion*. Trans. D. E. Green. Nashville, TN.

Foley, H. 1982. "The 'Female Intruder' Reconsidered: Women in Aristophanes' *Lysistrata* and *Ecclesiazusae*." *Classical Philology* 77:1–21.

Forbes, R. J. 1964. Vol. 4 of *Studies in Ancient Technology*. Leiden.

Ford, A. 1999. "Reading Homer from the Rostrum: Poetry and Law in Aeschines, *In Timarchus*." In *Performance Culture and Athenian Democracy,* ed. S. Goldhill and R. Osborne, 231–56. Cambridge, UK.

Ford, G. B., Jr. 1966. "An Analysis of *Amores* I.4." *Helikon* 6:645–52.

Fortin, E. L. 1994. Introd. to *Augustine: Political Writings,* ed. E. L. Fortin and D. Kries, vii–xxix. Indianapolis, IN.

Foucault, M. 1984. "On the Genealogy of Ethics: An Overview of Work in Progress." In *The Foucault Reader,* ed. P. Rabinow, 340–72. New York.

———. 1985. *The Use of Pleasure*. Vol. 2 of *The History of Sexuality*. Trans. R. Hurley. New York.

———. 1990. *The Care of the Self*. Vol. 3 of *The History of Sexuality*. Trans. R. Hurley. New York.

Foxhall, L. 1989. "Household, Gender and Property in Classical Athens." *Classical Quarterly* 39:22–44.

———. 1996. "The Law and the Lady: Women and Legal Proceedings in Classical Athens." In *Greek Law in Its Political Setting: Justifications Not Justice,* ed. Lin Foxhall and A. D. E. Lewis, 133–52. Oxford, UK.

Francotte, H. 1900. *l'industrie dans la Grèce ancienne*. Brussels.

Frazer, J. G. 1919. *Adonis Attis Osiris: Studies in the History of Oriental Religion*. Vols. 7–8 of *The Golden Bough: A Study in Magic and Religion*. 3rd ed. London.

Fredrick, D. 1997. "Reading Broken Skin: Violence in Roman Elegy." In *Roman Sexualities,* ed. J. Hallett and M. Skinner, 172–93. Princeton, NJ.

French, D. R. 1998. "Maintaining Boundaries: The Status of Actresses in Early Christian Society." *Vigiliae Christianae* 52:293–318.

French, R., and F. Greenaway, eds. 1986. *Science in the Early Roman Empire: Pliny the Elder, His Sources and Influence*. London.

French, V. 1986. "Midwives and Maternity Care in the Greco-Roman World." *Helios* 13.2:69–84.

Friedländer, L. 1908. *Roman Life and Manners under the Early Empire*. Trans. L. Magnus. 7th ed. London.

Frymer-Kensky, T. 1992. *In the Wake of the Goddesses: Women, Culture, and the Biblical Transformation of Pagan Myth*. New York.

Fuchs, W. 1995. "In Search of Herodotus' Poseidon at the Isthmos." *Thetis* 2: 73–78.

Fuks, A. 1951. "*Kolonos misthios*: Labour Exchange in Classical Athens." *Eranos* 49:171–73.

Furtwängler, A. E. 1980. "Zur Deutung der *Obeloi* im Lichte samischer Neufunde." In *Tainia, Festschrift für Roland Hampe*, ed. H. A. Cahn and E. Simon, 81–98. Mainz, Ger.

Gabrielsen, V. 1986. "*Phanera and aphanês ousia* in Classical Athens." *Classica et Mediaevalia* 37:99–114.

Gagarin, M. 2001. Review of *Law and Social Status in Classical Athens*, ed. V. Hunter and J. Edmonson. *Bryn Mawr Classical Review* 2001.10.3. http:// ccat.sas.upenn.edu/bmcr/2001/2001-10-03.html.

Galambush, J. 1992. *Jerusalem in the Book of Ezekiel: The City as Yahweh's Wife*. Atlanta.

Gallery, M. L. 1980. "Service Obligations of the *kezertu*-Women" *Orientalia*, n.s., 49:333–38.

Gallo, L. 1987. "Salari e inflazione: Atene tra V e IV sec. A. C." *Annali della Scuola Normale Superiore di Pisa* 17.1:19–63.

Gamel, M.-K. 1989. "*Nin sine caede*: Abortion Politics and Poetics in Ovid's *Amores*." *Helios* 16.2:183–206.

Garber, M. 1992. *Vested Interests: Cross-Dressing and Cultural Anxiety*. New York, London.

Gardner, J. F. 1986. *Women in Roman Law and Roman Society*. Beckenham, UK.

Gardner, R., trans. [1958] 1970. *Pro caelio*. Loeb Classical Library. Cambridge, MA.

Garlan, Y. 1980. "Le travail libre en Grèce ancienne." In *Non-Slave Labour in the Greco-Roman World*, ed. P. Garnsey, 6–22. Cambridge, UK.

———. 1982. *Les esclaves en Grèce ancienne*. Paris.

———. 1988. *Slavery in Ancient Greece*. Trans. J. Lloyd. Ithaca, NY.

Garland, R. 1995. *The Eye of the Beholder, Deformity and Disability in the Graeco-Roman World*. Ithaca, NY.

Garner, R. 1987. *Law and Society in Classical Athens*. London.

Garnsey, P., ed. 1980. *Non-Slave Labour in the Greco-Roman World*. Cambridge, UK.

Garnsey, P., and R. Saller. 1987. *The Roman Empire: Economy, Society, and Culture*. London.

Garrison, D. 2000. *Sexual Culture in Ancient Greece*. Norman, OK.

Garton, C. 1972. *Personal Aspects of the Roman Theatre*. Toronto.

Gassner, V. 1986. "Die Kaufläden in Pompeii." PhD dissertation, University of Vienna.

Gauthier, P. 1985. *Les cités grecques et leur bienfaiteurs, IVe-Ier siècle avant J.-C.* Bulletin de Correspondance Hellénique Supplement 12. Paris.

Geagan, D. 1994. "Children in Athenian Dedicatory Monuments." In vol. 4 of *Boeotia Antiqua: Papers on Recent Work in Boiotian Archaeology and History*,

163–73. McGill University Monographs in Classical Archaeology and History. Amsterdam.

Geffcken, K. A. 1973. *Comedy in the Procaelio*. Leiden.

George, A, ed. 2003. *The Babylonian Gilgamesh Epic*. 2 vols. Oxford, UK.

George, L. 2001. "Domination and Duality in Plautus' *Bacchides*." Διοτίμα: Materials for the Study of Women and Gender in the Ancient World. http://www.stoa.org/cgi-bin/ptext?doc=Stoa:text:2002.01.0001.

Gernet, L. 1955. *Droit et société dans la Grèce ancienne*. Paris.

Gibson, M. 1999. *Prostitution and the State in Italy, 1860–1915*. Columbus, OH.

Gilfoyle, T. J. 1992. *City of Eros: New York City, Prostitution, and the Commercialization of Sex, 1790–1920*. New York.

Gill, C., N. Postlethwaite, and R. Seaford, eds. 1998. *Reciprocity in Ancient Greece*. Oxford, UK.

Gilula, D. 1980. "The Concept of the *Bona Meretrix*: A Study of Terence's Courtesans." *Rivista di Filologia e di Istruzione Classica* 108:142–65.

Glassner, J.-J. 2001. "Polygynie ou prostitution: Une approche comparative de la sexualité masculine." Presentation to the Rencontre Assyriologique Internationale 47, Helsinki, Finland.

Glazebrook, A. 2005. "The Making of a Prostitute: Apollodoros's Portrait of Neaira." *Arethusa* 38.2:161–87.

Gleason, M. 1995. *Making Men: Sophists and Self-presentation in Ancient Rome*. Princeton, NJ.

Goldberg, Sander M. 1986. *Understanding Terence*. Princeton, NJ.

Golden, M. 1984. "Slavery and Homosexuality at Athens." *Phoenix* 38:308–24.

———. 1990. *Children and Childhood in Classical Athens*. Baltimore.

———. 1992. "The Uses of Cross-Cultural Comparison in Ancient Social History." *Échos du monde classique* 36:309–31.

———. 1998. *Sport and Society in Ancient Greece*. Cambridge, UK.

Goldhill, S. 1998. "The Seductions of the Gaze: Socrates and His Girlfriends." In *Kosmos: Essays in Order, Conflict and Community in Classical Athens*, ed. P. Cartledge, P. Millett, and S. von Reden, 105–24. Cambridge, UK.

Goldman, E. 1969. *Anarchism and Other Essays*. New York.

Goldman, M. S. 1981. *Gold Diggers and Silver Miners: Prostitution and Social Life on the Comstock Lode*. Ann Arbor, MI.

Goodfriend, E. A. 1992. "Prostitution (Old Testament)." In vol. 5 of *The Anchor Bible Dictionary*, ed. D. N. Freedman, 505–10. New York.

Goody, J. 1986. *The Logic of Writing and the Organization of Society*. Cambridge, UK.

Gophas, D. 1994. *Thallasa kai Synallages stin arkhaia Ellada*. Athens.

Gordon, L. 1986. "What's New in Women's History?" In *Feminist Studies/Critical Studies*, ed. T. de Lauretis, 20–30. Bloomington, IN.

Gourevitch, D. 1984. *Le mal d'être femme: La femme et la médecine dans la Rome antique*. Paris.

Gowers, E. 1995. "The Anatomy of Rome from Capitol to Cloaca." *Journal of Roman Studies* 85:23–32.

Graham, A. 1992. "Thucydides 7.13.2 and the Crews of Athenian Triremes." *Transactions of the American Philological Association* 122:257–70.

———. 1998. "Thucydides 7.13.2 and the Crews of Athenian Triremes: An Addendum." *Transactions of the American Philological Association* 128:89–114.

Grahame, M. 1999. "Recent Developments in Pompeian Archaeology." *Journal of Roman Archaeology* 12:567–75.

Green, M. 1989. "Women's Medical Practice and Health Care in Medieval Europe." *Signs* 14.2:434–73.

Greenwood, L. H. G., trans. [1928] 1959. Vol. 1 of *The Verrine Orations*. Loeb Classical Library. Cambridge, MA.

———, trans. [1935] 1988. Vol. 2 of *The Verrine Orations*. Loeb Classical Library. Cambridge, MA.

Gruber, M. 1986. "Hebrew *qedesh* and Her Canaanite and Akkadian Cognates." *Ugarit-Forschungen* 18:133–48.

Gruen, E. S. 1968. *Roman Politics and the Criminal Courts, 149–78 B.C.* Cambridge, MA.

———. 1974. *The Last Generation of the Roman Republic.* Berkeley, CA.

———. 1992. *Culture and National Identity in Republican Rome.* Ithaca, NY.

Gschnitzer, F. 1964. *Studien zur griechischen Terminologie der Sklaverei.* Vol. 1 of *Grundzüge des vorhellenistischen Sprachgebrauchs.* Wiesbaden.

Guilhembet, J.-P. 1996. "La densité des *domus* et des *insulae dans* les XIV Régions de Rome selon les *Régionnaires*: Représentations cartographiques." *Mélanges de l'École française de Rome: Antiquité* 108:7–26.

Gunderson E. 1998. "Discovering the Body in Roman Oratory." In *Parchments of Gender: Deciphering the Bodies of Antiquity,* ed. M. Wyke, 169–90. Oxford, UK.

———. 2000. *Staging Masculinity: The Rhetoric of Performance in the Roman World.* Ann Arbor, MI.

Gurney, O. R. 1982. "A Case of Conjugal Desertion." In *Zikir sumim: Assyriological Studies Presented to F. R. Kraus on the Occasion of His Seventienth Birthday,* ed. G. van Driel et al., 91–94. Leiden.

———, ed. and trans. 1983. *The Middle Babylonian Legal and Economic Texts from Ur.* Oxford, UK.

Guy, D. J. 1991. *Sex and Danger in Buenos Aires: Prostitution, Family, and Nation in Argentina.* Lincoln, NE.

Hall, J. 1981. *Lucian's Satire.* New York.

Hallett, J. P. 1984. *Fathers and Daughters in Roman Society: Women and the Elite Family.* Princeton, NJ.

———. 1989a. "Female Homoeroticism and the Denial of Roman Reality in Latin Literature." *Yale Journal of Criticism* 3:209–27.

———. 1989b. "Woman as *Same* and *Other* in Classical Roman Elite." *Helios* 16: 59–78.

Hallett, J. P., and M. B. Skinner, eds. 1997. *Roman Sexualities.* Princeton, NJ.

Halperin, D. 1990a. *One Hundred Years of Homosexuality and Other Essays on Greek Love.* New York.

———. 1990b. "Why Is Diotima a Woman? Platonic Eros and the Figuration of Gender." In *Before Sexuality: The Construction of Erotic Experience in the Ancient Greek World,* ed. D. Halperin, J. J. Winkler, and F. Zeitlin, 257–308. Princeton, NJ.

————. 1993. "Is There a History of Sexuality?" In *Lesbian and Gay Studies Reader*, ed. H. Abelove, M. A. Banale, and D. M. Halperin, 416–36. New York.

Halperin, D., J. Winkler, and F. Zeitlin, eds. 1990. *Before Sexuality: The Construction of Erotic Experience in the Ancient Greek World*. Princeton, NJ.

Halporn, J. 1993. "Roman Comedy and Greek Models." In *Theater and Society in the Classical World*, ed. R. Scodel, 191–213. Ann Arbor, MI.

Hamilton, C. [1909] 1981. *Marriage as a Trade*. London.

Hanawalt, B. A. 1998. *'Of Good and Ill Repute': Gender and Social Control in Medieval England*. Oxford, UK.

Hansen, M. H. 1991. *The Athenian Democracy in the Age of Demosthenes*. Oxford, UK.

————. 1996. "The Ancient Athenian and the Modern View of Liberty as a Democratic Ideal." In *Demokratia: A Conversation on Democracies, Ancient and Modern*, ed. J. Ober and C. Hedrick, 91–104. Princeton, NJ.

Hanson, A. E. 1990. "The Medical Writers' Woman." In *Before Sexuality: The Construction of Erotic Experience in the Ancient Greek World*, ed. D. M. Halperin, J. J. Winkler, and F. I. Zeitlin, 309–38. Princeton, NJ.

————. 1992. "Conception, Gestation, and the Origin of Female Nature in the *Corpus Hippocraticum*." *Helios* 19:31–71.

Harding, P. 1987. "Rhetoric and Politics in Fourth-Century Athens." *Phoenix* 42: 25–39.

Harris, D. 1995. *The Treasures of the Parthenon and Erechtheion*. Oxford, UK.

Harris, E. 2002. "Workshop, Marketplace and Household: The Nature of Technical Specialization in Classical Athens and Its Influence on Economy and Society." In *Money, Labor and Land: Approaches to the Economies of Ancient Greece*, ed. P. Cartledge, E. Cohen, and L. Foxhall, 67–99. London.

Harris E. M. 1985. "The Date of the Trial of Timarchus." *Hermes* 113:376–80.

————. 1995. *Aeschines and Athenian Politics*. Oxford, UK.

Harrison, A. R. W. 1968. *The Family of Property*. Vol. 1 of *The Law of Athens*. Oxford, UK.

Harsin, J. 1985. *Policing Prostitution in Nineteenth-Century Paris*. Princeton, NJ.

Harvey, D. 1988. "Painted Ladies: Fact, Fiction, and Fantasy." In *Proceedings of the 3rd Symposium on Ancient Greek and Related Pottery*, ed. J. Christiansen and T. Melander, 242–54. Copenhagen.

Hauschild, H. 1933. *Die Gestalt der Hetäre in der griechischen Komödie*. Leipzig.

Havelock, C. M. 1995. *The Aphrodite of Knidos and Her Successors: A Historical Review of the Female Nude in Greek Art*. Ann Arbor, MI.

Havet, L. 1905. "Études sur Plaute, *Asinaria* I: La seconde et la troisième scenes et la composition générale." *Revue de Philologie* 29:94–103.

Helbig, W. 1873. *Untersuchungen über die campanische Wandmalerei*. Leipzig.

Helm R. 1906. *Lucian und Menipp*. Leipzig.

Henderson, J. 1987a. *Lysistrata*. Oxford, UK.

————, trans. 1987b. "Older Women in Attic Old Comedy." *Transactions of the American Philological Association* 117:105–29.

————. [1975] 1991. *The Maculate Muse: Obscene Language in Attic Comedy*. 2nd ed. Oxford, UK.

————, trans. 1996. *Staging Women: Three Plays by Aristophanes*. New York

————. 2002. "Strumpets on Stage: The Early Comic Hetaera." *Dionisio* 1:78–87.

Henry, M. 1985. *Menander's Courtesans and the Greek Comic Tradition.* Frankfurt am Main.

————. 1987. "*Êthos, Mythos, Praxis:* Women in Greek Comedy." In "Rescuing Creusa: New Methodological Approaches to Women in Antiquity," ed. Marilyn Skinner. Special issue, *Helios* 13:141–50.

Herrmann, H.-V. 1979. *Kesselprotomen und Stabdreifüsse.* Vol. 2 of *Die Kessel der orientalisierenden Zeit.* Olympische Forschungen 11. Berlin.

Herter, H. 1957. "Dirne." *Reallexikon für Antike und Christentum* 3:1149–257.

————. 1960. "Die Soziologie der antiken Prostitution im Lichte des Leidnischen und Christ-lichen Schrifttums." *Jahrbuch für Antike und Christentum* 3:70–111.

————. 1985. "Il mondo delle cortigiane e delle prostitute." In *Le donne in Grecia,* ed. G. Arrigoni, 363–97. Rome.

Hervagault, M.-P., and M.-M. Mactoux. 1974. "Esclaves et société d'après Démosthène." In *Actes du colloque 1972 sur l'esclavage,* 57–102. Annales Littéraires de l'Université de Besançon 163. Paris.

Heskel, J. 1994. "Cicero as Evidence for Attitudes to Dress in the Late Republic." In *The World of Roman Costume,* ed. J. L. Sebesta and L. Bonfante, 133–45. Madison, WI.

Hill, M. W. 1993. *Their Sisters' Keepers: Prostitution in NewYork City, 1830–1870.* Berkeley, CA.

Hindley, C. 1991. "Law, Society, and Homosexuality in Classical Athens." *Past and Present* 133:167–83.

Höghammar, K. 1997. "Women in Public Space: Cos c. 200 B.C. to c. A.D. 15/20." In *Sculptors and Sculpture of Caria and the Dodecanese,* ed. I. Jenkins and G. B. Waywell, 127–33. London.

Holzberg, N. 1988. "Lucian and the Germans." In *The Uses of Greek and Latin,* ed. A. C. Dionisotti, A. Grafton, and J. Kraye, 199–209. London.

Hooks, S. M. 1985. "Sacred Prostitution in Israel and the Ancient Near East." PhD dissertation, Hebrew Union College.

Hopkins, M. K. 1965. "Contraception in the Roman Empire." *Comparative Studies in Society and History* 8:124–51.

Hopper, R. 1979. *Trade and Industry in Classical Greece.* London.

Howard, J. E. 1994. *The Stage and Social Struggle in Early Modern England.* London.

Hubbard, T. 1998. "Popular Perceptions of Elite Homosexuality in Classical Athens." *Arion* 6.1:48–78.

Hughes, D. O. 1983. "Sumptuary Law and Social Relations in Renaissance Italy." In *Disputes and Settlements: Law and Human Relations in the West,* ed. J. Bossy, 69–99. Cambridge, UK.

Humphreys, S. C. 1978. *Anthropology and the Greeks.* London.

————. [1983] 1993. *The Family, Women and Death.* 2nd ed. Ann Arbor, MI.

————. 1999. "From a Grin to Death: The Body in the Greek Discovery of Politics." In *Constructions of the Classical Body,* ed. J. Porter, 126–46. Ann Arbor, MI.

Hunt, P. 1998. *Slaves, Warfare, and Ideology in the Greek Historians.* Cambridge, UK.

Hunter, N. D. 1986. "The Pornography Debate in Context: A Chronology." In *Caught Looking,* ed. F.A.C.T. Book Committee, 26–29. New York.

Hunter, V. J. 1994. *Policing Athens: Social Control in the Attic Lawsuits, 420–320 B.C.* Princeton, NJ.

Jacquemin, A. 1999. *Offrandes monumentales à Delphes.* Paris.

Jacques, J. M. 1989. *Ménandre: La samienne.* Paris.

Jaggar, A. 1985. "Prostitution." In *Philosophy of Sex,* ed. A. Soble, 348–68. Totowa, NJ.

James, S. 1998a. "Constructions of Gender and Genre in Roman Comedy and Elegy." *Helios* 25.1:3–16.

——. 1998b. "From Boys to Men: Rape and Developing Masculinity in Terence's *Hecyra* and *Eunuchus.*" *Helios* 25:31–47.

——. 2003. *Learned Girls and Male Persuasion: Gender and Reading in Roman Love Elegy.* Berkeley, CA.

Jameson, M. 1977–78. "Agriculture and Slavery in Classical Athens." *Classical Journal* 73:122–45.

——. 1990. "Private Space and the Greek City." In *The Greek City from Homer to Alexander,* ed. O. Murray and S. Price, 171–95. Oxford, UK.

——. 1997. "Women and Democracy in Fourth-Century Athens." In *Esclavage, guerre, économie en Grèce ancienne: Hommages à Yvon Garlan,* ed. P. Brulé and J. Oulhen, 95–107. Rennes, Fr.

——. 2002. "On Paul Cartledge, 'The Political Economy of Greek Slavery.'" In *Money, Labor and Land: Approaches to the Economies of Ancient Greece,* ed. P. Cartledge, E. Cohen, and L. Foxhall, 156–66. London.

Jeffery, L. H. 1988. "Poseidon on the Acropolis." *Praktika tou XII Diethnous Synedriou Klassikis Archaiologias* 3:124–26.

Joannès, F. 1994. "Amours contrariées." *Nouvelles Assyriologiques Brèves et Utilitaires* 72.

——, ed. 2000. *Rendre la justice en Mésopotamie.* Paris.

Jocelyn, H. D. 1980. "A Greek Indecency and its Students: LAIKAZEIN." *Proceedings of the Cambridge Philological Society,* n.s., 26:12–66.

Johnston, S. I. 1995. "Defining the Dreadful: Remarks on the Child-Killing Demon." In *Ancient Magic and Ritual Power,* ed. M. Meyer and P. Mirecki, 361–89. Leiden.

Joly, R. 1969. "Esclaves et médecins dans la Grèce antique." *Sudhoffs Archiv* 53: 1–14.

Jones, C. P. 1986. *Culture and Society in Lucian.* Cambridge, MA.

Jongman, W. 1998. *The Economy and Society of Pompeii.* Amsterdam.

Jordan, D. R. 1985. "A Survey of Greek Defixiones Not Included in the Special Corpora." *Greek, Roman and Byzantine Studies* 26:151–97.

Joshel S., and S. Murnaghan. 1998. "Introduction: Differential Equations." In *Women and Slaves in Greco-Roman Culture,* ed. S. Murnaghan and S. Joshel, 1–21. London.

Just, R. 1989. *Women in Athenian Law and Life.* London.

Kane, S. 1993. "Prostitution and the Military: Planning AIDS Intervention in Belize." *Social Science and Medicine* 36:956–79.

Kanellopoulos, A. 1987. *Arkhaioellinika protypa tis Koinis Agoras.* Athens.

Kapparis, K. 1998. "The Law on the Age of the Speakers in the Athenian Assembly." *Rheinisches Museum* 141.3/4:255–59.

———, trans. 1999. *Against Neaira: [D] 59*. Berlin.

Kardos, M.-J. 2001. "l'*Vrbs* de Martial: Recherches topographiques littéraires autour des Épigrammes V.20 et V.22." *Latomus* 60.2:387–413.

Karras, R. M. 1996. *Common Women: Prostitution and Sexuality in Medieval England*. Oxford, UK.

Kauer, R., W. M. Lindsay, and O. Skutsch. [1926] 1961. *Comoediae*. Oxford, UK.

Kavoulaki, A. 1999. "Processional Performance and the Democratic Polis." In *Performance Culture and Athenian Democracy*, ed. S. Goldhill and R. Osborne, 293–320. Cambridge, UK.

Kazhdan, A. 1991. s.v. "Patria of Constantinople." Vol. 3 of *Oxford Dictionary of Byzantium*, 1598. Oxford, UK.

Keiser, R. 1986. "Death Enmity in Thull:Organized Vengeance and Social Change in a Kohistani Community." *American Ethnologist* 13:489–505.

Kellum, B. 1999. "The Spectacle of the Street." In *The Art of Ancient Spectacle*, ed. B. Bergmann and C. Kondoleon, 283–99. Washington, DC.

Kempadoo, K. 1998. "Globalizing Sex Workers' Rights." In *Global Sex Workers: Rights, Resistance, and Redefinition*, ed. K. Kempadoo and J. Doezema, 1–28. New York.

Kempadoo, K., and J. Doezema, eds. 1998. *Global Sex Workers: Rights, Resistance, and Redefinition*. New York.

Keuls, E. 1983. "The Hetaera and the Housewife: The Splitting of the Female Psyche in Greek Art." *Mededelingen van het Nederlands Historisch Instituut te Rome* 44/45:23–40.

———. 1985. *The Reign of the Phallus: Sexual Politics in Ancient Athens*. New York.

———. 1989. "Archaeology and the Classics: A Rumination." In *Classics: A Discipline and Profession in Crisis?* ed. P. Culham and L. Edmonds, 225–29. Lanham, MD.

Khatzibasileiou, B. 1981. *Ta dêmosionomika tês Kô*. Kôaka 8. Athens.

Kincaid, L. 1990. *Lucy*. New York.

King, H. 1993. "Producing Woman: Hippocratic Gynaecology." In *Women in Ancient Societies*, ed. L. Archer, S. Fischler, and M. Wyke, 102–14. London.

———. 1995. "Self-Help, Self-Knowledge: In Search of the Patient in Hippocratic Gynaecology." In *Women in Antiquity: New Assessments*, ed. R. Hawley and B. Levick, 135–48. London.

Kirschenbaum, A. 1987. *Sons, Slaves, and Freedmen in Roman Commerce*. Jerusalem.

Kissas, K. 2000. *Die attischen Statuen- und Stelenbasen archaischer Zeit*. Bonn.

Klapisch-Zuber, C. 1985. *Women, Family, and Ritual in Renaissance Italy*. Trans. L. G. Cochrane. Chicago.

Kleberg, T. 1957. *Hôtels, restaurants et cabarets dans l'antiquité romaine: Études historiques et philologiques*. Uppsala.

Klees, H. 1998. *Sklavenleben im klassischen Griechenland*. Forschungen zur antiken Sklaverei 30. Stuttgart.

Kleiner, D. E. E., and S. B. Matheson, eds. 1996. *I, Claudia: Women in Ancient Rome*. New Haven, CT.

Knigge, U. 1988. *Der Kerameikos von Athens*. Athens.

Knorr, Ortwin. 1995. "The Character of Bacchis in Terence's *Heautontimoroumenos*." *American Journal of Philology* 116:221–35.

Konstan, D. 1983. *Roman Comedy.* Ithaca, NY.

———. 1993. "The Young Concubine in Menandrian Comedy." In *Theater and Society in the Classical World*, ed. R. Scodel, 139-60. Ann Arbor, MI.

Korver, J. 1934. *De Terminologie van het Creditwesen in het Griekschk.* Amsterdam.

Koutorga, M. de. 1859. *Essai sur les trapezites ou banquiers d'Athènes.* Paris.

Kränzlein, A. 1975. "Die attischen Aufzeichnungen über die Einleiferung von *phialai exeleutherikai.*" In *Symposion 1971*, ed. H. J. Wolff, 255-64. Cologne.

Krenkel, W. 1988. "Prostitution." In *Civilization of the Ancient Mediterranean: Greece and Rome*, ed. M. Grant and R. Kitzinger, 1291-97. New York.

Kron, U. 1996. "Priesthoods, Dedications and Euergetism: What Part Did Religion Play in the Political and Social Status of Greek Women?" In *Religion and Power in the Ancient Greek World*, ed. P. Hellström and B. Alroth, 139-82. Boreas 24. Uppsala.

Kudlien, F. 1968. *Die Sklaven in der griechischen Medezin der klassischen und hellenistischen Zeit.* Forschungen zur antiken Sklaverei 2. Stuttgart.

Kurke, L. 1989. "Kapêlia and Deceit." *American Journal of Philology* 110:535-44.

———. 1994. "Herodotus and the Language of Metals." *Helios* 22:36-64.

———. 1996. "Pindar and the Prostitutes, or Reading Ancient 'Pornography.'" *Arion* 4.2:49-75.

———. 1997. "Inventing the *Hetaira*: Sex, Politics, and Discursive Conflict in Archaic Greece." *Classical Antiquity* 16.1:106-50.

———. 1999. *Coins, Bodies, Games, and Gold: The Politics of Meaning in Archaic Greece.* Princeton, NJ.

———. 2002. "Gender, Politics, and Subversion in the *Chreiai* of Machon." *Proceedings of the Cambridge Philological Society*, n.s., 48:20-65.

Kytzler, B. 1992. *Minucius Felix: Octavius.* Leipzig.

Lacey, W. 1968. *The Family in Classical Greece.* London.

LaFollette, L. 1994. "The Costume of the Roman Bride." In *The World of Roman Costume*, ed. J. L. Sebesta and L. Bonfante, 54-64. Madison, WI.

Lambert, W. G. 1960. *Babylonian Wisdom Literature.* Oxford, UK.

———. 1992. "Prostitution." In *Aussenseiter und Randgruppen: Beiträge zu einer Sozialgeschichte des Alten Orients*, ed. V. Haas, 127-57. Konstanz, Ger.

Landsberger, B. 1937. *Die serie ana ittišu.* Materialien zum sumerischen Lexikon 1. Rome.

Lane, R. 1991. *The Market Experience.* Cambridge, UK.

Lane Fox, R. 1994. "Aeschines and Athenian Democracy." In *Ritual, Finance, and Politics: Athenian Democratic Accounts Presented to David Lewis*, ed. R. Osborne and S. Hornblower, 135-55. Oxford, UK.

Lanni, A. 2004. "Arguing from 'Precedent': Modern Perspectives on Athenian Practice." In *The Law and the Courts in Ancient Greece*, ed. E. M. Harris and L. Rubinstein. London.

Larmour, D., P. Miller, and C. Platter. 1998. "Situating *The History of Sexuality.*" In *Rethinking Sexuality: Foucault and Classical Antiquity*, ed. D. Larmour, P. Miller, and C. Platter, 3-41. Princeton, NJ.

Laumonier, A. 1958. *Les cultes indigènes en Carie.* Paris.

Laurence, R. 1994. *Roman Pompeii: Space and Society.* London.

———. 1995. "The Organization of Space in Pompeii." In *Urban Society in Roman Italy*, ed. T. J. Cornell, and K. Lomas, 63–78. New York.

Lazzarini, M. L. 1982. "Weihgeschenk und Vormünzgeld: Obelòs in einer Statueninschrift des 6. vorchristlichen Jahrhunderts in Griechenland." In *Probleme des archaischen Griechenland*, 9–19. Xenia 2. Konstanz, Ger.

Lear, J. 1992. "Inside and Outside the Republic." *Phronesis* 37:184–215.

Lefkowitz, M., and M. B. Fant. 1992. *Women's Lives in Greece and Rome*, 2nd ed. Baltimore.

LeGrand, P. 1907. "Les Dialogues des courtisanes comparés avec la comédie." *Revue des études grecques* 20:176–231.

Legras, B. 1997. "La prostitution féminine dans l'Égypte ptolémaïque." In *Symposion 1995*, ed. G. Thür and J. Vélissaropoulos-Karakostas, 249–64. Köln.

Lentakis, A. 1998. *I Porneia*. Vol. 3 of *O erôtas stin arkhaia Ellada*. Athens.

———. 1999. *Oi etaires*. Vol. 4 of *O erôtas stin arkhaia Ellada*. Athens.

Leontsini, S. 1989. "Die Prostitution im frühen Byzanz." PhD dissertation, University of Vienna.

Lerner, G. 1986. "The Origin of Prostitution in Ancient Mesopotamia." *Signs* 11: 236–54.

Lesko, B. 2002. "Women and Religion in Ancient Egypt." Διοτίμα: Materials for the Study of Women and Gender in the Ancient World. http://www.stoa .org/cgi-bin/ptext?doc=Stoa:text:2002.01.0007.

Lévi-Strauss, C., and D. Eribon. 1991. *Conversations with Claude Lévi-Strauss*. Trans. P. Wissing. Chicago.

Lewis, D. 1959. "Attic Manumissions." *Hesperia* 28:208–38.

———. 1968. "Dedications of Phialai at Athens." *Hesperia* 37:368–80.

Lewis, D. M. 1955. "Notes on Attic Inscriptions (II) xxiii: Who Was Lysistrata?" *Annual of the British School at Athens* 50:1–36.

Licht, H. [1932] 1956. *Sexual Life in Ancient Greece*. Trans. J. H. Freese. London.

Lind, H. 1988. "Ein Hetärentum am Heiligen Tor?" *Museum Helveticum* 45: 158–69.

Linders, T. 1972. *Studies in the Treasure Records of Artemis Brauronia Found in Athens*. Stockholm.

Lindsay, W. M., ed. [1904] 1981. *Comoediae*. Oxford, UK.

Lipsius, J. [1905–15] 1966. *Das attische Recht und Rechtsverfahren*. 3 vols. Hildesheim, Ger.

Lloyd, A. B. 1988. Vol. 3 of *Herodotus, Book II*. Leiden.

Lloyd, G. E. R. 1987. *Polarity and Analogy: Two Types of Argumentation in Early Greek Thought*. Bristol, UK.

———. 1979. *Magic, Reason and Experience: Studies in the Origin and Development of Greek Science*. Cambridge, UK.

———. 1983. *Science, Folklore and Ideology: Studies in the Life Sciences in Ancient Greece*. Cambridge, UK.

Löhr, C. 2000. *Griechische Familienweihungen: Untersuchungen einer Repräsentationsform von ihren Anfängen bis zum Ende des 4 Jhs. v. Chr.* Rahden, Ger.

Loomis, W. 1998. *Wages, Welfare Costs and Inflation in Classical Athens*. Ann Arbor, MI.

Loraux, N. 1980–81. "l'acropole comique." *Ancient Society* 11/12:119–50.

———. 1993. *The Children of Athena: Athenian Ideas about Citizenship and the Division between the Sexes.* Trans. C. Levine. Princeton, NJ.

———. 1995. *The Experiences of Tiresias: The Feminine and the Greek Man.* Trans. P. Wissing. Princeton, NJ.

———. 2002. *The Divided City: On Memory and Forgetting in Ancient Athens.* Trans. C. Pache with J. Fort. New York.

Lowe, J. C. B. 1992. "Aspects of Plautus' Originality in the *Asinaria.*" *Classical Quarterly* 52:152–75.

Luck, G. 1974. "The Woman's Role in Latin Love Poetry." In *Perspectives of Roman Poetry: A Classics Symposium,* ed. G. K. Galinsky, 15–31. Austin, TX.

Lyne, R. O. A. M. 1980. *The Latin Love Poets.* Oxford, UK.

MacDowell, D. M. 1989. "The *Oikos* in Athenian Law." *Classical Quarterly* 39: 10–21.

———. 1995. *Aristophanes and Athens: An Introduction to the Plays.* Oxford, UK.

———. 2000. "Athenian Laws about Homosexuality." *Revue internationale des droits de l'antiquité,* 3rd ser, 47:13–27.

MacLaughlan, B. 1992. "Sacred Prostitution and Aphrodite." *Studies in Religion* 21/22:145–62.

Mactoux, M.-M. 1980. *Douleia: Esclavage et pratiques discursives dans l'Athènes classique.* Paris.

Mahood, L. 1990. *The Magdalenes: Prostitution in the Nineteenth Century.* London.

Maleuvre, J.-Y. 1998. *Jeux de masques dans l'élégie latine: Tibulle, Properce, Ovide.* Louvain, Bel.

Manville, P. B. 1990. *The Origins of Citizenship in Ancient Athens.* Princeton, NJ.

Marcadé, J. 1957. Vol. 2 of *Recueil des signatures de sculpteurs grecs.* Paris.

Martin, D. 1995. *The Corinthian Body.* New Haven, CT.

Martin, R. P. 1984. *The Spirit and the Congregation: Studies in 1 Corinthians 12–15.* Grand Rapids, MI.

Martini, R. 1997. "Sul contratto d'opera nell'Atene classica." In *Symposion 1995,* ed. G. Thür and J. Vélissaropoulos-Karakostas, 49–55. Köln, Ger.

Marx, K. 1970–72. *Capital.* 3 vols. Trans. S. Moore and E. Aveling. London.

Marzi, M., ed. 1979. *Lisia: Per ferimento premeditato.* Castello, It.

Mastrokostas, E. 1953. "*Latypê delphikê.*" In *Geras Antoniou Keramopoullou,* 635–46. Hetaireia Makedonikôn Spoudôn. Epistçmonikai pragmateiai. Seria Philologike kai theologike 9. Athens.

Mattusch, C. C. 1996. *Classical Bronzes: The Art and Craft of Greek and Roman Statuary.* Ithaca, NY.

McCarthy, B. 1934. "Lucian and Menippus." *Yale Classical Studies* 4:3–58.

McCarthy, K. 2000. *Slaves, Masters, and the Art of Authority in Plautine Comedy.* Princeton, NJ, and Oxford, UK.

McClure, L. 2003. *Courtesans at Table: Gender and Greek Literary Culture in Athenaeus.* New York.

McGarrity, T. J. 1980–81. "Reputation vs. Reality in Terence's *Hecyra.*" *Classical Journal* 76:49–56.

McGinn, T. A. J. 1994. s.v. "Prostitution." *Encyclopedia of Social History,* 588–91. New York.

——. 1998a. "Caligula's Brothel on the Palatine." *Échos du monde classique* 17: 95–107.

——. 1998b. "*Feminae probosae* and the Litter." *Classical Journal* 93:241–50.

——. 1998c. *Prostitution, Sexuality, and the Law in Ancient Rome.* Oxford, UK.

——. 1999. "The Social Policy of Emperor Constantine in *Codex Theodosianus* 4.6.3." *Tijdschrift voor Rechtsgeschiedenis* 67:57–73.

——. 2002. "Pompeian Brothels and Social History." In "Pompeian Studies," *Journal of Roman Archaeology* 47:S7–S46.

——. 2004. *The Economy of Prostitution in the Roman World: A Study of Social History and the Brothel.* Ann Arbor, MI.

McIntosh, M. 1978. "Who Needs Prostitutes? The Ideology of Male Sexual Needs." In *Women, Sexuality and Social Control,* ed. C. Smart and B. Smart, 71–92. London.

McKenzie, J. L. 1965. "Prostitution." In *Dictionary of the Bible,* 700–701. Milwaukee.

McKeown, J. C. 1987. *Text and Prologomena.* Vol. 1 of *Ovid, Amores: Text, Prolegomena, and Commentary.* Liverpool.

——. 1989. *A Commentary on Book One.* Vol. 2 of *Ovid, Amores: Text, Prolegomena, and Commentary.* Liverpool.

——. 1998. *A Commentary on Book Two.* Vol. 3 of *Ovid, Amores: Text, Prologomena, and Commentary.* Liverpool.

Menzel, B. 1981. *Untersuchungen zu Kult, Administration und Personal.* Vol. 1 of *Assyrische Tempel.* Rome.

Meritt, B. D. 1941. "Greek Inscriptions." *Hesperia* 10:38–64.

Meyer, M. 1988. "Männer mit Geld. Zu einer rotfigurigen Vase mit 'Alltagsszene.'" *Jahrbuch des Deutschen Archäologischen Instituts* 103:87–125.

Migeotte, L. 1992. *Les souscriptions publiques dans les cités grecques.* Geneva.

Millar, F. G. B. 1995a. "The Last Century of the Republic: Whose History?" *Journal of Roman Studies* 85:25–43.

——. 1995b. "Popular Politics at Rome in the Late Republic." In *Leaders and Masses in the Roman World: Studies in Honour of Zvi Yavetz,* ed. I. Malkin and W. Z. Rubinsohn, 91–113. Leiden.

——. 1998. *The Crowd in Rome in the Late Republic.* Ann Arbor, MI.

Miller, F. 1974. "The State and the Community in Aristotle's *Politics.*" *Reason Papers* 1:61–69.

Miller, P. A. 2004. *Subjecting Verses: Latin Erotic Elegy and the Emergence of the Real.* Princeton, NJ.

Millett P. 1991. *Lending and Borrowing in Ancient Athens.* Cambridge, UK.

Mirhady, D. 2000. "The Athenian Rationale for Torture." In *Law and Social Status in Classical Athens,* ed. V. Hunter and J. Edmonson, 53–74. Oxford, UK.

Mitchell, T. N. 1979. *Cicero, the Ascending Years.* New Haven, CT.

——. 1984. "Cicero on the Moral Crisis of the Late Republic." *Hermathena* 136: 21–39.

——, trans. 1986. *Verrines* 2.1. Atlantic Highlands, NJ.

——. 1991. *Cicero, the Senior Statesman.* New Haven, CT.

Monoson, S. 2000. *Plato's Democratic Entanglements: Athenian Politics and the Practice of Philosophy.* Princeton, NJ.

Montgomery, H. 1983. *The Way to Chaeronea: Foreign Policy, Decision-Making and Political Influence in Demosthenes' Speeches*. Bergen, Nor.

Moore, T. J. 1998. *The Theater of Plautus: Playing to the Audience*. Austin, TX.

Morris, I. 1996. "The Strong Principle of Equality and the Archaic Origins of Greek Democracy." In *Dêmokratia: A Conversation on Democracies, Ancient and Modern*, ed. J. Ober and C. Hedrick, 19–48. Princeton, NJ.

Morrow, G. [1960] 1993. *Plato's Cretan City: A Historical Interpretation of the Laws*. Princeton, NJ.

Mossé, C. 1983. *La femme dans la Grèce antique*. Paris.

Mras, Karl. 1916. "Die Personennamen in Lucians Hetärengesprächen." *Wiener Studien* 38:308–42.

Muecke, F. 1986. "Plautus and the Theatre of Disguise." *Classical Antiquity* 5: 216–29.

Munier, C., ed. and trans. 1995. *Saint Justin: Apologie pour les chrétiens* Paradosis 9. Fribourg, Swi.

Murray, A. S. 1890. "The Alcmene Vase Formerly in Castle Howard." *Journal of Hellenic Studies* 11:225–30.

Neils, J. 2000. "Others within the Other: An Intimate Look at Hetairai and Maenads." In *Not the Classical Ideal: Athens and the Construction of the Other in Greek Art*, ed. B. Cohen, 203–26. Leiden.

Nesselrath, H. G. 1990. "Lucian's Introductions." In *Antonine Literature*, ed. D. A. Russell, 111–40. New York.

Nevett, L. 1999. *House and Society in the Ancient Greek World*. Cambridge, UK.

Nicolet, C. 1980. *The World of the Citizen in Republican Rome*. Trans. P. Falla. Berkeley, CA.

Nieves, E. 2001. "Anxious Days in Bordello Country: Resort Plan Brings What Nevada Brothels Hate Most: Attention." *New York Times*, Sunday, August 19: A16.

Nightingale, A. 1995. *Genres in Dialogue: Plato and the Construct of Philosophy*. New York.

Nilsson, M. 1906. *Griechische Feste*. Leipzig.

Nissinen, M. 1998. *Homoeroticism in the Biblical World*. Minneapolis.

Nock, A. D. 1972. "*Synnaos theos*." In *Essays on Religion and the Ancient World*, ed. Z. Stewart, 202–51. Cambridge, MA.

North, H. 1977. "The Mare, the Vixen and the Bee: Sophrosyne as the Virtue of Women in Antiquity." *Illinois Classical Studies* 2:35–48.

Nutton, V. 1986. "The Perils of Patriotism: Pliny and Roman Medicine." In *Science in the Early Roman Empire: Pliny the Elder, His Sources and Influence*, ed. R. French and F. Greenaway, 30–58. London.

Ober, J. 1989. *Mass and Elite in Democratic Athens: Rhetoric, Ideology, and the Power of the People*. Princeton, NJ.

———. 1998. *Political Dissent in Democratic Athens: Intellectual Critics of Popular Rule*. Princeton, NJ.

———. 2001. "The Debate Over Civic Education in Classical Athens." In *Education in Greek and Roman Antiquity*, ed. Y. L. Too, 178–207. Leiden.

Ober, J., and C. Hedrick, eds. 1996. *Dêmokratia: A Conversation on Democracies, Ancient and Modern*. Princeton, NJ.

Oden, R. A. [1987] 2000. *The Bible without Theology: The Theological Tradition and Alternatives to It.* [San Francisco] Chicago.

Ogden, D. 1999. *Polygamy, Prostitutes and Death: The Hellenistic Dynasties.* London.

Ogilvie, R. M. 1970. *A Commentary on Livy, Books 1–5.* Rev. ed. Oxford, UK.

Olson, K. 2002. "*Matrona* and Whore: The Clothing of Roman Women." *Fashion Theory* 6:387–420.

———. 2003. "Roman Underwear Revisited." *Classical World* 96.2:201–10.

Oppenheim, A. L. 1955. "Siege Documents from Nippur." *Iraq* 17:69–89.

———. 1977. *Ancient Mesopotamia: A Portrait of a Dead Civilization.* Rev. ed. Chicago.

Oriental Institute. 1956–. *The Assyrian Dictionary.* Chicago.

Osborne, R. 1995. "The Economics and Politics of Slavery at Athens." In *The Greek World,* ed. A. Powell, 27–43. London.

Otis, B. 1938. "Ovid and the Augustans." *Transactions of the American Philological Association* 49:188–229.

Otis, L. L. 1985. *Prostitution in Medieval Society: The History of an Urban Institution in Languedoc.* Chicago.

Padel, R. 1992. *In and Out of the Tragic Mind: Greek Images of the Tragic Self.* Princeton, NJ.

Page, D. L. 1981. *Further Greek Epigrams.* Cambridge, UK.

Palmer, R. E. A. 1998. "Bullae insignia ingenuitatis." *American Journal of Ancient History* 14:1–69.

Palmer, S., and J. Humphrey. 1990. *Deviant Behavior: Patterns, Sources, and Control.* New York.

Paoli, U. 1976. *Altri studi di diritto greco e romano.* Milan.

Parker, D. 1969. "The Ovidian Coda." *Arion* 8:80–97.

Parker, H. N. n.d. "Metrodora: The Earliest Surviving Work by a Woman Doctor." Unpublished manuscript.

———. 1997. "The Teratogenic Grid." In *Roman Sexualities,* ed. J. P. Hallett and M. B. Skinner, 47–65. Princeton, NJ.

Parker, R. 1996. *Athenian Religion: A History.* Oxford, UK.

Parkins, H. M. 1997. "The 'Consumer City' Domesticated?: The Roman City in Élite Economic Strategies." In *Roman Urbanism: Beyond the Consumer City,* ed. H. M. Parkins, 83–111. London.

Parslow, C. 1999. "Beyond Domestic Architecture at Pompeii." *American Journal of Archaeology* 103.2:340–43.

Pateman, C. 1988. *The Sexual Contract.* Stanford, CA.

Patterson, C. 1981. *Pericles' Citizenship Law of 451–50 B.C.* New York.

———. 1987. "*Hai Attikai:* The Other Athenians." In "Rescuing Creusa: New Methodological Approaches to Women in Antiquity," ed. M. Skinner. Special issue, *Helios* 13.2:49–67.

———. 1990. "Those Athenian Bastards." *Classical Antiquity* 9:40–73.

———. 1994. "The Case against Neaira." *Athenian Identity and Civic Ideology,* ed. Alan L. Boegehold and Adele C. Scafuro. Baltimore.

———. 1998. *The Family in Greek History.* Cambridge, MA.

Pavan, E. 1980. "Police des moeurs, société et politique à Venise à la fin du Moyen Age." *Revue Historique* 536:241–88.

Pellizer, E., ed. and trans. 1995. *Dialoghi delle cortigiane.* Venice.

Perotti, E. 1974. "Esclaves *Khôris Oikountes.*" In *Actes du colloque 1972 sur l'esclavage,* 47–56. Annales Littéraires de l'Université de Besançon 163. Paris

Perrot, P. 1994. *Fashioning the Bourgeoisie: A History of Clothing in the Nineteenth Century.* Trans. R. Bienvenu. Princeton, NJ.

Perry, M. E. 1985. "Deviant Insiders: Legalized Prostitutes and a Consciousness of Women in Early Modern Seville." *Comparative Studies in Society and History* 27:138–58.

———. 1990. *Gender and Disorder in Early Modern Seville.* Princeton, NJ.

Pesando, F. 1987. *Oikos e ktesis: La casa greca in età classica.* Perugia, It.

Peschel, I. 1987. *Die Hetäre bei Symposion und Komos in der attisch-rotfigurigen Vasenmalerei des 6.-4. Jahrhunderts v. Christus.* Frankfurt.

Peiss, K. 1990. "Making Faces: The Cosmetics Industry and the Cultural Construction of Gender, 1890–1930." *Gender* 7:143–46.

Pierce, K. 1997. "The Portrayal of Rape in New Comedy." In *Rape in Antiquity: Sexual Violence in the Greek and Roman Worlds,* ed. S. Deacy and K. Pierce, 163–84. London.

Pinault, J. R. 1992. "The Medical Case for Virginity in the Early Second Century C.E.: Soranus of Ephesus, *Gynecology* 1.32." *Helios* 19.1/2:123–39.

Pirenne-Delforge, V. 1994. *l'Aphrodite grecque: Contribution à l'étude de ses cultes et de sa personnalité dans le panthéon archaïque et classique.* Kernos Supplement 4. Athens.

Plácido, D. 1997. "Los 'oikétai,' entre la dependencia personal y la producción para el mercado." In *Schiavi e dipendenti nell'ambito dell' "oikos" e della "familia,"* ed. M. Moggi and G. Cordianno, 105–16. Pisa.

Pohl, P. A. 1933. *Neubabylonishe Rechtsurkunden aus den Berliner Staatlichen Museen.* Analecta Orientalia 8. Rome.

Poljakov, F. B. 1989. *Die Inschriften von Tralleis und Nysa.* Pt.1 of *Die Inschriften von Tralleis.* Bonn.

Pomeroy, S. 1975. *Goddesses, Whores, Wives and Slaves.* New York.

Pope, M. 1962. "Fertility Cults." Vol. 2 of *The Interpreter's Dictionary of the Bible,* 265.

Popper, K. 1950. *The Open Society and Its Enemies.* Princeton, NJ.

Preger, T., ed. 1975. *Scriptores originum Constantinopolitanarum.* New York.

Pringsheim, F. 1955. "The Transition from Witnessed to Written Transactions in Athens." In *Aequitas und Bona Fides: Festgabe zum 70. Geburstag von August Simonius,* 287–97. Basel.

Rabe, H., ed. 1906. *Scholia in Lucianum.* Leipzig.

Rackham, H., ed. and trans. [1932] 1990. *Politics.* Loeb Classical Library. Cambridge MA

Rackham, H., W. H. S. Jones, and D. E. Eichholz, eds. and trans. 1938–63. *Natural History.* 10 vols. Loeb Classical Library. Cambridge, MA.

Raditsa, L. 1985. "The Appearance of Women and Contact: Tertullian's *De habitu feminarum.*" *Athenaeum* 73:297–326.

Ramage, E. S. 1983. "Urban Problems in Ancient Rome." In *Aspects of Greco-Roman Urbanism: Essays on the Classical City,* ed. R. T. Marchese, 61–92. Oxford, UK.

Ramsay, W. M. 1883. "Unedited Inscriptions of Asia Minor." *Bulletin de Correspondance Hellenique* 7:276–77.

Randall, R. 1953. "The Erechtheum Workmen." *American Journal of Archaeology* 57:199–210.

Raubitschek, A. E. 1950. "Another Drachma Dedication." *Yale Classical Studies* 11:295–96.

Reden, S. von. 1992. "Arbeit und Zivilisation. Kriterien der Selbstdefinition im antiken Athen." *Münstersche Beiträge z. antiken Handelsgeschichte* 11:1–31.

———. 1995. *Exchange in Ancient Greece.* London.

———. 1997. "Money, Law and Exchange: Coinage in the Greek Polis." *Journal of Hellenic Studies* 117:154–76.

———. 1998. "The Commodification of Symbols: Reciprocity and Its Perversions in Menander." In *Reciprocity in Ancient Greece,* ed. C. Gill, N. Postlethwaite, and R. Seaford, 255–78. Oxford, UK.

Reinach, T. 1892. "l'impôt sur les courtisanes à Cos." *Revue des Études Grecques* 5:99–102.

Reinhold, M. 1971. "The Usurpation of Status and Status Symbols in the Roman Empire." *Historia* 20:275–302.

Reinsberg, C. 1989. *Ehe, Hetärentum und Knabenliebe im antiken Griechenland.* Munich.

Renger, J. 1975. "Heilige Hochzeit." In Vol. 4 of *Reallexikon der Assyriologie,* ed. E. Ebeling, 250–59. Berlin.

Rhodes, P. 1981. *A Commentary on the Aristotelian Athenaion Politeia.* Oxford, UK.

Richards, D. A. J. 1982. *Sex, Drugs, Death and the Law: An Essay on Human Rights and Overcriminalization.* Totowa, NJ.

Richardson, L., ed. 1977. *Elegies I–IV.* Norman, OK.

Richardson, L. J. D. 1961. "The Origin of the Prefix *Bou-* in Comedy." *Hermathena* 95:51–63.

Richlin, A. 1983. *The Garden of Priapus: Sexuality and Aggression in Roman Humor.* New Haven, CT.

———. 1984. "Invective against Women in Roman Satire." *Arethusa* 17.1:67–80.

———. 1992a. *The Garden of Priapus: Sexuality and Aggression in Roman Humor.* Rev. ed. Oxford, UK.

———. 1992b. "Julia's Jokes, Galla Placidia, and the Roman Use of Women as Political Icons." In *Stereotypes of Women in Power,* ed. B. Garlick, S. Dixon, and P. Allen, 63–91. New York.

———. 1993a. "The Ethnographer's Dilemma and the Dream of a Lost Golden Age." In *Feminist Theory and the Classics,* ed. N. S. Rabinowitz and A. Richlin, 272–303. New York.

———. 1993b. "Not before Homosexuality: The Materiality of the Cinaedus and the Roman Law against Love between Men." *Journal of the History of Sexuality* 3.4:523–73.

———. 1995. "Making Up a Woman: The Face of Roman Gender." In *Off with Her Head: The Denial of Women's Identity in Myth, Religion, and Culture,* ed. W. Doniger and H. Eilberg-Schwartz, 185–213. Berkeley, CA.

———. 1997. "Carrying Water in a Sieve: Class and the Body in Roman Women's Religion." In *Women and Goddesses,* ed. K. King, 330–74. Philadelphia.

Riddle, J. M. 1992. *Contraception and Abortion from the Ancient World to the Renaissance.* Cambridge, MA.

Riddle, J. M., J. W. Estes, and J. C. Russell. 1994. "Birth Control in the Ancient World." *Archaeology* 47.2:29–35.

Ritti, T. 1973–74. "l'uso di 'immagini onomastiche' nei monumenti sepolcrali di étà greca." *Archeologia Classica* 25/26:639–60.

Robert, L. 1970. *Études anatoliennes: Recherches sur les inscriptions grecques de l'Asie Mineure.* 2nd ed. Amsterdam.

Robertson, B. G. 2000. "The Scrutiny of New Citizens at Athens." In *Law and Social Status in Classical Athens,* ed. V. Hunter and J. Edmondson, 149–74. Oxford, UK.

Robinson, D. J. 1997. "The Social Texture of Pompeii." In *Sequence and Space in Pompeii,* ed. S. E. Bon and R. Jones, 135–44. Oxford, UK.

Rodenwaldt, G. 1932. "Spinnene Hetären." *Archäologischer Anzeiger7*–22.

Rolfe, J. C., trans. 1914. *Suetonius.* 2 vols. Loeb Classical Library. Cambridge, MA.

Roller, M. 2003. "Horizontal Women: Posture and Sex in the Roman *Convivium.*" *American Journal of Philology* 124:377–422.

Rose, S. 1999. "Cultural Analysis and Moral Discourses: Episodes, Continuities, and Transformations." In *Beyond the Cultural Turn: New Directions in the Study of Society and Culture,* ed. V. Bonnell and L. Hunt, 217–40. Berkeley, CA.

Rosenmeyer, P. A. 2001. "(In-)Versions of Pygmalion: The Statue Talks Back." In *Making Silence Speak: Women's Voices in Greek Literature and Society,* ed. A. Lardinois and L. McClure, 240–60. Princeton, NJ.

Rosivach, V. 1989. "*Talasiourgoi* and *Paidia* in *IG* 2² 1553–78: A Note on Athenian Social History." *Historia* 38:365–70.

———. 1998. *When a Young Man Falls in Love: The Sexual Exploitation of Women in New Comedy.* London.

Rossiaud, J. 1988. *Medieval Prostitution.* Trans. L. G. Cochrane. Oxford, UK.

Roth, M. T. 1987. "Age at Marriage and the Household: A Study of Neo-Assyrian and Neo-Babylonian Forms." *Comparative Studies in Society and History* 29:715–47.

———. 1988a. "'She Will Die by the Iron Dagger': Adultery and Marriage in the Neo-Babylonian Period." *Journal of the Economic and Social History of the Orient* 31:186–206.

———. 1988b. "Women in Transition and the *bīt mār banî.*" *Revue d'Assyriologie* 82:131–38.

———. 1989. *Babylonian Marriage Agreements, 7th–3rd Centuries B.C.* Alter Orient und Altes Testament 222. Neukirchen-Vluyn, Ger.

———. 1991–93. "The Neo-Babylonian Widow." *Journal of Cuneiform Studies* 43–45:1–26.

———. 1998. "Law and Gender: A Case Study from Ancient Mesopotamia." In *Gender and Law in the Hebrew Bible and the Ancient Near East,* ed. V. Matthews, B. Levinson, and T. Frymer-Kensky, 173–84. Sheffield, UK.

———. 2000. *Law Collections from Mesopotamia and Asia Minor.* In vol. 6 of *Writings from the Ancient World,* ed. Piotr Michalowski. 2nd ed. Atlanta.

Rouse, W. H. D. [1902] 1975. *Greek Votive Offerings.* Cambridge, UK.

Rueschemeyer, D. 1984. "Theoretical Generalization and Historical Perspective in the Comparative Sociology of Reinhard Bendix." In *Vision and Method in Historical Sociology*, ed. T. Skocpol, 129–69. Cambridge, UK.

Ruggiero, G. 1993. *Binding Passions: Tales of Magic, Marriage, and Power at the End of the Renaissance*. New York.

Savunen, L. 1997. *Women in the Urban Texture of Pompeii*. Pukkila, Fin.

Scafuro, A. 1994. "Witnessing and False Witnessing: Proving Citizenship and Kin Identity in Fourth Century Athens." In *Athenian Identity and Civic Ideology*, ed. Alan L. Boegehold and Adele C. Scafuro, 156–98. Baltimore.

———. 1997. *The Forensic Stage: Settling Disputes in Graeco-Roman New Comedy*. Cambridge, UK.

Schaps, D. 1979. *Economic Rights of Women in Ancient Greece*. Edinburgh.

Schneider, K. 1913. "Hetairai." In vol. 8 of *Real-Encyclopädie der klassischen Altertumswissenschaft*, 1331–72.

Schodorf, K. 1905. *Beiträge zur genaueren Kentnis der attischen Gerichtssprache aus den Zehn Redners*. Beiträge Zur historischen Syntax der griechischen Sprache 17. Würzburg, Ger.

Scholl, A. 1994. "Polutalanta mnemeia: zur literarischen und monumentalen Überlieferung aufwendigen Grabmäler im spätklassischen Athen." *Jahrbuch des Deutschen Archäologischen Instituts* 109:239–71.

Scholz, B. 1992. *Untersuchungen zur Tracht der römischen matrona*. Köln.

Schonbeck, H.-P. 1981. *Beiträge zur Interpretation der plautinischen "Bacchides."* Düsseldorf.

Schrage, W. 1999. Vol. 3 of *Der Erste Brief an die Korinther 3 (1Kor 11.17–14.40)*. Evangelisch-Katholischer Kommentar zum Neuen Testament 7. Zurich.

Schuhl, P. 1953. "Adêla." *Annales publiées par la Faculté des Lettres de Toulouse, Homo: Études philosophiques* 2:86–93.

Schuller, W. 1985. *Frauen in der griechischen Geschichte*. Konstanz, Ger.

Schulz, Fr. 1934. *Prinzipien des römischen Rechts*. Munich.

Schulze, W. 1904. *Geschichte lateinischer Eigennamen*. Berlin.

Schuster, B. 1995. *Die freien Frauen: Dirnen und Frauenhäuser im 15. und 16. Jahrhundert*. Frankfurt.

Schwartz, J. 1965. *Biographie de Lucien de Samosate*. Brussels.

Schwimmer, E. 1979. "The Self and the Product: Concepts of Work in Comparative Perspective." In *The Social Anthropology of Work*, ed. S. Wallmann, 287–315. London.

Scodel, R. 1993. *Theater and Society in the Classical World*. Ann Arbor, MI.

Scullard, H. H. 1984. *From the Gracchi to Nero: A History of Rome from 133 B.C. to A.D. 68*, 5th ed. London.

Seaford, R. 1994. *Reciprocity and Ritual*. Oxford, UK.

———. 1998. "Introduction." In *Reciprocity in Ancient Greece*, ed. C. Gill, N. Postlethwaite, and R. Seaford, 1–11. Oxford, UK.

Sealey, R. 1990. *Women and Law in Classical Greece*. Chapel Hill, NC.

Sebesta, J. L. 1994a. "Symbolism in the Costume of the Roman Woman." In *The World of Roman Costume*, ed. J. L. Sebesta and L. Bonafante, 46–53. Madison, WI.

——. 1994b. "*Tunica ralla, tunica spissa:* The Colours and Textiles of Roman Costume." In *The World of Roman Costume,* ed. J. L. Sebesta and L. Bonafante, 65–76. Madison, WI.

——. 1997. "Women's Costume and Feminine Civic Morality in Augustan Rome." *Gender and History* 9.3:529–41.

Sebesta, J. L., and L. Bonafante, eds. 1995. *The World of Roman Costume.* Madison, WI.

Segal, E. 1987. *Roman Laughter: The Comedy of Plautus,* 2nd ed. Oxford, UK.

Seltman, C. T. 1953. *Women in Greek Society.* London.

——. 1956. *Women in Antiquity.* London.

Senior, O. 1992. *Working Miracles: Women's Lives in the Engligh-Speaking Caribbean.* Bloomington, IN.

Sensi, L. 1980–81. "Ornatus e status sociale delle donne romane." *Annali della Facoltà di Lettere e Filosofia, Università degli Studi di Perugia* 18:55–92.

Shackelton Bailey, D. R., ed. [1965] 1999. Vol. 3 of *Cicero's Letters to Atticus.* Loeb Classical Library. Cambridge, MA.

Shipton, K. 1997. "The Private Banks in Fourth-Century B.C. Athens: A Reappraisal." *Classical Quarterly* 47:396–422.

Shrage, L. 1994. *Moral Dilemmas of Feminism: Prostitution, Adultery, and Abortion.* New York.

Sigerist, E. 1970. *Der Arzt in der griechischen Kultur.* Esslingen, Ger.

Silver, M. 1995. *Economic Structures of Antiquity.* Westport, CT.

Sissa, G. 1999. "Sexual Bodybuilding: Aeschines against Timarchus." In *Constructions of the Classical Body,* ed. J. Porter, 147–68. Ann Arbor, MI.

Sjöberg, Ã. W. 1977. "Miscellaneous Sumerian Texts, II." *Journal of Cuneiform Studies* 29:3–45.

Skinner, M. B. 1993. "Woman and Language in Archaic Greece, or, Why Is Sappho a Woman?" In *Feminist Theory and the Classics,* ed. N. S. Rabinowitz and A. Richlin, 125–44. New York.

Slater, N. W. 1985. *Plautus in Performance: The Theatre of the Mind.* Princeton, NJ.

Smith, M. S. 1998. "The Death of 'Dying and Rising Gods' in the Biblical World: An Update, with Special Reference to Baal in the Baal Cycle." *Scandinavian Journal of the Old Testament* 12:257–313.

Snodgrass, A. M. 1989–1990. "The Economics of Dedication at Greek Sanctuaries." *Scienze dell'antichita: Storia, archeologia, antropologia (Rome)* 3/4:287–94.

Soards, M. L. 1999. *New International Biblical Commentary: 1 Corinthians.* Peabody, MA.

Soren, D. 1997. "Hecate and the Infant Cemetery at Poggio Gramignano." In *Excavation of a Roman Villa and Late Roman Infant Cemetery near Lugnano in Teverina, Italy,* ed. D. Soren and N. Soren, 619–31. Rome.

Soren, D., T. Fenton, W. Birkby, and R. Jensen. 1997. "The Infant Cemetery at Poggio Gramignano: Description and Analysis." In *Excavation of a Roman Villa and Late Roman Infant Cemetery near Lugnano in Teverina, Italy,* ed. D. Soren and N. Soren, 477–530. Rome.

Sourvinou-Inwood, C. 1988. *Studies in Girls' Transitions: Aspects of the Arkteia and Age Representation in Attic Iconography.* Athens.

——. 1995. "Male and Female, Public and Private, Ancient and Modern." In *Pandora: Women in Classical Greece*, ed. E. D. Reeder, 111–20. Princeton, NJ.

Spano, G. 1920. "La illuminazione delle vie di Pompei." *Atti della reale accademia di archeologia, lettere, e belle arti di Napoli* 7:3–128.

Stallybrass, P., and A. White. 1986. *The Politics and Poetics of Transgression*. Ithaca, NY.

Stamm, J. J. 1939. *Die Akkadische Namengebung*. Mitteilungen der Vorderasiatische-Aegyptischen Gesellschaft 44. Berlin.

Stansell, C. 1987. *City of Women: Sex and Class in New York, 1789–1860*. New York.

Ste. Croix, G. de. 1981. *The Class Struggle in the Ancient Greek World*. London.

Steiner, D. 1994. *The Tyrant's Writ*. Princeton, NJ.

Steinkeller, P. 1999. "On Rulers, Priests, and Sacred Marriage: Tracing the Evolution of Early Sumerian Kingship." In *Priests and Officials in the Ancient Near East*, ed. K. Watanabe, 103–38. Papers of the Second Colloquium on the Ancient Near East: The City and Its Life. Heidelberg.

Stewart, A. 1979. *Attika: Studies in Athenian Sculpture of the Hellenistic Age*. Society for the Promotion of Hellenic Studies Supplementary Paper 14. London.

——. 1997. *Art, Desire and the Body in Ancient Greece*. Cambridge, UK.

Stocks, J. 1936. "Scholê." *Classical Quarterly* 30:177–87.

Stockton, D. 1971. *Cicero: A Political Biography*. Oxford, UK.

Stol, M. 1991. "Old Babylonian Personal Names." *Studi epigrafici e linguistici sul Vicino Oriente antico* 8:191–212.

——. 2000. *Birth in Babylonia and the Bible*. Groningen, Neth.

Stone, S. 1994. "The Toga: From National to Ceremonial Costume." In *The World of Roman Costume*, ed. J. L. Sebesta and L. Bonafante, 13–45. Madison, WI.

Storey, G. R. 1997. "The Population of Ancient Rome." *Antiquity* 71:966–78.

Strassmaier, J. N. 1889. *Inschriften von Nabuchodonosor, König von Babylon*. Leipzig.

——. 1890. *Inschriften von Cyrus, König von Babylon*. Leipzig.

Strauss, B. 1987. *Athens after the Peloponnesian War: Class, Faction, and Policy, 403–386 B.C.* Ithaca, NY.

Stroh, W. 1971. *Die Römische Liebeselegie als werbende Dichtung*. Amsterdam.

——. 1979. "Ovids Liebeskunst und die Ehegesetze des Augustus." *Gymnasium* 86:323–52.

Strom, I. 1992. "*Obeloi* of Pre- and Proto-Monetary Value in Greek Sanctuaries." In *Economics of Cult in the Ancient World*, Boreas 21, ed. T. Linders and B. Alroth, 41–51. Uppsala.

Strong. R. A. 1997. "The Most Shameful Practice: Temple Prostitution in the Ancient Greek World." PhD dissertation, University of California, Los Angeles.

Stroud, R. 1998. *The Athenian Grain-Tax Law of 374/3 B.C.* Hesperia Supplement 29. Princeton, NJ.

Stumpf, G. 1986. "Ein athenisches Münzgesetz des 4. Jh. V. Chr." *Jahrbuch für Numismatik und Geldgeschichte* 36:23–40.

Stumpp, B. 1998. *Prostitution in der römischen antike*. Berlin.

Swain, S. 1996. *Hellenism and Empire: Language, Classicism and Power in the Ancient Greek World AD 50–250*. Oxford, UK.

Sweet, R. 1994. "A New Look at the 'Sacred Marriage' in Ancient Mesopotamia." In *Corolla Torontonienseis: Studies in Honor of Ronald Morton Smith,* ed. E. Robbins and S. Sandahl, 85–104. Toronto.

Tatum, W. J. 1999. *The Patrician Tribune: Publius Clodius Pulcher.* Chapel Hill, NC.

Taylor, Q. P. 1998. "St. Augustine and Political Thought: A Revisionist View." *Augustiniana* 48:287–303.

Taylor, R. 1997. "Two Pathic Subcultures in Ancient Rome." *Journal of the History of Sexuality* 7.3:319–71.

Teeter, E. 1999. "Temple Life." In *Women of the Nile,* ed. J. Freeman, 25–26. San Jose.

Temkin, O., trans. [1956] 1991. *Soranus' Gynecology.* Baltimore.

Theokhares, R. 1983. *Arkhaia kai Byzantini Oikonomiki Istoria.* Athens.

Thomas, R. 1989. *Oral Tradition and Written Record in Classical Athens.* Cambridge Studies in Oral and Literate Culture 18. Cambridge, UK.

Thompson, W. 1983 "The Athenian Entrepreneur." *l'Antiquité classique* 51:53–85.

Thornton, B. 1997. *Eros: The Myth of Ancient Greek Sexuality.* Boulder, CO.

Tod, M. N. 1950. "Epigraphical Notes on Freedmen's Professions." *Epigraphica* 12:3–26.

Todd, S. 1990. "The Purpose of Evidence in Athenian Courts." In *Nomos: Essays in Athenian Law, Politics and Society,* ed. P. Cartledge, P. Millett, and S. Todd, 19–39. Cambridge, UK.

———. 1993. *The Shape of Athenian Law.* Oxford, UK.

———. 1997. "Status and Gender in Athenian Public Records." In *Symposion 1995,* ed. G. Thür and J. Vélissaropoulos-Karakostas, 113–24. Köln.

Tomlinson, R. A. 1977. "The Upper Terraces at Perachora." *Annual of the British School at Athens* 72:197–202.

Trachtenberg, J. 1961. *Jewish Magic and Superstition.* Cleveland.

Travlos, J. 1937. "*Anaskafai Hieras Hodou.*" *Praktika* 25–41.

Treggiari, S. 1971. "Libertine Ladies." *Classical World* 64:196–98.

Trendall, A. D., and T. B. L. Webster. 1971. *Illustrations of Greek Drama.* London.

Trexler, R. C. 1981. "La prostitution florentine au XVᵉ siècle." *Annales (Économies, Sociétés, Civilisations)* 36:983–1015.

Umholtz, G. 2002. "Architraval Arrogance? Dedicatory Inscriptions in Greek Architecture of the Classical Period." *Hesperia* 71:261–93.

van Bremen, R. 1996. *The Limits of Participation: Women and Civic Life in the Greek East in the Hellenistic and Roman Periods.* Amsterdam.

van der Toorn, K. 1989. "Female Prostitution in Payment of Vows in Ancient Israel." *Journal of Biblical Literature* 108:193–205.

———. 1992. "Prostitution (Cultic)." In vol. 5 of *The Anchor Bible Dictionary,* 510–13.

Vanoyeke, V. 1990. *La prostitution en Grèce et a Rome.* Paris.

Van Straten, F. T. 1981. "Gifts for the Gods." In *Faith, Hope and Worship. Aspects of Religious Mentality in the Ancient World,* ed. H. S. Versnel, 65–151. Studies in Greek and Roman Religion 2. Leiden.

———. 1995. *Hiera Kala, Images of Animal Sacrifice in Archaic and Classical Greece.* Leiden.

Vernant, J.-P. 1971. *Mythe et pensée chez les Grecs.* 2 vols. 4th ed. Paris.

———. 1983. "Hestia-Hermes, the Religious Expression of Space and Movement in Ancient Greece." In *Myth and Thought among the Greeks*, ed. J. P. Vernant, 127–75. London.

Veyne, P. 1988. *Roman Erotic Elegy: Love, Poetry, and the West*. Trans. D. Pellauer. Chicago.

Vidal-Naquet, P. 1986. *The Black Hunter: Forms of Thought and Forms of Society in the Greek World*. Trans. A. Szegedy-Maszak. Baltimore.

Von Staden, H. 1991. "*Apud nos foediora verba:* Celsus' Reluctant Construction of the Female Body." In *Le latin médical: La constitution d'un language scientifique*, ed. G. Sabbagh, 271–96. Mémoirs du Centre Jean Palerne 10. Saint-Étienne, Fr.

———. 1992. "Women and Dirt." *Helios* 19.1/2:7–30.

Vout, C. 1996. "The Myth of the Toga: Understanding the History of Roman Dress." *Greece & Rome* 43:204–20.

Wacker, M.-T. 1992. "Kosmisches Sakrament oder Verpfändung des Körpers? 'Kultprostitution' im biblischen Israel und im hinduistischen Indien. Religionsgeschichtliche Überlegungen im Interesse feministischer Theologie." *Biblische Notizen* 61:51–75.

Wade-Gery, H. T. 1940. "The Inscriptions on Stone." In *Architecture, Bronzes, Terracottas*, ed. H. Payne, 256–67. Vol. 1 of *Perachora, the Sanctuaries of Hera Akraia and Limenia: Excavations of the British School of Archaelogy at Athens, 1930–1933*. Oxford, UK.

Wake, G. 1932. *Sacred Prostitution and Marriage by Capture*. New York.

Waldstein, C., ed. 1902. Vol. 1 of *The Argive Heraeum*. Boston.

Walkowitz, J. R. 1992. *City of Dreadful Delight: Narratives of Sexual Danger in Late-Victorian London*. Chicago.

Wallace, R. 1993. "Personal Conduct and Legal Sanction in the Democracy of Classical Athens." In *Questions de responsabilité*, ed. J. Zlinzsky, 397–413. Miskolc, Hun.

———. 1994a. "The Athenian Laws of Slander." In *Symposion 1993*, ed. G. Thür, 109–24. Köln.

———. 1994b. "Private Lives and Public Enemies: Freedom of Thought in Classical Athens." In *Athenian Identity and Civic Ideology*, ed. A. Scafuro and A. Boegehold, 205–38. Baltimore.

———. 1995. "On Not Legislating Sexual Conduct in Fourth-Century Athens." In *Symposion 1995*, ed. G. Thür and J. Vélissaropoulos-Karakostas, 151–66. Köln.

———. 1996. "Law, Freedom, and the Concept of Citizens' Rights in Democratic Athens." In *Demokratia: A Conversation on Democracies, Ancient and Modern*, ed. J. Ober and C. Hedrick, 105–20. Princeton, NJ.

Wallace-Hadrill, A. 1989. "Patronage in Roman Society: From Republic to Empire." In *Patronage in Ancient Society*, ed. A. Wallace-Hadrill, 63–87. London.

———. 1994. *Houses and Society in Pompeii and Herculaneum*. Princeton, NJ.

———. 1995. "Public Honour and Private Shame: The Urban Texture of Pompeii." In *Urban Society in Roman Italy*, ed. T. J. Cornell and K. Lomas, 39–62. New York.

———. 2001. "Emperors and Houses in Rome." In *Childhood, Class and Kin in the Roman World*, ed. S. Dixon, 128–43. London.

Weber, C. 1996. "Roscius and the *roscida dea*." *Classical Quarterly* 46:298–302.

Webster, T. B. L. 1972. *Potter and Patron in Classical Athens*. London.

———. 1995. *Monuments Illustrating New Comedy.* 3rd ed., rev. and enl. by J. R. Green and A. Seeberg. Bulletin of the Institute of Classical Studies, supp. 50. London.

Wegner, J. R. 1991. "The Image and Status of Women in Classical Rabbinic Judaism." In *Jewish Women in Historical Perspective,* ed. J. R. Baskin, 94–114. Detroit.

Wehrli, F. 1936. *Motivstudien zur griechischen Komödie.* Zurich.

———, ed. 1969. Vol. 7 of *Die Schule des Aristoteles.* 2nd ed. Basel.

Weiss, E. 1923. *Griechisches Privatrecht auf rechtsvergleichender Grundlage.* Leipzig.

Weissler, C. 1991. "Prayers in Yiddish and the Religious World of Ashkenazic Women." In *Jewish Women in Historical Perspective,* ed. J. R. Baskin, 159–81. Detroit.

Weitzer, R. 2000. "The Politics of Prostitution in America." In *Sex for Sale: Prostitution, Pornography and the Sex Industry,* ed. R. Weitzer, 159–80. New York.

Welch, K. 1999. "Subura." *Lexicon topographicum urbis romae* 4:379–83.

Welwei, K.-W. 1974. Vol. 1 of *Unfreie im Antiken Kriegsdienst.* Stuttgart.

Westbrook, R. 1984. "The Enforcement of Morals in Mesopotamian Law." *Journal of the American Oriental Society* 104:753–56.

———. 1990. "Adultery in the Ancient Near East." *Revue biblique* 97:542–76.

———. 1994. "The Old Babylonian Term *napɵarum.*" *Journal of Cuneiform Studies* 46:41–46.

Westenholz, J. G. 1989. "Tamar, qedēšā, qadištu, and Sacred Prostitution in Mesopotamia." *Harvard Theological Review* 82:245–65.

White, L. 1990. *The Comforts of Home: Prostitution in Colonial Nairobi.* Chicago.

White, R. 1975. *Artemidorus, oneirokritika.* Park Ridge, NJ.

Whitehead, D. 1986. *The Demes of Attika 508/7–ca. 250 BC: A Political and Social Study.* Princeton, NJ.

Whitehorne, J. E. G. 1975. "Golden Statues in Greek and Latin Literature." *Greece & Rome* 22:109–19.

Whitmarsh, T. 2001. *Greek Literature and Beyond: The Politics of Imitation.* Oxford, UK.

Wijers, M. 1998. "Women, Labor, and Migration: The Position of Trafficked Women and Strategies for Support." In *Global Sex Workers: Rights, Resistance, and Redefinition,* ed. K. Kempadoo and J. Doezema, 69–78. New York.

Wilamowitz-Moellendorff, U. von, et al. 1912. *Die griechische und lateinische Literatur und Sprache.* Die Kultur der Gegenwart I.8. Leipzig and Berlin.

Wilcke, C. 1980. "*šumṣulum,* 'den Tag verbringen.'" *Zeitschrift für Assyriologie* 70: 138–40.

Wiles, D. 1989. "Marriage and Prostitution in Classical New Comedy." In vol. 11 of *Themes in Drama,* ed. J. Redmond, 31–48. Cambridge, UK.

Wilhelm, A. 1909. *Beiträge zur griechischen Inschriftenkunde.* Vienna.

Wilhelm, G. 1990. "Marginalien zu Herodot Klio 199." In *Lingering Over Words: Studies in Ancient Near Eastern Literature in Honor of William L. Moran,* ed. T. Abusch et al., 505–24. Atlanta.

Williams, C. A. 1999. *Roman Homosexuality: Ideologies of Masculinity in Classical Antiquity.* Oxford, UK.

Williams, D. 1983. "Women on Athenian Vases: Problems of Interpretation." In *Images of Women in Antiquity,* ed. A. Cameron and A. Kuhrt, 92–106. London.

Williams, G. 1968. *Tradition and Originality in Roman Poetry*. Oxford, UK.

Wilson, L. M. 1924. *The Roman Toga*. Baltimore.

———. 1938. *The Clothing of the Ancient Romans*. Baltimore.

Wilson, P. 1996. "Tragic Rhetoric: The Use of Tragedy and the Tragic in the Fourth Century." In *Tragedy and the Tragic: Greek Theater and Beyond*, ed. M. S. Silk, 310–31. Oxford, UK.

Winkler, J. J. 1990. *The Constraints of Desire: The Anthropology of Sex and Desire in Ancient Greece*. New York.

Wiseman, T. P. 1985. *Catullus and His World: A Reappraisal*. Cambridge, UK.

Witherington, B., III. 1995. *Conflict and Community in Corinth: A Socio-Rhetorical Commentary on 1 and 2 Corinthians*. Grand Rapids, MI.

Wohl, V. 1999. "The Eros of Alcibiades." *Classical Antiquity* 18.2:349–85.

Wollstonecraft, M. 1983. "A Vindication of the Rights of Men." In *A Mary Wollstonecraft Reader*, ed. B. H. Solomon and P. S. Berggren, 239–63. New York.

Wolpert, A. 2002. *Remembering Defeat: Civil War and Civic Memory in Ancient Athens*. Baltimore.

Wood, E. 1988. *Peasant-Citizen and Slave: The Foundations of Athenian Democracy*. London.

Wood, S. E. 1999. *Imperial Women: A Study in Public Images, 40 BC–A.D. 68*. Leiden and Boston.

Woolf, V. [1929] 1957. *A Room of One's Own*. New York.

Wright, F. A. [1923] 1969. *Feminism in Greek Literature: From Homer to Aristotle*. Port Washington, NY.

Wycherley, R. 1957. *The Athenian Agora*. Vol. 3 of *Literary and Epigraphical Testimonia*. Princeton, NJ.

Wyke, M. 1994. "Woman in the Mirror: The Rhetoric of Adornment in the Roman World." In *Women in Ancient Societies: An Illusion of the Night*, ed. L. J. Archer, S. Fischler, and M. Wyke, 134–51. New York.

Wyse, W. [1904] 1967. *The Speeches of Isaeus*. Hildesheim, Ger.

Yardley, J. C. 1987. "Propertius 4.5, Ovid *Amores* 1.6 and Roman Comedy." *Proceedings of the Cambridge Philological Society* 213:179–89.

———. 1991. "The Symposium in Roman Elegy." In *Dining in a Classical Context*, ed. W. J. Slater, 149–54. Ann Arbor, MI.

Young, J. 1956. "Studies in South Attica. Country Estates at Sounion." *Hesperia* 25:122–46.

Zaccagnini, C. 1994. "Feet of Clay at Emar and Elsewhere." *Orientalia* 63:1–4.

———. 1995. "War and Famine at Emar." *Orientalia* 64:92–109.

Zagagi, N. 1980. *Tradition and Originality in Plautus: Studies of the Amatory Motifs in Plautine Comedy*. Göttingen, Ger.

Zanker, P. 1988. *The Power of Images in the Age of Augustus*. Trans. A. Shapiro. Ann Arbor, MI.

Zeitlin, F. 1990. "Thebes: Theater of Self and Society in Athenian Drama." In *Nothing to Do with Dionysos?: Athenian Drama in Its Social Context*, ed. J. J. Winkler and F. I. Zeitlin, 130–67. Princeton, NJ.

Zweig, B. 1993. "The Primal Mind: Using Native American Models for the Study of Women in Ancient Greece." In *Feminist Theory and the Classics*, ed. N. S. Rabinowitz and A. Richlin, 145–80. New York.

Contributors

PHYLLIS A. BIRD is professor emerita of Old Testament interpretation at Garrett-Evangelical Theological Seminary and author of *Missing Persons and Mistaken Identities: Women and Gender in Ancient Israel* (1997). Her research interests center on the intersections of religion and culture in the world of ancient Israel and the literature of the Hebrew Bible, with particular attention to issues of women and gender.

STEPHANIE L. BUDIN holds a PhD in ancient history from the University of Pennsylvania. Her main interests are religion, sex and gender, and cross-cultural connections between the classical world and the Near East. Her first book was on the origin of Aphrodite, and she is currently working on two others: one on the iconography of the "Nude Goddess" and another on the origin and evolution of the myth of sacred prostitution. She teaches at Temple University

EDWARD E. COHEN is an adjunct professor of ancient history and classical studies at the University of Pennsylvania. He also serves as chairman of the board and chief executive officer of Resource America, Inc. Among his books are *The Athenian Nation* (2000) and *Athenian Economy and Society: A Banking Perspective* (1992).

ANNE DUNCAN is assistant professor of classics in the Department of Languages and Literatures at Arizona State University. She has published articles on performance issues in Greek and Roman drama. Her book *Performances and Identity in the Classical World* is forthcoming from Cambridge University Press.

CHRISTOPHER A. FARAONE is a professor of classics at the University of Chicago. He is author of *Talismans and Trojan Horses: Guardian Statues in Ancient Greek Myth and Ritual* (1992) and *Ancient Greek Love Magic* (1999) and a number of articles on Greek poetry, religion, and gender. He is coeditor of *Initiation in Ancient Greek Rituals and Narratives: New Critical Perspectives* (2003).

KATE GILHULY is an assistant professor of classics at Wellesley College. She is the author of a doctoral thesis, "Excess Contained: Prostitution and the Polis in Classical Athens," completed at the University of California at Berkeley, and is currently working on a manuscript about the construction of gender in classical Athens.

ALLISON GLAZEBROOK is an assistant professor of classics at Brock University. Her research relates to the social and cultural history of ancient Greece and focuses on gender and sexuality, prostitution, and ancient rhetoric. She has written articles on [Demosthenes] 59 and constructions of gender in Greek vase painting.

SHARON L. JAMES is an associate professor of classics at the University of Chapel Hill at North Carolina. She is the author of *Learned Girls and Male Persuasion: Gender and Reading in Roman Love Elegy* (2003) and several articles on elegy, Roman Comedy, and Vergil.

CATHERINE M. KEESLING is an associate professor of classics at Georgetown University. Her publications include *The Votive Statues of the Athenian Acropolis* (2003) and articles on ancient Greek sculpture, epigraphy, and commemorative monuments. She is currently writing a book on the epigraphical evidence for Greek portraiture and the afterlives of Greek portrait statues.

SUSAN LAPE is an associate professor of classics at the University of Southern California. Her recent interests include Greek drama, law, and political theory. She has just completed *Reproducing Athens: Menander's Comedy, Democratic Culture, and the Hellenistic City* (2004). She is currently working on a project on the history of the citizen in ancient Greece.

LAURA K. MCCLURE is a professor of classics at the University of Wisconsin–Madison. Her books include *Spoken Like a Woman: Speech and Gender and Athenian Drama* (1999) and *Courtesans at Table: Gender and Greek Literary Culture in Athenaeus* (2003). She has also written articles on tragedy, women in antiquity, and the classical tradition.

MARSHA MCCOY is a visiting assistant professor of classics at Austin College. Her doctoral dissertation studies Ciceronian political reform, considering the literary, philosophical, legal, and cultural aspects of Cicero's efforts to reform Roman civil society. Her interests in civil society have led to work on Augustus, Vergil, and war, and to a current study of Petronius, in which she is examining the anxieties of gender, sexuality, humor, and politics in Nero's Rome.

THOMAS A. J. MCGINN is an associate professor of classical studies at Vanderbilt University. He is author of *Prostitution, Sexuality, and the Law in Ancient Rome* (1998), *The Economy of Prostitution in the Roman World: A Study of Social History and the Brothel* (2004), and a number of articles on Roman marriage, concubinage, and adultery. He is also coauthor, with Bruce W. Frier, of *A Casebook on Roman Family Law* (2003).

KELLY OLSON is an assistant professor of classical studies at the University of Western Ontario, Canada. She has published articles on Roman clothing and adornment as well as several book chapters and reviews. She is currently at work on a book-length study of female appearance in ancient Rome entitled *Fashioning the Female in Roman Antiquity: Self-Presentation and Society.*

MARTHA T. ROTH is a professor of Assyriology at the Oriental Institute of the University of Chicago. She is the editor in charge of the Chicago Assyrian Dictionary. Her research interests are in Mesopotamian law and society. Her publications include *Babylonian Marriage Agreements 7th–3rd Centuries B.C.* (1989) and *Law Collections from Mesopotamia and Asia Minor* (1995, 2nd rev. ed. 2000).

Index

Note: This general index includes subjects, names, and words discussed in the text. Specific textual references can be located using the *index locorum* that follows.

Index Locorum

Alexis Fr.:
36 (119n76)
98 (221)
Alkiphron:
4 (119n69)
4.19 (115n17)
Amos, 7:17 (44)
Ana ittišu:
VII ii 23–26 (28)
VII iii 7–10 (29)
Anaxilas Fr. 22 (K-A), (98)
Andocides:
1.38 (121n90)
1.111 (136n8)
Anthologia Palatina. See Palatine Anthology
Antiphanes, *Alestria* Frs. 21–24 (119n76)
Aristophanes:
Acharnians 551 (122n98)
Clouds 53–55 (119n75)
Ecclesiazusae 215 (119n76)
Frogs 1349–51 (119n75)
Lysistrata: 30 (214); 41 (214); 78–84
(281); 133 (209); 341–49 (213);
342–43 (213); 403–29 (211); 519–20
(119n75); 525 (214); 536–37 (119n75);
551–54 (215); 638–48 (212); 728–30
(119n75); 729–34 (210); 740–52 (214);
828ff (210); 831–34 (216); 860 (216);
1108–11 (217); 1184–88 (219)
Wealth 149 55 (115)
Aristotle:
The Constitution of the Athenians 49.4
(117n50)

Oeconomicus A.5.1 (117n42)
Politics: 1253b6–7 (102); 1253b33–
1254a1 (104); 1269b20–25 (281);
1334b29–1335b37 (116n30);
1335b38–1336a2 (116n30);
1344a27–29 (119n66)
Rhetorica: 1361a (123n112);
1367a30–33 (100); 1417a3–
8 (136n11)
Artemidorus, *Interpretation of Dreams:*
1.45 (283)
1.80 (283)
Athenaeus, *Deipnosophistae:*
13.573c–d (65)
13.573e–f (9)
13.574c–d (66)
13.590d–e (76n43)
13.591b (59) (76n42)
13.591b–c (66)
13.591d (68)
13.594d–595a (59)
Augustinus:
Civitas Dei 14.18 (176n43)
Ordine (70–72) (167–68); 1.1 (175n33);
2.11 (175n39); 2.12 (167)

Catullus, 55.11–12 (195)
Cicero:
Ad Familiares 9.26 (240)
De Officiis: 1.126 (175n34); 1.127
(175n34); 3.22–23 (175n36); 3.26–
27 (175n36); 3.32 (175n36); 3.85
(175n34)

353

WISCONSIN STUDIES IN CLASSICS

General Editors
William Aylward, Nicholas D. Cahill, and Patricia A. Rosenmeyer

---

E. A. THOMPSON
Romans and Barbarians: The Decline of the Western Empire

JENNIFER TOLBERT ROBERTS
Accountability in Athenian Government

H. I. MARROU
A History of Education in Antiquity
Histoire de l'Education dans l'Antiquité, translated by George Lamb

ERIKA SIMON
Festivals of Attica: An Archaeological Commentary

G. MICHAEL WOLOCH
Roman Cities: Les villes romaines by Pierre Grimal, translated and edited by
G. Michael Woloch, together with A Descriptive Catalogue of Roman Cities by
G. Michael Woloch

WARREN G. MOON, editor
Ancient Greek Art and Iconography

KATHERINE DOHAN MORROW
Greek Footwear and the Dating of Sculpture

JOHN KEVIN NEWMAN
The Classical Epic Tradition

JEANNY VORYS CANBY, EDITH PORADA,
BRUNILDE SISMONDO RIDGWAY, and TAMARA STECH, editors
Ancient Anatolia: Aspects of Change and Cultural Development

ANN NORRIS MICHELINI
Euripides and the Tragic Tradition